EXCEL BASICS TO BLACKBELT

Second Edition

This second edition of *Excel Basics to Blackbelt* capitalizes on the success of the first edition and leverages some of the advancements in visualization, data analysis, and sharing capabilities that have emerged over the past five years. As with the original text, the second edition is intended to serve as an accelerated guide to decision support designs for consultants and service professionals. This "fast track" enables a ramping up of skills in Excel for those who may have never used it to reach a level of mastery. This advancement will allow them to integrate Excel with widely available associated applications, make use of intelligent data visualization and analysis techniques, automate activity through fundamental Visual Basic for Application (VBA) designs, and develop easy-to-use interfaces for customizing use. In other words, this book provides users with lessons on and examples of integrative Excel use that are not available from alternative texts.

Elliot Bendoly is an associate professor at Emory University's Goizueta Business School. He serves as an associate editor for the *Journal of Operations Management*, a senior editor for *Production and Operations Management*, and an associate editor for *Decision Sciences*. His research has been published in several academic journals including *MIS Quarterly*, *Information Systems Research*, and the *Journal of Applied Psychology*. He is the co-editor of *Strategic ERP Extension and Use* and of the *Handbook of Research in Enterprise Systems*, as well as the author of the first edition of *Excel Basics to Blackbelt*. He holds a Ph.D. from Indiana University.

EXCEL BASICS TO BLACKBELT

An Accelerated Guide to Decision Support Designs
Second Edition

ELLIOT BENDOLY
Emory University, GA

CAMBRIDGE UNIVERSITY PRESS

CAMBRIDGE UNIVERSITY PRESS
Cambridge, New York, Melbourne, Madrid, Cape Town,
Singapore, São Paulo, Delhi, Mexico City

Cambridge University Press
32 Avenue of the Americas, New York, NY 10013-2473, USA

www.cambridge.org
Information on this title: www.cambridge.org/9781107625525

First published 2008
Second edition published 2013

Printed in the United States of America

A catalog record for this publication is available from the British Library.

Library of Congress Cataloging in Publication Data
Bendoly, Elliot.
Excel basics to blackbelt : an accelerated guide to decision support designs / Elliot Bendoly,
Emory University, GA. – Second edition.
pages cm
Includes bibliographical references and index.
ISBN 978-1-107-62552-5 (pbk.)
1. Decision support systems.   2. Microsoft Excel (Computer file)   I. Title.
HD30.213.B46   2013
005.54–dc23   2012051702

ISBN 978-1-107-62552-5 Paperback

Additional resources for this publication at www.excel-blackbelt.com

Contents

Associated Links

Main course portal: www.excel-blackbelt.com

Example workbooks from the text: www.experimental-instruments.com/ BlackBelts/Examples/, followed by the chapter number and the filename (provided in the text). For example, to access Chp11_TickerPFunction_12.xls, use www.experimental-instruments.com/BlackBelts/Examples/Chp11/Chp11_ TickerPFunction_12.xls

Add-ins described in text: https://sites.google.com/site/exceladdinsdirectory

Demonstration blackbelt projects: http://experimental-instruments.com/Gallery .htm

LinkedIn group (which contains non-English-language subgroups): http://www .linkedin.com/groups?gid=3124035&trk=myg_ugrp_ovr

Preface

The world changes all the time. Technological resources advance at such a clip it seems hard to keep up. But not all technological developments really need shadowing. What we really need to keep up with are developments that help us do the great things we've been doing all along...only more effectively.

Such is the case with spreadsheet applications. New interfaces and bells and whistles appear in each new version. Some are wonderful; however, not all are particularly useful. And sadly, some of the best features often get left behind (I always give as an example the losses in macro writing capabilities and graphical direct-editing we lost after MS Excel 2007 replaced Excel 2003). But that's history. We need to keep looking forward, and where new capabilities replace older ones, we are not necessarily left in the lurch. After all, MS Excel and VBA provide the remarkable ability to be expanded and customized to our particular needs, even in ways that can replicate some of what we loved about previous versions, and even in ways we might expect future versions to automate (but which are not yet in place).

With that in mind, the second edition of *Excel Basics to Blackbelt* capitalizes on many of the recent developments made available by more contemporary versions of Excel (while retaining a nod to the features of the past). Furthermore, this edition looks forward to capabilities that are not currently standard through the introduction of a series of newly developed Excel add-ins. The application and description of these are peppered throughout the second-edition text with an aim to augment the text and fill in the capability gaps that were present in the original edition.

Throughout the second edition we also see additional examples of how the various tools available through Excel – and associated add-ins and bolt-on applications (for example, Palisade, MapPoint, XLStat, WorldWide Telescope, and Outlook) – can be integrated and leveraged. Numerous new graphical capabilities and tactics are explored, as are a range of analytical techniques not present in the original edition. Furthermore, this text is accompanied by a wealth of supplemental material, ranging from example workbooks, free access to recently developed add-ins, and connections to a twenty-thousand-strong user community.

This is what I love to teach. It's ostensibly one of the greatest environments to execute creative problem solving and tool development. I sincerely hope you find as much enjoyment in learning about these insights as I have found in teasing them out and expanding upon them.

Best wishes in all that you do,
Dr. Elliot Bendoly, Emory University

Section 1
Getting Oriented

1

Necessary Foundations for Decision Support

People make decisions every several minutes. Some of these decisions may appear trivial, such as what shirt to wear or what to have for lunch. Some decisions may appear routine: Should I provide my PIN number? Should I respond to a question from a colleague? Others are more complex: Should I recommend that my client invest in a particular firm? Should I offer to take on additional work? Should I purchase a new technology? Should I recommend a settlement in a lawsuit? These aren't simple questions and they don't have obvious answers and outcomes. Sometimes, we need help with decisions. The sources of help can vary, but increasingly these sources tend to have two things in common: analytical strength and ease of use. These sources of assistance often take the form of prepackaged off-the-shelf software tools. However, they can also be uniquely customized, and more and more frequently, this customization is being developed by individual users.

We can describe these tools by listing their potential benefits. Some of them appear in Figure 1.1. For many developers and analysts, only a few of those attributes are listed important. For others, the full complement of potential benefits must be considered. Toward this goal, visualization is very important. Indeed, one could argue that the application of visualization in data analysis is critical to the development of Decision Support Systems (DSS).

Consider the following key principles described in *Beautiful Evidence* by Edward Tufte, a world-renowned scholar on data and relational visualization:

1) *Enforce Wise Visual Comparisons*: Comparison is a critical element in the development of an understanding of anomalies in data. Therefore, it is also critical in the practical application of findings from analysis. Comparison allows for the illustration of practical relevance of effects and decisions that may give rise to them. Wise visual comparisons are the mechanisms by which analytical and theoretical findings are vetted by real-world experience. They encourage faith in the

analyst, and hence in most systems, as well as on the framework, that the analyst is recommending.

2) *Show Cause*: Most practical researchers cringe when amateurs claim "causality" because these assertions so often lack evidence. However, in some cases, certain reasoned explanations can be convincing. The task of the developer is to provide his or her reader with enough temporal and situational information for causal suggestions, either stated or implied, to be clear. The developer should also be able to show criticism of data where appropriate. Developers should further allow audiences to draw their own conclusions regarding causality rather than rely on their own hypotheses as pure fact.

3) *The World We Seek to Understand Is Multivariate, as Our Displays Should Be (AND as our analysis that supports them should be)*: This is the classic story of the blind men and the elephant. Considering one dimension of data gives only limited and potentially flawed understanding of the big picture. However, not all pieces of information are useful. A little bit of rationality goes a long way in analysis. Hence, one should push for multidimensional analysis and visualization but only as needed.

4) *Completely Integrate Words, Numbers, and Images*: Inconsistency between data and graphics weaken arguments. In some cases, inconsistent information misinforms. Analysts need to view numerical and textual content as reinforcement only. People need to understand text and graphics at a glance. This is another key to generating faith in the analyst and his or her tool.

5) *Most of What Happens in Design Depends upon the Quality, Relevance, and Integrity of Content*: Garbage fed into a graph results at best in beautiful garbage (but it still stinks). Know your audience. Understand the practice. Be fully aware of what needs to be analyzed and do it the right way. Mistakes and irrelevant detail can weaken your work.

Regardless of the technical nature of decision support tools, a serious consideration of these principles during development helps guarantee future generations' use.

Aside from these recommendations, it is essential to reinforce a point here, particularly for those new to DSS development: Decision support systems refer to applications that are designed to *support*, not *replace*, decision making. Unfortunately, DSS users too often forget this concept, or the users simply equate the notion of intelligent support of human decision making with automated decision making. Not only does that miss the point of the application development, but it also sets up a sequence of potentially disruptive behaviors. These include excessive anthropomorphism, poor or impractical decisions, disastrous results, and the scapegoating of IT technicians. *It's easy for decision makers to view decision support systems as remedies for difficult work, particularly if they can blame others when things don't work.*

Although it is often difficult to codify, there is an implied contract between those who attest to deliver intelligent tools and those who accept their use:

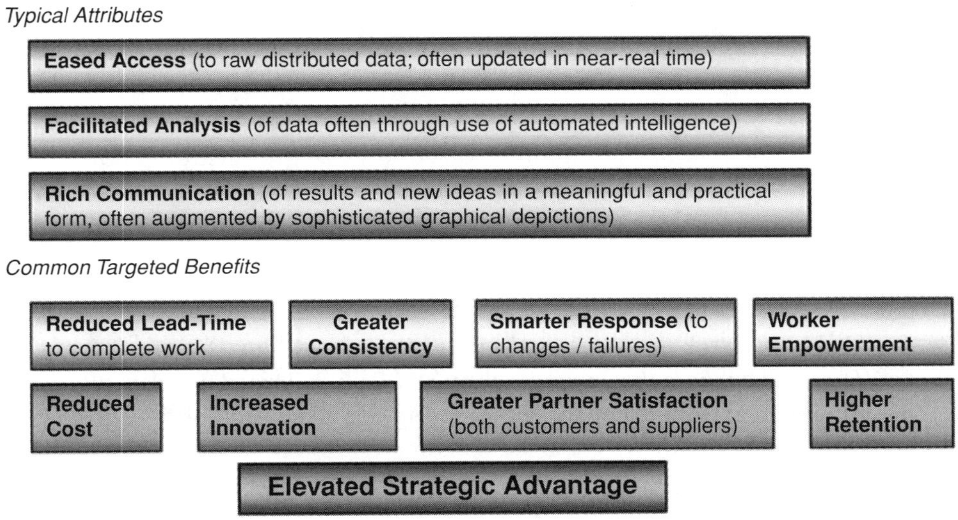

Typical Attributes

Eased Access (to raw distributed data; often updated in near-real time)

Facilitated Analysis (of data often through use of automated intelligence)

Rich Communication (of results and new ideas in a meaningful and practical form, often augmented by sophisticated graphical depictions)

Common Targeted Benefits

Reduced Lead-Time to complete work	**Greater Consistency**	**Smarter Response** (to changes / failures)	**Worker Empowerment**
Reduced Cost	**Increased Innovation**	**Greater Partner Satisfaction** (both customers and suppliers)	**Higher Retention**

Elevated Strategic Advantage

Figure 1.1. Elements of DSS.

namely, an agreement that the analyst will not attempt to intentionally mislead the user. Ultimately, these issues contribute to the accountability and ethics of organizations, as well as the personal accountability of those developing the applications. If you want to develop a strong decision support tool, you have to identify your desk as where the buck stops. But if you want to be able to share the tool, you have to pay attention to how your applications might be used by others. It is critical here to guide built-in assistance in analysis, clear visualization of how characteristics of problems and solutions relate, and formally structured interfaces that deter, if not prohibit, misuse. In my opinion, it is difficult to distinguish between those who intend to use their positions dutifully and those who will use it to deter others.

Unlike many in the field, this book is prepared both for the developer and the ultimate user. When reading these chapters, readers will learn what to expect from DSS and from those already using DSS tools. DSS is increasingly available for nonprogrammers, and this text illustrates the arrival of that inevitability.

This book uses published examples to enrich instruction on decision support. The first section, titled "Getting Oriented," will ease people into the Excel 2007 environment as a platform for tool development and visualization. Navigation and data acquisition are central themes, as are discussions of the pros and cons for their application. Sections of the book will discuss the most valuable and often underused Excel functions. Data resources like MapPoint and the Internet will be discussed, as well several free user add-ins.

In the second section, "Harvesting Intelligence," I discuss the structuring of decision-making problems that are meaningful to those in practice. Newly published visualization tools will be covered, several of which are free (bivariate normal confidence interval plotter, heatmap add-ins, and so on). MapPoint will come up again in discussion of graphical capabilities. I will describe methods to simplify large data sets as a prelude to leveraging problem structures and solution technologies. There is also a discussion of Excel's Solver and Palisade's RISKOptimizer package along with XLStat.

In the third section, "Leveraging Dynamic Analysis," I describe the design and construction of simulations from a number of different angles. DataTables will be discussed along with their combined use with other applications and Excel summary tools like PivotTables. Use of controls to simplify the management of simulations is discussed, as are approaches to simulation optimization. I will introduce Macro recordings in one section and demonstrate their use in a range of methods and with a variety of tools.

In the fourth section, "Advanced Automation and Interfacing," we deal with work that could not easily be conducted in a spreadsheet (even one as advanced as Excel's). Instead, the Visual Basic developer is ideal. I will give examples of Macro editing, the creation of new functions, application calls, integrated automation, and advanced interface development (references are available at www.excel-blackbelt.com).

As a reminder to the reader, this is not a textbook designed for an advanced programming course. Nor is it a statistics text or a single-source dictionary defining all things Excel. This is a guide for professionals who want to utilize their own skills and need only the right coaching, inspiration, and reinforcement to demonstrate these skills. The content is not designed to inundate, but rather to illuminate. Because readers come to this text at various skill levels, you should feel free to pick and choose among the chapters. Even those looking for unusual references will find value in these pages. However, the real hope is that this book will open the world of DSS development to a community that is otherwise unfamiliar with software-supported analysis. Everyone deserves to know how accessible DSS design can be and the potential that it holds. It's time to shatter the wall between the programmer and the professional, and the confluence of those skills can start here.

2

The Development Environment

Before attempting to construct a home, architects and builders need to know what resources they have at their disposal and how they can access these resources. The same holds in decision support development, but as you'll learn in subsequent chapters, the tools available to Excel developers are more numerous than a typical user would imagine. In this chapter, we'll start with the low-hanging fruit by becoming acquainted with the general nature of Excel's front-end development environment. Figure 2.1 provides an annotated view of what people typically see when they open a new file in Excel. Only a few key elements of this interface are central to our initial discussion.

Excel files are called "workbooks." They contain any number of worksheets (spreadsheets) that can be used in tandem. For the vast majority of its use in practice Excel is relegated to storing information. This is largely because most users don't know what else Excel can do. Not that storing information in Excel is bad, but there are often better alternatives available for storage, such as databases, in the case of very large sets of data. Functionally, the storage capability of Excel represents only the bare tip of this technological iceberg.

Regardless, knowing how the cell structure in a spreadsheet works is a good place to start, and this knowledge is essential to further discussion. Cells in spreadsheets can contain:

- *Fixed data*: Data you've entered, numerical or otherwise.
- *Formatting*: Background color, border thickness, font type, and so on.
- *Labels*: References other than the standard ColumnRow reference.
- *Comments*: Notes regarding the contents.
- *Formulae*: Can be mathematical or statistical, text-based, or a range of other types such as logic-based or search oriented.
- *Live data links*: Data that are drawn from an externally linked source, such as a database or the Internet.

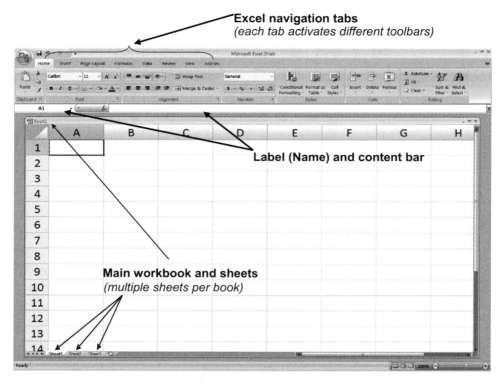

Figure 2.1. Basic front-end elements of the Excel environment.

2.1 Fixed Data

Data entry in Excel is about as basic as it gets – just click and type. And it's probably the only thing that people universally know how to do in Excel. But Excel makes some kinds of data entry easier in ways that many current users don't realize. For example, Excel has an automatic pattern-recognition element that, by default, will attempt to aid you in filling in additional cells of data. Although it's not always successful, it's often convenient. Let's say I want to enter the number 1 into five cells in the first row. I can start by entering the number 1 into cell A1. This is shown in Figure 2.2.

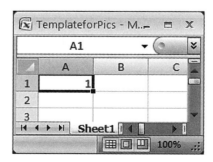

Figure 2.2. Initial entry.

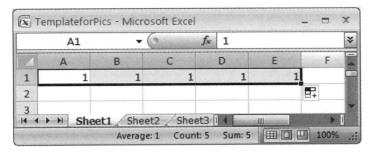

Figure 2.3. After copying across.

Note that when cell A1 is selected, its border is bold and a small square appears at the bottom right of the cell. That small square is the copy prompt. If I pull that square either to the right or down, Excel will attempt to fill in all other cells I highlight with the pattern – in this case, the number 1. By pulling the square to the right and highlighting the next four cells, I get the results shown in Figure 2.3.

At this point, with all five cells selected, I could pull the copy prompt down two rows and get the spreadsheet shown in Figure 2.4. Ascending values and alternating text values are also recognized. For example, take a look at Figure 2.5.

Or, consider the copy shown in Figure 2.6.

Although this may not be exactly what we wanted (the alphabet isn't extrapolated here), we are provided with a potentially meaningful sequence based on Excel's existing pattern recognition. Some results of pattern recognition by Excel are less intuitive, however. For example, take a look at Figure 2.7.

Here, as in the previous examples, Excel is trying to figure out what pattern the user is trying to specify. However, not every pattern that seems natural to us is encoded in these rules, and other mathematical rules may have automatic priority in Excel. There are a lot of options for trying to recognize and continue numeric patterns; in this case, the option selected isn't the one

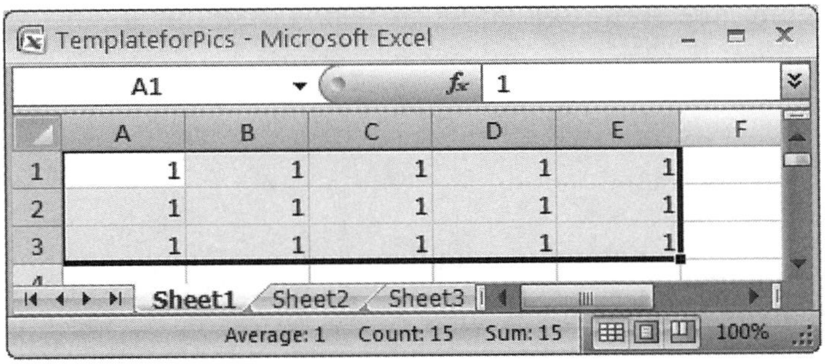

Figure 2.4. After copying the row down.

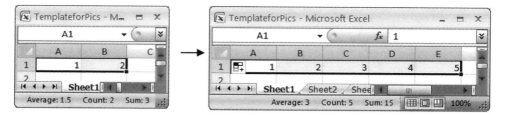

Figure 2.5. Initial sequential entry, followed by copy.

we expected. Excel has considerable intelligence built into it, and sometimes it just tries too hard.

There are several simple ways to avoid ending up with an Excel extrapolated pattern that doesn't fit a user's need. One method is to completely avoid relying on pattern recognition and instead use a formula that generates the pattern you want. For example, type "=A1" into cell E1, press Enter, and use the copy prompt on E1 to pull that entry into all other cells in that row. This formula essentially duplicates the pattern in cells A1–D1 for as long as you want it repeated.

If you would prefer to rely on Excel's pattern-recognition mechanisms, you could also try entering your numbers as text. Excel's options for intelligently identifying and extending text patterns are more limited, and this might generate unexpected results. To enter numbers as text in any given cell, precede the number with an apostrophe, such as '1 or '2. This will ensure that Excel interprets the entry as text – at least as far as pattern recognition is concerned. Within the spreadsheet, Excel will still let you perform mathematical functions using the numbers following that apostrophe, but this is an added step that may create other difficulties in formatting and contribute to more advanced use of data down the line, so it isn't an approach that's often used.

Still another mechanism to augment existing pattern-recognition capabilities is available through the Edit Custom Lists button. In Excel 2007, this can be found under "Options" accessed through the Office Button. In Excel 2010, these Options are found under the File tab in the upper left-hand corner. An image of the Popular options is presented in Figure 2.8.

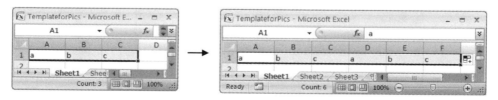

Figure 2.6. Initial text sequential entry, followed by copy.

Figure 2.7. Initial switching sequence, followed by copy.

Regardless of the version of Excel, clicking on the Edit Custom Lists button will open the Custom Lists dialog box, as seen in Figure 2.9. This functionality allows you to view the existing custom lists, generate new lists, and import other lists that aren't currently being recognized by the workbook.

2.2 Formatting

Formatting can be applied to a wide range of elements within Excel. The most common is cell formatting. The following sections explore static and conditional cell formatting.

2.2.1 Static Formatting for Cells

Static formats can be modified in a variety of ways. Access to formatting options is gained by either right-clicking on the desired cell and then selecting Format Cells in the shortcut window that appears (as shown in Figure 2.10), or by selecting Format>Format Cells from the standard toolbar. Whether choosing Format Cells from the shortcut menu or selecting Format>Format Cells, the Format Cells dialog box appears. The formatting options in this dialog box include:

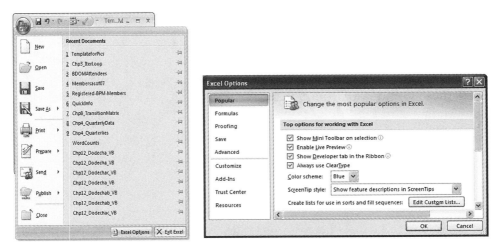

Figure 2.8. Excel Options access and access to Edit Custom Lists.

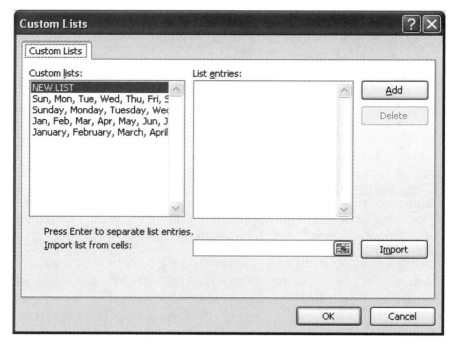

Figure 2.9. Edit Custom Lists interface.

Figure 2.10. Accessing cell-formatting options.

- *Number*: Allows modification of the type of numeric or text presentation for that cell. For example, this allows numbers that represent percentages to be presented as such (that is, with a % sign), numbers that represent dates to be presented in month-day format, and very large or very small numbers to be presented in scientific notation (for example, 3.45E8 instead of 345,000,000, or 3.45E-8 instead of 0.0000000345).
- *Alignment*: Allows changes to the horizontal and vertical alignment of contents within cells, as well as whether cells will merge with neighboring cells, and whether text within a cell will run outside the boundary of the cell or if it will wrap (as it would in a paragraph in MS Word) based on the boundary of the cell.
- *Font*: Self-explanatory. Pick a font, any font. Not to mention color, bold, italics, underline, and so on.
- *Border*: Allows changes in the appearance of the cell boundary. Line thickness, color, and line type are options.
- *Fill*: Allows changes in the appearance of the interior background of the cell. Pattern selection (for example, striped or hatched) and color fill are options.
- *Protections*: When accompanied by sheet security options, prevents unauthorized users from modifying the contents or other attributes of the cell.

2.2.2 Conditional Formatting

Unlike static formatting, conditional formatting offers a more dynamic approach to highlighting the contents of cells. Any cell or set of cells subject to conditional formatting will take on a special appearance only when it contains special values. In the current, standard versions of Excel, each cell can have multiple conditional formatting rules associated with it in addition to the default cell format.

Click the Conditional Formatting button in the Home tab. A drop-down menu appears with a list of conditional formatting options (shown in Figure 2.11). From here, you can select which type of conditional formatting you want to apply.

If you select the Manage Rules option, the Conditional Formatting Rules Manager opens, and you can add, edit, and delete rules from the same window. Basically, this dialog box allows you to spell out rules or conditions and to specify fonts, borders, and patterns to apply when the cell(s) take on specific values or ranges of values. In the example shown in Figure 2.12, cells subjected to the conditional format will take on one colored background pattern when their values are less than 0.4, whereas those with values greater than 0.6 will take on an alternate pattern.

Occasionally, the focus of formatting is not the content of the cell you want to format, but rather some other cell in which data exist and potentially change. The formatted cell then takes on the role of presentation. Figure 2.13 provides an example of a cell (say, B3) that has been formatted conditionally on the values contained in cells A3 and A4. If the equality in the

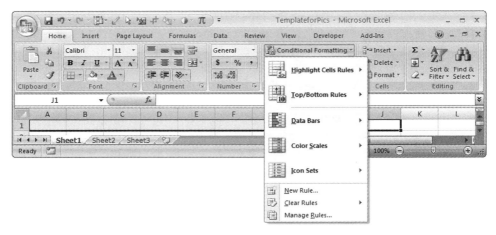

Figure 2.11. Accessing conditional formatting.

parentheses depicted in the first rule's formula (a4=1) is true, then B3 will appear blue (regardless of what value it contains at this point). If false, then the second rule's formula is checked and the formatting is applied, if needed.

Any other default, such as static formatting, will apply to cells that don't meet either criterion. In this case, the static format of these cells involves no background shading of any kind, so cells with values between 0.4 and 0.6 are unshaded. Furthermore, the rules that have been applied obey a strict hierarchy. If the top rule is met, any later rules that would override that formatting will not play out. If the order of the hierarchy needs changing (for example, the "red" rule should have precedence over the "blue" rule), the order can be changed by selecting a rule and then clicking on the up or down arrow buttons available in the form.

Figure 2.12. Developing conditional formatting rules.

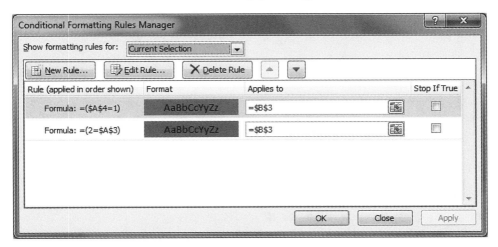

Figure 2.13. Conditioning on the value of OTHER cells.

There are a few points I'd like to make about formatting multiple cells:

- All static formatting and conditional formatting actions can be applied to multiple cells simultaneously by selecting a group of cells prior to beginning any of the previously mentioned procedures. A group of adjacent cells can be selected by selecting a cell at a corner of the range desired, holding down the mouse button, and highlighting all other cells in the adjacent range. A group of nonadjacent cells can be selected by holding down the Control (Ctrl) key and then clicking on each of the cells in the desired group. When selected, the same access to both static and conditional formatting windows is available.
- A number of special multicell conditional formatting options exist that format cells according to their relative magnitude. These include data bars, color scales, and icon sets. Upon selecting a range of cells for formatting, any of these options can be selected to portray a rich visual representation of these cell values.
- If you've already formatted a single cell in a particular way and would like to replicate that format in other cells, the Format Painter is a handy tool for copying that format to new cells. You can access the Format Painter by clicking the paintbrush icon in the Home toolbar. Select the cell with the appropriate format you want to copy, click the Format Painter icon, and select the set of additional cells to which you would like to apply your format.

2.3 Labeling (Naming)

Labels, or names, as they are called by standard, provide a way of referencing cells in a meaningful fashion other than the generic terms A1 or C12. For example, a cell that is consistently used to contain estimated shipping cost data might more meaningfully be labeled ShippingCost, as opposed to

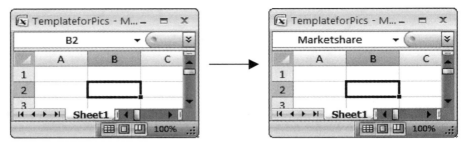

Figure 2.14. Making use of names or labels to reference cells.

G4. If cell H13 contains the rate of return on an investment, a more mean-ingful name for this cell might be RateofReturn.

Clearly labeled cells can be helpful for at least a couple of reasons. First, other users can more easily understand what the cell contains. For example, when calculating a formula, it's beneficial for others to know what terms you are referring to in the calculation. Excel makes it easy to visually associate terms with the data they represent by highlighting cells on a spreadsheet when cells with a formula are selected. A second reason for clear labeling is that you'll know what you were thinking after you built a tool (when you may want to modify that tool).

Labels can be assigned to cells by selecting the desired cell and then enter-ing a new label for that cell in the label box (Name box), which is usually located near the upper-left corner of the spreadsheet.

When unlabeled cells are initially selected, their column-row reference will appear in that label/name box. Click the Label box, enter the new label or name for the cell, and then press Enter. The new name for the cell, such as Marketshare, will display in the Name box (Figure 2.14).

The cell may now be referenced by either its column-row designation or its new label. More conveniently, however, if at any point the developer wants to move the location of that cell and its contents, the new label will go along with it. This can be very helpful in avoiding confusion when other cells or applications depend on being able to locate the cell's information after such a move.

2.3.1 Handling Name/Label Typos and Changes

If a typographical error in labeling is made, or if the developer later wants to change the name of the cell, the most secure route to correct this issue is to select Name Manager from the Formulas menu to open the Name Manager dialog box. This dialog box enables the user to delete the undesired label and add other labels. All existing labels in a workbook can be modified from the Name Manager (Figure 2.15).

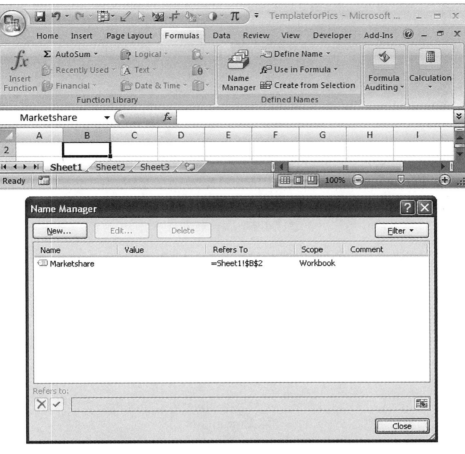

Figure 2.15. Managing names assigned to elements in a workbook.

2.3.2 Cell Range Labels

As with formatting, multiple cells can be selected simultaneously and assigned a specific label. For example, if cells A1:A30 reference information on the profitability of ten leading firms, the cells can be labeled Top10Companies. The use of range labels becomes more meaningful in advanced applications, but they remain extremely useful in helping others understand the design of a developer's tool.

2.3.3 Worksheet Labels

Referring back to the idea that Excel documents are really workbooks that contain multiple worksheets, each worksheet has a name that can be relabeled as well. Changing the label of a worksheet is extremely straightforward. Just double-click the tab label corresponding to the worksheet of

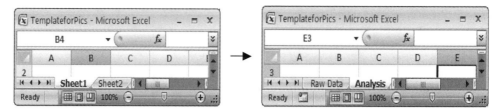

Figure 2.16. Modifying sheet labels.

choice (for example, Sheet1 as shown in Figure 2.16), and type in a new name for that sheet (for example, Raw Data).

2.3.4 Object Names

Objects include items such as drawn shapes (for example, circles), controls (for example, option buttons), charts (for example, a bar graph), inserted media (for example, .wav files), and embedded tools (for example, Map-Point maps). Each of these items can be assigned labels/names for reference (Figure 2.17). Labels for cells and objects are universal across all worksheets in a specific workbook. In other words, if on Sheet1 you label cell A1 PRICE, you can still refer to that cell as PRICE for anything done on Sheet2 in that workbook.

2.4 Comments

Along with the labeling of cells to provide better reference mechanisms, comments can be added to specific cells to add greater clarity when needed. For example, aside from labeling a cell Cost, a developer might add the text shown in Figure 2.18 to appear in comment form when the cursor passes over the cell. Comments are added to selected cells by right-clicking on the

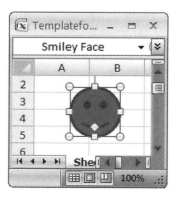

Figure 2.17. Assigning names to objects.

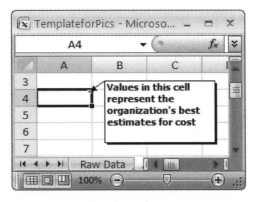

Figure 2.18. Application of a comment to a cell.

cell and then selecting Insert Comment from the shortcut menu. The developer will then be able to modify the text within the new comment bubble, as well as manipulate the height and width of that bubble.

2.5 Hyperlinks

Although hyperlinks (links to Web pages and pages on local drives) can be embedded within cells, they require that the cell content be used entirely for this purpose. Why waste a cell this way when hyperlinks can be assigned to noncell objects, such as drawn circles? Honestly, I've never found a good reason; however, the option is available by either right-clicking and selecting Hyperlink from the shortcut menu, or by selecting a cell and then selecting Hyperlink from the Insert tab on the main menu.

2.6 Formulae

Some formulae are basic, such as adding the contents of two cells, or dividing the contents of one by another and then subtracting a third. The syntax of others is less obvious. Excel 2007 and 2010, when loaded with Palisade software, has more than 500 functions already built in for use within cells. This is probably more than any one person will ever want, but it's nice to have these functions available.

After you select a cell in which to embed a built-in function, follow the Formulas>Insert Function menu path. The Insert Function dialog box (shown in Figure 2.19) will display.

The great thing about this dialog box is that the functions are organized into a set of approximately ten fairly intuitive categories, plus the

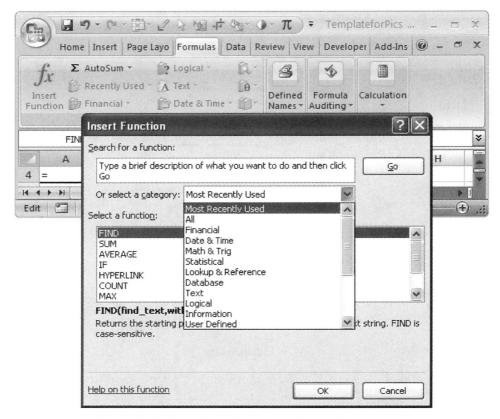

Figure 2.19. Selection of functions for use by category.

all-encompassing All category and User Defined items. Even better, this dialog box gives you instructions on the types of inputs each function takes and what each function does with these inputs. (I'll show a couple of examples shortly.) The following is a list of some of the options available in the Insert Function dialog box:

- *Financial*: Anything from interest-accrual calculations to net present value (NPV) to yields on T-bills. Useful stuff (makes you wonder why you were ever forced to memorize any formulae in finance classes).
- *Date & Time*: Getting and working with current date and time representations.
- *Math & Trig*: Common calculations that come up in business models such as sums (Σx), products (Πx), factorials ($x!$), exponentials (e^x), and rounding. Other, more sophisticated calculations that greatly assist in large-scale data consolidations are also available. These include SUMPRODUCT(x,y), which allows an array of x values to be multiplied by an array of y values of the same dimension. Each component in x is multiplied by its corresponding value in y and the sum of these products serves as the output.

- *Statistical*: Averages, counts, normal distribution (such as z-scores) calculations, quartiles, F-tests, and even things like the Poisson distribution.
- *Lookup & Reference*: Some of the neatest and most useful functions are in this category. Sifting through data can be frustrating for a manager, but these functions make the task a lot easier, quicker, and potentially more accurate. INDIRECT is an example of a simple reference tool that allows for an alternative means of accessing information elsewhere in a workbook. Providing a cell reference or cell label in quotation marks as the argument of this function will return the value in the corresponding cell. For example, if cell A1 is labeled FirstCell and contains the value 12, the INDIRECT(A1) or INDIRECT(FirstCell) will provide the value of 12 when called.

The Lookup & Reference function is often used in conjunction with other functions in a workbook. For illustration, the following sidebar provides an example of how often some functions (VLOOKUP, MATCH, and OFFSET) might be used in integration.

Sidebar on Function Use: VLOOKUP, MATCH, and OFFSET

In the workbook Chp2 IdentitiesList, we have an example where a class roster is used to look up a fake ID associated with a student's name (B2 relabeled Name) in a table (StudentInfo). As shown in Figure 2.20, the ID is in the second column of the table. (This function needs the exact spelling of the name.)

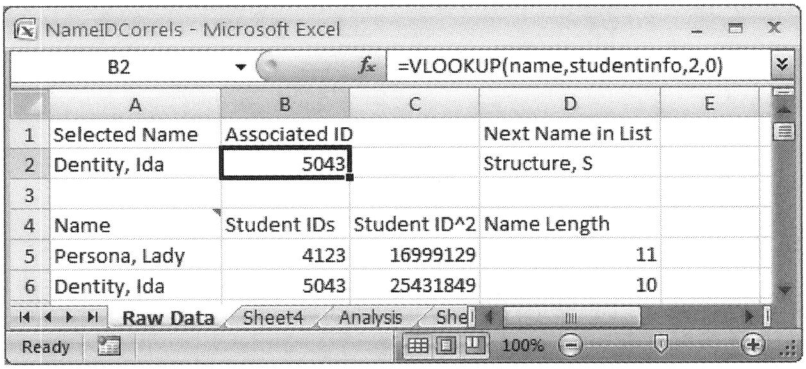

Figure 2.20. Example of VLOOKUP function in use.

Although I may already have an understanding of how to use this (and other functions), Excel won't leave me in the dark if I don't. If I select Insert Function, I'm given a full list of all the parameters associated with the function, some of which may be optional. In the case of OFFSET, for example, the Functions Argument dialog box opens (shown in Figure 2.21). For an example of integrated use, see Figure 2.22.

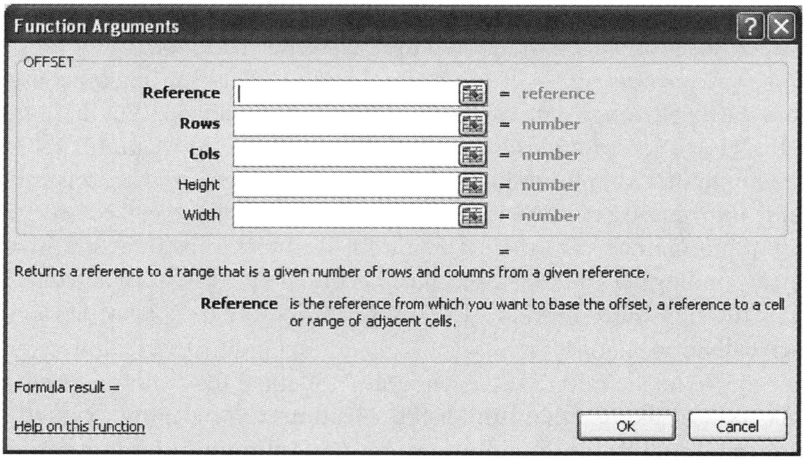

Figure 2.21. Example of assisted field interface for the OFFSET function.

In Figure 2.22, I used the MATCH function to determine which row a student's name is in (within just the Names column, NamesList), and I selected the student's name that appears just after it using the OFFSET function (my starting base is the Nameheader cell – A4 – in this table).

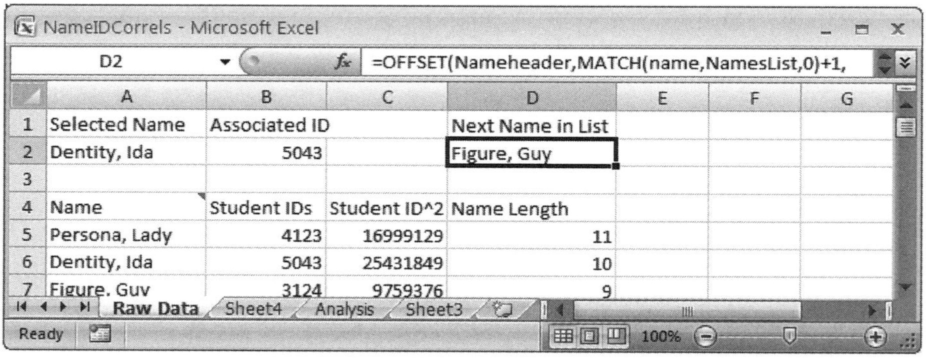

Figure 2.22. Example of combined use of MATCH and OFFSET.

- *Database*: Not an impressive list, but handy when interfacing Excel with databases. Provides averages, sums, and other summaries based on the contents of fields in databases.
- *Text*: Functions that allow you to merge text into a single string [such as CONCATENATE("alien", "ate") = "alienate"], determine the length of a string [such as LEN("alienate") = 8], extract a portion of text in a cell [such as MID("alienate",2,4) = "lien"], or simply find text within a large text [such as FIND("nate", "alienate") = 5 or FIND("nation", "alienate") = #VALUE!, which

essentially represents an error because nation cannot be found anywhere in the text "alienate"].

- *Information*: Provides information on the contents on cells, such as whether the number contained is odd, whether it's a number at all, or whether the cell contains an error as an output of the function within it (taking the square root of a negative number would provide the error term #NUM).
- *Engineering*: This is probably not that useful to you, but it allows for options such as the translation of binary to hexadecimal notation (for use in computer science) and calculations with imaginary complex numbers (for use in physics).
- *Logical*: Short list, but a critical one in decision support – especially the IF statement. IF can be applied to both numerical and text inquiries. It allows you to test whether the value in another cell is equal to, not equal to, or in some way related to (for example, greater than) other specifications, and it allows you to specify which calculation you want to be active in this cell under either condition (for example, if true or if false).

Examples: IF(B2=B3, B3*B3, "Not Applicable")
             IF(OFFSET(Nameslist,1,1)=MAX(B2:B3), "Maximum", "-")

Other extremely useful Logic functions include combinations of the IF statement concept with arithmetic functions (COUNTIF, SUMIF, AVERAGEIF), which allow only select values from an array of cells to be included in such calculations.

For more insights into the scope of the usefulness of conditional statements in general, see the Chapter 2 Supplement. For those not familiar with the nature of logical statements (perhaps from past philosophy or computer science coursework), this supplement will provide essential insights. Similar ways of thinking will be assumed throughout subsequent chapters in this text.

2.7 Copying Content and Formats

As shown in the use of the copy prompt in copying fixed data across cells, and in doing so making implicit use of Excel's pattern recognition capability, functions of all kinds, as well as cell formats and other attributes, can easily be pulled across (or down) ranges of other cells. However, a few caveats are worth mentioning. Cells conditionally formatted relative to a group of other cells (for example, as available through Excel 2007's group-relative formatting capabilities) may impact the conditional appearance of other cells in the original range. If not expected, this can occasionally prove frustrating, particularly if new cells in the formatted group represent outliers of some kind. They may reduce the apparent distinctiveness of certain cells in the originally formatted group.

Another caveat deals with functions that include cell references (as many do). When cells with such functions are copied, if they use soft-references to cells [for example, "=MATCH(B3, A1:A20,0)"], Excel will automatically change referenced cells as well [for example, "=MATCH(B4, A2:A21,0)"], if the cell copied to is one row below. Obviously, this is often not what a user wants. In this case, a user would probably not want the key range A1:A20 to change. To avoid this change, the use of cell and cell range names can do the trick beautifully because Excel will not attempt to alter the use of such labeled ranges as it copies among other cells.

Alternatively, one can use hard referencing to prevent any such changes in references as they are copied. A hard-referenced cell in a formula has its column and row each preceded by a dollar sign ($), such as $A$1 or $A$1:$A$20. When typing such a reference into a cell or function within a cell, you can toggle between soft and hard referencing by pressing the F4 key on the keyboard, or, more directly, by adding a $ as needed. Partial hard references that allow changes in either row (for example, $A1) or column (for example, A$1), but not both, can also come in handy, as we'll see in some of the more advanced examples presented throughout this book. Of course, if there are only a handful of cells or cell ranges that you plan to regularly reference, then the best tactic is to use the cell and range labeling approaches discussed previously.

2.8 Built-In Tools and Matrix Functions

Functions that provide singular outputs are incredibly useful. Being familiar with the functions covered up to this point would distinguish you from 90 percent of Excel users to date. But there's no reason to stop here – sometimes you need to perform a more sophisticated task that can't be handled easily by a set of functions. Here's where Excel's tools and data-manipulation devices come in handy. Generally, they are found in the Data tab. In the interest of time, we'll review only a few elements found in the Data tab menus. We'll start with Sort. Select a range of cells (for example, the StudentInfo range from the last exercise); select Data>Sort to open the Sort dialog box. Then, select which column you want to sort by (and how). Figure 2.23 shows the result of choosing the StudentID column for sorting.

You can apply a hierarchical sort by adding "Then by" requirements in the window above (for example, first sort by "Program" to get all the BBA and LAS students separated, then sort by "StudentID").

Another helpful tool is the Data Filter. This one is handy for tables that you've already constructed. You can select any cell in the table and go to Data Filter. Excel will automatically convert your table headers into drop-down menus that you can use to selectively present specific records of

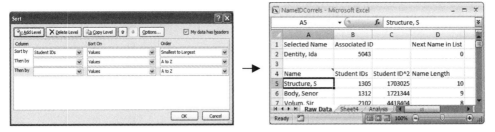

Figure 2.23. Example of the Sort capability in Excel.

interest. For example, having used the Autofilter on this table, I have the choice of filtering out all but the LAS students.

Many other convenient tools are also available for working with data in Excel. Many come standard with an Excel installation but are not "active" until you specify that you want them to be. These are the common add-ins such as the Analysis ToolPak and Solver. Other tools don't come with Excel but can be acquired from external sources (that is, through freeware or through purchase from vendors: See www.excel-blackbelt.com). Fortunately, many of the most useful nonstandard tools available from other sources (user-developed add-ins) are activated in the same way as the standard add-ins.

You can access add-ins in Excel 2010 by clicking on the File tab in the upper-left corner of the screen (in Excel 2007, the Office Button is used). This is depicted in Figure 2.24.

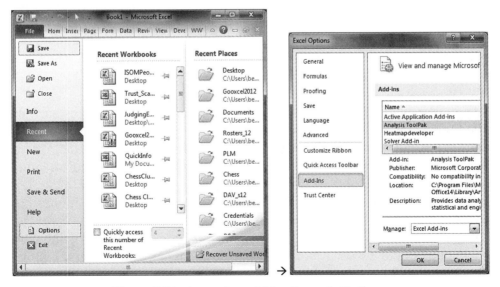

Figure 2.24. Accessing add-ins through Options.

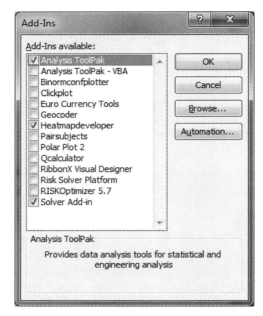

Figure 2.25. Add-Ins activation interface.

The resulting interface provides a host of options for changing the way your particular version of Excel works on your computer, including many advanced interfacing features we'll look at when discussing designs for use. In order to view the add-in availability, select the Add-Ins tab and then select "Excel Add-ins" on the lower "Manage" drop-down menu. Clicking on Go will generate a new dialog box that displays the set of add-ins immediately available. An example of what you might see is given in Figure 2.25. These files are stored in a folder on your computer and you can add more tools to them in the future (we'll return to this when we discuss the backend coding environment). Clicking on the Analysis ToolPak checkbox will activate the add-in and, in this case, make the Data Analysis tool accessible through the command ribbons

A reader who is new to add-ins may have immediate questions such as "Why do I have to go through so many steps to access something that comes with my installation?" and "Why aren't they all already activated?" There are numerous reasons for this, including computer resource use and an interest in keeping the Excel user interface simple (more add-ins can make the interface a noisy environment). However, there is another important reason: Some add-ins can actually interfere with the use of others – especially those designed by well-intentioned, but otherwise independent developers, who may, for example, assign a short-cut key to activate a feature of their add-ins that is already in use. For these reasons, when you don't need an add-in to be active, you should deselect it from your availability list.

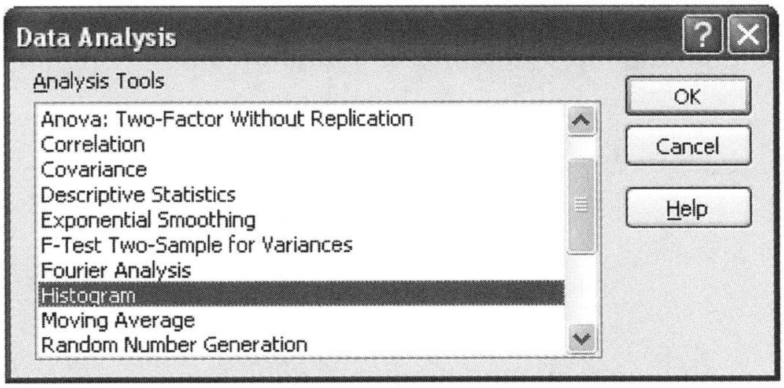

Figure 2.26. Data Analysis pop-up interface.

As for the power of add-ins, let's start to discuss in depth the one we've just activated. The Data Analysis add-in provides access to a range of tools; some are more useful to certain types of work than others. For example, let's try the Histogram tool using the data on the Analysis sheet of the Looku-pExample workbook. From the Data Analysis dialog box, select Histogram and then click OK (see Figure 2.26).

Imagine that we're interested in a histogram of the length of student names. The Histogram dialog box (Figure 2.27) is divided into two sections: Input and Output options. In the Input section, fill in the Input Range (the data that you want the histogram to display), as well as a Bin Range (the upper limits of each bar in the histogram). I've created a Bin Range within cells $H$8:$H$13 on the example worksheet and I use it here. In the Output options section, select the Output Range option button to determine where the bin summaries are provided and where a graphical output, if requested,

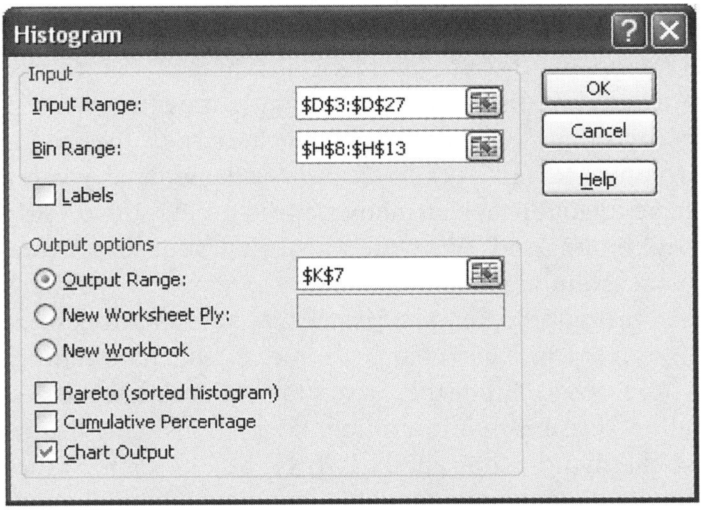

Figure 2.27. Specification of Histogram inputs.

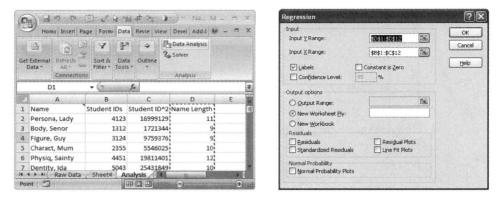

Figure 2.28. Specification of Regression inputs based on structure of spreadsheet.

is to be generated. The completed Histogram dialog box is shown in Figure 2.27.

In this particular case, the appropriate information provides a listing of the bins specified, the upper cut-off values for each bin, the number of observations that fall within it (count), as well as a histogram (as requested). You could get the same numbers that appear in the new Frequency column by using built-in formulae (see the contents of the Count column to the left of the new table). Another issue to consider here is the fact that the numbers in the new table are static. In other words, if the calculations behind the original data change (which might shift the data), this table won't change. In contrast, the numbers in the Count column will change because they are dynamically linked to the actual data by a function.

Let's consider another tool in the pack: Regression. Choosing this option provides a pop-up screen as shown in Figure 2.28. It allows you to specify a dependent (y) variable and any number of x variables that you might want to include in a regression. If we're interested in whether or not student IDs are somehow predictive of the length of student names (we must have hit our heads when coming in today), we could include both the student IDs and the square of those IDs (we really hit our heads hard) as x variables in the regression. The results provided, shown in Figure 2.29, are fairly rich from the perspective of the needs of a typical analyst who desires a quick snapshot of possible data relationships.

As with the histogram example, the results here are also static, meaning that they are not responsive to changes in the original data. This is an artifact of the Data Analysis tool, but there are other, more dynamic capabilities in Excel that allow for similar informational depictions. One of the most convenient is a building function called LINEST. Unlike some of the previously discussed functions that provide single outputs into single cells, the output of LINEST spans multiple cells (when used appropriately). The nature

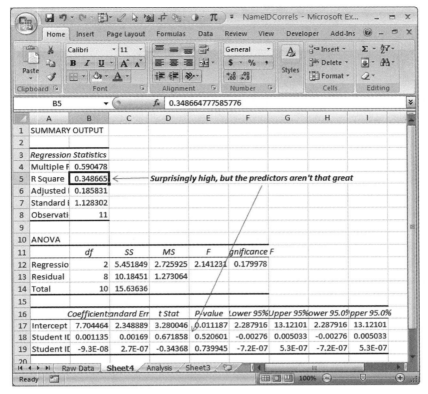

Figure 2.29. Sample annotated output of the Regression tool.

of this output is more akin to that of matrix functions such as MMULT that allow two-dimensional matrices to be multiplied by one another (the result of which may be more than a single cell of values). In order to use LINEST to regress an array of *y* values (for example, A1:A100) as a function of up to fifteen *x* values (for example, B1:P100), the following could be entered into an anchor cell: =LINEST(A1:A100,B1:P100,1,1). The third and fourth parameters specify whether a constant should be included in the model estimation and whether all statistical details of the regression are desired.

The result will be a single value in that cell. However, if that cell is selected as the start of a larger range selection (multiple rows and columns), and Ctrl-Shift-Enter is hit while the cursor is in the formula bar when it contains the LINEST function, all regression estimates can be presented in turn. Figure 2.30 provides an annotated example of LINEST in action. Estimated coefficients and standard errors around them are in the first two rows. Descriptions of overall fit are placed below. Note the curled brackets around the LINEST function as it appears in the formula bar. This denotes that a matrix function is being used.

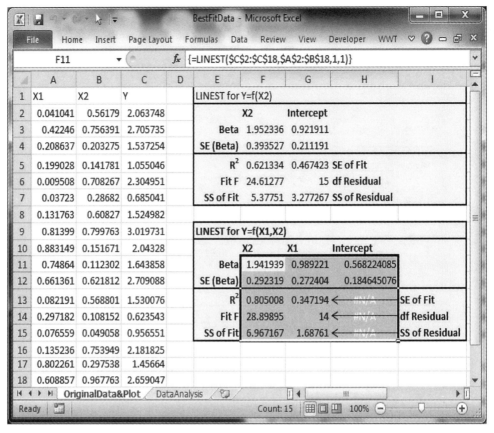

Figure 2.30. Selected range showing example output of LINEST for Y=f (C, X1, X2).

The nice thing, of course, is that when any of the original data (in A1:P100) is changed, as a live function, LINEST will react to those changes and change all the output cells accordingly, which is considerably more flexible than the Data Analysis function, albeit less straightforward for the casual user to initiate. Keep in mind that, regardless of the tactic used in analyzing data, statistical strength in a single analysis can be misleading. Taken alone it can even indicate patterns among unrelated random numbers, so be cautious. In general, it's always valuable to question the kinds of results that tools provide, so touch base with reality before you take the output of analysis as infallible.

Supplement: Logic and Structure in Conditional Statements

In most management settings, decisions that are made at one point in time affect the kinds of decisions that need to be confronted down the road. For

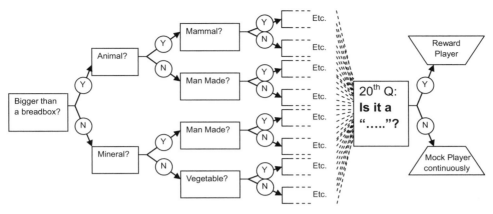

Figure 2.31. Example tree structure for determining identity.

example, consider the choice to expand the number of services offered by a firm to its clients.

If an option to expand is rejected, perhaps no additional decisions on the matter need to be made. However, if an option to expand is accepted, additional questions need to be answered. Should the expansion be targeted toward acquiring new clients, or toward better serving existing clients? If we simply want to better serve existing clients, is our end goal to increase their patronage, or to increase the likelihood of retention? Are we concerned about encouraging mid-term or long-term retention?

The structure of these complex multiphase decisions can be mapped out in a decision tree, a straightforward and commonly used framework. Decision tree structures (shown in Figure 2.31) are useful not only in outlining the course of a decision-making process, but also in outlining the course of a set of questions that might be asked in an attempt to assess the specific state of a management scenario. We can draw an analogy here with the common game of 20 Questions, using answers that are true or false (we stick to this assumed limitation for now).

Different types of questions may be relevant when trying to determine what calculations to make based on the current information available to a business analysis (such as data contained in a spreadsheet). For example, let's say we're a firm that manages large advertising projects for other businesses. We have a facility with a limited number of rooms, and we typically assign an individual room to a single advertising project. Other rooms may be used for a variety of other activities that we manage: for example, printing, secretarial duties, storage, management offices, and maintenance offices for ongoing campaigns. Occasionally, we may run short of space and need to consider renting additional space. We might want to determine the risk of an event in planning for rentals. But our calculation of risk might be based on a

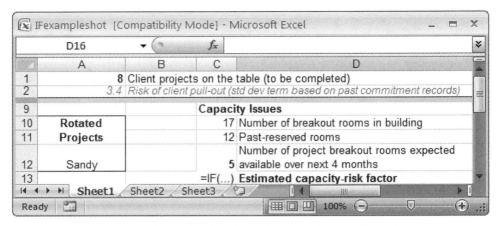

Figure 2.32. Example professional application of a conditional statement.

complex set of issues including the number of projects, past space reserved, managers involved, nature of the projects and clients, and so on.

It wouldn't take much for the calculation of risk, conditional on so many variables, to become complex, but we could consider mapping it out in a spreadsheet (see Figure 2.32). Let's say that based on the information we've started to lay out, the nature of risk (or uncertainty) we face regarding our need for capacity might be spelled out in a decision tree as shown in Figure 2.33. Calculating this risk can become convoluted (especially since there are implied differences in the risk-dynamics of coordinating different mixes of projects). But no matter how strange or complex the conditions of a work system may be, they shouldn't be ignored; rather, they should be captured as faithfully as possible with regard to their potential impact on decision

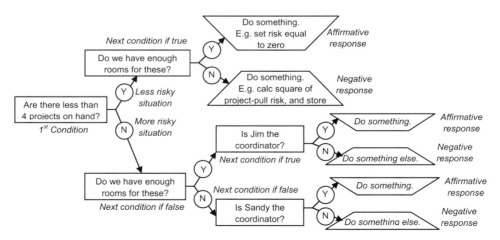

Figure 2.33. Tree structure characteristic of current professional application.

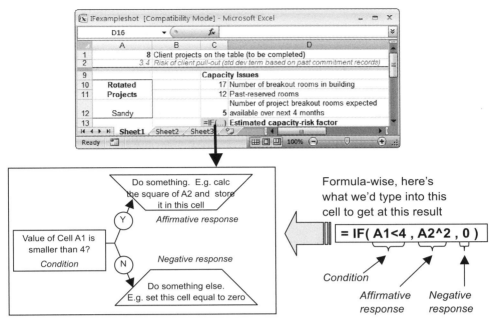

Figure 2.34. Relationship between conceptual tree structures and use of IF statements.

making and performance. Similar decision structures, as well as much simpler ones and much more complex ones, are possible in Excel.

The simplest form of the IF statement has three components:

1) A condition to test for (should be something that can be shown to be either TRUE or FALSE)
2) An affirmative response (what to do if TRUE)
3) A negative response (what to do if FALSE)

Using the space rental example, consider a much simpler version of 20 Questions to figure out the risk level facing the firm. Rather than 20 Questions, this game can be called 1 Question. One question is asked (one condition is tested) and one of two results (either an affirmative or a negative response) will be recorded (in cell C13, shown in Figure 2.34).

However, we don't have to limit ourselves to games of 1 Question when it comes to using IF statements. In a single cell in a worksheet, we may want to ask a sequence of questions that are each appropriate given the result of earlier questions (conditions). We do this using embedded or compound IF statements. Figure 2.35 shows an example using the first three levels of the earlier example (shown in alternate shades of gray). Note that each gray-shaded set of parentheses always encloses three elements: a condition, an affirmative response, and a negative response.

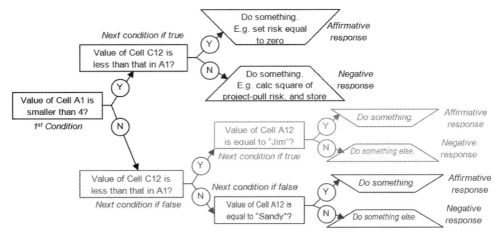

Figure 2.35. Gray-shaded representation of tree structure (specific to content in a spreadsheet).

The IF statement that embodies this structure is as follows; again, note that each set of parentheses always encloses three elements: a condition, an affirmative response, and a negative response.

= IF(A1<4, IF(C12<A1, 0, A2^2), IF(C12<A1, IF(A12="JIM", *something, something else*), **IF(A12="SANDY",** *something, something else*)))

It's worth noting a couple of major limitations of the IF statement in the spreadsheet. (Incidentally, these are limits that don't apply if we're coding behind the scenes, which is something we'll get into further on in this book.)

1) The result of an IF statement developed in a spreadsheet can only come in the form of cell content (for example, a number or text).
2) This content can only appear in the cell in which the IF statement resides.

However, the usefulness of the IF statement concept can (and often does) extend beyond the contents of any single cell. For example:

1) We could use conditional formatting to have the cell appearance change as the contents change (subject to the results of the IF statement).
2) Other cells in the spreadsheet may have their values based on the contents of that cell.
3) Similarly, in recursive use (iteration mode), we can use an IF statement in a single cell to basically serve as an ON/OFF switch for a host of other automated activities in the spreadsheet (such as data record construction, Monte Carlo simulations, and so on).

As a final note on how Excel interprets "conditions" or "logic" statements, it is worth mentioning that whenever we use a statement such as A11>12 as part of an IF statement, it triggers a response in Excel. Excel recognizes it as either TRUE or FALSE. If you type =(A11>12) into a cell in a spreadsheet, the result will be either True or False, depending on what value is in cell A11. However, Excel also uses numerical representations for True and False. In Excel, True is equal to 1, and False is equal to 0. If you multiply a True by a True, Excel will give you the value 1 ($1 \times 1 = 1$). If you add a True to two Falses, Excel will give you the value 1 as well ($1 + 0 \times 0 = 1$).

This dual interpretation can come in extremely handy when you want to do quick calculations with existing data that already contain True or False responses. For example, say you're trying to keep track of the capacity of a network of warehouses. In one column of a spreadsheet you might have records of the storage space for each warehouse. In the adjacent column you might have True or False statements on whether the space is accessible on a given date (perhaps some of these are in regions you can't get to, don't allow you to store what you want to, or simply have been shut down). You could create a third column that multiplies the first (#) and the second (True or False) and have a sum at the base of that column to let you know how much space is really available.

PRACTICE PROBLEMS

Practice 2.1

All of the minor methods discussed in this chapter can be used together to get some otherwise tedious work done in a quick but user-friendly way. For example, let's work to develop a threshold table for z-scores.

1) Type the following text into the cells of a new spreadsheet: In A1, type z-score; in B1, type Cumulative; in C1, type Density.
2) In the cells below A1, create a list of numbers from -3, -2.9, -2.8, up through 3. Use the copy prompt to do this. Label the full numeric range of cells z-scores.
3) In the cells below B1, use the NormsDist function to convert the values in the range z-scores (using the label as your reference, not the column-row designation) into percentages (fixed format them to be viewed as %). Use the copy prompt to copy down the rest of column B. Label that full numeric range of cells Cumulative.
4) In cell C2, type =Cumulative. In cell C3, type =Cumulative-B2. Use the copy prompt to copy the contents of C3 down to the rest of the cells in column C.
5) In D1, type Threshold =, and in D2, type some number between 0 and 0.04. Label D2 Threshold.
6) Use conditional formatting to make the background of any cell in column C green if it is greater than that threshold.

Practice 2.2

Select an approximately 200-word paragraph to analyze. This doesn't need to be relevant to your area of expertise, although that might make the exercise more meaningful to you. Import the paragraph into a single cell in a new workbook. Using the FIND and MID functions, decompose it into a list (column in Excel) of individual words. Use the COUNTIF function to create a second column that specifies how many times each word is found in the list you created. Then, use conditional formatting to color numbers (in that second column) red if they are greater than 2 and green if they are equal to 1.

3

Getting Data: Acquisition, Linkage, and Generation

Aside from typing information into Excel, there are a number of other ways to get new data into spreadsheets. These methods include opening structured, plain-text files in ways that are meaningful to Excel (for example, raw-data.txt); using other desktop applications as data sources (such as tables in MS Word and tabular results from SPSS); drawing information from structured or nonstructured online sources (such as content from COMPUSTAT or even the whitepages.com); and developing systems that create or simulate large volumes of data with desired characteristics (mainly for use in illustrating or testing the robustness of proposed management policies). In this chapter, we'll touch on each of these methods at some level.

3.1 Text File Imports and Basic Table Transfers

If you have a text file that contains information, such as a survey or database data in text-file format, it can be opened into Excel as a new file. You simply need to specify how data in that file are organized, such as separated by spaces, tabs, commas, and so on. As an example, imagine a text file titled Chp3_MultRespsFinal.txt. Each record in this file occupies a new row, and the information relating to each record is organized sequentially with each field separated by a comma. This kind of data organization is referred to as "comma delimited." Select Home>Open in Excel and then find and select this text document. The Step 1 of the Text Import Wizard opens, as shown in Figure 3.1.

In this case, we have what is referred to as a "delimited" file. It's relatively easy to import raw files such as these into other programs – certain markers such as commas help designate where a type of data ends and another begins. Most applications are designed to be able to make sense out of data organized this way. Comma delimitation (or delimitation of some other kind) is specifically designated in the Delimiters section of Step 2 of the Text Import

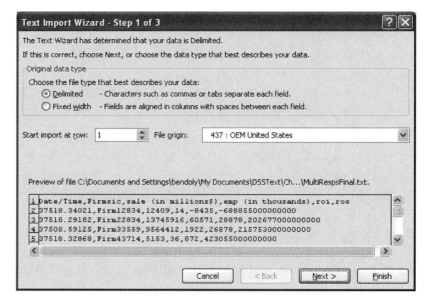

Figure 3.1. Text Import Wizard interface.

Wizard, shown in Figure 3.2. In this case, selecting Comma provides you with a preview of how the data will appear in the spreadsheet once Finish is selected.

What you end up with in the spreadsheet is a relatively intuitively structured display of the contents of that file, if done correctly (Figure 3.3).

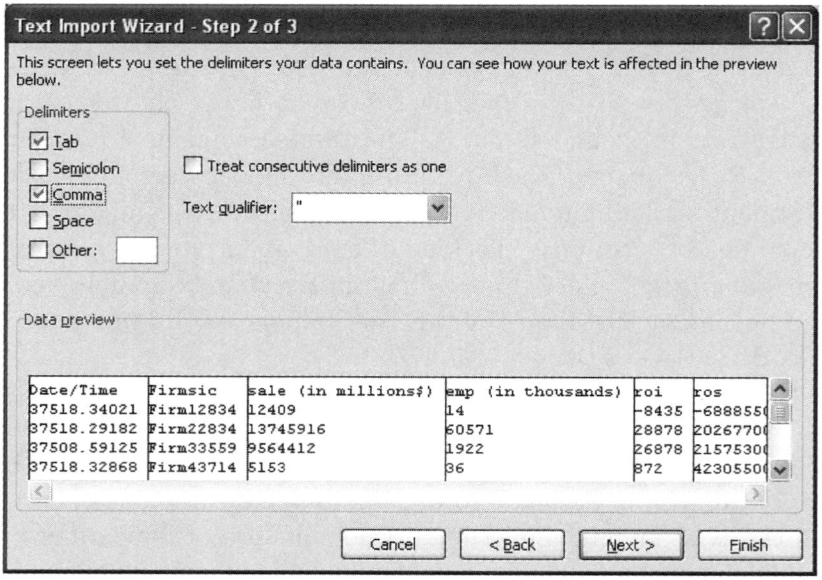

Figure 3.2. Specification of comma delimitation.

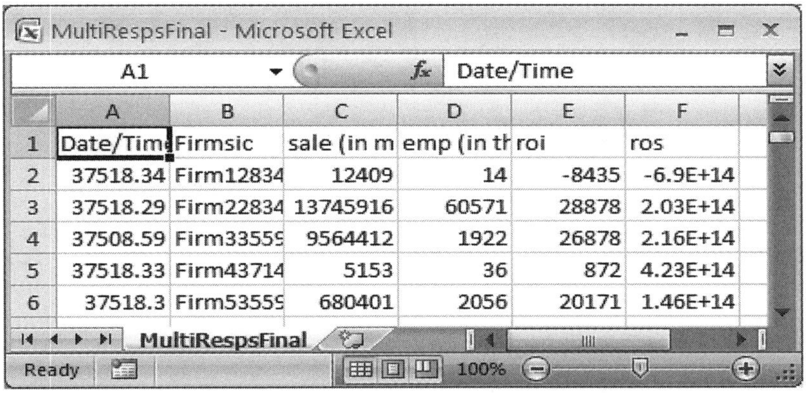

MultiRespsFinal - Microsoft Excel

A1 | Date/Time

	A	B	C	D	E	F
1	Date/Tim	Firmsic	sale (in m	emp (in th	roi	ros
2	37518.34	Firm12834	12409	14	-8435	-6.9E+14
3	37518.29	Firm22834	13745916	60571	28878	2.03E+14
4	37508.59	Firm33559	9564412	1922	26878	2.16E+14
5	37518.33	Firm43714	5153	36	872	4.23E+14
6	37518.3	Firm53559	680401	2056	20171	1.46E+14

MultiRespsFinal

Ready 100%

Figure 3.3. Spreadsheet content once imported.

Direct imports from other MS office programs (such as tabular data in MS Word) or non-MS programs that use tabular structures (for example, SPSS) are even easier. In most cases, select the table or range of data of interest, copy it, select a starting cell in your spreadsheet, and then paste the data into it by pressing Ctrl-V. Alternatively, you can select Edit>Paste and achieve the same result.

3.2 More Sophisticated Application Transfers

Few meaningful corporate decisions can be made without some implied, if not explicit, consideration for the geographical surroundings in which the firm is set (local demand, local labor, environmental regulations, international law, and so on). Fortunately, if we want to account for geography, infrastructure, and demographics, we have a number of resources already available to us. One of those is MS MapPoint, shown in Figure 3.4.

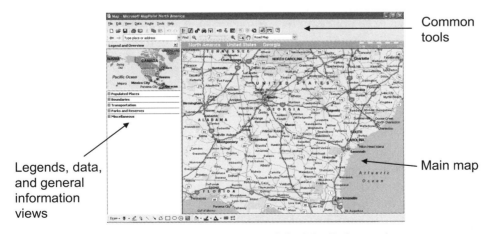

Figure 3.4. Basic front-end elements of the MapPoint environment.

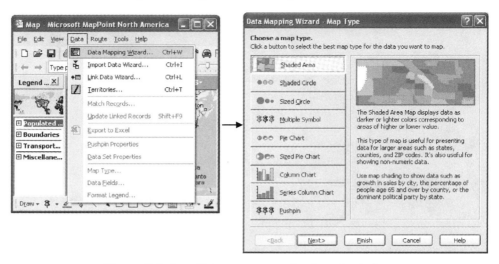

Figure 3.5. Specifying map type for data depiction.

3.2.1 MapPoint Data Sources

MapPoint is more than a mapping program. It's also a geographic information system (GIS) with geo-data already built into it. You can access this data through the Data Mapping Wizard as shown in Figure 3.5.

The wizard starts by presenting several different ways to graphically represent this geo-data. After you select a presentation type, you'll need to specify what data you want to present. For example, you might be interested in graphing demographic data relating to specific areas in the United States (Figure 3.6).

MapPoint can then present a host of demographic options specific to your needs (depending on what MapPoint database you have access to). When those data are fully specified, you can then tweak some of the aesthetics of the map you want to generate (see Figure 3.7). Before you know it, you have a geographic representation of data to which you can add information, pan across, and zoom in and out.

We'll spend more time on the graphical capabilities of MapPoint in Chapter 4. However, at this point in our discussion of data access, it's enough to recognize that these maps are both data-rich and interactive in terms of making specific instances of that data available. Specifically, if you place your cursor over certain areas or features, comment boxes will pop up to provide specific details.

Another tool that assists with understanding the data depicted in a MapPoint map is the Location Sensor shown in Figure 3.8. When the Location Sensor is turned on, you can move the cursor over a location (for

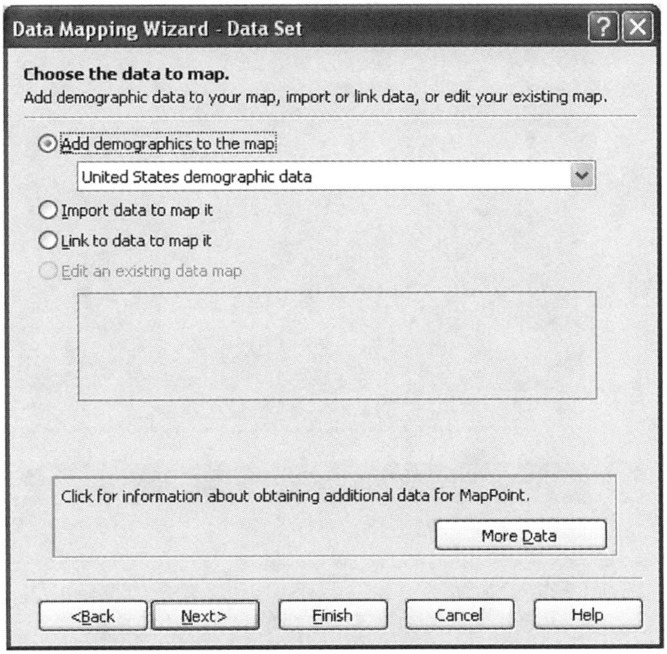

Figure 3.6. Initial data specification.

example, Monroe Heights, VA) and see a summary of the data mapped at that location as well as the longitude and latitude. This could come in handy for some quick approximations of distances between a variety of locations.

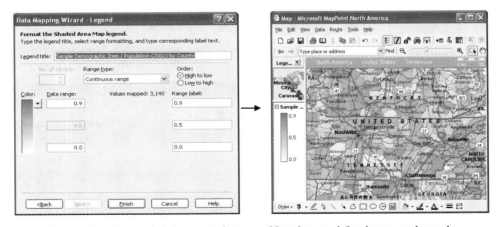

Figure 3.7. Potential demarcation specification and final mapped result.

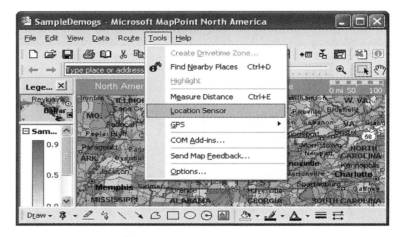

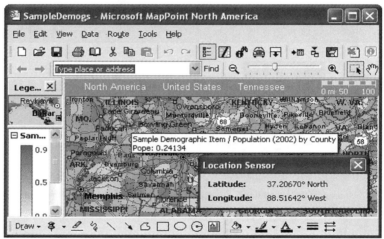

Figure 3.8. Activating and using the Location Sensor by panning.

3.2.2 Pulling Data from MapPoint

It is easy to export MapPoint data into Excel where the data can be manipulated. There are several approaches worth going over for those interested in leveraging this data. In MapPoint, the most direct method is Data>Export to Excel, as seen in Figure 3.9.

Alternatively, if you want to export a specific geographic region, select that region in MapPoint and then conduct an export only. Using the numerous drawing tools available (such as the radius tool), you can select a geographically relevant area of interest (100 miles around Nashville, TN, for example), and restrict the export of data to that area. This is demonstrated in Figure 3.10. And the nice thing is that you are getting exactly what you want without the burden of having to wait for a much larger volume of data to otherwise be exported.

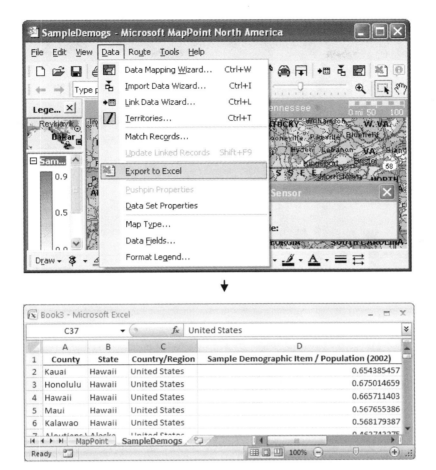

Figure 3.9. Requesting an export to Excel and the resulting spreadsheet.

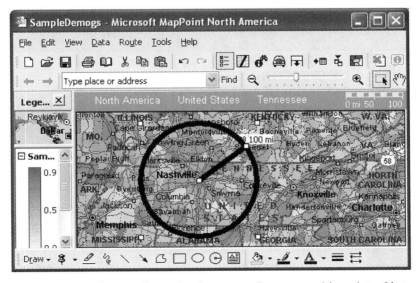

Figure 3.10. Example of radius selection around a geographic point of interest.

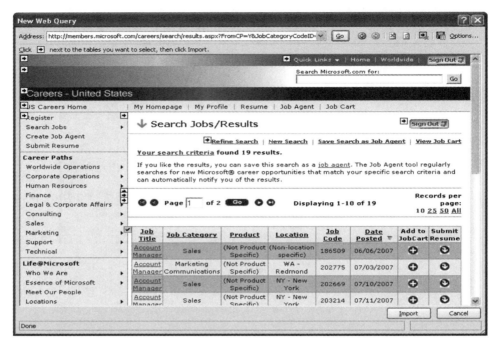

Figure 3.11. Example of Web Query interface.

3.3 Online Data Acquisition

The integration of alternative data-rich applications with Excel has the potential to open up numerous opportunities for developers and managers who might otherwise be unaware of these convenient resource integrations. At this point, let's look at how we can bring the Internet into our discussion of data resources.

3.3.1 Generalized Web-Data Pulls

Many online sources of potentially valuable data are already publicly available and updated on a regular basis. The number of these sources is on the rise. The implication of this, however, is that what the sources said yesterday may not be relevant to a decision that needs to be made today. In Excel, Web queries are used to draw information from online resources. Similar to data analysis, a Web query is a tool that comes standard in Excel. Select Data>Web Query to open the New Web Query dialog box. Specify from where the data will be drawn, such as the URL. Figure 3.11 shows an example of the public job site hosted by Microsoft.

Newer versions of Excel have an updated interface for selecting what you want to import. In the previous example, only the job specification table has been selected (shown as a gray check-marked box here; however, in a live document it would appear as a green check-marked box as, opposed to an unselected one marked by a yellow arrow). You can toggle between selecting and deselecting these elements with the click of the mouse.

Click Import after making the table selections (check marks will appear). You will then be asked where you want the results of the query to be placed in your spreadsheet. Specify somewhere in the upper-left corner "where" exactly you want the input data to start. I usually pick cell A2 for simplicity. After you provide location information, the first importation of data will occur. The data you're interested in will start somewhere to the right of and below the cell you selected, depending on the table structures on that Web page.

Consider doing additional work to the right or below the import space, so updates don't overwrite other work on the worksheet. Losing information can be frustrating, so I recommend saving various versions as you develop your spreadsheet. After a new Web query is created (or just prior to import), further specifications can be made by selecting Properties from the Data tab. This opens the External Data Range Properties dialog box, as shown in Figure 3.12.

This dialog box enables you to set a number of properties for your Internet imported data. In this example, I've made additional specifications that the data be updated every ten minutes; updates do not change the column widths on the spreadsheet and all formats are preserved. Further on in this chapter, we'll take a look at how this might be important when building a tool for collecting Web data over time.

A caveat to the use of general Web Queries is the fact that many sources will not structure data targeted for import in a way that is immediately useable in Excel. For illustration, let's look at an alternative to the job site example. Specifically, let's consider the content-sharing capabilities provided by Google Documents. The Google sheets can be used as targets for Web Queries. However, unless the source is the published version of the sheet, the resulting import may contain content that you don't want. Figure 3.13 provides a clip of a sample Google sheet and the associated Excel Web Query. Content such as row and column headers comes along for the ride, as does an unneeded progress message.

This additional data won't be a serious barrier to the use of the imported data, but it might create an impetus to take additional action to improve the presentation of the query. Other import results from a variety of sites that contain data of interest are much messier. What solutions exist? Here is where the use of Excel functions come up again. Particularly useful are functions such as MATCH (for finding key markers in the imported data, beyond which critical data exist), OFFSET (for pulling out data located near

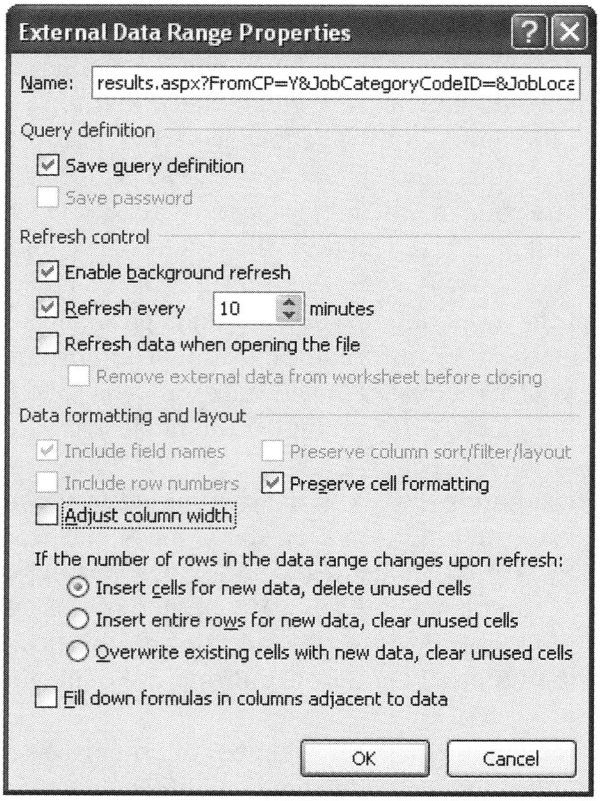

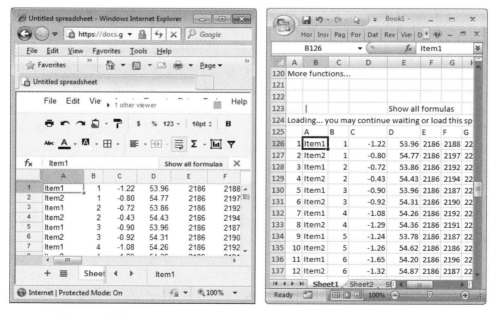

Figure 3.12. Example of specifications for Web query.

Figure 3.13. Google sheet and Web Query of that sheet in Excel.

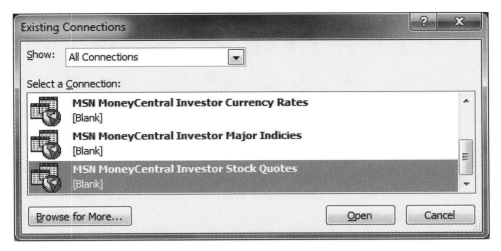

Figure 3.14. MSN stock data connection.

the result of MATCH), and both FIND and MID (for parsing data that gets imported as merged with other content).

3.3.2 Specialized Web-Data Pulls

Fortunately, those interested in developing pulls of data from the Web have alternatives in certain circumstances that guarantee structure. Some of these come standard with Excel. A fantastic example is that of Excel's MSN MoneyCentral connections, found under Get External Data>Existing Connections. Figure 3.14 shows the options available under this category, including a source of highly structured stock quotes, which are refreshed regularly throughout the day.

Other sources capitalize on both Excel and Google capabilities, such as the GoogleMaps API. One such example is the Geocoder add-in developer by David Wichman (a student of mine), which is available on the Excel Black-belts directory (https://sites.google.com/site/exceladdinsdirectory/home/main-directory) along with documentation. In order to make this add-in, or any external add-in, available to your version of Excel, store the unzipped file in your "\Roaming\Microsoft\AddIns" folder. Yours might be more like: "C:\Users\smith\AppData\Roaming\Microsoft\AddIns," replacing "smith" with your user name. I examine and use external add-ins so frequently that I've actually made a shortcut to this folder on my desktop. This is the folder that Excel will look for an add-in within. When you open the Excel application and go to Options>Add-ins>Manage Add-ins>Go, you should see all such files available (as in our previous discussion of the activation of Excel's Data Analysis ToolPak).

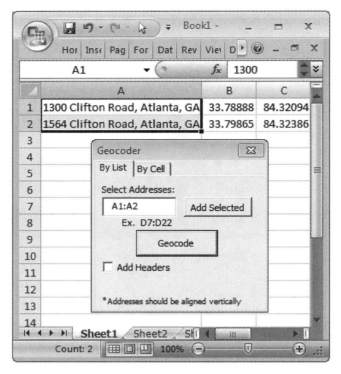

Figure 3.15. Use of the GoogleMaps API in the Geocoder add-in.

An example of the Geocoder add-in in use is provided in Figure 3.15. The resulting longitude and latitude coordinates of all addresses requested are consistently presented in columns B and C.

3.4 Simulating Continuous Data: The Basics

When acquired data are not available or do not sufficiently character- ize future scenarios, developers often rely on random numbers to portray dynamics. There are many different ways to calculate random numbers in Excel. The following sections discuss some of the more common methods (refer to Chp3_RandomNumbers.xls).

3.4.1 Uniformly Distributed Random Values

Basically, these are random values ranging from some minimum value (*a*) to some maximum value (*b*). To create a random number based on this distribution in Excel, start with the random number generation func- tion Rand(). Rand() automatically gives you a random number between 0 and 1. To change that to a range from *a* to *b*, enter the following information into a cell (replacing *a* and *b* with real numbers): = a + Rand() * (b, a).

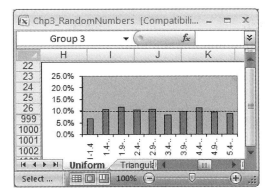

Figure 3.16. Example of sample population from uniform distribution.

If a = 1 and b = 5 for 1,000 random numbers, we might get what's demonstrated in Figure 3.16. Note that you can press F9 to generate new random numbers.

3.4.2 Triangularly Distributed Random Values

These distributions also represent random values ranging from some minimum value (*a*) to some maximum value (*b*). However, unlike uniformly distributed random values, the chance of picking a number in this range peaks at some value (*c*), and is essentially zero at both *a* and *b*. Excel uses the IF statement along with the Rand() function to provide the following form:

= IF (Rand()<(c-a)/(b-a); for example, is Rand() below the peak?
a+SQRT((b-a)*(c-a)*Rand()); for example, if yes, then use this calculation.
b-SQRT((b-a)*(b-c)*(1-Rand()))); for example, if no, then use this calculation instead.

If a = 1, b = 5, and c = 4 for 1,000 random numbers, we might get what's demonstrated in Figure 3.17.

3.4.3 Normally Distributed Random Values

You're probably familiar with this one (at least, in theory – for example, the bell curve). Fortunately, Excel makes this simple: = NORMINV(Rand(), μ, σ). If $\mu = 3$ and $\sigma = 1$ for 1,000 random numbers, we might get what's shown in Figure 3.18.

Excel's built-in functions allow for several other common distributions to be handled the same way (such as CHIINV() for the χ-dist, FINV() for F-dist, TINV() for t-dist, and so on).

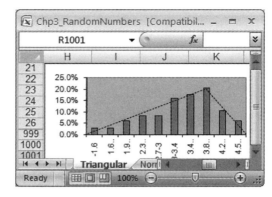

Figure 3.17. Example of sample population from triangular distribution.

3.5 Discrete Random Number Generation

Sometimes, it's useful to consider the chances that alternative discrete events occur. For example, a person decides to buy Brand X instead of Brand Y; or three people don't show up for hotel room reservations on Friday (as opposed to one person, or two or four people); or a competing firm decides to build its new facility in Jacksonville instead of Des Moines or Toledo; or items 2 and 17 are dropped from a federal bill outlining tax incentives for small exporters.

Each of these events is discrete – it either happens or it doesn't. If it does happen, the implication is that alternative events that could have occurred in its place didn't, at least for the specific timeframe considered. Sometimes, the alternative events are related in an ordinal fashion – for example, three people not showing up is greater than two people not showing up. Sometimes, alternative events are simply nominal; they're not easily comparable

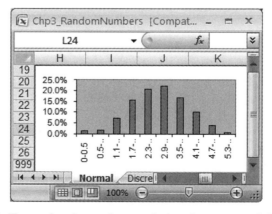

Figure 3.18. Example of sample population from normal distribution.

by a single measure but they're distinct from one another nevertheless (buying Brand X instead of Brand Y, for example). The consideration of these kinds of variables and their uncertainty are just as important to good decision making as is the consideration of more continuous variables (those that can take on meaningful decimal values).

3.5.1 Uniform Discrete Randoms

These are the simplest variables that describe multiple discrete events, with each event having exactly the same chance of occurring at a given point in time. Regardless of what each event is, it can be represented by coding, such as Event 1, Event 2, and so on, up to Event n. This makes it easy to use Excel to generate random events with equal (uniform) chances of occurring. For n random events, we can use:

$$= \text{RANDBETWEEN(1,n), or } = \text{INT(n*RAND()+1)}$$

Both will provide equally weighted random integers between 1 and n that can correspond to each of the n events under consideration.

3.5.2 Bernoulli Discrete Randoms

In some circumstances, we are interested in only one of two events taking place, such as a potential customer either signing up or not signing up for an offered service contract. The chances of either event are often not equal. These are called Bernoulli events, and the outcomes are typically coded numerically as 0 (doesn't sign up) or 1 (does). If the probability of 1 occurring is p percent(29%, 73%, 8%, or another percentage), we can generate a 0,1 variable value in Excel by using the following IF-based statement:

$$= \text{IF(RAND()<=p, 1, 0)}$$

We could even replace the 0,1 coding directly with meaningful information, such as:

$$= \text{IF(RAND()<=29\%, "Signs up", "Doesn't sign up")}$$

3.5.3 Custom Discrete Randoms

In some circumstances, we have multiple (more than two) alternative events, each of which has its own probability of occurring. Because these are true alternatives, adding up the chances of each event should give us 100 percent (all possible outcomes need to be accounted for). We can consider these events and their probabilities in a tabular format. Consider an example from

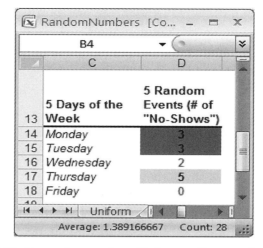

Figure 3.19. Example sample pulls from a discrete distribution.

the hotel industry. Past data show that the following number of no-shows occur by these probabilities regardless of the day of the week:

Number of no-shows	Probability of that number of no-shows occurring (%)	Cumulative (%)
0	9	0
1	12	9
2	22	21
3	28	43
4	19	71
5	10	90

An easy way to draw random values from this table is to use the VLOOKUP function again with the RAND() function. Specifically, using the last two columns in the previous table, VLOOKUP will return the row with the Cumulative probability <= RAND() (see Figure 3.19) and will return the value in the second of those two columns:

$$= VLOOKUP(RAND(),LastTwoColumns,2)$$

3.6 Living Data Records: The Basics

The standard calculation mode in Excel is noniterative automatic, meaning that every time you make a change in the workbook, all cells are updated. But sometimes you want to have more control over your data. The iteration option enables you to gain some of that control.

Iteration allows for actions such as setting the value in cell A1 equal to the value in A1 + 1 (for example, it enables you to enter the "A1=A1+1"

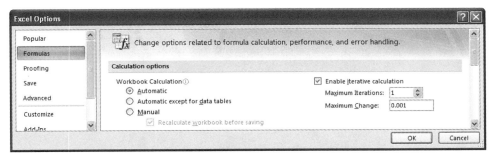

Figure 3.20. Specification of iteration mode in Excel.

equation into cell). In general, this is referred to as a circular loop because you're asking the computer to base the value of something off itself. If the computer were told to do this continuously, that value would soon become huge (and would keep growing). When faced with this situation, some software will give you an error message saying something like a circular loop has been detected and the value in the cell will not stabilize.

Iteration mode allows developers to say exactly how many times the computer should do the calculation before stopping, thus avoiding problems usually caused by circular loops. To switch into iteration mode, click the Office Button (2007) or the File tab (2010) and then select Options>Formulas to open the Excel Options dialog box. Under the Calculation options section, check the Enable iterative calculation checkbox (see Figure 3.20). For most cases, one iteration, maximum, is appropriate. Select that and click OK to enable this setting. Note that you should use iteration mode only when it's your best option. Trying to create other types of spreadsheet workbook tools can be tough in this mode, as well as frustrating. Most work is done in the noniterative mode.

Under the iteration setting, calculations begin with the upper-left cell (such as A1), and then progress through the first row of the spreadsheet from left to right until that row comes to an end (cell IV1). Calculations then resume, starting at the first column of the next row and progressing again from left to right, until all cells containing calculations are handled (see Figure 3.21).

In iteration mode, recalculations are started by pressing the same key used to refresh or generate new random values in normal modes. In the single iteration mode, if there is a calculation to be made in cell A1, whenever F9 is pressed Excel will base that calculation off all information currently available (including information that currently appears in A1). If there is subsequent calculation to be made in cell B1, that calculation will take into account all current information as well as the value calculated for A1. Similarly, any calculation for B2 would involve the updated values for both A1

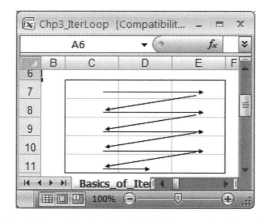

Figure 3.21. Order of refresh calculations under iteration mode.

and B1. After calculations are made for cells during a single iteration (by pressing F9), they will not change until another iteration is started. This holds true for all mathematical calculations, logic statements, and text functions, as well as random number generation.

The spreadsheet Chp3_IterLoop.xls contains examples of how the iteration mode might be applied. The first example is basically the baseline example that illustrates how a typical circular loop is constructed, and how cell calculations based on it are changed upon each iteration (each time F9 is pressed). In this example, I have set up fourteen cells such that the values contained in thirteen of them are based on the value of the cell before it. I've depicted this dependency with dashed lines. (Notice that it is in the opposite direction of the order by which cell calculations are made in the iteration mode. I did that on purpose.) The value in the fourteenth cell is calculated by increasing itself by 1 (D18 is set to =D18+1, as shown in Figure 3.22).

The specific structure of this series of calculations is often referred to as a "bottom-up" design. This design allows new data generated in lower cells to "percolate" up to cells above them (or to the left). This movement is possible only because of the "top-down" nature of iteration mode calculations (shown in Figure 3.21).

In this case, I've also restricted calculations to particular situations (that is, only when the value for a cell labeled Restart is set to True). In the spreadsheet, this value can be either modified directly through typing or it can be toggled using the associated check box (we'll talk about creating check boxes later). The calculations begin when Restart is True and I press F9. But after the first iteration, the only cell that should appear to change is cell D18 (=0+1=1). All others are recalculating as well. However, they only take on the value of their assigned neighbors – and because that value is 0 to start,

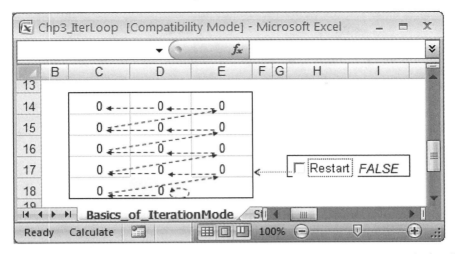

Figure 3.22. Example of living record cell interdependency: data "percolation."

no changes appear to occur. After a second iteration, D17 takes on D18's value (1) and D18 becomes 2. After ten iterations, we get what's shown in Figure 3.23.

3.7 Living Records in Practice

To give you a better feeling for how the iteration mode can become a critically valuable resource in practice, it's worth considering a couple more sophisticated examples in which it's applied.

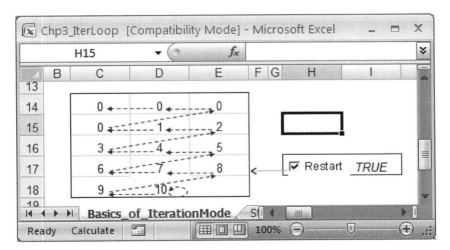

Figure 3.23. Associated result of example living record update.

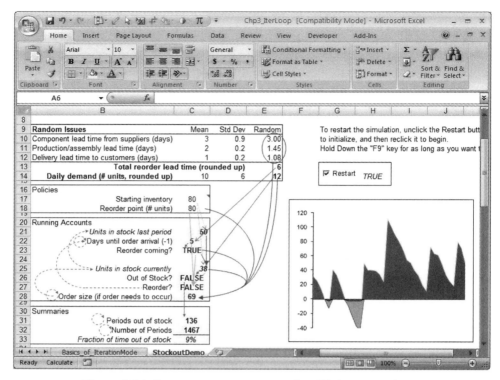

Figure 3.24. Inventory system example of living record use.

3.7.1 Example: Simulated Histories (A Preview of System Simulations)

The first in-practice example (found on the StockoutDemo worksheet of the previous workbook) is considerably more complex in terms of the number and nature of cell dependencies. As in the previous example, I've illustrated where both forward (solid lines) and circular or backward dependencies (dashed lines) exist, as well as how starting conditions are applied (light dotted lines). Also, in this example, one of the variables (Units in Stock) is tied to a live data record and an associated graph (see Figure 3.24).

This example shows how far an individual might be able to leverage the iteration mode and living records. The live data record that the graph is working off of is no more complex that the previous fourteen-cell numeric example.

Basically, we have one cell at the bottom that continues to update itself (see Figure 3.25). This cell is based off the most recent value representing units in stock, while cells above it take on values of those below them (that is, values from the past).

Note that the form of the plot shown is a simple line graph with the x-axis assumed to be time. Therefore, it is depicting changes in inventory positions as time progresses.

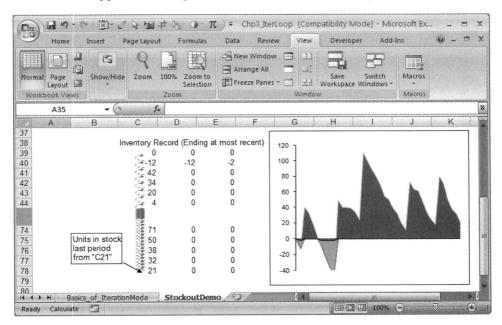

Figure 3.25. Specific structure of living record in inventory system example.

3.7.2 Example: Web-Import Histories

Having already discussed the potential of acquiring data from the Web, and given the example of building a living record based on randomly generated data, we now have the basic tools necessary to construct a live-data recording mechanism based on data updates from external sources.

With online data provided by external sources, it often makes sense to record new data only when we're sure that they're different from past data, and then to collect the time at which these changes are detected. This way, you can get a good idea of how data change over time without having too much redundant information. In a spreadsheet, this will mean basically selecting two columns in which you want to store records (one column for your imported data, another for the time at which the data are recorded). This approach requires limited (four, in this case) kinds of cell calculations. In this case, two of these calculations will be repeated throughout most of your data record. A typical spreadsheet layout for this purpose is described in the following clip from Chp3_nrtRecords.xls. It's fully annotated and duplicates much of the logic we've discussed (see Figure 3.26).

Supplement: Unique Data Generation and Sharing Tactics

Graphics need not be solely the "outcome" of data collection efforts. They can also facilitate data development. Similarly, Excel doesn't need to be the

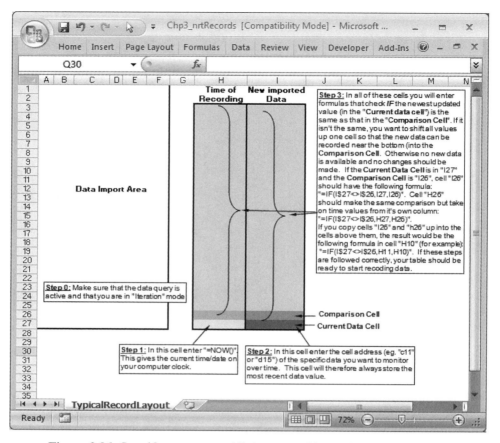

Figure 3.26. Specific structure of living record in Web query example.

final destination for developed data. Freely available add-ins make graphics-driven data generation and data exporting to online sources possible (in contrast to our discussion of data importing, but something that can certainly be used in tandem).

The ClickPlot add-in, developed by In-Wook Yoo (a student of mine) allows individuals to effectively generate data points by moving their mouse and clicking on targeted locations in scatter or bar charts. The add-in and documentation is downloadable from the Excel Blackbelts directory (https://sites.google.com/site/exceladdinsdirectory/home/main-directory). Ctrl-P activates the add-in and generates a userform pop-up that will allow you to specify the kind of graphical-data development you want. It will also allow you to manage the development process (stop, start, delete, and so on). An example of this add-in in use is presented in Figure 3.27.

In this particular case, an image (taken from GoogleMaps) of the Cleveland area and surrounding cities, has been inserted and the ClickPlot chart template, set up as a scatter plot, and given a transparent backing so that

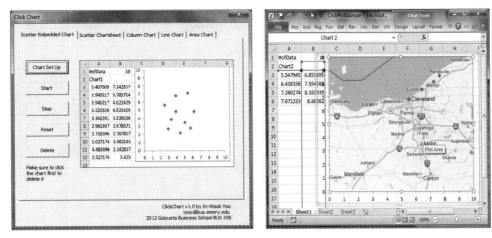

Figure 3.27. ClickPlot add-in applied to the x–y mapping of geographic points of interest.

the map image is visible. In this way, the relative x–y position of points of interest, or even paths of transit, can quickly be recorded for later use.

Now, let's say you'd like to quickly share that generated data, or any data for that matter, with the world. Everyone else can clearly query data from a Google sheet through Excel, as we saw in Section 3.3. We can also post to such sheets if we make use of tools such as the GoogleWriter add-in, a tool co-developed by Harry Taylor and also available on the Excel Blackbelts add-in directory. The inputs to this beta version add-in are similar to what is shown in Figure 3.28 when it is activated.

Inputs associated include specifications for the area of data in the Excel worksheet to be sent out, the URL destination (a Google sheet), the start cell for transfer at that destination, and Google doc username and password details as needed. Hitting the Post Data to File button, assuming the Google sheet exists and you are able to post data to it, will transfer the described data online. Default settings are also available so that a regularly used URL, data range, and username and password need not be retyped every time the tool is used. To reiterate the previous discussion in Section 3.3.2, store the unzipped file in your "\Roaming\Microsoft\AddIns" folder in order to make these add-ins, or any external add-ins, available to your version of Excel.

PRACTICE PROBLEMS

Practice 3.1

Select a set of data to map; then select a portion of the map and export the data into Excel. Modify the data to your liking, perhaps by replacing some of it with other

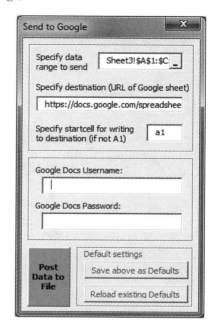

Figure 3.28. GoogleWriter add-in interface.

random values or a simple mathematical function. Click Update Now to see the resulting change in mapping.

Practice 3.2

Create a stock-value generator that picks values of a stock based on a random mechanism for selecting recently observed values of that stock. Create a stock-value collector for an individual company (your choice), using the iterative mode Web query and recording method discussed in this chapter. Run the collector for a two-hour period (start early to make sure you have it working) and then use the collected record and the RAND function to pick values from the list. Use whatever technique you think may be appropriate.

Practice 3.3

Use a Web query to import a page from *The New York Times* job database. Use the following URL stem, and add the last digit of your birth date to it to signify the page number being referenced: http://jobsearch.nytimes.monster.com/jobs/where=New_2DYork_2DCity_2C_2DNY&rad=75&sort=dt.rv.di&cy=us.

  For example, if my student ID ended with 0, I'd include a 1 at the end of the above URL stem for this particular practice problem. Assume that interest in job locations (state information) is uniformly distributed (for example, there's a one-in-fifty chance that someone will be interested a job in a particular given state). Use that information to draw a random state, and create a count of the number of jobs located at that randomly drawn state.

Section 2

Harvesting Intelligence

4

Structuring Problems and Option Visualization

Decision modeling describes the use of data and logic to clarify the specific nature of a situation for which assistance in the decision-making process may be needed. The hope is that in clarifying such details, the development of meaningful suggestions and solutions may be easier to create. Most management problems for which decisions are sought can be represented by three standard elements: objectives, decision variables, and constraints.

Objectives
Maximize profit
Provide earliest entry into market
Minimize employee discomfort and turnover

Decision variables
Determine what price to use
Determine the length of time tests should be run on a new product or service
Determine the responsibilities to assign to each worker

Constraints
Can't charge below cost
Must test enough to meet minimum safety regulations
Ensure responsibilities are shared by two workers at most

All of these elements can be visualized graphically, often to the benefit of analysis and general insights. Our initial discussion will be limited to objectives and decision variables; we'll discuss constraints further on in this chapter. In most business scenarios, managers are faced with making a set of decisions that impact a final outcome (objective). This tends to make the decision process more complex, and sometimes the rationale for making specific decisions is difficult to describe.

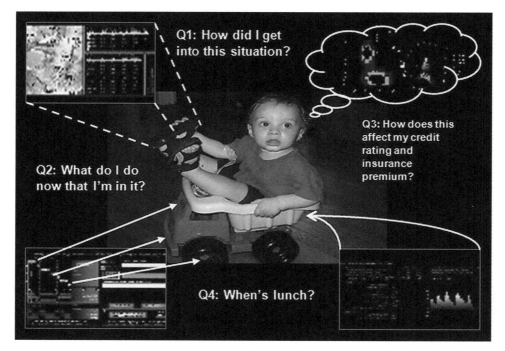

Figure 4.1. Value and limitations in visualization.

4.1 Value of Data Visualization

As the old saying goes, a picture is worth a thousand words (Figure 4.1). Some pictures are cute but may say very little to professionals – at least, initially. Misleading suggestions can throw a decision maker off his or her game. It's the responsibility of individual charged with providing decision support to clarify what limitations exist in a graphical representation – that is, what to take with a grain of salt, and where consistency and relevance exist.

There are plenty of graphs that can be built through Microsoft Office products, ranging from basic pie charts and bar charts to more sophisticated plots. For example, geographic mappings such as that featured in Figure 4.2 (integrated through MS MapPoint and discussed in the previous chapter) are at one extreme.

Ultimately, nongeographic plots can be just as aesthetically sophisticated as mapped data, and they are often more directly meaningful. For example, the basic scatter plot can be used to show how a group of publicly traded firms (for example, by industry) compare along two performance measures or strategic orientations. Figure 4.3 shows a plot of Inventory/Sales (x-axis) and Earnings Per Share or EPS (y-axis) plots for a set of firms in the chemical and materials fabrication industries. Figure 4.3 is a time shot that depicts a single instance in time.

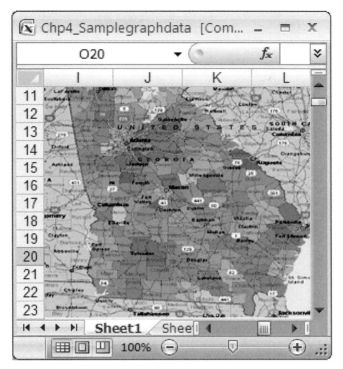

Figure 4.2. Sample map generated by MapPoint embedded in Excel.

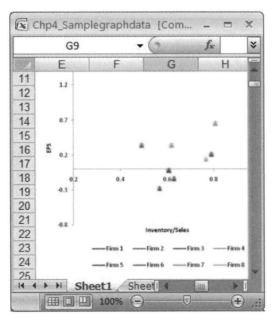

Figure 4.3. First quarter 2004 numbers for a range of Chem/Mat firms.

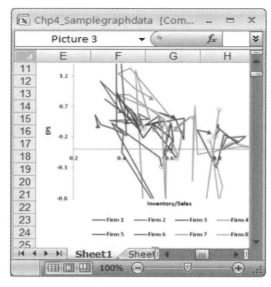

Figure 4.4. All quarters from 2001–2004 linked chronologically per firm.

What can we gather from this plot? If the answer is "not much," we might want to rethink whether we are depicting the right kind of information in the right kind of format to either (1) draw inferences or (2) get a particular point across. Of course, if we have more data (for example, data relating to prior periods), we can attempt to show them, as well. We might even link data from a single firm together to show the path taken in the pursuit of changing inventory costs and EPS (Figure 4.4).

However, something is left to be desired in such a depiction. A lot of information is being shown in a potentially meaningful way, but, as a whole, the rendering and the nature of noise incorporated in the graph is detracting. Alternatively, the right mix of information can be helpful. As shown in Figure 4.5, the estimates from only the first quarter of 2001 and the first quarter of 2004 are depicted.

Here, the graph becomes useful. For example, most firms that started with negative EPS levels decreased their average inventory positions (and increased turns). Those same firms also significantly increased their EPS into the positive region. Similar observations are made when we limit ourselves to the average 2001.1–2002.4 values and the average 2003.1–2004.4 values.

The critical intelligence depicted by a graph is contingent not only on the selected form of the graph, but also on the selected subset of data presented. Mastery of graphical attributes can only get you so far without an appropriate understanding of the ultimate visualization goal. Fortunately, the basic logic required to create and manipulate any graph in Excel is the same. Given a selected subset of data to graph, you need to specify how to use

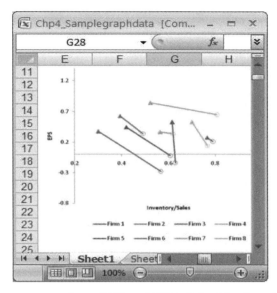

Figure 4.5. First quarters from 2001 and 2004, linked by firm for comparison.

it (for example, as a label, or as data to be plotted) and then specify the particular aesthetic features of the resulting graphical presentation. For this reason, we will review the construction and manipulation of three representative types of graphs – bar charts, scatter plots, and surface graphs – and we will devote the rest of our discussion to analytical intelligence and the dynamic enrichment of visualizations.

4.1.1 Bar Charts

Because bar charts represent a fairly expansive range of graphing possibilities, from the simplistic to the information packed, they serve as a useful foil for describing the various options available when developing visuals in Excel. Here, we'll start small and build up to much more complex variants of bar chart construction.

4.1.1.1 The Basics

Basic bar charts are useful when you have a small set of categories, each of which describe and compare along a single measure. For example, we might want to chart the efficiency of inventory use for a single firm across each financial quarter starting from 2001 onward (that is, twenty observed records).

First, select the data. The AllData sheet in Chp4_QuarterlyData provides a good starting point. If the categorical data that interest you (year.quarter, for example) is not located adjacent to the comparison data (inventory and

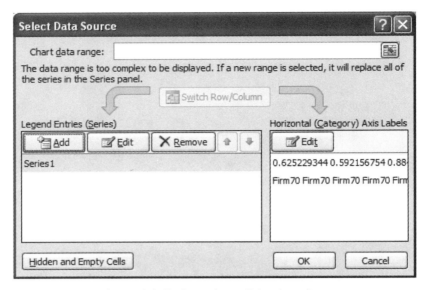

Figure 4.6. Series value editing interface.

sales), we can hold down the Ctrl key while selecting the appropriate cells. When selected, choose the desired chart type from the Insert tab, such as the Column chart type chosen here.

Next, select the type of graph you want (such as the standard graph in the upper left of the options). At this point, Excel will attempt to provide what it thinks you want, and often it's wrong. It's not uncommon for Excel to pick the wrong way to transform selected data into a plot. We might want our categories (x-axis for this kind of graph) to come from cells Z3882:Z3898 and our comparison data from cells T3882:T3898; however, this might not be Excel's first intuitive stab at depicting the data.

Fortunately, we can correct for Excel's initial stumble and ultimately generate exactly what we want. We simply need to get comfortable with how to make the necessary requirements clear to Excel. Once any chart is created in Excel, the Chart Tools menu automatically displays at the top of the screen. This menu will allow us to modify any part of the chart, including the misinterpreted data. Clicking on Select Data from the Design tab displays the screen in which both the series of values and the series of labels can be manipulated (corrected, in this case). The value editing interface in this example (again, with the initial incorrect configuration) appears as follows (Figure 4.6).

Click on Edit in the left-hand pane to select the appropriate series values; we want the data in "AllData!$T$3882:$T$3898" as the series values. The name of this series is defaulted to "Series1" but we could change it at this point as well, for example, by typing in "Inventory/Sales" given the nature

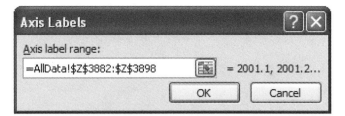

Figure 4.7. Series label editing interface.

of our data. Click Edit in the right-hand pane to change the category axis labels. We want to choose "AllData!$Z$3882:$Z$3898" for our horizontal axis labels (Figure 4.7). After making these adjustments, the following chart is displayed with year and quarter along the x-axis and Inventory/Sales along the y-axis (Figure 4.8).

We may now have a chart that will work, but we can probably do better in terms of presentation. We can use the Layout tab of Chart Tools menu (Figure 4.9) to modify axis titles, chart titles, legends, data labels, axes,

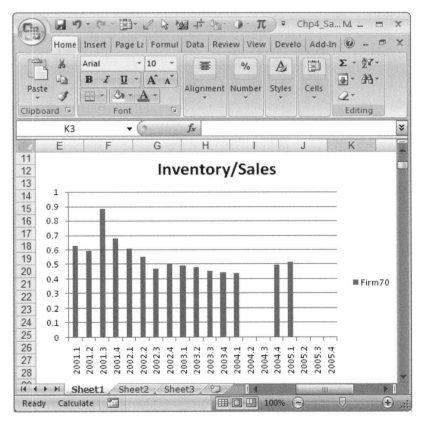

Figure 4.8. Simple bar chart example.

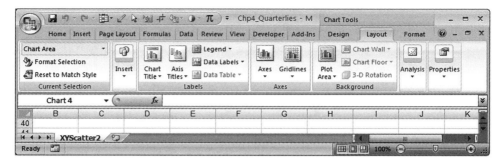

Figure 4.9. Various options for modifying charts.

gridlines, or the entire plot area. All of this can be done after the chart is created in Excel. Additionally, we can click on any element in the chart (such as the gridlines or the legend) to manipulate it. For example, if we don't want gridlines, we can select them and press Delete. We can also add a chart title by selecting Chart Title from the Layout tab.

At this point, we can also add additional series of data. For example, perhaps we want to compare Firm70 to another comparable firm in its industry, such as Firm172. We could click the Add Series button and make the appropriate additional specifications based on the location of the series in our spreadsheet. The graph shown in Figure 4.10 displays these modifications.

We could then continue to make additional aesthetic changes to elements such as the bars and background. Click Plot Area>More Plot Area Options>Picture or Texture Fill to open the Format Series dialog box (Figure 4.11). From here, we can replace the existing area-fill or background with something more visually pleasing, such as a marble texture.

Double-click the bars within the graph and then select Format Selection from the Format tab to access graph formatting options. Here, we can modify other elements such as the gaps between the bars and the extent to which they overlap. We can also make color changes to them at this point using features such as gradient fills. The Legend itself can also be transposed (made horizontal rather than vertical) and moved around. Basically, we can change anything in the graph that we can click.

4.1.1.2 Compound (Stacked) Bar Charts

Compound bar charts are somewhat more complex. These charts are often used to depict compound concepts. For example, rather than viewing only inventory efficiency, we might want to look at how capital-resource costs contribute to total expenditures relative to sales. We'll build this new variable (Plant and Equip Costs/Sales) on the right-most column of the data table, and select the last twenty quarters of a particular firm along with this

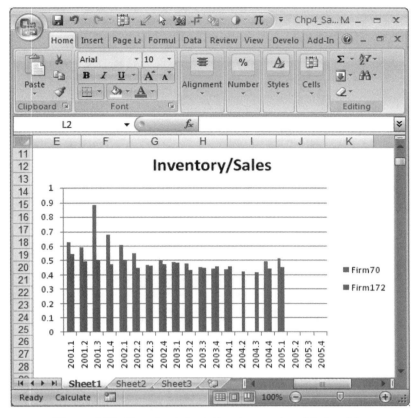

Figure 4.10. Bar chart depicting two series side by side.

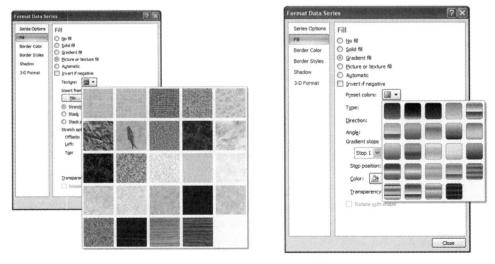

Figure 4.11. Sampling of graphic fill options.

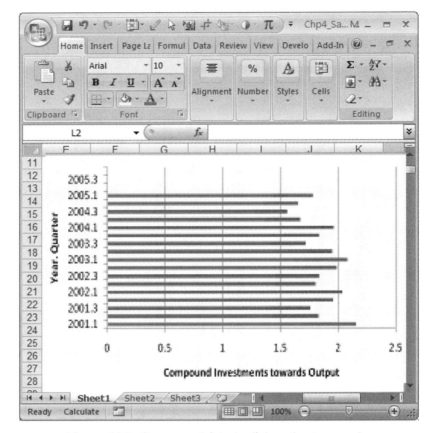

Figure 4.12. Compound (stacked) bar chart example.

new variable. The new chart we'll build is called a stacked or compound bar chart. By specifying the correct information for each axis and making some quick modifications to the appearance of the graph, we can generate a chart for a particular firm similar to that in Figure 4.12.

By copying and pasting this graph, we get a duplicate that we can then edit to develop a comparable graph for yet another set of data. We could even make most of the subsequent plot transparent by selecting None as an area and line coloring option. With a little careful positioning, we could overlay it on top of the original graph for comparison. Figure 4.13 shows an example of a chart along these lines reflecting data on a couple of firms.

In contrast to the graph in Figure 4.11 that showed only inventory investments for a couple of firms, the compounded graph shows much more information that could be comparatively valuable. In this particular case, the data (drawn from a COMPUSTAT) suggest that Firm B has much less money tied up in capital resources, relative to its investments in inventory. This may indicate a greater focus on productivity than on input efficiency

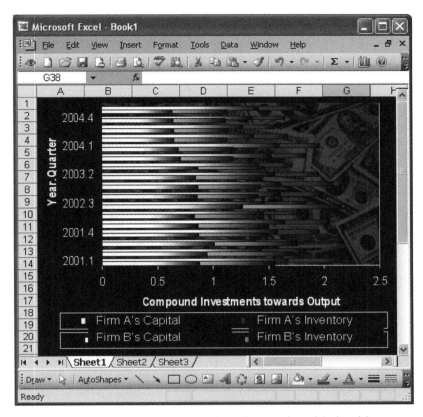

Figure 4.13. Two compound bar chart series, side by side.

(vis-à-vis Firm A). Furthermore, Firm B seems to be gaining ground along this single measure over time as compared to Firm A. This may demonstrate an overall distinguishing strategy in place at Firm B.

Still, we need to be cautious about trying to throw too much into aesthetic features while providing rich detail. The example in Figure 4.13 goes far beyond minimal concerns for visual overcrowding – laughably so. When confusion grows faster than insight, it's time to rethink the design and the purpose behind it. The fancy background graphics in Figure 4.13 could definitely be dropped, and higher contrast colors could be used. The use of gradient fills might also be reconsidered. Remember that just because you can enhance multiple graphic aspects doesn't mean you should.

Note that Gantt charts, which are popular in project management, are another variety of stacked bar charts. In such cases, each of the y-axis categories (in Figure 4.13 Year.Quarter) could be an individual activity that follows a chronological sequence in a project. The two series data you would want to use to build a Gantt would be Activity Start Time and Activity Duration. By coloring the Activity Start Time bar portions as transparent, or the

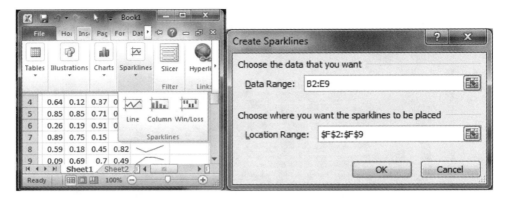

Figure 4.14. Example of Sparklines in Excel 2010.

same color as the background, the Activity Duration bars gain the appearance of hanging in place – in thin air, so to speak. We'll see an example of one of these Gantt charts when we discuss nonlinear optimization topics.

4.1.2 Cell-Embedded Sparklines

With Excel 2010 came a number of innovations in graphical capabilities. Among these was the Sparklines feature. This tool allows any unidimensional series, sequenced series, or series otherwise divided into discrete bins to be depicted visually within cells of the spreadsheet. Although the vast number of chart formatting options covered in the previous section are not available, the results are often visually straightforward. These are often viewed as easier to manage by those desiring nothing more than a quickly generated display of differences and trends. In Excel 2010, Sparklines are found under the Inter tab. A userform pop-up will ask for the location of the series and the destination for the resulting Sparkline graphic. As shown in Figure 4.14, Sparklines for multiple series can be generated simultaneously. As with embedded charts in Excel, any changes to the source data will automatically be reflected in the Sparklines graphics.

4.2 Visualizing Continuous Data

Not all data are best examined in discrete units. Much of the world's data are better understood by looking at potential relationships that connect observations rather than differences or changes over time. Scatter plots are perhaps the most popularly used graphics for illustrating and examining the relationship (or lack thereof) between two variables depicted along the x-axis and y-axis. To construct a scatter plot, select any data available on your spreadsheet (for example, on Chp4_QuarterlyData.xls, PullFromPivot2 sheet) that relate two variables of interest. For example:

1) Average inventory and sales figures for companies in the Industrial Equipment industry as the *x* variable
2) Average earnings per share for those same companies as the *y* variable

From the Insert tab, select Scatter and then select the desired scatter type. Select the first type of scatter plot (unconnected points) unless you have reason to believe that the data to be plotted represent a sequence of observations (for example, x–y pairs changing over time).

Of course, a lack of direct connections between points in a series doesn't preclude the ability to depict an underlying relationship embedded in the data. Such a relationship might very well be described by a line, straight or otherwise, and not just a current sequence muddied by the existence of multiple sources of variation in the data. Because of this, scatter plots are often designed to consist not only of individual points, but also of general trendlines (for example, regression lines) that attempt to depict relationships that are not always immediately obvious.

4.2.1 Adding in Trendlines and Their Statistics

Right-click any data set on a scatter plot to be presented with the option of adding a trendline: a best fit, based on the type of relationship you believe might exist, such as linear, quadratic (parabolic), and so on (Figure 4.15). You also have the option of specifying what summary numbers for that best fit should appear on your graph, such as regression coefficients, R-squared values, and so on.

In contrast to the detailed results provided by regression analysis, trendline fits to a data set in a graph do remain live. This means that the fit coefficients and R-squared value will change as the data points change. This can be handy when different data sets or different levels of simulated variation in data might be worth considering. It's also handy when you want to duplicate graphs for alternate variable combinations – just cut, paste, and change the source data to which the graph is referring. The regression equations will automatically adjust for you (Figure 4.16).

4.2.2 Kicking Up Scatter Plot Graphics

Scatter plots aren't just used to depict associations. They can also be used to describe general closeness or proximity among comparable observations. For example, we could compare multiple firms with respect to the dimensions of Cost (*x*) and Quality (*y*) to see which firms seem to dominate various positions and which seem to lag behind. Or, we might want to simply show how various firms are located, relative to one another in some geographically

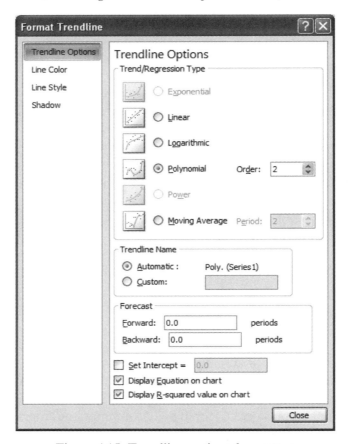

Figure 4.15. Trendline options for scatter.

meaningful space, such as Latitude (*x*) and Longitude (*y*). If we we're interested in comparing distinct entities rather than estimating relationships, we
might want more meaningful depictions of those entities. In other words,
we might want to pick something other than a dot to depict these entities;
maybe a picture of a paper airplane, for example (Figure 4.17).

These kinds of graphic substitutions are amazingly simple in Excel. If you
have a particular picture in mind, you can import it into Excel by choosing Insert>Picture>From File to open the My Pictures dialog box. Choose
the picture you want to insert into Excel and then click OK. After your
picture appears in Excel, you can make it smaller, combine it with a text
box, adjust color contrasts or transparency, and so on. You can also copy
it (right-click and choose Copy), select any individual point in the scatter plot (or all of the points simultaneously), and paste it (right-click and
choose Paste) on that point. The picture will then respond to any changes
in the graph and associated data the same way that any traditional point
would.

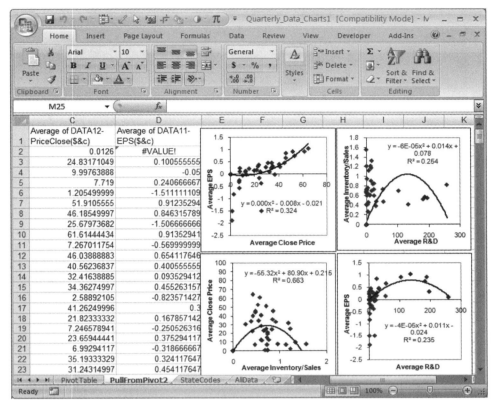

Figure 4.16. Example use of plot-embedded line fits and equations (live).

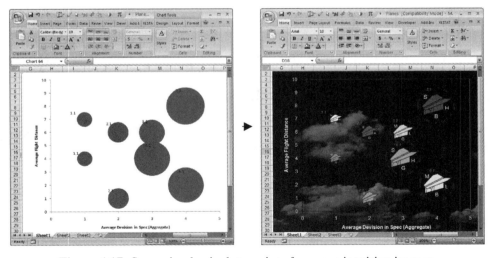

Figure 4.17. Swapping basic data points for more intuitive images.

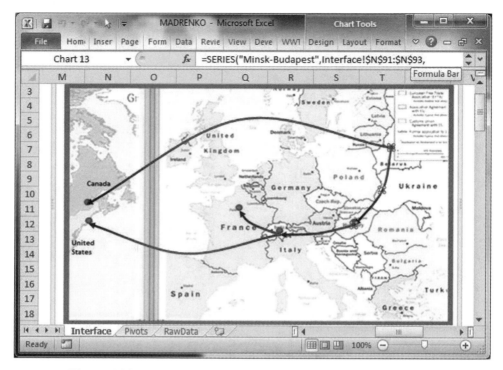

Figure 4.18. A multiseries connected scatter plot depicting flow.

4.2.3 Depicting Flow in Scatter Plots

Another nice thing you can depict with scatter plots is the "connectedness" of things. Many scatter plot examples you will encounter contain sets of x–y data points that do not have a clear relationship. However, there are many alternative examples in which x–y pairs are ordered, and these represent a series of interrelated data points. The simplest examples are x–y pairs that are ordered across time (year one x–y, year two x–y, and so on). Connecting these points (using the "scatterplot with line") can demonstrate how the history of how these x–y pairs has changed.

Connected scatter plots can also be used to portray paths across space. An example is shown on Figure 4.18. In this particular depiction (from the Chp6_Madrenko file that we'll look at again further on), each arc between the x-y pairs is defined as a separate set in the scatter in order to provide an easy mechanism to turn selected arcs on or off. An intermediate point is used to enforce curvature in the arc.

To see how these coordinates are put together in the first place and how they allow connecting arcs to be turned on and off, we need to look inside the cells themselves. Looking at the cell that contains the x coordinate for Minsk, we see the product of some cell (Q91) and the result of a VLOOKUP.

The VLOOKUP is pulling the designated x coordinate that is representative of Minsk (which is being stored elsewhere in the sheet, among other coordinates of other cities).

The cell Q91 contains a value that is either $+1$ or -1, which itself is dependent upon the result of a decision higher in the sheet (in this example, whether the route is being used for shipping). When the value is $+1$, the coordinates are positive, and the arc appears in the positive quadrant of the scatter plot. When the value is -1, it appears in the negative quadrant, but because the scatter plot's axes are fixed and nothing below (0,0) is displayed, the negative arcs never show up.

4.3 Less Conventional Depictions of Means and Variance

One thing that individuals – analysts and nonanalysts alike – are biased toward is simplified depiction of reality. This isn't our fault because most of what we are educated on either comes in the form of assumed facts or measures of central tendency (averages, medians, and so on). Although professionals are aware that averages are only one representation of a distribution of values, the vast majority of professional decisions are still based on considerations that exclude other characteristics, such as variance. Even our graphical depictions of data tend to be light on depictions of variance – exceptions include control charts, spreads, and full-surface depictions. However, the latter can be cumbersome in depicting the dynamics of variance.

For this reason, among others, interest has grown in the ability to depict variance in multiple dimensions. The result was a project spearheaded by the Council for Ubiquitous Intelligence (CUbInt). The result was an add-in referred to as the Bivariate Normal Confidence Interval Plotter. This tool, freely available on the Excel Blackbelts site, takes the means and standard deviations of a series of x and y distributions, along with correlations of each pair of x and y distributions, and plots confidence intervals for each pair. Figure 4.19 provides an illustration of the tool in use. In this example, two potentially related variables are examined (Georgia county population and farm density). For each decade from 1950 to 2010, the joint distribution characteristics of these two variables are used to create forty-percent confidence intervals in comparing changes in averages and variance over time. The result is a fairly rich depiction of the relationship of these two factors.

4.4 Depictions in More Than Two Dimensions

There are many ways to depict more than two dimensions in Excel. Most remain unknown to the casual user. However, these approaches can be

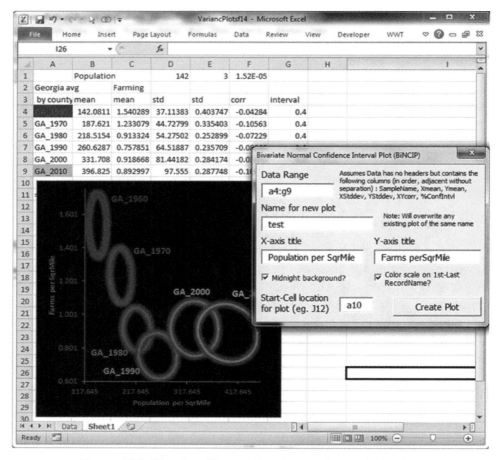

Figure 4.19. Bivariate Normal Confidence Interval plotting.

incredibly powerful in capturing the nuanced relationship of variables – relationships that more often than not involve the interaction of effects.

4.4.1 Surface Templates and Three-Dimensional Plots

Aside from looking cool, surface templates and plots are useful when you want to depict the relationship among three variables. For now, we'll talk about the generic structure of surface plots and what you need to create them. Further on in this chapter, we'll present an example that directly relates to the options encountered by management decision-makers.

First, you need a set of x and y values that occur multiple times or that can be roughly categorized into a set of discrete values, which seem to be meaningful multiple times across the data set as a whole. These can be ordinal categories (for example, increasing whole numbers, or equidistant fractions such as 0.25, 0.50, 0.75, 1.0, 1.25). The more x and y categories you choose, the more complex your plot will be, but it will be potentially more informative as well.

For generalization, let's assume we have three entities; they could be firms, machines, or consumer populations. Each entity has two distinct attributes (an *x* variable and a *y* variable). The *x* variable might be the entity's value in the marketplace, and the *y* variable might be some measure of associated liability. Both variables have a central value (a mean), and can be described as having a certain amount of variation over time (that is, standard deviation). If these attributes are normally distributed, we can describe the probability of both *x* and *y* variables taking on specific values and we can then show how those probabilities (or intensities) decrease as we move further away from the central (average) attribute values.

A simple way to describe this might be with a table that includes various *x* and *y* values and their associated intensity levels (that is, a third variable that might be dependent on the other two). We could even use conditional formatting to color cells in the table to add emphasis to the variations in intensity (probability) levels for differing levels of *x* and *y*. In J through AE (shown in Figure 4.20), we have a conditionally formatted table describing intensity levels depending on where we are in the x-y grid. This could be cool and informative, depending on what we're trying to make sense of.

On the other hand, we have all the elements we need to develop a three-dimensional surface map: specific *x* and *y* values and values of a third associated variable (in this case, probability or intensity). If we select the data in the conditionally formatted, large table shown in Figure 4.20, and we then select the three-dimensional surface graph option, we can generate a rough form of a three-dimensional image (Figure 4.21). We can format and edit this in the same way we have with other graphs.

Incidentally, these graphs don't need to be static. If we believe that values change over time according to some meaningful dynamic or process, we could build that into the parameters on which the graph was originally based. All of these graphs are ostensibly live and ready for updating, based on our needs. In this case, a simple press of the F9 key advances the random number generation that lends to a living appearance of our graphs. We'll get into the details of dynamic visualization in Chapter 10.

4.4.2 Basic Cartesian Bubble Charts

What is typically lost in the use of surface plots is the flexibility otherwise associated with scatter plots. Surface plots demand the preestablishment of a spreadsheet structure, and as a result they usually require a lot of space in a spreadsheet. Changes to such a setup can be cumbersome. Furthermore, a large portion of the data never even appear uniquely on the plot (see the

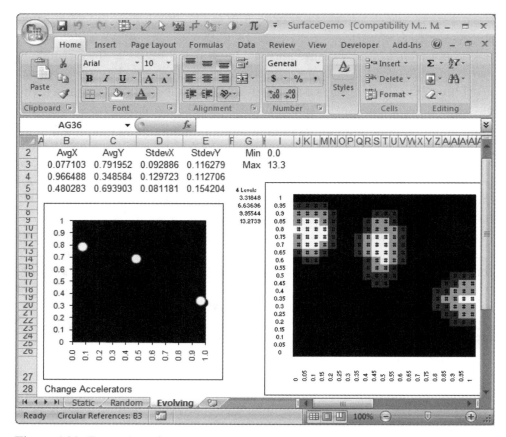

Figure 4.20. Example using conditional formatting to develop intensity pseudo-graphs.

black areas in Figure 4.21). Fortunately, there are some nice alternatives available in Excel when drawing out a third dimension.

Like surface plots, bubble charts are found under Other Charts in the Insert menu bar. Also like surface plots, bubble charts require three sets of related data. However, unlike surface plots, the data can simply be arranged as three adjacent (or nonadjacent) columns without additional data structuring. The first two columns in the bubble chart data serve as the standard x–y Cartesian value. The third column selected will be depicted in terms of the size of the bubbles. You have the option to depict negative values in the third column in a color that is distinct from positive values.

Let's take the following example data set (in TernaryPolar.xlsx) containing records with four distinctions and one potentially related attributed ($x1$, $x2$, $x3$ and y). Graphing three of the variables in a bubble chart (as in the left-most panel of Figure 4.22, with positive value of y in blue and larger by magnitude of y) provides some indication of regularity.

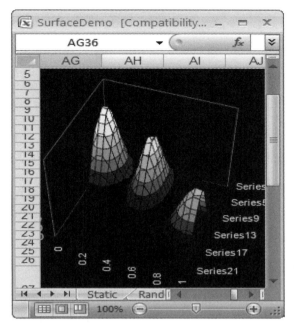

Figure 4.21. Example surface plot to depict intensity.

Unfortunately, regardless of whether a standard bubble chart or a surface plot is used, adding a third dimension won't guarantee clear, additional insights. In the present case, it's not easy to extract a meaningful description of existing relationships. Certainly, some complex relationship is apparent, but putting it into words may be difficult.

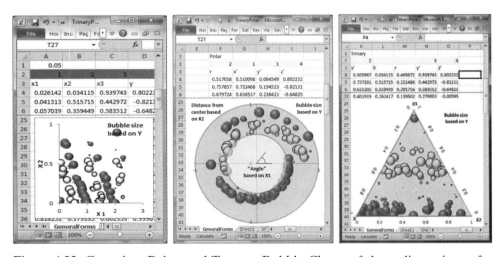

Figure 4.22. Cartesian, Polar, and Ternary Bubble Charts of three dimensions of a data set.

4.4.3 Polar Bubble Charts

Another possible way to depict data is through transformation. Polar coordinate depiction can provide surprising insights in some cases. This is certainly not the typical way to depict data in the social sciences, which is all the more reason why insights drawn from these depictions appear surprising.

Polar plots are specified based on distance from a center (radius) and angle (0–360 degrees, or $0-2\pi$). In the plot on the right, the angle is based on $x1$ in the original data, and distance on $x2$. Bubble size is still y. It appears that the lower-right quadrant (which contains certain ranges of $x1$ values) only contains records with positive (blue) values of y. It also shows less spread with regard to distance from the center (and so less variance in $x2$). This might say something important about the risk and value of such $x1$ values. For details in the calculations used to convert polar data into a form that a standard bubble chart can use (with a result similar to that in the center panel of Figure 4.22), the reader is referred to the Chp4_TernaryPolar workbook. An Add-in designed to quickly convert data in an $x1$, $x2$, $x3$ format into a Ternary plot is also available through the Excel Blackbelt add-in directory.

4.4.4 Ternary Bubble Charts

If your interest in attempting to depict a fourth dimension in a graphic, depending on the nature of the data, a Ternary plot may be an option. In this case, the values $x1$, $x2$, and $x3$ sum to 1. This is actually a well-established graphical technique used in depicting the properties of material mixtures in engineering. This technique is also beginning to show its value in other professional fields. For example, perhaps these three component variables ($x1$, $x2$, $x3$) represent a percentage of budget allocations to various activities such as research and development, human-resources training, and maintenance.

If y represents some outcome, using the same original data set depicted in the polar projection, it now appears that there is a clear band of activity to avoid, and two distinct regions that seem to hold some promise for future planning. The mathematical conversion required to transform three compositional attributes (such as $x1$, $x2$, and $x3$) into x–y coordinates that can be plotted in a bubble chart is provided in Chp4_TernaryPolar.xlsx. With images of diagonal axis superimposed, the result might appear similar to that in the right-most panel of Figure 4.22.

4.4.5 Depicting Depth with Bubble Charts

Finally, there are occasions where yet another means of leveraging bubble charts can come in handy. For example, the points in all bubble charts will,

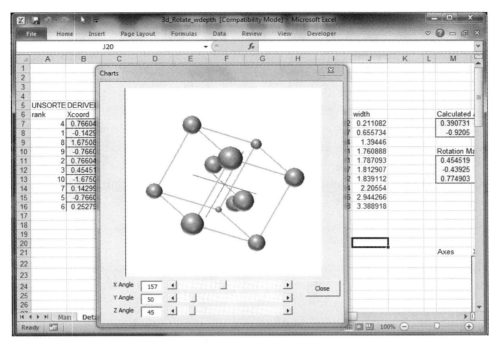

Figure 4.23. Using the Rank function to back-set points in a Bubble Chart.

by their very nature, appear "stacked" in a plot (unless they are transparent). The points at one end of the column of data may appear to partially or completely cover those at the other end, which is not always ideal. Sometimes, large bubbles effectively hide smaller ones as a result (again, unless some level of transparency is applied). Alternatively, we can reorder these points for a more ideal depiction.

Again, as with polar and ternary plots, we can draw on the experience of the sciences. Figure 4.23 provides as depiction common to chemistry and materials science text books. It's a depiction of atomic structure (or could be one ostensibly). In the workbook Chp4_3d_Rotate_wdepth, you have the option of rotating the reference frame of this data set. However, calculations are made simultaneously with rotations to determine which points should appear "closer" to the screen. The data are then effectively re-sorted, and the re-sorted set is used for inputs in the bubble chart. Excel worksheet functions that we've already encountered in Chapter 2 – RANK, MATCH, COUNTIF, and VLOOKUP – are key to this automatic sorting mechanism. In this case, the top-most sorted points are also depicted as larger to leverage natural perspective. However, this need not be the case.

Basically, this is just another example where a bit of math and Excel spreadsheet function capability are being leveraged to augment graphical depictions.

4.5 Complex-Form Heat Mapping

The previously discussed examples provide a way of describing information that is otherwise associated with two dimensions by incorporating the graphical depiction of a third dimension. This third dimension may represent the intensity or magnitude of a third variable fairly meaningfully if data are available in the form $(x1, x2, y)$. That isn't exactly the case in many real-world data visualization tasks. In many cases, y values are associated with an area on the $x1$-$x2$ plane rather than a single point. When these areas are complex (not simply squares on a grid), other graphical techniques must be sought out to assist with visualization.

4.5.1 Basic Heat Mapping

Heat mapping is a general term that refers to the colored or shaded distinction of areas in a larger graphical depiction (typically, two dimensional) in which each distinct color or shade is associated with different levels of a trait shared by each area. These maps are also commonly referred to as choropleths. Geographic maps (as introduced with MapPoint in Chapter 3) are the most common examples of applied heat mapping. Other examples in practice involve the heat mapping of levels of quality across the components of a manufactured good, the level of foot traffic intensity in a mall or hospital, or the levels of injury sustained to a human body or organ. These latter examples are not the kinds of things that geographic information systems are typically equipped to handle. Fortunately, there are free, publicly available tools and techniques for generating preexisting structures. One of these tools is the HeatmapDeveloper add-in (available under the Heat Mapper heading in the Excel Blackbelt add-in directory – a link to the add-in and documentation is available at www.excel-blackbelt.com).

The associated interface allows for the generation of more than fifty image sets in the larger library categories of geography-national, geography-global, geography-city, anatomy, art, and blueprints. An example of the userform pop-up that appears after activating the heat mapper tool is given in the left panel of Figure 4.24, where a user has selected the shape set Car_Model1 and its associated images. The resulting heat map is shown in the right panel, along with the column A listing of all images and associated token values of "heat" (for example, damage to vehicle) provided in column B.

Other examples of area-based depictions through this heat mapping tool are provided in Figure 4.25.

All images in the sets are drawn polygons (scalable vector graphics on a sort). If a user would like to leverage an image set on a regular basis that is

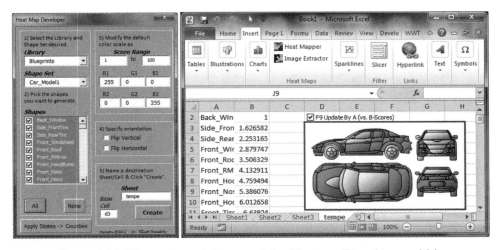

Figure 4.24. Illustration of the use of the HeatmapDeveloper add-in.

not available in the shape libraries, the Excel Blackbelts group on LinkedIn has a procedure for allowing contributions to these libraries from all users.

4.5.2 Mapping Excel Data in MapPoint

Data stored or created in Excel can also be imported into MapPoint; however, the more MapPoint-related data you add to an Excel project, the more time it will take for functions such as zooming, panning, analysis, and so on

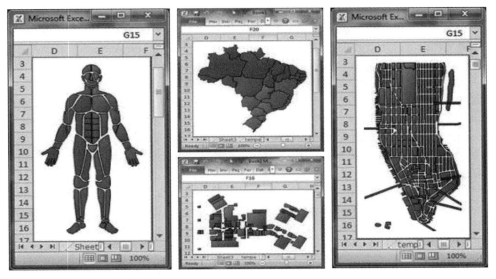

Figure 4.25. HeatmapDeveloper: human body, Brazil, Tallahassee mall, lower Manhattan.

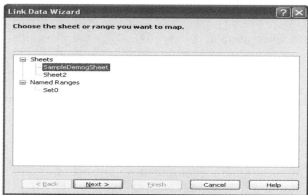

Figure 4.26. Using the Link DataWizard to tie MapPoint maps to Excel data (refreshable).

to work. So, if you are interested in a select set of data, such as data associated with a relatively specific geographic area such as New York, it's worth avoiding importing and exporting large volumes of unrelated data. The Link Data Wizard is particularly useful if you want to import updateable data from Excel – for example, data that you might want to eventually change in both Excel and MapPoint. To open the Link Data Wizard, start by selecting Data>Link Data Wizard (Figure 4.26). In the first page of the wizard, choose the Excel spreadsheet from which you want to retrieve the data and then click Next.

The wizard will then ask for a unique reference key to designate each record in the data you want to import. That reference code can be numeric or text-based, but it has to be unique. In other words, each record must have a value for that key that is not used by another record. This is an important point to keep in mind with geo-data because many geo-names, such as Springfield, Monroe, Oakville, and so on, are used by numerous cities throughout the United States.

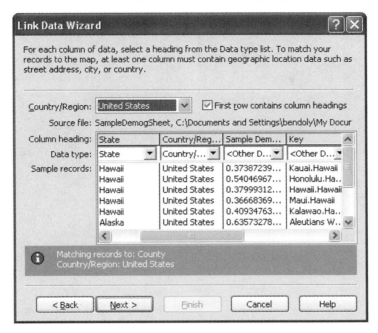

Figure 4.27. Specifying reference keys and other information being linked to a map.

After the key is selected, designate what each record attributes match concepts in MapPoint (see Figure 4.27). For example, MapPoint recognizes geographic areas including cities, counties, states, and countries and has additional data for each of these. There may be more data than you would like to import that MapPoint isn't familiar with, and MapPoint will be happy to graph that for you, but that's about all you can expect as far as MapPoint's understanding is concerned.

The Link Data Wizard can update your map without much additional work on your part. For example, try setting up a data link using the Chp4_SampleDemogs file. When mapped, edit the data by adding sound or taking the square of the data and copying over the original. Click the scale/legend in MapPoint and select the Update Now option to update your map in MapPoint. You are not limited to previously exported data that you have simply modified in Excel. You can always pick an entirely new series to export into MapPoint from Excel.

For example, if you used some kind of marketing model to assess the likelihood that residents of specific census tracts would seek your services from a specific geographically located firm, you might import and graph those newly derived data (Figure 4.28). Or, as shown on the right side of Figure 4.27, if similar analysis helped designate which of a set of competing firms were dominant in a geographic market space, you could import and graph that information.

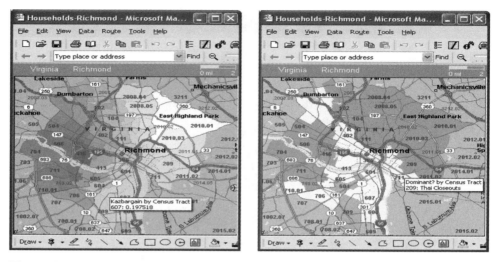

Figure 4.28. Examples of imported data for the same region showing variable intensity

4.5.3 Excel (MapPoint): Embedded Maps

MapPoint objects can also be imported into Excel. To do this, select a cell within the range of data and reference-key designations you want; then, select Insert>Object to open the Object dialog box (Figure 4.29). Scroll down to Microsoft MapPoint North America Maps, and click OK to embed a map of the United States into Excel. Double-click the map to activate the MapPoint toolbar in Excel, shown in Figure 4.30.

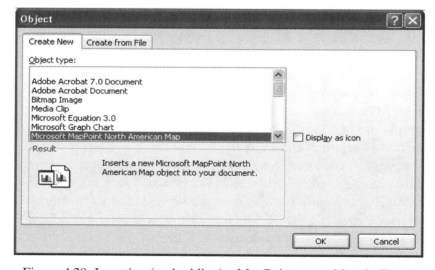

Figure 4.29. Inserting (embedding) a MapPoint map object in Excel.

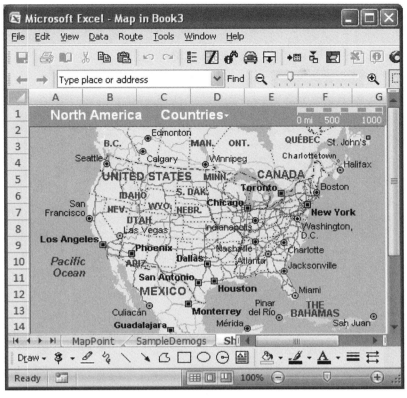

Figure 4.30. Appearance of a MapPoint map embedded in Excel.

Click the Link Data Wizard to initiate a series of pop-up windows prompting you to specify where the data are located in the workbook. Browse for your Excel filename (in this example, Chp4_SampleDemogs.xls). From the Link Data Wizard, select the worksheet name where your data are stored. Depending on compatibility, you may need to resave your Excel file as an earlier version of the worksheet prior to linking or MapPoint might not recognize it. Otherwise, it's the same procedure that we followed when we discussed the Link Data Wizard.

In many cases, Excel may graph your data using a method you might not want (using pushpins rather than colored regions, for example). But, as with all graphs in Excel, this can be easily changed by selecting the map and clicking the Shaded Area button in the Data Mapping Wizard – Map Type page. (See Figure 4.31; note that this page is available only after a map is embedded.)

In the case of maps embedded in Excel, you might find the updating process more convenient at some level (for example, if the spreadsheet containing the source data also contains the mapping of that data). Unfortunately,

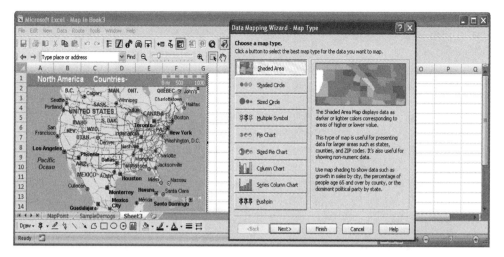

Figure 4.31. Editing an embedded map in Excel.

graphical updates are not as dynamic as those with Excel plots. You still need to double-click the map, right-click the legend, and then click Update Now. To perform this update, only Excel needs to be open; you don't have to switch between programs.

4.5.4 Routing Information and Insights through MapPoint

Aside from data storage and visualization, MapPoint's Routing tool provides fairly accurate estimates for travel distance, time, and cost. To activate this tool, select the automobile icon on the main MapPoint toolbar, or choose Route>Route Planner. This provides the opportunity to add any number of sites to a constructed route. Selecting Get Directions will do just that: provide a set of step-by-step directions for carrying out the route in the sequence specified, as well as a graphical mapping of that sequenced route. Additional summary measures of the specified sequence also comes in the form of total trip distance, time estimates, and cost (Figure 4.32).

Some sequences specified in routes are less ideal than others. Visual inspection alone would suggest that driving directly to Atlanta first in this example might not be ideal. Fortunately, MapPoint makes the visually driven, manual manipulation of route sequences fairly straightforward by allowing any site to be selected and shifted in its order of sequence in a route (Figure 4.33).

After a sequence is modified, associated route directions can be updated (by clicking Get Directions again) to provide a new set of directions, summary of total route distance, time, and cost (Figure 4.34). I don't have to do all of that in MapPoint directly. I can accomplish the same thing using a

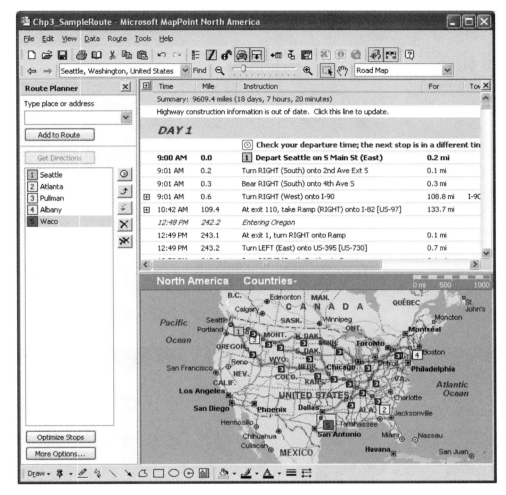

Figure 4.32. Example of route specification, derived directions, and route mapping.

map embedded in Excel (that is, I don't actually have to deal with MapPoint directly to get this done; however, it often runs faster).

As with everything else, all these data are subject to export into Excel for further analysis, manipulation, and subsequent feeds back into MapPoint. The key here is that these products can be used in a back-and-forth dialogue to develop meaningful insights that any one of these applications might not provide alone. A quick note on resequencing: It may already have become obvious, but manual resequencing with the intention of minimizing costs or distance can be substituted by MapPoint's built-in route optimization mechanism (Optimize Stops on the Route Planner frame). We will discuss the mechanics of route optimization in Chapter 5 and Chapter 7. The art of route optimization is not a simple one, and there are many approaches that can be taken. Some will be better than others, and this is subject to the specific

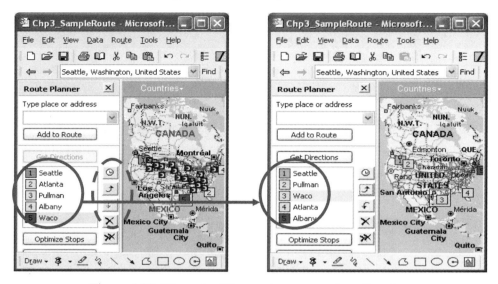

Figure 4.33. Manual editing and resequencing of routes.

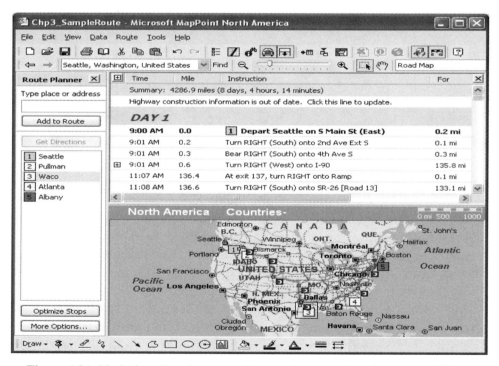

Figure 4.34. Updating directions, graphics, and summaries after route editing.

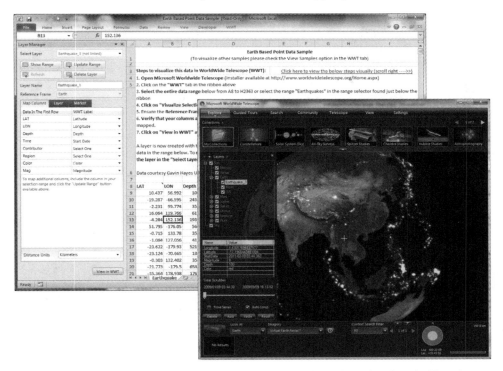

Figure 4.35. WorldWide Telescope depiction of earthquake data in Excel.

goals of the analyst or DSS developer. For now, it is sufficient to recognize that whatever method is used, MapPoint continues to provide an excellent mechanism through which to visualize solutions.

4.5.5 WorldWide Telescope

As mentioned, one common drawback encountered by new users of Map-Point is the relatively static nature of the graphics (relative to other charts available in Excel). Aside from using smaller tools like the HeatmapDeveloper for smaller geographic mapping tasks, other solutions exist that have challenged MapPoint graphic capabilities. One of these alternatives is also a brainchild of Microsoft research – namely, the WorldWide Telescope (WWT; http://www.worldwidetelescope.org/).

WWT works off of Excel spreadsheet data and allows data specified by longitude and latitude to be plotted. Size and color attributes can be used to distinguish plotted points (additional attributes of those points). Points can also be distinguished by date of occurrence and subsets of such data scrolled through to depict moving histories of events (for example, movement of material, changes in demographics, and so on). One example that comes with WWT is a data set that contains recent earthquake data including magnitude attributes, depth, and timing (see Figure 4.35).

Figure 4.36. Geographic area distinctions in WWT.

Like MapPoint and HeatmapDeveloper, polygon areas can also be distinguished graphically (sets of latitude and longitude required to define each area). An example is provided in Figure 4.36.

Unlike MapPoint, WWT provides a time scrubber tool that allows one to pan a data set through time and see how the distributed data have evolved historically. A similar function can be quickly adapted with HeatmapDeveloper, but WWT provides a far sexier presentation.

4.6 Selective Pruning for Presentation and Analysis

We've already breezed through filtering, which is one way to limit data presentation in Excel. But the Filtering tool can be somewhat limiting. If you plan to filter along one categorical variable, it only allows you to pick a single value of that variable to filter along. For example, if filtering along the Industry variable, you might select chemical, consumer electronics, or aerospace, but never all but chemical. If filtering along a variable such as year, you can filter along 2003 or 2006, but not just 2003 and 2006. Also, filtering doesn't provide much insight into summary data relating to how multiple categorical variables jointly impact other issues of interest.

Filtering also doesn't have a standard mechanism for summarizing data that take on numerous values for the same filterable categories. For example, if you have a categorical variable such as Industry and a large number of

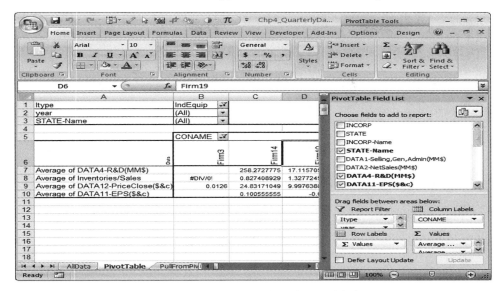

Figure 4.37. General nature of a PivotTable interface.

firms that fall into each of its categories, it might be more useful to present the average value calculated across the selected set of firms on a specific year, opposed to every observation separately. Standard filtering won't give that to you. To attempt to make up for these deficits, Excel provides PivotTables, which are alternative filtering and data presentation tools.

A final caveat on filtering, and something I've seen people make mistakes with again and again: Filtered data, at least in existing versions of Excel, are still present within the spreadsheet. The downside to this is that some functions that act across the filtered cells (for example, Lookup functions), and most add-ins, are not going to work off only the information displayed, and the filtered data are often still incorporated, which can lead to some misleading (critically so) conclusions.

4.6.1 How to Build and Modify PivotTables

Consider the PivotTable that already exists on the PivotTable sheet of the Chp4_QuarterlyData workbook. Click on the table to view available options (shown in Figure 4.37).

The following describes the three mechanisms you can use to prune presentation and analysis data using PivotTables.

- *Pages (global filters)*: These allow you to restrict data presented in the table as a whole to certain cases (for example, firms in the industrial equipment industry and nothing else, students at the Junior rank and nothing else). Add a page filter by using the cursor to drag and drop a variable (for example, firm type, or student type) from the field list (shown in the right portion of Figure 4.37) to the Page Fields box above the PivotTable. You can also drag and drop a variable to the Report Filter box at the bottom of the PivotTable Field List.

* *Row and Column filters (local filters)*: These allow you to restrict the data presented in specific rows and columns of the table to certain cases (for example, each row provides summaries across a single state. Fifty rows of information would then supposedly be presented). Add a row or column filter by using the cursor to drag and drop a variable (for example, firm type or student type) from the field list to the Row Fields box at the left of the PivotTable or the Column Fields box on table header. You can also drag and drop a variable to the Column Labels or Row Labels box at the bottom of the PivotTable Field List.

* *Data elements*: These allow you to restrict what is actually summarized in the meat of the table. For example, you might want to see how any number of issues (for example, earnings per share, spending on research and development depending on location and size of firms, and so on). If you divide your table by placing location categories (for example, state) in the Row Field box, the size categories (for example, 100–999 employees or 1,000–9,999 employees) in the Column Field box, and earnings per share (or spending on research and development) in the Data Items box at the center of the table, you would be able to see such comparisons.

By default, Excel's PivotTables tend to pull data in as counts (that is, how many pieces of data exist for the row-column combination, as opposed to averages in the data selected for that combination). If you are summarizing a single variable in the data field, you can double-click on the data header that appears in the upper left corner of the table, and switch to average or any other summary you want. You can change this by right-clicking on any header and selecting Value Field Settings. You'll have the option to specify what kind of data summary pops up at that point.

In a PivotTable you can also generate cross-summaries for multiple variables at the same time (that is, multiple variables in the Data field). Unfortunately, the task of requesting an alternative form of the data other than the default count becomes less intuitive here; however, it can still be done by selecting Value Field Settings from the Values box shown in Figure 4.38, or by right-clicking on the Data column and selecting Value Field Settings. A dialog box permitting choice of average, max, variance, and so on will display.

4.6.2 Selective Pruning by Row and Column

Aside from limiting the entirety of the data viewed in PivotTables by what you put in the Data Fields and Page Fields boxes, you also have the opportunity to limit the number of rows and columns for which data are shown. For example, if you have placed a location category (for example, state)

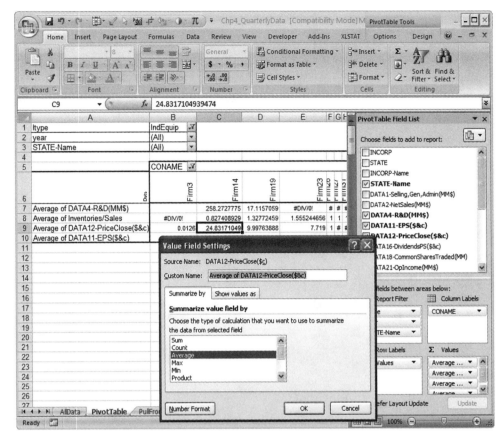

Figure 4.38. Modifying field settings in PivotTables (for example, pruning by general data content).

in the Rows Field and are only interested in comparing specific locations (for example, California, Oregon, and Washington, as opposed to all fifty states), you have the ability to do so easily in a PivotTable. Such selective pruning of presented data can greatly increase the clarity of points you may be trying to make with the data. Click on the category listing you want (for example, STATE-Name) and then check off the items for which you want data displayed (for example, California). This is shown in Figure 4.39.

4.6.3 PivotCharts

Anything created in a PivotTable can be transferred into a graphical form using the built-in PivotChart function. With a PivotChart, you are given a graphical interface with which to directly prune the kind of graphical data being presented (often in bar-chart form). I find PivotCharts fairly limiting because they allow only certain presentation styles (for example, bar charts

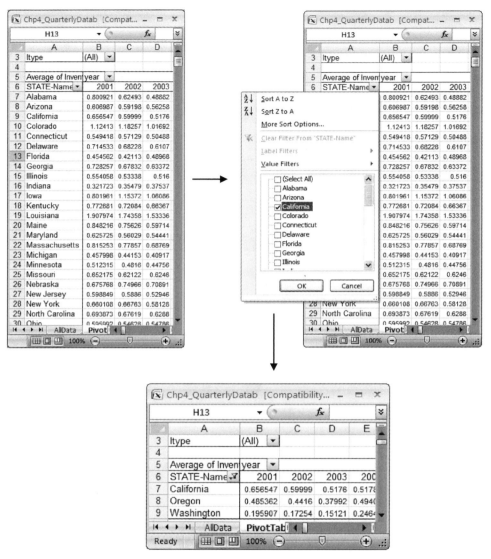

Figure 4.39. Pruning by selective data inclusion/exclusion.

but not scatter plots). I usually create a separate page that duplicates the PivotTable data and then I develop my own graphs based on those duplicates.

4.7 Visualizing Constraints

Up to this point, we have been fiddling with good ways to demonstrate the possible impacts of one variable or another (or differences in dynamics of certain elements of a system – for example, a restaurant). Unfortunately, this can be misleading if we don't account for unavoidable limitations in

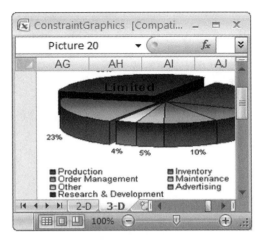

Figure 4.40. Three-dimentional pie chart depicting allocation constraints.

the decisions we make and the performance we attain. We also need to be familiar with methods by which to graphically depict constraints.

Constraints come in the form of rules like:

Can't charge below cost.
Must test enough to meet minimum safety regulations.
Must make sure responsibilities are shared by two workers at most.

Constraints can include financially based considerations, as shown in Figure 4.40. They can also include geographically based considerations (Figure 4.41).

Sometimes, constraints are even more sophisticated and require us to recognize dependent relationships between various decisions and relevant variables. For example, as the price goes up by $x, expected demand will fall by y%. Additional product tests will require that additional specialists to be assigned to assessment. The more new responsibilities we create, the less focused our workforce may become, and the less productive they may become in existing duties. These consequences get to the heart of the trade-off aspect of constraints. Specifically, when constraints are active, and we always have something constraining us, we need to consider the costs and benefits of picking specific decisions over others. In other words, constraints ensure that we can't have it all, so to speak.

The overall impact of multiple constraints and relationships may be hard to put into a few words, which is why we often rely again on visualization in the early phases of complex decision making. Visualization is equally important when we first get our hands on a set of data that we believe is relevant to our decision making. For example, consider the classic economic trade-off example of guns versus butter (most people who took basic economics

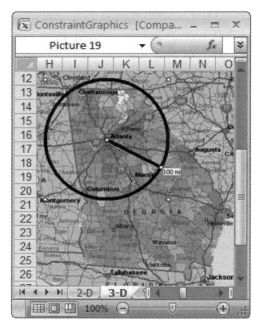

Figure 4.41. MapPoint generated embedded graph, depicting constraints.

courses in the last twenty years are familiar with this scenario). The constraint here is a relational one. We have fixed resources and can devote them to either activity, but we can only assign more resources to one manufacturing activity by pulling from another (see Figure 4.42).

More complex relational constraints can also be depicted using surface graphs. For instance, in a restaurant example, the number of barstools, two-seat tables, and four-seat tables may be individual decisions that planners may have to make, but given limited floor space, the managers may want to visually depict the trade-offs of increasing one of these types of seating elements over the others. Figure 4.43 shows two views (top-down and center-in) of a hypothetical feasibility plot for the space use at a restaurant. The legend to the right of each graph is used to demark quantity (for example, four-seat tables) possible for positioning given specific decisions regarding the quantity of the other two variables (for example, barstools and two-seat tables).

In the classic form of the guns versus butter economic problem, any option along the production-possibilities frontier makes full use of resources and is superior to more interior points (at least from a resource-utilization standpoint). On the other hand, there may be additional constraints that limit our ability to consider certain production options. There may be some minimally required level of gun and butter production needed to maintain other parts of society. Furthermore, regulations might place an upper limit on the number of guns manufactured (probably a good thing). As additional limits continue to build up, our ability to choose from a variety of alternatives

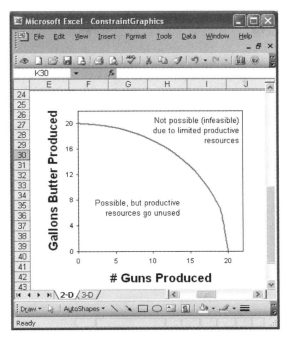

Figure 4.42. Connected scatter plot relational constraints.

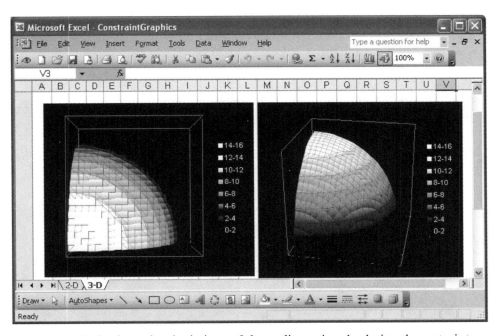

Figure 4.43. Surface plot depictions of three-dimensional relational constraints.

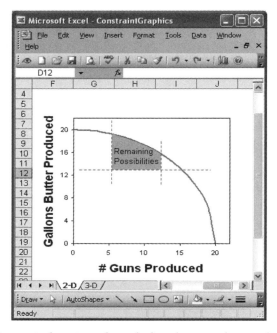

Figure 4.44. Connected scatter plot relational constraints and absolute limits.

becomes more and more limited (see Figure 4.44), as does our ability to excel in terms of other performance measures (for example, police force readiness, NRA self-esteem, and international baking contests). Figure 4.45 shows the three-dimensional equivalent of Figure 4.44.

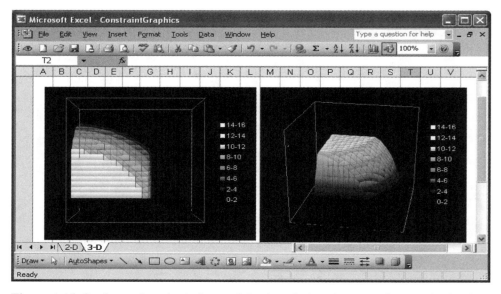

Figure 4.45. Surface plot depictions of both relational constraints and absolute limits.

PRACTICE PROBLEMS

Practice 4.1

Develop two scatter plots based on the data in Chp4_Samplegraphdata.

First plot: A on the x-axis; C on the y-axis.
Second plot: B on the x-axis; C on the y-axis.

Add best-fit parabolas (also known as second-order polynomial fits) to each plot.

Practice 4.2

If we assume that both A and B independently impact C, what would a plot of C as a function of both A and B look like? (Graph this using a three-dimensional surface plot.)

Practice 4.3

Create two columns of numbers. The first column should contain integers from 0 to 20. Label this column Apples. The second column should contain the following formula:

$$= SQRT(20^2 - \{ \text{Whatever \# of Apples are in the adjacent cell} \}^2)$$

Call the second column Oranges. Create a line-connected scatter plot of the two columns, and call the plot Production Frontier.

Pick one cell in the sheet and label it Location. Label the cell to the right of it Direction. Use the following to define the value inside Location: = Location + Direction.

Use an IF statement within the Direction cell that makes Direction equal to 1 if Location is 0, or equal to −1 if Location is equal to 20, or unchanged at all levels in between. (I'll let you figure that out.)

Use a VLOOKUP to set two additional cells in the sheet (below the Location cell) equal to the number of apples and number of oranges that are given in the row corresponding to the value of Location (for example, the 0th row, the 1st row, the 20th row). Add that x-y data point as a new series to your plot. In iteration mode, F9 should move that point back and forth along the production frontier you've plotted.

Note that you may want to include an IF statement in the Location cell tied to a Restart (or Toggle) cell so that you can make sure that things start the way you want them to (that is, at Location=0) when the iterations begin.

5

Simplification Tactics

There is a clear truism in George Box's 1979 statement that "all models are wrong, some models are useful." We attempt to model reality to see how changes can affect it – hopefully, for the better. But models of reality are, by their very nature, incomplete depictions, which tend to be misleading. Still worse are models and associated solutions that faithfully attempt to do justice to reality by incorporating many facets of reality into their structures. Unfortunately, a common result is an overemphasis on certain issues in decision making that, although interesting, are far less relevant to effective decisions than other issues that have been overlooked.

Ultimately, any approach to decision making is a balancing act between an appropriate accounting of relevant reality (that is, the objectives, decision variables, and constraints discussed in Chapter 4) and avoiding details that only obscure or mislead. When we attempt to rationalize all of the factors that might go into a decision-making process, as well as possible solutions that might be practically viable, we often "satisfice," a term used to describe making a decision about a set of alternatives that respects the limitations of human time and knowledge.

Of course, there are some decision makers who are extremely effective at coming up with quick, effective solutions to otherwise complex problems, whereas others are less capable. The difference often comes down to a familiarity with tried-and-true rules of thumb, applied consciously or unconsciously, which fit specific settings or simply help decision makers consolidate knowledge, regardless of settings. Fast and frugal heuristics (codified approaches to developing ideas, decisions, or solutions) embody this by employing a minimum of time, knowledge, and computation to make adaptive choices in real environments. (The interjection *Eureka!* derives from the same Latin stem as heuristics.) Fast and frugal heuristics are characterized by consolidations and simplifications of solution-search procedures. To the surprise of many managers and practitioners across fields, the simplest models and solutions are often the best.

5.1 Heuristics in Decision-Making Practice

Given this introduction to the general benefits of simplification in decision making, it is worth providing an overview of some of the simplest and most commonly used rules of thumb that exist in practice.

5.1.1 The Recognition Heuristic

One of the simplest examples of an effective fast and frugal heuristic is the *recognition heuristic*. Rather than assuming that people act as unboundedly rational individuals (strangely, a common assumption in academic literature to date), the recognition heuristic assumes that human ignorance not only exists, but is also an important factor in determining the strength of specific decision options. In fact, the foundation of this heuristic relies on at least some level of human ignorance to develop good solutions to problems.

As an example, consider a study performed by Bernhard Borges and his colleagues (1999), which is detailed in *Simple Heuristics that Make Use Smart*. Borges et al. examined the ability of lay individuals to develop high-performing stock portfolios based on their personal, albeit limited, exposure to corporate information.

> *Objective*: Develop a portfolio with consistently high returns relative to the market average.
> *Decision Variables*: Which publicly traded firms should be bought or shorted?
> *Constraints*: In the case of the heuristic, the ability of individuals to recognize companies in domestic and foreign markets (which obviously differs by expertise).

Certain companies in the United States are widely recognized by career financial workers and lay people overseas. Likewise, in the United States, we recognize only a relative handful of foreign companies by name. Does that signify anything? The assumption of the recognition heuristic is: Yes. This recognition probably indicates the ability of a brand name to penetrate foreign markets, as well as the resiliency of the reputation it has developed within those markets. In most cases, we'd assume this resilient reputation to be positive because companies with negative reputations don't last very long, and thus aren't resilient.

But can something as simple as name recognition by lay individuals predict performance even close to the level of highly sophisticated financial techniques? More sophisticated approaches, aside from being vastly more complex, are often proprietary in nature (not so publicly accessible); however, more alarmingly, they often don't do that well. In fact, the history of major U.S. investment management and mutual companies suggests that the favored selections of many highly experienced financial professionals perform worse than the market as a whole. This suggests that sophistication and experience might bias professionals toward misleading decision-making approaches. Perhaps less sophistication and experience might avoid such biases, at least in some cases.

To compare the recognition heuristic to more sophisticated and expert solutions, a research team asked average people and financial experts in the United States to specify from a list those companies in Germany that they recognized. They did the same thing in Germany with a list of U.S. companies. How well did the ten most-recognized U.S. stocks do, chosen on the basis of German recognition?

Those top-ten German choices (again, based on the recognition heuristic) beat the Dow 30 by about 10 percent, along with a number of funds supposedly based on sophisticated intelligence. They did much better than a random portfolio method. Granted, sophisticated methods of field experts showed better performance against random portfolio assembly as well (but, of course, it costs to hire such professionals – one might question the value of the incremental gain against the recognition heuristic here). Even better was the top-ten portfolio based on U.S. recognition of German firms. The average Joe was able to outperform the Dax 30 by 23 percent over the six-month test period, and similarly over subsequent periods studied.

In subsequent studies, this phenomenon has been retested with mixed results, largely by those financial professionals who have a clear interest in suggesting that simple techniques have limitations relative to proprietary expertise. This may be true in some cases, but these and other related results certainly cast critical doubt on what it means to be a financial *expert*. This is not to suggest that there won't be successfully sophisticated selection procedures developed in the future to consistently beat lay recognition; however, perhaps the best approach would be to incorporate simplistic rules into sophisticated models.

5.1.2 Nearest Next: A Routing Heuristic

Another well-established fast and frugal heuristic can be taken from the history of the shipping and transportation industry. Before computing power was abundant, shippers relied on professional planners to use their own modes of judgment to develop shipping routes and schedules that economized on cost but still met the service levels their clients expected. The types of problems about which these planners had to make decisions were highly complex.

Imagine a central facility, a single vehicle, and seven locations to which we need to make deliveries. Obviously, it might be in our best interest to find

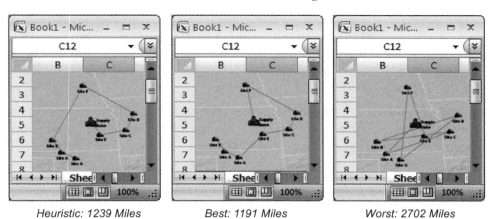

Heuristic: 1239 Miles   Best: 1191 Miles   Worst: 2702 Miles

Figure 5.1. Heuristic versus best and worst routing solutions.

the most time- and cost-effective route to carry off those deliveries. Basically, what we want is a good sequence of stops. But how many ways can we sequence seven stops? As it turns out, quite a few (7*6*5*4*3*2*1 = 5,040). Do we really want to compare 5,040 stops to find the best one, and then do this every time we need to find a new route? The *nearest next heuristic* provides a shortcut. Its rule is "Go to the closest site next," and then repeat this until all sites are visited.

Objective: Minimize total time or cost of transit.

Decision Variables: Sequence of sites to be visited in turn.

Constraints: Visit each site once, and in the case of this heuristic, the next site visited is the next closest site available.

Figure 5.1 shows an example comparing the heuristic solution to the absolute worst and absolute best options. It doesn't quite hit the best solution, but it's closer to the best solution than it is to the worst one.

The number of calculations (actually, just searches) needed to determine the nearest next solution is only 7+6+5+4+3+2+1 (28). In general, *nearest next* needs n*(n+1)/2 searches (where *n* is the number of sites) whereas a comprehensive search for the absolute best needs *n*! (that is, *n* factorial) searches (assuming no other ancillary heuristics are applied). So, if we needed to find a decent solution for n = 15 sites, the nearest next heuristic would give a solution after thirty searches, whereas a complete review of all possible solutions would require 1.3 trillion searches. Not a trivial task for many computers. Is it worth it? What if n = 30 sites?

Routing applications today tend to use a mixture of simple heuristics and complex, large-scale analysis to arrive at highly effective solutions. We continue to see improvements made in these applications with increases in computing power (that is, speed and memory); hence additional elements of reality can be practically included without an abandonment of fundamentally crucial aspects. Some of the most recent additions to routing applications now attempt to account for the human aspects of shipping, such as individual psychology, relationships between drivers and clients, and morale. Fast and frugal heuristics continue to have their place in these applications. Furthermore, these heuristics continue to provide benefit for managers who need to make decisions on the fly (for example, immediate rerouting responses to real-time road closures).

5.1.3 MinSlack and SPT: Two Project-Management Heuristics

Resources, such as workers and machines, often constrain the processes managed by an organization. These hurdles are common in project management, regardless of industry. The process of deciding which activities will be given access to potentially limited personnel first is a critical one in these settings, and these decisions need to be made quickly. For this reason, a large number of fast and frugal heuristics have been developed by managers in an attempt to make these decisions simple.

Two common fast and frugal heuristics are MinSlack and Shortest Processing Time (SPT). MinSlack assigns resources and starts comparing activities based on which ones will be most costly or problematic to project completion times, if they are otherwise delayed. The idea here is that limiting activities should be addressed as soon as possible so they don't delay subsequent activities.

SPT assigns resources and starts comparing activities based on which ones can be completed quickest. If you can get these activities done quickly, you can free up resources and assign them elsewhere while allowing the start of other activities that might not need those resources.

5.1.4 The Punchline: Relevance to DSS Designs

I could keep giving examples of heuristics that have been used in practice to make quick decisions in complex decision-making settings, but that's not really the goal here. Some may be of the mindset that they don't want a simple approach; they want the best solution. Aside from the perception that a single, best solution to all management settings exists, this mindset seems to assume that simple approaches cannot be as effective as ones that require several tools used together to deliver ideal solutions.

Each of the heuristics I've discussed represents a structured set of rules that somebody came up with because the rules made sense in a specific setting. For people who develop decision support systems, there are at least three reasons to provide structured rules that are backed by logical explanations.

1) By definition, the rules tend to be both easy to apply and informative.
2) The rules can offer a great starting place for more sophisticated support.
3) Perhaps most important, the rules can offer a performance benchmark from which to gauge the efficacy of more sophisticated solutions. This, in turn, helps to convince users of the support system that is providing to benefit them. The effectiveness of decision support system designs comes largely from selling the effectiveness of the support they are designed to provide.

For DSS designers, the question of the practical application of heuristics comes down to how much is gained and lost through the use of such techniques, and, perhaps more fundamentally, whether these techniques can be automated for integration with other techniques useful in the DSS design.

The supplement to this chapter discusses a rough approach to automating the nearest next heuristic. We will see, however, that there are better ways to implement simple decision-making rules behind the scenes for DSS designs.

5.2 Heuristics Applied to Data Rationalization

Whereas the application of simple rules for developing solutions can be critical, another discussion of simplification relates to the nature of the data used to define both the types of management problems we face and the solutions provided. Increasingly, professionals are bogged down in vast amounts of available data. The seemingly basic task of selecting which data should be used to develop solutions often becomes a stumbling block and slows the development of meaningful analysis and solutions. The overwhelming nature of large amounts of data applies to all aspects of decision making, particularly to the ability to apply logically designed heuristics to solution development. Can the concept behind heuristics (that is, easily applied rules for simplification) be applied to the rationalization of data as well?

Experience (even for lay persons) leads us to recognize that what to leave in or take out isn't always obvious. Fortunately, both DSS designers and users don't have to limit themselves to omitting data and issues in their attempts to clarify the decision-making processes. They also have the option of consolidation.

There are basically two general perspectives relevant to considering data consolidation. The first approach is to select a set of attributes that represent similar or associated issues, and then somehow consolidate them into a smaller set of representative characteristics for each data record. Here,

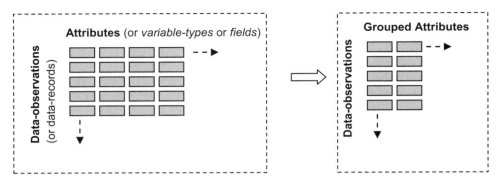

Figure 5.2. Consolidating attributes of large data sets.

we are grouping together attributes (elements that describe records of people, places, and things), and the consolidated result should have the same number of individual data observations but with a consolidated number of characteristic attributes (see Figure 5.2).

Principle Components Analysis (PCA) is one common form of this consolidation approach and is often preferred as a method for data reduction. (Note that other related methods such as Principle Factor Analysis are also discussed in more complex structural analysis, but a discussion of PCA will be sufficient here.)

The other approach, as you might guess, deals with grouping together similar kinds of data observations (that is, people, places, or things) to reduce the noise that may be inherent across individual observations. A simple example would be to designate groups of students (for example, by year, major, or fraternity) and create averages of the attributes by which they are characterized (for example, GPA, starting salary, summers spent as interns). We would be left with a set of consolidated data with the same number of attributes, but with much fewer observations (see Figure 5.3).

Ultimately, we could do both – again, attempting to reduce the complexity of the decision-making task – while avoiding the actual elimination of specific types of data or descriptors.

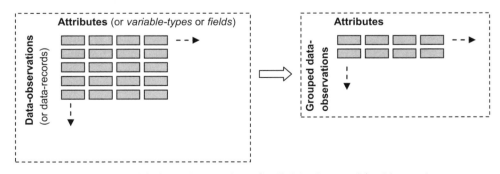

Figure 5.3. Consolidating observations (individual records) of large data sets.

5.3 Attribute Grouping Approaches

If you think you simply have way too many attributes describing the people, places, or things that you have data on, and you feel that several of these attributes may actually represent the same issue (or closely related issues), you have a number of options available to you for consolidating your data.

5.3.1 Trivial Consolidation Approaches

One of the simplest ways to consolidate a group of attributes is by creating an average value across them. If you create an unweighted average (that is, simply add attribute x + attribute y + attribute z, and divide by 3 to create some new overall attribute, xyz), the critical point is to make sure the attributes are similar in units and scale so that the calculation actually makes sense. For example, it might make sense to average the three student attributes – *grade in BUS330*, *grade in BUS331*, and *grade in BUS432* – to create something general (perhaps referring to it as "average Organization and Management area grade"). It would make less sense to average *score on 330 final*, *bowling score*, and *score on breathalyzer test* (which are different scales and hopefully unrelated issues).

Alternative ways to consolidate attributes may be to take advantage of other standard functions in Excel. For example, if it makes more sense to create something similar to "max performance in Organization and Management," you might use the MAX function to consolidate all final grades in organization and management classes into a single, best attribute. Similarly, if you're less interested in the overall performance of students and more interested in their tendency to perform inconsistently in a particular discipline, you might calculate the STDEV across related scores. Maybe those who tend to perform more inconsistently in a discipline are doing so for a particular reason that might be meaningful to you.

These are examples that hit close to home for a typical management student, but the same simplified attribute-grouping technique is used in the marketplace:

- Maybe we don't care what consumers spend on individual items, but rather what they spend on groups such as all perishables, electronics, and so on.
- Maybe we don't care about how much all stocks vary on an hourly basis, but we are concerned with their morning and afternoon averages.

In any case, the methods suggested put the responsibility of consolidation decisions entirely on the shoulders of individual decision makers or DSS designers. They are assumed to be entirely conscious of why certain attributes should be grouped together, and why either unweighted averaging or the use of other summary measures is appropriate. Furthermore, an unmentioned assumption in these examples is that the these schemes are applicable regardless of the nature of the sample population as a whole (that is, they would provide the same summary results per record, regardless of how many records are involved).

5.3.2 Consolidations Using Statistically Derived Weightings

Sometimes, we don't really have a strong feeling about how attributes should be consolidated, only that there's probably some redundancy in the information they provide and that our decision process would be easier if we could crunch them down to more generalized (yet still meaningful) groupings. Fortunately for us, someone has already done the work here. Again, one popular method freely available to us is Principle Components Analysis (PCA). As mentioned previously, PCA is a statistical technique that attempts to create a reduced subset of attributes based on a larger set of potentially closely related (perhaps redundant) attributes. It is not constrained to the assumption that all attributes have equivalent relevance in such consolidation, but it does base its statistical approach to the development of weighting schemes on the entire sample of data as a whole (and hence can be sensitive to the size and constituency of that sample).

As an example of results that might be derived through PCA consolidation, consider the case of Dodecha Solutions, Ltd. Dodecha is a small consulting firm that manages a number of information technology implementation projects over the course of a year. It has been collecting both preproject selection and postimplementation data for several years and now wants to base its consideration of future client requests on that data.

Early on, Dodecha had the foresight to recognize that many preproject characteristics could not be assessed by anything but subjective (opinionated) reports from their consultants. They developed a highly structured set of evaluation questions for their consultants to fill out every time they were given a potential client project to consider. They specifically designed multiple questions aimed at revealing similar higher-level issues (for example, potential problems with client participation in projects, uncertainty relating to specific technologies), knowing that the use of only a handful of potentially biased questions could provide an extremely misleading view of project potential.

Table 5.1 provides the full list of the higher-level issues (left column) and the specific sets of questions (right column) Dodecha's consultants were instructed to answer for each proposed client project. Managers evaluated each of these questions on a scale from 1 to 7 (1 = strong disagreement with

Table 5.1. *Items Thought to Reflect Higher-Level Management Issues for Dodecha*

	A1 :	Will require redesign of many processes
	A2 :	Will require elimination of many processes
Ops Fit Issues	A3 :	Will require resequencing of many processes
	A4 :	Will require addition of many processes
	A5 :	Will require changes in work assignments
	B1 :	Tech capabilities in client industry change frequently
Industry Instability	B2 :	Process capabilities in client industry change frequently
	B3 :	Market of client industry changes frequently
	C1 :	Client demonstrates poor information sharing
	C2 :	Client demonstrates lack of interest in involvement
Inter-Org Concerns	C3 :	Client demonstrates poor worker-resource sharing
	C4 :	Client requires fairly limited time windows for system access/change
	C5 :	Client requires fairly restricted access to stakeholders
	D1 :	New technology untested by related firms
New Tech Concerns	D2 :	We lack familiarity with nuances of the technology
	D3 :	Patches to new technology are forthcoming
	D4 :	Value of new technology to market still uncertain
	E1 :	Will require new training for our project staff
Expertise Issues	E2 :	Will require work outsourcing to experts
	E3 :	Will require repeated contacts with vendor
	F1 :	Much data stored in legacy systems to be replaced
	F2 :	Much data formatting based on noncompliant standards
Legacy Concerns	F3 :	Culture of use/championship of legacy system
	F4 :	User skills highly tuned to legacy system need changing
	F5 :	Many ties to external systems customized to legacy
	G1 :	Client has demonstrated process design and control problems
Client Issues	G2 :	Client has demonstrated managerial leadership problems
	G3 :	Client has demonstrated poor technical know-how
	H1 :	Involves many separate facilities of client
	H2 :	Involves many functional groups of client
Org Complexity	H3 :	Involves many decision makers at client
	H4 :	Involves many stakeholders at client

the statement, and 7 = strong agreement with the statement) prior to making the decision to accept proposed projects for each of Dodecha's 115 past projects. The full data set along with the complete set of analyses to follow is provided in the Chp5_DodechaSolutions workbook.

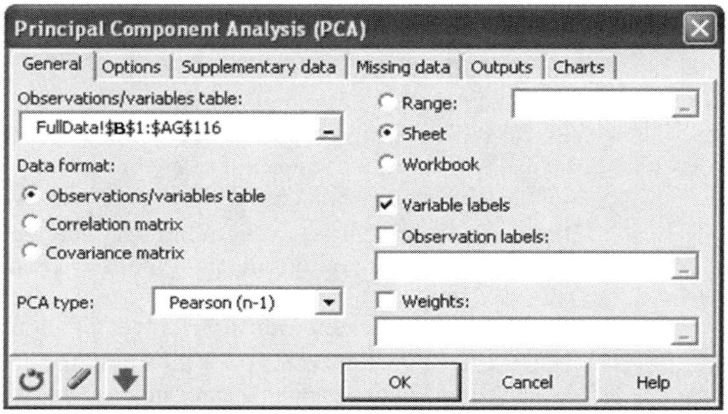

Figure 5.4. Specifying data ranges to be analyzed through PCA with XLStat.

Again, Dodecha went back to the full data set and attempted to consolidate it into the original eight factors that the management highlighted as being useful in later categorization and analysis, because the company was aware that any one of these items alone might provide a misleading impression of how managers viewed these projects prior to their acceptance. In doing so, Dodecha would be reducing their analysis set from essentially 115*33 (3,680) pieces of data into what they consider to be a more meaningful set of 115*8 (920) pieces of data. To do this, they will use PCA.

To demonstrate the use of the PCA consolidation technique (as well as other data simplification tactics), we'll be relying on another tool that goes beyond the typical boundaries of Excel functionality: XLStat (available at www.xlstat.com). XLStat has become one of the industry standards for extended spreadsheet analysis, and it is particularly useful in our discussions given the range of tools it makes available, in addition to the flexibility that it provides to DSS developers (as we will see in Chapter 12).

When installed, XLStat functions similar to any other add-in in Excel. In this particular case, we're interested in making use of its PCA function, which is located under Add-ins>XLStat>Analyzing Data>Principle Components Analysis (PCA). This opens the Principle Components Analysis (PCA) dialog box.

The application of the PCA tool can be fairly straightforward. The critical step required by the dialog box is the selection of the data set to be consolidated and some impression of how to consolidate the selected attributes (for example, into eight factors). Although numerous options are made for professional use, and professional users of this technique are certainly encouraged to investigate the benefits of these options, a demonstration of the basic types of results that can be expected is sufficient for discussion here. Figures 5.4 and 5.5 provide images relating to the specific settings used in the Dodecha case.

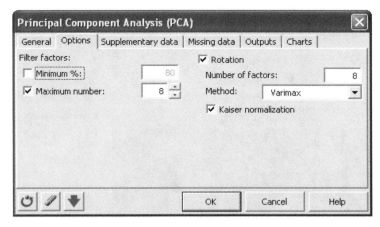

Figure 5.5. Target factor specification for PCA with XLStat.

The next steps happen largely behind the scenes; however, the output provided by XLStat is extremely rich (and beyond the scope of this text). In the most familiar terms for our purposes, the task completed by the PCA algorithm can be viewed as the following:

Objective: Construct new factors based on the existing set of attributes, such that the new factors are as uniquely distinct from one another (uncorrelated) as possible.

Decision Variables: The extent to which each attribute contributes to each new factor (for example, coefficients in each factor equation).

Constraints: Construct exactly eight new factors based on thirty-two original attributes (in the Dodecha Solutions, Ltd., case).

Figure 5.6 provides an annotated version of the XLStat PCA results in this case. Assisted by a little conditional formatting, we see an output table of component scores, which are greater the more each item relates to one of the eight factors derived from analysis.

Although there is no guarantee that individual attributes will naturally group into the eight factors originally conceived by the question designers, in this case there does seem to be some correspondence between what was originally conceptualized and the PCA results. It is also clear, as is usually the case, that the items don't load purely on one factor alone – that is, some attributes provide information that is helpful in forming other factors as well. The specific values of these coefficients are far from immediately intuitive. This is clearly not an equal-weighting scheme as might be derived through a simple averaging approach to attribute consolidation, and it is certainly not one that could be guessed.

Overall, the major conceptual breakouts seem to be well represented, suggesting it might be reasonable to apply the original eight-factor labels to the results. In the end, Dodecha can have some faith in the interpretability of

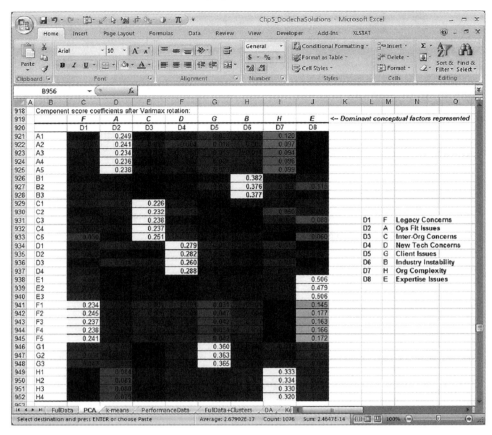

Figure 5.6. Example of PCA results (color coded through added conditional formatting).

the PCA data simplification. In end, the real product of PCA is the consolidated statistically weighted factor scores as shown in Figure 5.7. These will form the bases of further analysis by Dodecha.

5.4 Data Grouping Approaches

Similar to the discussion of grouping attributes, we can start this discussion by considering approaches that might be relevant, provided we have a strong

Factor scores after Varimax rotation:

	F	A	C	D	G	B	H	E	<-- Dominant conceptual factors represented		
	D1	D2	D3	D4	D5	D6	D7	D8			
Obs1	0.104	-0.447	1.911	-1.070	0.775	-0.588	-0.481	-0.898	D1	F	Legacy Concerns
Obs2	1.277	0.983	-1.454	0.004	-1.046	0.402	0.946	-1.086	D2	A	Ops Fit Issues
Obs3	-0.995	-1.056	-1.799	0.193	0.032	0.057	0.509	0.748	D3	C	Inter-Org Concerns
Obs4	-1.019	-1.572	0.763	1.049	-0.641	-0.583	-1.312	-1.057	D4	D	New Tech Concerns
Obs5	-0.976	1.133	0.911	-1.473	-0.746	-0.372	-1.441	-0.815	D5	G	Client Issues

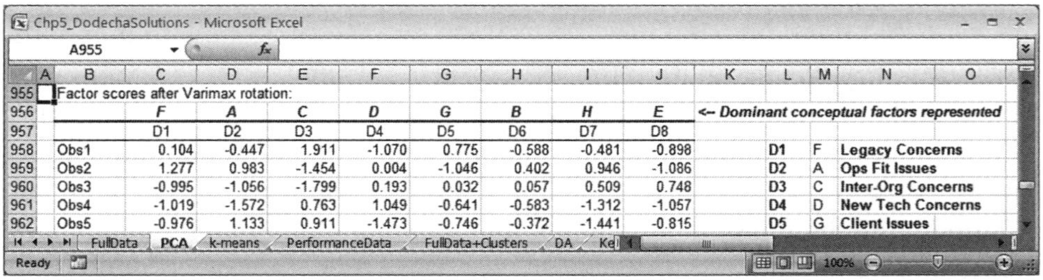

Figure 5.7. The eight-factor scores for each observation involved in the PCA analysis.

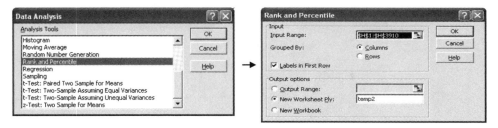

Figure 5.8. Rank and percentile analysis for observation grouping.

understanding of how we should group, based on simple statistics. We can then proceed to discuss approaches where such group structures are fairly unknown. In some real-world cases, decision makers already have a logical notion of which types of records should be similar enough to group together as a subsample (for example, maybe we have a reason for grouping student data by major, or companies by industry, or projects by technology type). If this is the case, we have a preexisting and well-reasoned structure for grouping. On the one hand, if this categorization scheme sufficiently reduces the complexity of our decision-making process, we're set and can move on to other forms of analysis and decision making.

On the other hand, maybe the scheme doesn't sufficiently reduce complexity. Or maybe we don't have sufficient reason for grouping our data by some prespecified category. Or maybe we just want to group by some numerically driven scheme, such as a ranking, where we divide our data based on whether it ranks in the top quarter, bottom quarter, or one of the quartiles in between. We can easily do this in Excel.

5.4.1 Quartile-Based Categorization

One of the many additional features of the Analysis tool box – the Rank and Percentile tool (introduced in Chapter 2) – is relevant to this discussion (Figure 5.8). This tool asks you for a set of observations (for example, 3,909 quarterly EPS figures for various firms in a spreadsheet) and the location of the relative ranking of the observations based on a single attribute. As would be expected, the more data you have, the lengthier the ranking process.

As an example of how to use this tool in a consolidation effort, I've done a simple ranking based on no other criteria other than quarterly sales across all quarters, for which we have data, from the previous QuarterlyData spreadsheet (see Chapter 4). Figure 5.9 shows an example of the results generated by the Ranking and Percentile tool. Note that the data had already been ranked in ascending order prior to using the tool.

A few things to note:

1) Look at the rankings. Notice that some ranking numbers (10, 16) are repeated whereas others (11, 17) are absent. What does this mean?

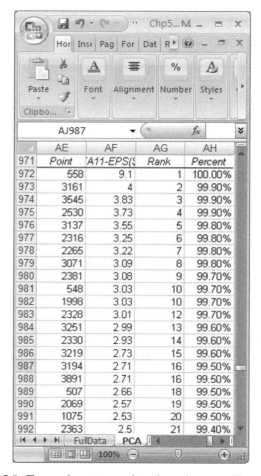

Figure 5.9. Example output of rank and percentile analysis.

2) Regarding the previous point, why might this be different than simply selecting the first, second, third, and fourth sets of twenty-five records out of a total of one hundred originals?

3) We could use these rankings to help us group data into the top 25 percent, the bottom 25 percent, and so on. How could we use an IF statement to automatically generate such groupings at this point?

5.4.2 Categorization Based on p-levels and z-scores

Measures of standard deviation from the mean provide other meaningful and related approaches to grouping (provided that the issue you are grouping generates data that are normally distributed). There's nothing stopping you from calculating a mean and standard deviation for sets of values and determining the z-scores and associated p-level of that observation;

Table 5.2. *Example Structure of Quartile Cross-Binning*

		EPS (earnings per share)			
		Bottom	Third 25%	Second 25%	Top 25%
R&D Investment	Bottom				
	Third 25%		*Cross-tab summaries of other measures (for example, profitability) for firms that fall into each cross-bin*		
	Second 25%				
	Top 25%				

however, whether that's statistically appropriate for the given data set is another question.

After you have a z-score associated with each data observation, you have the basis for designating whether that observation is a typical (for example, z-scores between -1 and 1) or atypical (for example, outlying z-scores that are greater than 2 or less than -2). How you define the bounds of the outlying region is yet another decision to make, but, in general, this can be as meaningful as (or more than) the kinds of splits and groupings derived from a ranking procedure.

5.4.3 Multidimensional Bins

If you think that there may be multiple, independent, noncategorical measures that could meaningfully distinguish subsets of your data, make use of them. Imagine you believe that certain firms – such as those that are simultaneously on the fringes of both (a) EPS performance and (b) research and development (R&D) investment – are relatively unique with regard to other aspects of their operations or financial performance. You have the ability to designate such groups independently, so do that, and then use a tool like a PivotTable to create cross-tabs (a table of summary measures, for example, of averages for each grouping combination as shown in Table 5.2).

These can provide a great deal of insight into the effects of multiple factors on additional performance measures. Such insight might suggest further investigations into specific regions of the data (for example, those firms in the third 25 percentile in R&D but the top 25 percent in EPS).

It is also worth noting, however, that although the number of data records that fall into each of the four categories for either the EPS or R&D splits

Table 5.3. *Example of Subpopulations Associated with Quartile Cross-Binning*

		EPS (earnings per share)			
		Bottom	Third 25%	Second 25%	Top 25%
R&D Investment	Bottom	2	8	9	5
	Third 25%	4	5	7	9
	Second 25%	8	6	5	6
	Top 25%	11	6	4	4

may be equal, there's nothing that will guarantee that the number of observations in each cell of a cross-tab will be similar. Consider the example in Table 5.3, where I've entered the number of records that fall into each cross-bin. There are big differences in the sizes of these bins. Does this make it more difficult to compare other performance measures based on some of the smaller groups?

5.4.4 Cluster Analysis for Multidimensional Splits

You might have the belief that your data are split across multiple dimensions but in ways that can't necessarily be described by post-hoc combination of independent splits (as done with cross-tabs). That is, maybe there are more complex relationships among the attributes of your data records that tend to group observations in weird but potentially informative ways.

To try to illustrate this, consider a bunch of points characterized by three attributes: x, y, and z. Upon visual inspection, in this three-dimensional space you might see these attributes cluster into four rough groups. Maybe you could even draw some dividing planes to emphasize those separations. But what if their clustering was less clear? What if there were more points or multiple ways to subjectively split them up? (See Figure 5.10.)

Consolidating observations through nonobvious (although perhaps statistically supported and managerially meaningful) divisions of their attribute space usually falls into the realm of what is called cluster analysis. This technique for grouping data is popular in marketing, where firms attempt to classify specific groups of customers based on a wide ranges of characteristics (attributes). But how would a somewhat complex and unintuitive approach to classifying data be useful to a manager? Suppose you collect data on individual entities such as:

• Customers of a business
• Stores of a retail chain
• Students of a university
• IT implementation projects (as in the Dodecha case)

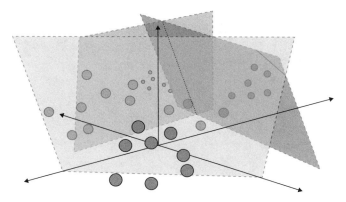

Figure 5.10. Multidimensional complexity in group distinction.

And let's say these individual entities can be characterized by a range of specific attributes or higher-level factors such as:

- For customers: age, monthly income, loyalty, tech savvy
- For stores: geo location, sales, market presence, efficiency
- For students: grades in different courses, determination
- For projects: anticipated costs, interorganizational concerns

To make these data useful, a decision maker or manager might want to identify smaller groups of individuals based on their similarities to one another (that is, the similarity of their attributes) and then make separate policy decisions for each group, rather than trying to come up with an all-encompassing and perfect solution for everyone. What kinds of distinct policy decisions might be realistic?

- Designing and deploying different marketing campaigns for different market segments of customers characterized by distinct interests
- Designing and deploying different business and operating strategies to promote
- Sales in different groups of stores facing different challenges
- Designing different courses, programs of study, or sources of assistance based of strengths and weaknesses of different groups of students
- Designing response plans for dealing with (or rejecting) specific projects requested by existing or future clients

The key to applying customized strategies is being able to know for whom or what you are customizing (that is, the nature and distinction of the group). Conceptually, the decision maker or analyst must be able to make these distinctions, often prior to designing customized policies. This conceptual goal translates into the following analytical task of cluster analysis.

Objective: Identify a set of fairly distinct groups of entities (records) in the data set, based on some measure of group separation (for example, minimizing the

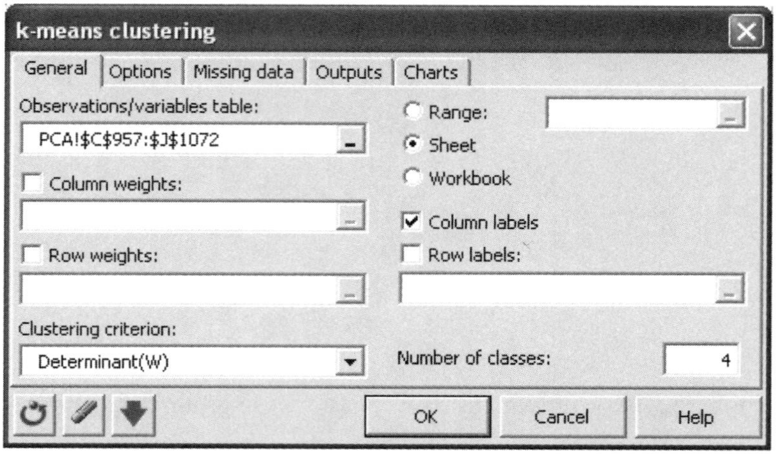

Figure 5.11. Specifying k-means clustering inputs and parameters for evaluation by XLStat.

ratio of within-group to between-group variance, with variation of the entire sample based on the full set of record attributes used for grouping).

Decision Variables: Which entities or records should belong to which group.

Constraints: Often, some criteria for limiting the number of groups that might be formed (for example, limit to the formation of four clusters of projects in the case of Dodecha Solutions, Ltd.).

That is, the algorithms used in cluster analysis are designed to locate clusters of data records that possess similar characteristics (whatever those attributes might be), which are distinguishable from other clusters and ideally have few records in between (where group membership is less clear). Returning to the Dodecha example, we might consider how a tool like XLStat could be used to provide a consolidation of records (projects in this case) into more generalized groupings through the use of cluster analysis. Again, we'll be making use of the Analyzing Data functionality under XLStat and, specifically, the Cluster Analysis tool.

Again, I'm going to specify a few points before letting the analysis run: specifically, the range of data – in this case, the eight-factor scores for all 115 projects derived earlier from PCA – and a request for the algorithm to limit itself to the formation of four groups (see Figure 5.11). As with PCA, many other options exist and professionals who are interested in the use of clustering are encouraged to look further into these. However, a critical point to stress here is that there are many possible combinations for a clustering algorithm to consider. In this case, with 115 projects and four groups of projects, we're talking about 1.72544×10^{69} combinations for a comprehensive search. That's basically a 2 followed by 69 zeros – a huge number that makes a routing example involving fifteen or thirty sites seem like child's play.

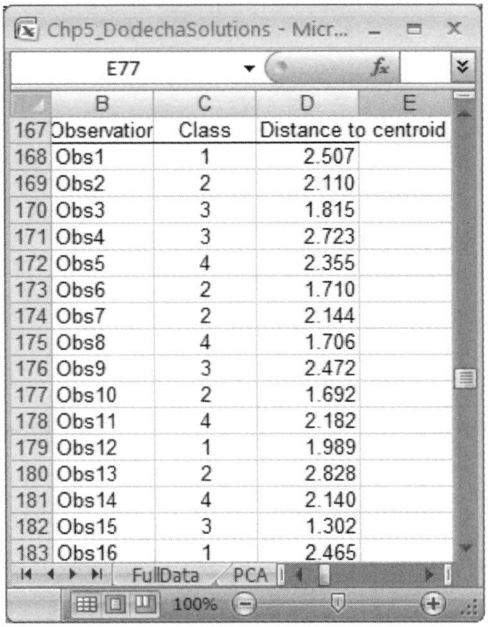

	B	C	D	E
167	Observation	Class	Distance to centroid	
168	Obs1	1	2.507	
169	Obs2	2	2.110	
170	Obs3	3	1.815	
171	Obs4	3	2.723	
172	Obs5	4	2.355	
173	Obs6	2	1.710	
174	Obs7	2	2.144	
175	Obs8	4	1.706	
176	Obs9	3	2.472	
177	Obs10	2	1.692	
178	Obs11	4	2.182	
179	Obs12	1	1.989	
180	Obs13	2	2.828	
181	Obs14	4	2.140	
182	Obs15	3	1.302	
183	Obs16	1	2.465	

Figure 5.12. Clustering results (classes/groups assigned) from k-means approach.

Clustering algorithms are not going to be conducting comprehensive searches; instead, they have their own heuristics built in, driven in part by statistical cues and some random guesses. For this reason, even on the same data set, clustering results are subject to variation. For professionals faced with the realization that results may be somewhat subject to chance, the best possible solution is to look at multiple runs of a cluster analysis to see if some consistent group formations are apparent, which gives greater credence to those group formations.

In any event, the main take-away from cluster analysis will be the derived group constituencies. These are what policy makers are looking for. In the results outlined in Figure 5.12, the Observations represent each of the 115 projects that have been grouped. Clustering results are only as good as the intelligence brought to bear in their use. Assuming the clusters themselves are fairly robust to other clustering methods that could have been applied, at least two sets of immediate implications typically come into consideration:

1) How do the groups differ across the set of factors upon which they were based?
2) Are only some of these factors critical in distinguishing these groups?

At first look, we might try to represent such differences visually. A radar plot is a common visualization tool used in cluster analysis. Fortunately, Excel comes to our aid again because radar plots are yet another type of

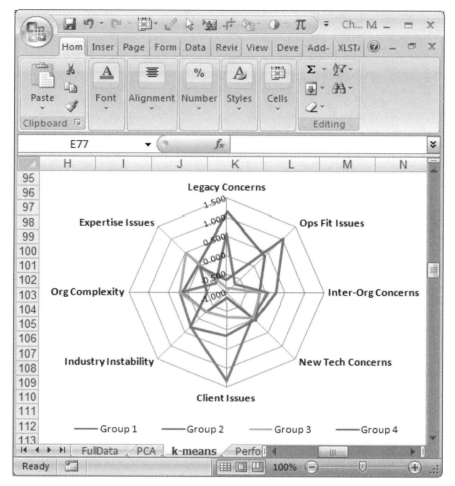

Figure 5.13. Radar plot of group distinctiveness across all factors considered by k-means.

graph made available for representing data. Figure 5.13 shows two versions of radar plots created for the present example.

Not all of the eight factors seem to have been very helpful in distinguishing these groups – for example, look at the New Tech Concerns factor. Unfortunately, the existence of less distinguishing factors tends to deemphasize the distinctiveness of the derived groups as depicted by measures such as the ratio of within-group to between-group variance. (This ratio will tend to go up as more factors are included that don't contribute to group distinction.) However, we don't need to be thrown by a single measure taken out of context. Our focus should be on distinctions that are salient in the data set. For example, consider a few key factors, along which the greatest differences exist. Use a similar radar plot approach to visualization (Figure 5.14).

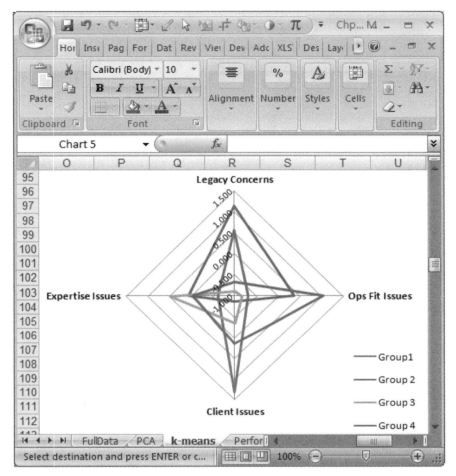

Figure 5.14. Radar plot of group characteristics across four seemingly key distinguishing factors.

Although it may be that no one factor could easily distinguish each of these groups (for example, each of the four factors describing Group 2 reflected in Figure 5.14 seem to be similar to at least one other group), it does appear that a multifactor story could be told relating to differentiation extracted by the clustering protocol. But even more relevantly, we don't necessarily need to limit our consideration of group distinctiveness to preproject data. After all, these are completed projects. Postproject performance data would not be available for categorizing future projects into such groups, but Dodecha would surely be interested in knowing how these groups might ultimately differ in performance as well. Which leads to our natural follow-up question for analysis: How do the groups differ across other related outcome or performance measures that might be of interest to managers?

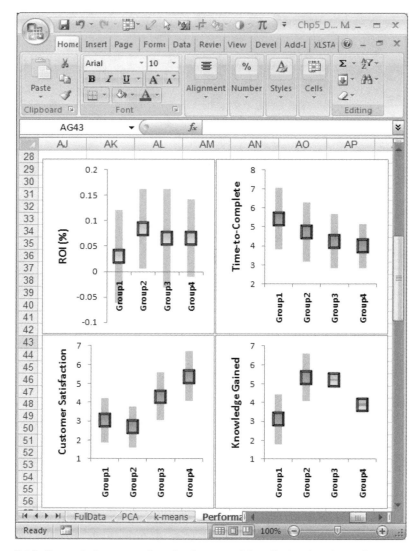

Figure 5.15. Spread charts used to further consider distinction in variance as well as group means.

For the purpose of motivating this discussion, the same workbook (Chp5_DodechaSolutions) includes performance data on the 115 projects analyzed, including ROI (%), Time-to-Completion (in weeks), and two subjective scales that report overall customer satisfaction and perceptions of knowledge gained by project team members. Figure 5.15 shows a variant of high-low-close plots (common to Excel) used to summarize how each of the four derived groups differ along these performance measures.

What kind of a story might this tell?

1) It seems as if projects that are deemed particularly problematic with regard to client issues (Group 1 projects) may also be slightly more likely to perform

poorly with regard to Dodecha's ROI, take a particularly long time to complete, not provide much in terms of customer satisfaction, and certainly don't add to the general knowledge of Dodecha's teams. It might be worthwhile to avoid such projects in the future.

2) Projects that lack client issues but pose concerns with regard to legacy and operational fit issues (Group 2) nevertheless tend to provide decent ROI ranges and team-learning opportunities, although they potentially face risks with customer satisfaction. If customer satisfaction isn't an issue for a particular client (for example, the customer would complain regardless), such projects present valuable opportunities. However, the issue of customer satisfaction would certainly need to be carefully considered on a client-by-client basis.

3) Projects whose primary distinctive concern centers on expertise issues (Group 3) provide an interesting opportunity for shoring up expertise through knowledge gains. These projects tend to be conducted in fairly short time windows and don't have major shortcomings with regard to customer satisfaction. They may be quick opportunities to gain knowledge in a way that is relatively free of risk.

4) Regarding Group 4 projects, these are also quick ones, but there is not nearly as much knowledge to be gained as with Group 3. However, there is some potential, as far as customer satisfaction and potential word of mouth are concerned. This may all be due to a naïveté on the part of the client with regard to what he truly needs and how to get some basic tasks done, but these projects could be handy in a pinch if testimonials are needed for marketing purposes. A more cynical view might be that these projects are the kinds that other less-scrupulous consulting firms might take advantage of, and they represent an opportunity for Dodecha to play an important interventional role from a market-citizenship perspective.

These are just some sample views of what Dodecha might consider, based on the results at this point.

5.5 Giving Form to Future Categorization

As much as past analysis might be interesting, the focus is still on the past. To truly leverage the findings from the use of consolidation processes such as PCA and cluster analysis, it will be particularly helpful to know if there was some simple way to use future preproject data to help identify where a new project might fall, and therefore whether it should be pursued. It would be even more helpful if some basic rules of thumb could be developed to quickly categorize ideal project opportunities.

To close this discussion with an eye on future applications of these results, we'll introduce yet another statistical tool made available by XLStat and the work structure available in the Chp5_DodechaSolutions workbook: Discriminant Analysis (DA). The aim of DA is to make use of a select set of predictive attributes to create some simple formulation that places specific records or entities (characterized by attributes) into groups to which they

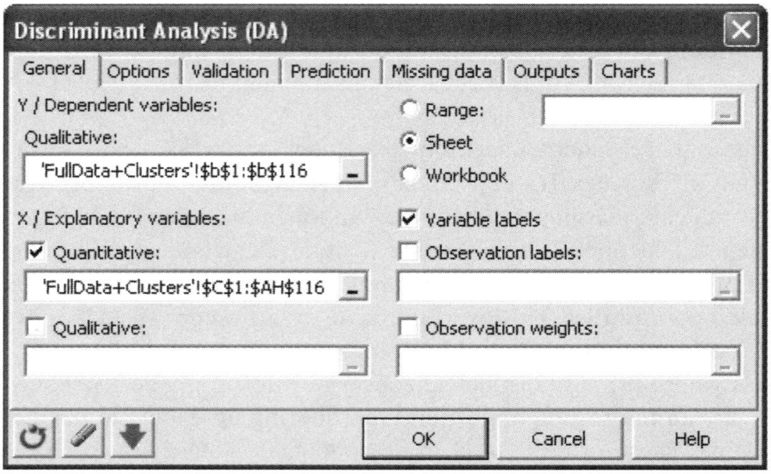

Figure 5.16. Discriminant analysis parameterization through XLStat.

are thought to belong. In this sense, DA is a nice complement to clustering, which developed group membership based on a set of attributes or factors but it typically does not provide a functional form or an equation that would formally predict such membership. As with all other XLStat tools discussed thus far, the DA option is found under the Analyzing Data menu.

On the FullData+Clusters worksheet in the Chp5_DodechaSolutions workbook, we can find the full set of the original thirty-two items along with the designations into which each derived cluster project has been placed. The hope is that DA can make use of this or some subset of this original attribute data to come up with a consistent categorization scheme for future projects. Let's first consider what it would come up with given the full set of attributes (expecting some to be much less useful than others). Figure 5.16 shows the settings I'll be using, which allow me to specify the qualitative data to predict (that is, the groups, in this case) and the quantitative data on which I want prediction equations based.

The task of the DA algorithm will be something like this:

> *Objective*: Generate a set of equations that makes use of the predictive data (attributes) in an attempt to identify, with a high level of accuracy, to which of the preestablished groups each observation already belongs.
> *Decision Variables*: Coefficients of the predictive equations.
> *Constraints*: Only the specified predictive variables (could be the whole set or a subset) should be used in the equations formed.

Figure 5.17 shows what the analysis provides in this case.

These are essentially a set of coefficients for four equations (one for each group), one coefficient for each of thirty-two predicting variables

	1	2	3	4
586 Classification functions:				
587				
588	1	2	3	4
589 Intercept	-97.493	-78.720	-59.137	-71.414
590 A1	-4.738	-4.521	-5.250	-4.049
591 A2	-0.851	2.190	2.544	2.458
592 A3	-0.706	-2.556	0.025	-0.918
593 A4	3.884	5.581	2.684	5.760
594 A5	4.318	3.392	1.267	1.247
595 B1	7.464	6.623	4.915	6.120
596 B2	-2.619	-2.159	-2.323	-0.875
597 B3	4.037	1.049	3.274	1.968
598 C1	-4.744	-0.682	-0.232	0.088
599 C2	-4.174	-2.213	-2.931	-2.246
600 C3	-0.452	-0.905	-1.082	-1.266
601 C4	5.262	2.596	4.094	3.259
602 C5	5.488	3.735	3.571	3.753
603 D1	-4.882	-3.399	-3.764	-2.964
604 D2	-0.035	0.127	0.451	0.478
605 D3	3.277	4.156	3.432	4.390
606 D4	6.669	4.402	4.026	2.784
607 E1	-8.146	-7.020	-4.250	-4.229
608 E2	0.571	3.499	2.407	0.823
609 E3	7.493	5.892	4.836	5.015
610 F1	6.483	7.476	6.097	5.324
611 F2	-2.675	-2.234	-1.053	-1.653
612 F3	11.214	6.783	3.579	5.914
613 F4	-8.258	-4.417	-6.419	-6.622
614 F5	-0.413	0.774	0.686	0.638
615 G1	7.667	5.491	4.750	5.367
616 G2	5.919	-0.405	2.604	1.893
617 G3	-2.578	-1.719	-2.667	-2.230
618 H1	-0.752	1.419	0.941	1.992
619 H2	-4.419	-3.760	-4.054	-4.594
620 H3	13.393	7.088	8.695	9.097
621 H4	-4.156	-0.838	-1.266	-2.944

Figure 5.17. Classification function showing individual item roles on cluster prediction.

(attributes) in this case, plus an intercept. This is the same kind of thing you'd see as an output from a regression analysis. How are these equations used in group-membership prediction? For any record/entity (that is, each of the 115 projects), and for any of the four discriminant functions (in this case), simply multiply coefficients to their associated attribute values and create a sum of these multiples that includes the intercepts. Formulaically:

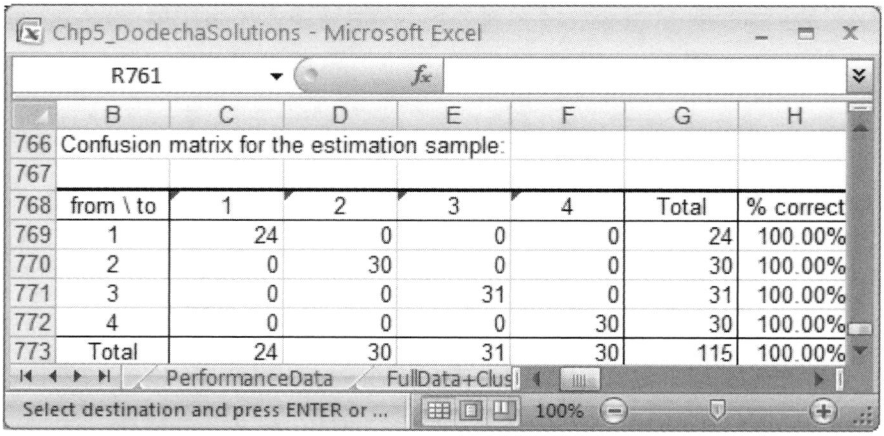

Figure 5.18. Overview of ability of all items to categorize observations in developed groups.

The spreadsheet shows:

Chp5_DodechaSolutions - Microsoft Excel

Cell R761

from \ to	1	2	3	4	Total	% correct
1	24	0	0	0	24	100.00%
2	0	30	0	0	30	100.00%
3	0	0	31	0	31	100.00%
4	0	0	0	30	30	100.00%
Total	24	30	31	30	115	100.00%

(766: Confusion matrix for the estimation sample:)

PerformanceData | FullData+Clus

$$\text{Value of function "k" for record "n"} = Intercept_k + \sum_{i}^{\#attributes} \beta_{k,i}\chi_{n,i}$$

The results of the four functions for a single record or entity are then compared. If the first function provides the highest sum, that record is classified into the first group. If the second function is the highest of the set, the record is classified into the second group, and so on. As is often the case with regression analysis, the hope is that a set of equations is able to accurately classify preexisting data and accurately classify future data. Looking at Figure 5.18, how well do the functions based on the thirty-two attributes classify? Perfectly. So, the next question is: Do we really need all of these to provide for a decent guess as to where (that is, into what clusters) new projects might fall? It would certainly be nice to rely on only a few key questions to figure out whether it's worth playing ball with a client request.

Let's consider the top five of these items based solely on something as simple as the range of their roles in the classification function (going with the top five in terms of overall impact might be a better approach, but we'll use this for demonstration purposes).

C1 (*under Inter-org Concerns*): Client demonstrates poor information sharing
E1 (*under Expertise Issues*): Will require new training for our project staff
F3 (*under Legacy Concerns*): Culture of use/championship of legacy system
G2 (*under Client Issues*): Client has demonstrated managerial leadership problems
H3 (*under Org Complexity*): Involves many decision makers at client

Running an almost identical analysis, except for greater constraints on the range of attributes available to the discriminant functions, we get the summary of classification strength shown in Figure 5.19.

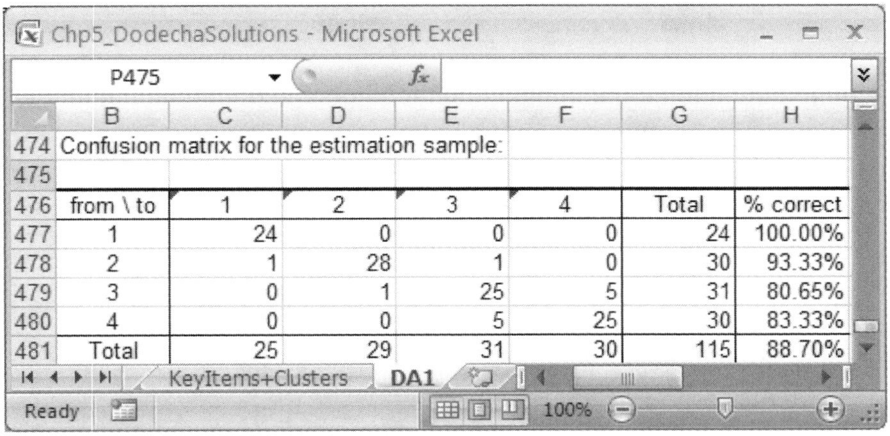

from \ to	1	2	3	4	Total	% correct
1	24	0	0	0	24	100.00%
2	1	28	1	0	30	93.33%
3	0	1	25	5	31	80.65%
4	0	0	5	25	30	83.33%
Total	25	29	31	30	115	88.70%

Figure 5.19. Ability of only five select items to categorize observations in developed groups.

Not bad for a using a five-question approach rather than a thirty-two-question one. If this was an acceptable level of accuracy, it might make type-assessments and subsequent strategies for handling a heck of a lot easier and quicker.

References

Borges, B., G. Goldstein, A. Ortmann, and G. Gigerenzer, "Can Ignorance Beat the Stock Market?" In *Simple Heuristics that Make Use Smart*, edited by G. Gigerenzer, P. M. Todd, and the ABC Research Group (Oxford University Press, 1999).

Box, G. E. P., "Robustness in the Strategy of Scientific Model Building." In *Robustness in Statistics*, edited by R. L. Launer and G. N. Wilkinson (Academic Press: New York, 1979).

Supplement: Making Heuristics Automatic (the Inelegant Way)

One of the key advantages of information technologies is that they allow you to automate rules and processes that you would not want to perform manually, even if you could explain how to actually perform the rule or process to the computer.

In decision support systems, the ability to automate tasks such as fast and frugal heuristics can be considerably helpful, especially because they eliminate the need to explain the heuristics to personnel and they eliminate the need to manually run through tasks (which may be relatively time consuming and error prone). Some heuristics are best automated through the use of computer programming, whereas others can be handled at some level purely through the design of data and cell linkages within a spreadsheet. These

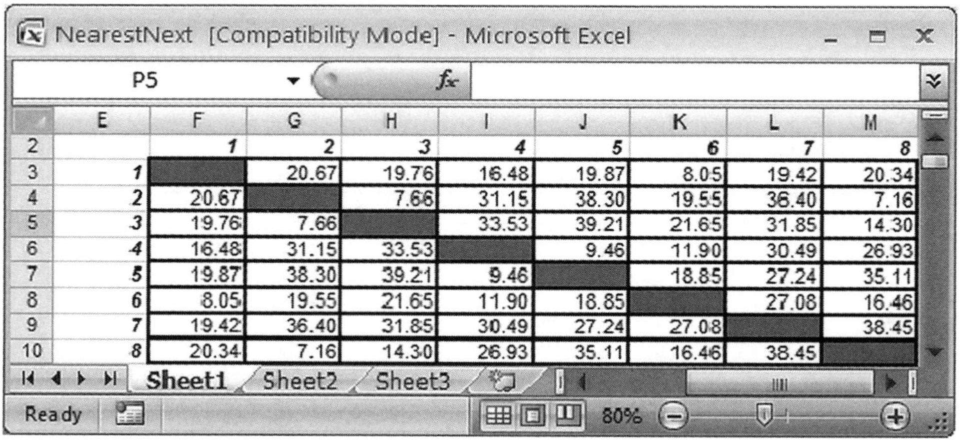

	E	F	G	H	I	J	K	L	M
2		1	2	3	4	5	6	7	8
3	1		20.67	19.76	16.48	19.87	8.05	19.42	20.34
4	2	20.67		7.66	31.15	38.30	19.55	36.40	7.16
5	3	19.76	7.66		33.53	39.21	21.65	31.85	14.30
6	4	16.48	31.15	33.53		9.46	11.90	30.49	26.93
7	5	19.87	38.30	39.21	9.46		18.85	27.24	35.11
8	6	8.05	19.55	21.65	11.90	18.85		27.08	16.46
9	7	19.42	36.40	31.85	30.49	27.24	27.08		38.45
10	8	20.34	7.16	14.30	26.93	35.11	16.46	38.45	

Figure 5.20. Starting set of inter-site distances defining the problem.

automations often do not appear as elegant as their programming equivalents, but they have the advantage of being something that nonprogrammers can create and understand.

Let's go over how we might automate one of the previously discussed heuristics: the nearest next heuristic (as might be applied to vehicle routing). Figure 5.20 is a matrix that shows the distance between any two sites, with the starting point represented by site #1. So, the distance from site #1 (row) to site #5 (column) equals 19.87 miles.

Visually, we can see that the site closest to our starting point (site #1) is actually site #6 (8.05 miles). But we could also use the MIN and HLOOKUP functions to get that result from Excel, provided we tell it to look for the MIN value in the row of our starting point (site #1). Figure 5.21 shows the same matrix with a few items added. Hence, I have the first step in this heuristic solved (that is, first go to site #6). If I change the distance numbers in this matrix, my solution might change (automatically).

Now, let's create a second matrix of similar form just below it. In this one, I'm no longer concerned about dealing with site #1 (been there, done that). All I care about is moving on from the last pick (site #6) to the next site closest to it. So, I want to eliminate site #1 from consideration, as shown in Figure 5.22.

Second Stage of the Nearest Next Heuristic Automated

Most of the structure here is the same as in Figure 5.21. I'm feeding the value of the last pick (site #6) into the associated new start cell, but I've also excluded everything about site #1. (I've filled its cells with spaces – not zeros, because that would be misleading.) I'm doing this automatically using

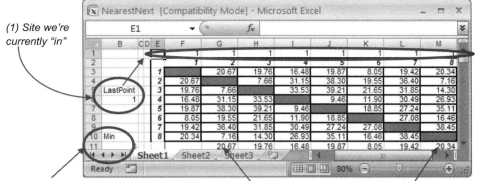

(1) Site we're currently "in"

(3) Using the MIN function on the bottom-most row, and then HLOOKUP to find the site # associated with that distance

(2) Distance between current site and the site on the column header 1,2,3… (using the OFFSET function)

Figure 5.21. Mechanism for assessing set of possible next distances (to find nearest).

an IF statement that basically says, "if the row or column header is equal to the LastPoint designated in the previous step (site #1), put a space in this cell; otherwise, copy the value from the previous table." As seen in Figure 5.23, more of the same is repeated throughout the spreadsheet (essentially duplicated *n* times; where *n* is the number of total sites under consideration).

Admittedly, there are more elegant ways to approach this, and the method I demonstrated takes up some space (especially if the number of sites increases considerably), but in the end what we have is a completed routing solution that will change any time we update the original distances.

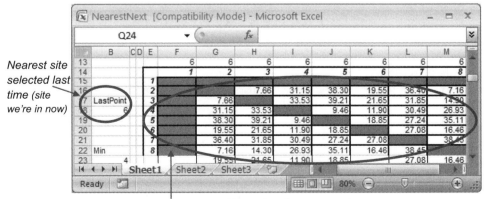

Nearest site selected last time (site we're in now)

Remaining set of inter-site distances under consideration (site #1 no longer relevant)

Figure 5.22. Second stage of the nearest next heuristic automated.

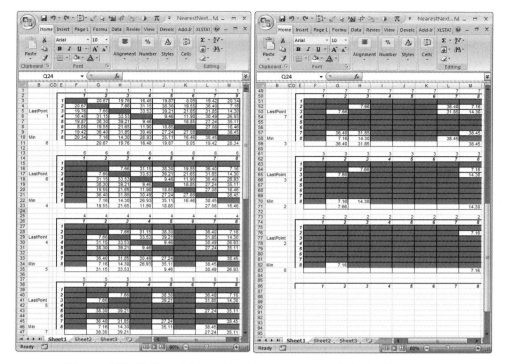

Figure 5.23. Full multistage implementation and derived solution.

The solution itself is a decent one that doesn't require an exhaustive search or any formal programming. Relying on code rather than the spreadsheet to crank out this answer would be much more elegant and efficient, but it's worth showing that there's more than one way to accomplish this task, and it doesn't always mean that we need to rely on programming skills.

PRACTICE PROBLEMS

Practice 5.1

The file Chp5_PractPCAClust.xls contains earnings-per-share data for 144 firms in three broad industry classifications. It also contains ratings provided by managers that describe the extent to which they invest in each of several research and development activities (for example, logistics research through customer testing).

1) Use all Research and Testing variables in a Principal Components Analysis to consolidate those attributes into two composite measures. How well do the ratings seem to match expectations with regard to interpretations of the two factors? Does there appear to be some conceptual consistency?
2) Use those two measures to form four clusters of your data records (remember to account for the bug in the cluster labeling part of that program). Discard any

Table 5.4. *Classic Prisoner's Dilemma*

		Prisoner 2 Squeals?	
		Yes	No
Prisoner 1 Squeals?	Yes	2, 2	0, 3
	No	3, 0	1, 1

clusters that are fewer than eight in size. Attempt to generate labels for these groups based on how they distinguish themselves along the two factors.

3) Use your clustering results to create a PivotTable that shows the average EPS of firms that fall into specific Industry (as your row headers) and R&D-type clusters (as column headers). What do the summaries in the PivotTable suggest regarding R&D strategies (clusters) for specific industries?

4) Use Discriminant Analysis subsets of the original items to attempt to determine whether a small number of questions can provide the similar classifications and therefore predictive capabilities, as far as EPS is concerned.

Practice 5.2

If performance differences are so critical, one might ask, "Why not just group by performance to begin with and then see what premeasures might be useful in predicting membership in performance groups?" Aside from getting into issues related to potential robustness in the results, the fact is that such seemingly straightforward approaches, as simple as they may be, often don't yield very strong mechanisms for future prediction (and may turn out not to be all that useful).

Using the existing Dodecha Solutions data set, give this a try. What are the apparent differences in predictive capabilities? Outline the pros and cons in the predictive capabilities of this approach relative to the one reviewed in this chapter.

Practice 5.3 (Challenge)

A common mechanism for attempting to model the choices that potentially competitive entities may make when faced with a variety of alternative options is provided in the area of what is now called Game Theory (popular in sociology, political science, and management).

Game Theory assumes that parties competing against each other have at least partial (if not complete) information regarding the payoff structures that each other faces – payoff structures that are dependent not only on their own decisions, but also on the decisions of those with whom they are competing. This means that although they may be able to understand where their best outcomes may be, they may have no means of securing those outcomes if they are not able to form prior agreements with their competitors (which is often the case).

A classic example in Game Theory is the prisoner's dilemma. In Table 5.4, we present the number of years each will get depending on what each crook reports.

Table 5.5. *Dominance Applied to Prisoner's Dilemma*

		Prisoner 2 Squeals?	
		Yes	No
Prisoner 1 Squeals?	Yes	2, 2 (y)	0, 3 (n)
	No	3, 0 (n)	1, 1 (n)

Obviously, the best each could do is no years of time. The worst is three years. Perhaps an acceptable compromise might be one year each. But how do the players choose the action that will benefit the most, given that they can't actually communicate on the issue?

The suggested solution is to follow what might be called the *dominance heuristic*. Each individual, not knowing what the other might do, tries to figure out if there is one best policy that will do well regardless of what the other individual decides to do, as shown in Table 5.5.

A quick assessment suggests that the dominant policy for each party is to squeal. If Prisoner 1 follows this policy and Prisoner 2 keeps his mouth shut, Prisoner 1 will do no time. If Prisoner 2 follows this heuristic as well, he will do two years instead of three. Of course, both results are worse for Prisoner 2 than for Prisoner 1, but again that's the nature of heuristics: They're very simple and usually provide semidecent outcomes – but they're often not the best.

Your task is to use a method similar to that presented in the discussion of automating the nearest next heuristic to automate instances of the dominance heuristic. Table 5.6 shows a sample matrix from which to base your structure and perform testing.

Basically, each player has five options from which he or she is trying to maximize a payoff. In each cell we see the total payoff given to Player 1, then that for Player 2 separated by a comma. So, Player 1 gets four points and Player 2 gets three points if Player 1 chooses his second option and Player 2 chooses his first.

We can see that Player 1's best option is either Option 1 or Option 5 depending on what Player 2 does (other options for Player 1 never do better than either of these options). Therefore, we could eliminate the other options from consideration. If Player 2 makes the same assumption, he recognizes that his own best option (given that Player 1 might rationally only pick Option 1 or 5) would be to pick Option 2. Subsequently, if Player 1 foresees this conclusion, he would select Option 1. The result is that Player 1 picks Option 1, and Player 2 picks Option 2.

Making that decision "automatic" might not appear straightforward, but here is one foundation for consideration: Start with Player 1. Find the maximum payoff possible for each option that Player 2 might take. Use a lookup function to find out which of Player 1's options is represented by that maximum payoff (which may be more than one). If any single option is always the best (or tied for the best) under each decision Player 2 might make, build a new matrix that eliminates the remainder of Player 1's options. If any two options are always the best (or tied for the best), perform a similar elimination. Do the same if the best solution crosses over three or four options. Keep the matrix intact if nothing can be eliminated.

Table 5.6. *Dominance in Gaming Example*

		Player 2's Options				
		1	2	3	4	5
Player 1's Options	1	5, 4	3, 7	3, 4	5, 4	4, 5
	2	4, 3	2, 6	2, 3	5, 6	3, 2
	3	3, 2	1, 7	3, 3	5, 6	2, 2
	4	3, 1	2, 4	3, 6	5, 1	4, 1
	5	4, 2	2, 8	4, 4	5, 5	6, 2

Do the same kind of thing for Player 2, using the "reduced" matrix, then create a second, still more reduced matrix. Create subsequent matrices until only one option remains (Note that in this case there is a final resolution to the game, although with other numbers we might not be able to determine a single best rational conclusion; still we should become aware of that fact pretty early on when attempting to reduce our decision space).

6

The Analytics of Optimization

Excel gives us Solver, a great tool that helps us determine what specific decisions (values of our decision variables) should be used to obtain our objectives that are subject to the issues constraining us. Generally, Solver can be accessed under the Data tab in the Analysis section (Figure 6.1). If you do not find Solver in your Excel Data tab, it means that either Solver was not selected for installation at the time your copy of Excel was installed, or it is currently not activated. To activate Solver, click Options>Add-Ins. Select Excel Add-Ins in the Manage drop-down menu and then click Go. The Add-Ins dialog box opens, which enables you to choose Solver Add-In (Figure 6.2).

6.1 Optimization with Solver

The general structure of Solver fits perfectly with the description in Chapter 4 of the three key elements of decision structuring: objectives, decision variables, and constraints (Figure 6.3). Solver is designed to provide the best solutions possible, based on the information we provide. It has its limits (it breaks down with extremely complex or large problems), but it does a nice job for smaller problems that still present challenges to decision makers.

Rather than talk about the theory and math behind simple optimization, we'll take a page from some of the most successful texts on teaching the value and use of this tool by diving right into a few examples in depth. (We'll pick up in Chapter 7 on how Solver succeeds, and in some cases fails, in its work.)

6.1.1 Example #1: Atlanta Professional Training

Atlanta has been an up-and-coming hot spot for young professionals over the past few years. As more 20-somethings migrate to Atlanta, they are finding it more and more difficult to land a dream job. Extensive market research

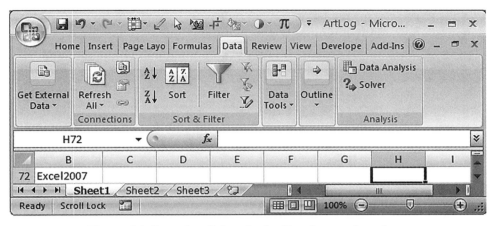

Figure 6.1. Locating Solver in the Excel menu interface.

with the major employers in the area indicates that these job seekers are lacking one of two key job skills: substance (analytics, number crunching, data analysis, and so on) or style (communication, poise, etiquette, and so on). Dorian McAnderstein, a recent MBA graduate, jumped at the opportunity to share his expertise in both of these areas. To do so, Dorian founded a professional training facility that caters to the needs of these clueless individuals.

He has decided to charge $3,500 for each substance-lacking student (termed "beatnik"), and $2,800 for each style-suppressed student (termed

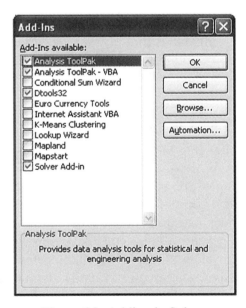

Figure 6.2. Adding-in Solver.

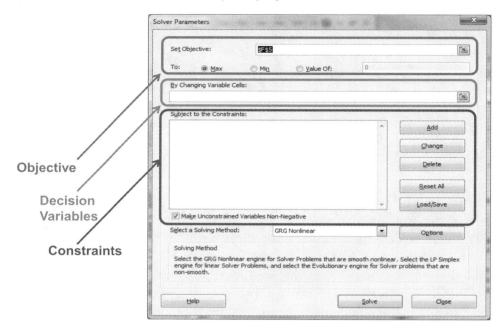

Figure 6.3. Objective, decision, and constraint specification fields in Solver.

"geek"). There are two professional training boot camps: Beatnik students need fourteen hours of training in number crunching and analysis and seven hours of training in communication and etiquette, whereas geeks need only six hours of training in number crunching and analysis but eleven hours of training in communication and etiquette.

Dorian teaches the style courses, and he can work up to 114 hours per month. Dorian's partner handles the substance sessions and can work up to 107 hours per month. In addition, Dorian does not feel that the students benefit from class sizes smaller than nine students. The question is: What mix of geek and beatnik students should Dorian admit?

6.1.1.1 Structuring Models for Optimization

One of the most challenging tasks for those new to optimization methods is figuring out how to translate a story problem into something a computer application (for example, Solver in this case) can make sense of and help solve. The three critical components to all business problems – objectives, decision variables, and constraints – are critical to the use of Solver.

Beginners need to get into the practice of asking what falls into each of these bins for every problem they tackle. In the professional training example, what's the objective? Although not explicitly stated, one assumption might be that Dorian is interested in finding a mix of students that will maximize total profit. In lieu of cost figures, we might assume the maximization of revenue to be an adequate proxy. Of course, if Dorian has other issues in mind, such as market growth, quality, or even civic virtue, such an objective might be shortsighted.

For the benefit of discussion, let's remain shortsighted and go with revenue maximization as our objective. The formulaic form of the revenue function might look like #beatniks*$3500 + #geeks*$2800. What about the decision variables? These appear to be fairly obvious here. Specifically, a set of decision variables needs to be defined so that we can clearly identify how many beatniks and how many geeks should be admitted.

Although there may be several approaches to this, it is true that there are often better (that is, more effective) approaches and worse (that is, more misleading) approaches that might be applied. For example, we could define our decisions directly as the number of beatniks admitted and the number of geeks admitted.

In contrast, a less effective way to define the decisions would be how many students in total should be admitted and what percentage should be geeks. However, if our objective function can be defined as the simple linear combination previously outlined, it would require a bit of multiplication between these latter two variables to get to a similar definition. Unfortunately, Solver often has difficulties when objectives are not linear functions of decision variables; therefore, such a definition might provide for undesirable (suboptimal) results. We'll talk more about these complications in Chapter 7, but for the purpose of optimization the basic rule for structuring the mathematical forms of story problems is to "Keep it simple" (often translating into "Keep it linear").

Regarding constraints, we'll try to keep things as direct as possible. We know Dorian and his partner have a limited number of hours to devote to students, and that student training requires time. The total amount of time required for substantive training (#beatniks*14hrs + #geeks*6hrs) must be less than or equal to the amount of time available from Dorian's associate (107 hours). A similar constraint relates the enrollment numbers to the maximum hours available by Dorian's sidekick. A third constraint ensures that total enrollment (#beatniks + #geeks) is not fewer than nine. As with decision variables, the "Keep it simple" ("Keep it linear") rule often serves the analyst best.

In Chp6_Examples, I've put all of the information (and the mathematical structure just outlined) from that story problem into some meaningful order on a spreadsheet. I've also added some graphics, but more important, I've provided sufficient annotation to let you know exactly what each of the numbers on this page refers to. As per Chapter 2, I've also labeled relevant cells and cell ranges with names (for example, TotRevenue, NofEachStudent) for easier reference (see Figure 6.4).

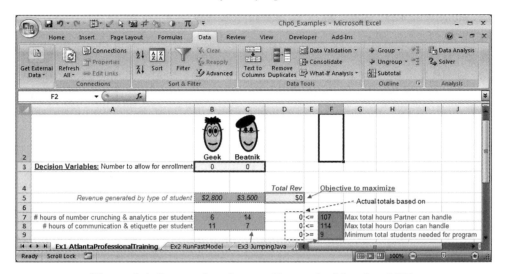

Figure 6.4. Structuring the enrollment decision for APT.

6.1.1.2 Getting to the Solution

If we didn't have any additional decision support mechanisms to help us at this point, we might start by trying out various values of our decision variables in an attempt to meet our objectives without violating any of our constraints:

> If I enter three geeks and three beatniks, I get total revenue of $27K.
> If I enter five geeks and three beatniks, I get total revenue of $45K.
> If I enter seven geeks and seven beatniks, I get total revenue of $63K, but this requires more hours than either instructor has available.

Obviously, a manual search for a good solution, even in this case, could take some time. Solver makes it easy for us. Figure 6.5 illustrates how the fields in the Solver interface might be populated to accommodate this problem.

Because all of the information is entered in some intelligent fashion into the spreadsheet with decisions linked both to the objective and the issues subject to constraint, we're already set up for Solver to help us. Note how the objectives, decision variables, and constraints correspond among the spreadsheet and fields in Solver. The intelligent naming of cells allows for a meaningful representation of the problem in the Solver interface, facilitating error checking. Solver is smart enough to interpret "NofEachStudent>=0" as "all the cells in the NofEachStudent range must be greater than 0" (no antimatter students, please).

In this case, the problem presented to Solver is the simplest kind. All relationships between the decision variables are linear ones. That is, although the decision variables are multiplied by constants at various points, nothing

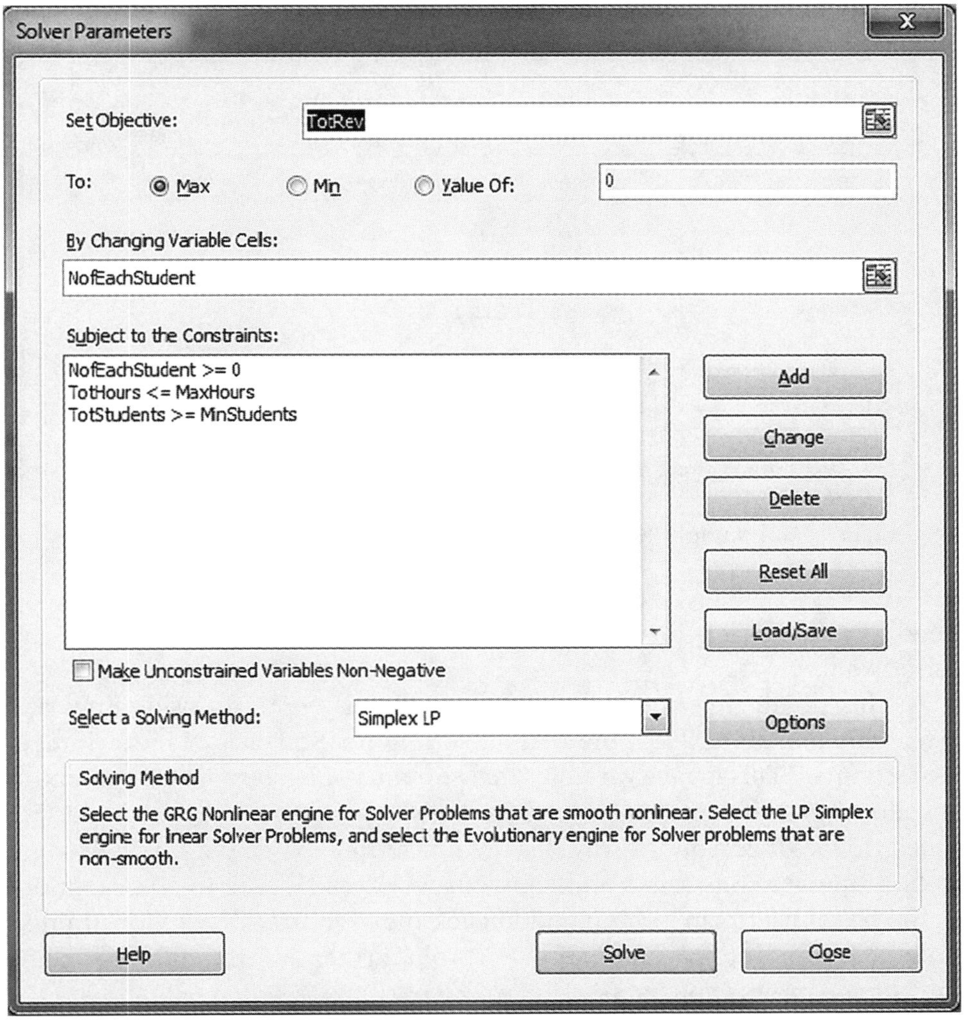

Figure 6.5. Specifying the problem structure for APT in Solver.

more complex than the addition of these products takes place. The decision variables are not multiplied by one another, or divided by one another, or transformed in any other way resulting in nonlinear effects: for example, $1/x$, $\ln(x)$. Because of this, we can guarantee that Solver will find an optimal solution for us. We can get Solver to find it using its most fast and frugal approach to these problems: the Simplex LP (linear programming) method. We'll learn a bit more about the other solution methods in Chapter 7.

With these selections made, hitting Solve should provide the following solution (Figure 6.6).

Let's think about this solution. Are 7.56 students or 4.40 students reasonable options in this problem? If partial students are not acceptable, we'll

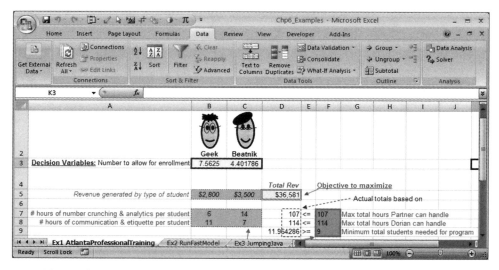

Figure 6.6. Example solution to one specification of constraints for APT.

need to add another constraint limiting our solution to integer-only options, as shown in Figure 6.7.

At this point, we need to provide a cautionary note on using Solver in Excel circa 2010. In 2010, the default setting for Solver is "Ignore Integer Constraints." This means variables that should, in fact, be whole numbers, as specified by constraints, might take on nonwhole-number values. There's not much rhyme or reason for why this default setting exists, but if you do want to have integer constraints apply in your work, make sure to go to Options in the Excel userform pop-up and unclick the "Ignore Integer Constraints" option. Setting Integer Optimality (%) to 0 further enforces interest in any integer constraints you list (see Figure 6.8).

A more reasonable solution for Atlanta Professional Training then emerges from this setup. To maximize revenues subject to the constraints listed, enrollment should include six geeks and five beatniks. This leaves some extra time for both Dorian and his partner. However, that's often the

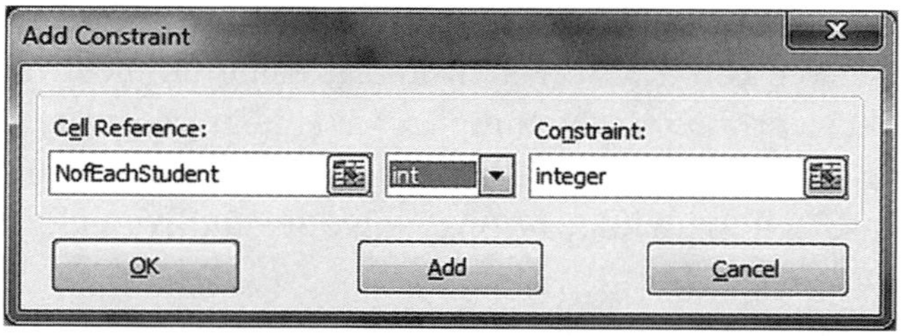

Figure 6.7. Adding the integer constraint on the decision variables.

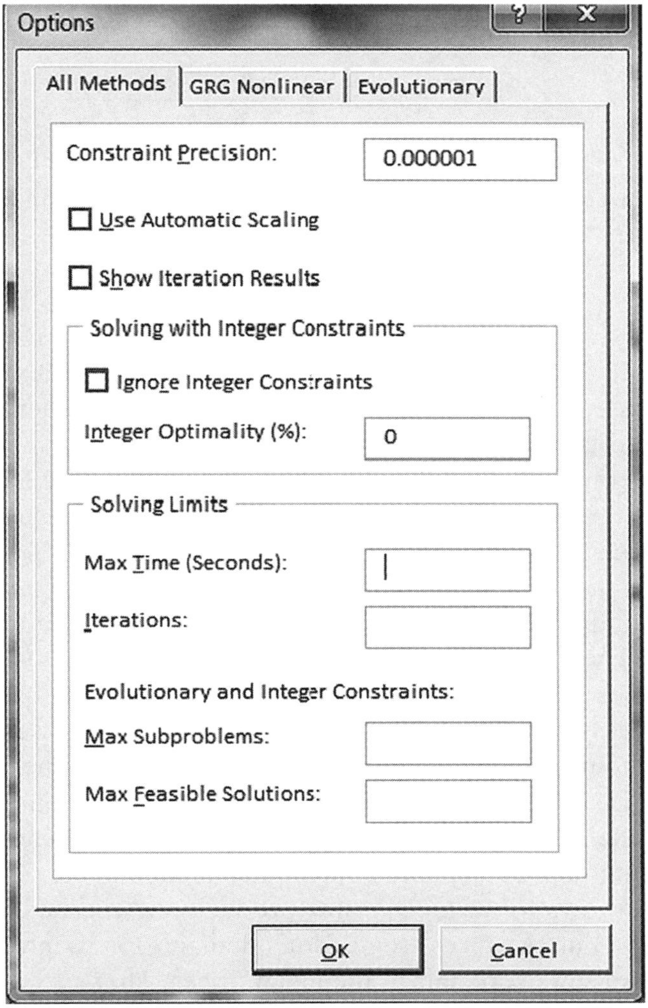

Figure 6.8. Enforcing integer constraints in Solver circa 2010.

nature of real-world solutions. We'll talk more on the interpretation of "slack" in solutions later on.

6.1.2 Example #2: RunFast, Inc.

RunFast manufactures running shoes used to supply specialty-running retailers throughout the southeast. RunFast currently produces three types of running shoes: basic, track, and trail. RunFast wants to determine how many pairs of each type to produce next month. The process of assembling each pair is highly automated, followed by manual inspection of each individual pair to ensure it meets the high quality standards set by RunFast. Each

Table 6.1. *Requirements Specifications for a Production*

	Shoe Type		
Production Method	Basic (min/pair)	Track (min/pair)	Trail (min/pair)
Blazer620	6.75	4.80	6.00
Inspection Area	15.30	17.40	14.25

component of the shoe (sole, laces, air wick, insole, and so on) is placed onto a belt that feeds through an assembly machine called the Blazer620. After each shoe is assembled, it passes onto manual inspection, where its quality is checked and tested.

Each of the three types of shoes must be processed on the Blazer620, and each pair must be inspected. The times required for these two processes for each shoe type are specified in Table 6.1.

There are ninety hours of Blazer620 time available for assembly of these shoes next month. Not all of the hours must be used, but no more than ninety can be used. The inspection team has 125 hours available for testing these products next month.

The accounting department at RunFast has provided $6.38 as the production cost per hour for using the Blazer620. This cost should be considered in this decision. Likewise, the direct labor cost for the inspection team is $0.151 per minute. The revenue and overall profit that each pair generates and the cost of the materials used in each pair are specified in Table 6.2.

RunFast is known for its high-quality products and special testing of each pair of shoes. RunFast faces tremendous demand for its products, and is confident it can sell every pair at the given prices. There is one catch: One of RunFast's largest customers has already placed an order for thirty pairs of the track shoes to be delivered next month. The marketing department

Table 6.2. *Cost and Revenue Details for a Production*

	Shoe Type		
	Basic ($/pair)	Track ($/pair)	Trail ($/pair)
Revenue	23.85	19.88	18.00
Material Cost	7.80	7.34	6.30
Direct Production Cost	3.03	3.14	2.79
Profit Margin	13.02	9.41	8.91

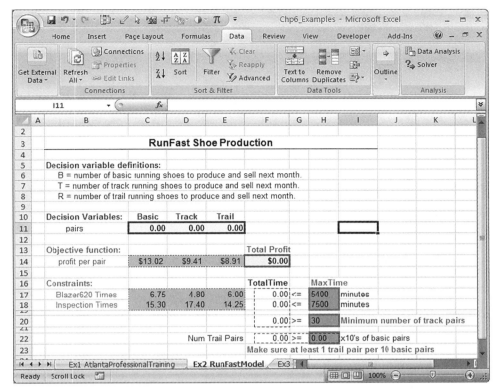

Figure 6.9. Structuring the production decision.

wants to ensure that RunFast maintains a full product line to stave off the competition encroaching on its territory, and the department has requested that at least one pair of trail shoes be produced for every ten basic pairs that are produced next month.

We now formally state the decision problem confronting RunFast:

Determine a production plan that specifies how many basic, trail, and track running shoes should be produced next month in order to maximize total monthly profit.

What constraints do we face?

1) Don't use more than ninety hours of Blazer620 time.
2) Don't use more than 125 hours of inspection time.
3) Do produce at least three pairs of track shoes.
4) Do produce at least one pair of trail shoes for every ten basic pairs.

Figure 6.9 shows a structure that we might use to outline our decision variables, and how they relate to the objectives and constraints we're faced with. Given the appropriate labeling of cells and cell ranges for reference purposes, Figure 6.10 shows how we'd convey that information to Solver.

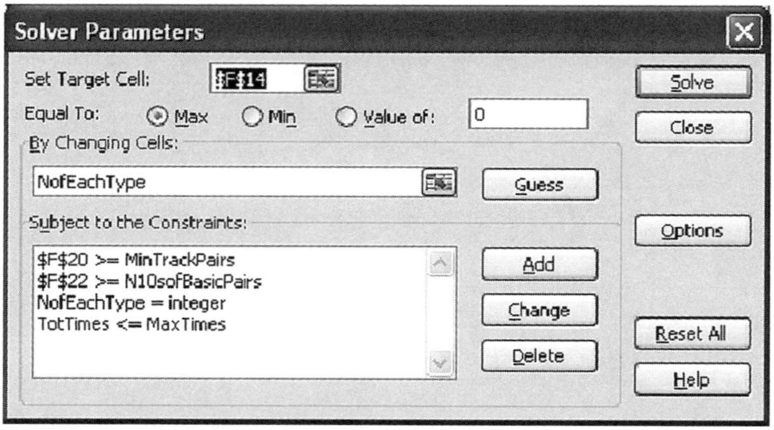

Figure 6.10. Specification of the production objective, decisions, and constraints.

Note that, as with the previous example, we would like an integer solution. Therefore, we need to make sure Solver is not going to ignore the integer constraints we've added (see Figure 6.8). We can also leverage the Simplex LP in this case. The solution that Solver gives us is shown in Figure 6.11.

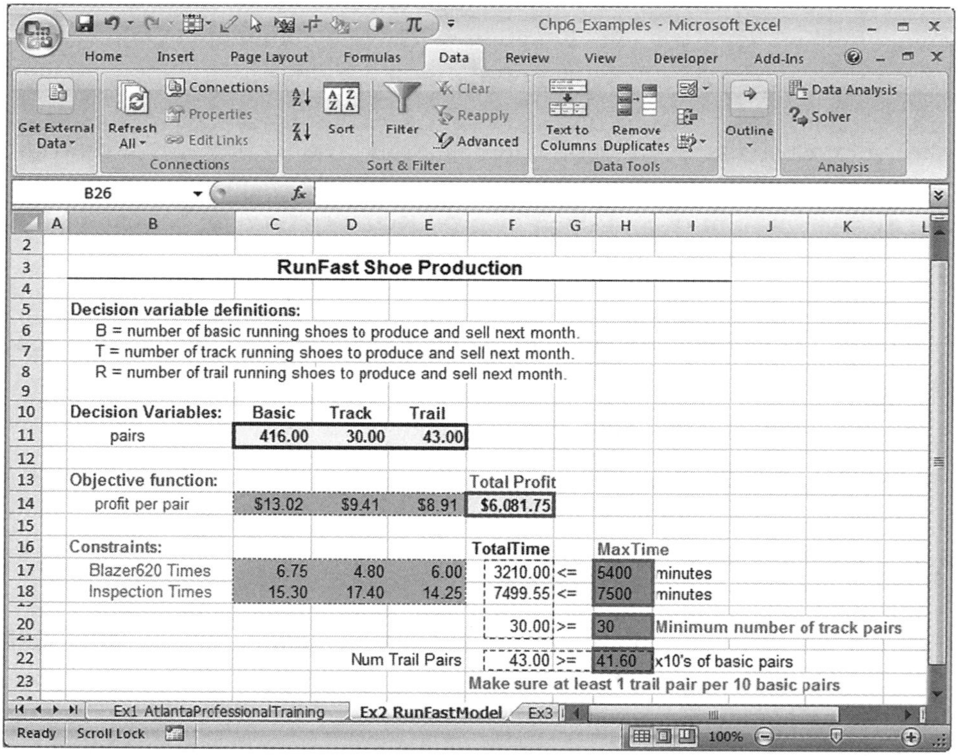

Figure 6.11. Solver's suggested optimal production solution based on specification.

Table 6.3. *Details for Employee Staffing Example*

Day	Shift Time	Minimum Number of Employees Needed
Monday	1 (midnight–4 A.M.)	4
Monday	2 (4 A.M.–8 A.M.)	11
Monday	3 (8 A.M.–noon)	16
Monday	4 (noon–4 P.M.)	21
Monday	5 (4 P.M.–8 P.M.)	18
Monday	6 (8 P.M.–midnight)	8
Tuesday	1 (midnight–4 A.M.)	3
Tuesday	2 (4 A.M.–8 A.M.)	13
Tuesday	3 (8 A.M.–noon)	17
Tuesday	4 (noon–4P.M.)	22
Tuesday	5 (4 P.M.–8 P.M.)	15
Tuesday	6 (8 P.M.–midnight)	11

6.1.3 *Example #3: Jumping Java*

The Jumping Java coffee shop located on a local college campus is open twenty-four hours per day. Jumping Java employs mostly students who enjoy the flexibility of four-hour shifts, (6 per day). All shifts start at four-hour intervals that begin at midnight. The minimum number of employees required in each time interval over a two-day cycle is given in Table 6.3. This table gives a sample of the staffing requirements for two consecutive days (Monday and Tuesday).

Note that in this example, we are assuming that these staffing requirements repeat every two days. This is a major simplification, but it's useful to sufficiently demonstrate the structure of the logic and overall nature of the model. In reality, each day of the week may have different staffing requirements.

Staff members can work either four- or eight-hour shifts. Employees choosing to work an eight-hour shift receive $13.50 per hour. Those working only a four-hour shift receive $12.75 per hour. The coffee shop also incurs an overhead cost of $7.50 per person working either shift. Therefore, the total cost of having one person work for eight hours is $(8 \times 13.50) + 7.50 = \$115.50$. The total cost of having one person work one four-hour shift is $(4 \times 12.75) + 7.50 = \$58.50$. So, the question is: How many employees should be working in each time period on each day to minimize total staffing costs (subject to minimum staffing requirements)?

In this particular problem, because there are two separate kinds of staffers (four-hour-shift and eight-hour-shift people), and because we are concerned with assigning those staffers to specific time slots, the description of the decision variables might seem a little more complex than in the previous

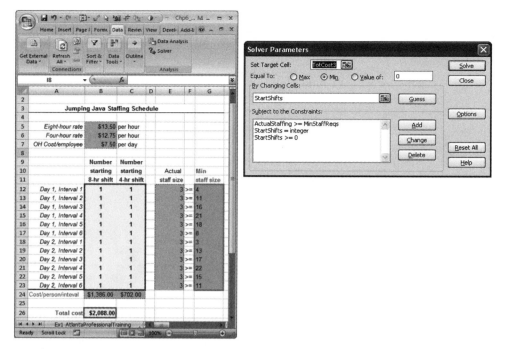

Figure 6.12. Spreadsheet construction and Solver setup for staffing problem.

examples. It would help if we could design decision variables that would simplify the model regardless of whether we were using a manual search or Solver.

The most straightforward definition might at first seem to be just deciding on and keeping track of the number of people working in each of the time intervals for each day. Unfortunately, if we know only the total number of people (of a given shift type) working from midnight to 8 A.M., we don't know how many of these people are eight-hour employees and how many are four-hour employees. Even if we kept track of these workers separately, we would not know how many eight-hour shift workers were ending as opposed to beginning their shifts in that interval. We could easily get confused in our policy using that approach.

To clarify the schedule and avoid this problem, we define variables that tell us how many people of each type simply begin their shift in each time interval. With this information, we can compute total employment costs as well as determine the total number of people working in each of the twelve four-hour time intervals. Figure 6.12 shows how we might structure the problem in a spreadsheet and in Solver.

Provided we make sure Solver does not ignore integer constraints (Figure 6.8), Figure 6.13 provides an example of what Solver might show us. Consider trying to come to this solution through a manual trial-and-error approach!

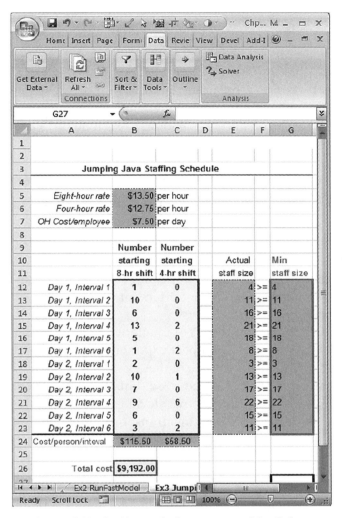

Figure 6.13. Staffing solution suggested by Solver.

Now, if you give this problem to Solver, you might not get exactly the same solution. The final objective function might be the same, but the decision variable values might not be the same. This isn't a mistake. There's actually a good reason for this kind of a discrepancy. What distinguished this problem from the previous two examples is the sheer number of variables relative to the constraints. The increased number of variables introduces some additional flexibility. It so happens that in this case there are multiple ways to get to the same total cost number in this problem. These are akin to multidimensional isoquant frontiers, borrowing from economic-speak, each peppered with several potentially different variants on decision variable value sets. The one that gives the lowest cost is the "optimal frontier" and this might have several solutions along it as well. Which one Solver comes up with depends on a few things, including the nature of the install and the starting solution you give Solver. However, aside from proposing different decisions, if all you care about is "optimizing the objective subject to constraints," that shouldn't matter much.

If your interests are a bit more nuanced, however, it might be worth considering alternative solutions along that "optimal frontier" (perhaps derived from alternative starting solutions). We'll get into this notion more in Chapter 7.

6.1.4 Example #4: Madrenko Fine Art Galleries

As a final example, consider the work of Madrenko Fine Art Galleries. Madrenko is a buyer and reseller of fine Eastern European paintings and sculpture. Based on input from local staff, top management foresees a likely need to restock its galleries in Montreal, Paris, and New York in the next six months. Madrenko has identified works in its Minsk, Budapest, and Zurich offices that have not received recent offers for purchase, but are likely to do well in their more Westerly markets.

The Montreal, Paris, and New York galleries are also better equipped to showcase these pieces. Based on past experience, top management doesn't believe it matters which works each of these galleries receive, as long as *most* of the anticipated gallery need is covered (equal sales prospects). However, it does want to get formal buy-ins from local gallery chiefs, to check against unanticipated issues, before making transport arrangements. All told, it anticipates a demand for three additional units in Montreal, ten in New York, and six in Paris. Surplus of two units exist in Zurich, five in Budapest, and eleven in Minsk. Madrenko already sees that not all expected demands will be covered; regardless, it would like to cover as much of that demand as possible at the lowest cost. What lowest-cost reallocation of works should top management propose?

Figure 6.14 provides an example set-up for this problem, including details on the costs of transit (in $100s) between the six cities (see Chp6_Madrenko). These costs supposedly include transport as well as courier fees and the cost of paperwork filing and international tariffs.

6.2 Deeper Insights into Optimization Solutions

Although Solver can give us an optimal solution to a problem spelled out in math form, often the specific details that we provide have some uncertainty associated with them. Sometimes, the parameters we use in specifying the problem are more like estimates than hard facts. To make a problem simpler to solve, we sometimes exclude the possibility that we could modify these parameters (albeit at some additional cost). Sometimes, situations are

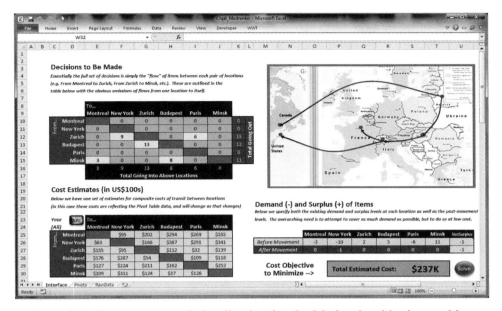

Figure 6.14. Facts, setup, and visualization for the Madrenko shipping problem.

simply subject to change – we might want to consider the implications of such changes to the parameters assumed.

For example, in a hypothetical routing or facility location problem, on one hand, we could start with an assumption that we have only four cities to work with, but, on the other hand, we might assume we have the opportunity to consider a six-city scenario to solve this problem if we're willing to add in further cost structure. In a different management problem, we could assume workers work at a particular pace; or we could assume the possibility of increasing that pace (at cost) and see how Solver's solution to our problem changes. All of this might alter obstacles that could be preventing us from doing better in our objective. That is, altering certain constraints of the problem can have a significant impact on how well we do.

But not all issues listed as constraints end up having a major impact on the solution that Solver provides. Those that do are referred to as binding constraints. Those rules that are active but are less severe than binding constraints, and therefore don't actually hold us back, are called non-binding.

The concept of a binding constraint is analogous to the concept of a bottleneck in operations management. Bottlenecks are always the key elements that hold us back, even if other rules simultaneously apply. Managers are (or at least should be) always trying to find ways to break down bottlenecks, and find new ones to tackle. When bottlenecks (binding constraints) are broken, we expect other limitations (originally nonbinding constraints) to take their place (that is, essentially become binding). Make sense?

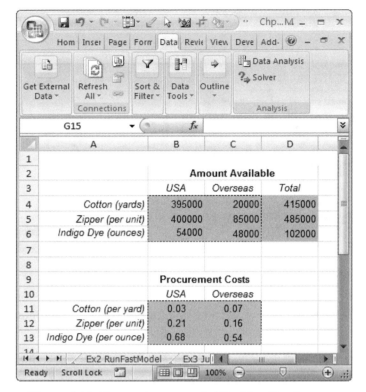

Figure 6.15. Facts relevant to the Fashion Denim case.

Solver provides a few handy mechanisms for describing which specific constraints in a problem are binding, how much they can be modified (presumably at some cost) before becoming nonbinding, and to what degree other currently nonbinding constraints can be modified (often at some marketable gain) before becoming binding themselves. We're going to focus on the interpretation of the most straightforward tool: Answer Reports.

Answer Reports from Solver tells us specifically which constraints are binding. It does this by reporting on cell references involved in a problem – that is, cells containing decision variables (and implied decisions based on these) and the cells that contain the limits to which these decisions are subject.

6.2.1 Example #5: Fashion Denim, Inc.

Fashion Denim, Inc., is a designer jeans manufacturer that currently produces all their goods in the United States. To cut costs, Fashion Denim is considering sourcing some of its materials from overseas for next month's production. Three of the major raw materials used in jeans manufacturing (cotton, zippers, and indigo dye), as well as how much of each material is available, is shown in Figure 6.15.

	A	B	C	D	E	F	G	H
16		**Purchase Allocation**			**Acquired**		**Production**	
17		*USA*	*Overseas*		**Materials**		**Requirements**	
18	*Cotton (yards)*	0	0		0	>=	300000	yards
19	*Zipper (per unit)*	0	0		0	>=	100000	zippers
20	*Indigo Dye (ounces)*	0	0		0	>=	25000	ounces
23	**Total Cost**	$0						

Figure 6.16. Possible spreadsheet structuring purchasing problem.

In addition, the procurement costs of each material from the United States and overseas are shown. Next month, Fashion Denim wants to produce 100,000 pairs of jeans. The raw material requirements for this plan are as follows:

Cotton (yards): 300,000
Zippers: 100,000
Indigo Dye (ounces): 25,000

Comparing this to the total amount of components available, this goal seems generally achievable. However, given high import tariffs on certain goods purchased overseas, Fashion Denim needs to limit the quantity of zippers and dye imported to 50,000 and 1,500, respectively. What portion of materials should Fashion Denim acquire from the United States and overseas to minimize the total cost, meet production requirements, and limit import tariffs? To find the answer, we might set up the problem as shown in Figure 6.16. Provided integer constraints are not ignored, Solver gives us the solution shown in Figure 6.17 (when specified appropriately).

	A	B	C	D	E	F	G	H
16		**Purchase Allocation**			**Acquired**		**Production**	
17		*USA*	*Overseas*		**Materials**		**Requirements**	
18	*Cotton (yards)*	300000	0		300000	>=	300000	yards
19	*Zipper (per unit)*	50000	50000		100000	>=	100000	zippers
20	*Indigo Dye (ounces)*	23500	1500		25000	>=	25000	ounces
23	**Total Cost**	$44,290						

Figure 6.17. Solution to purchasing problem by Solver.

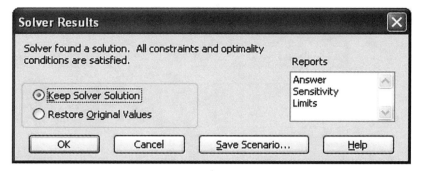

Figure 6.18. The Answer Report option.

But before it does so, it also asks us what kinds of reports we might be interested in. Figure 6.18 shows what we get if we select Answer in the Report scroll box. Figure 6.19 shows what we'd get on a separate tab.

We could figure out most of this information from the solution provided, but it's explicit in the report. Solver is revealing the potentially alterable constraints that critically bind our decision. Keep in mind that integer constraints are always binding. We might ask what the situation would be if import tariffs were eased on zippers (which would essentially break the binding nature of this constraint). If we eliminated that constraint entirely, Figure 6.20 shows what we'd get.

This is good news because our total cost drops to $41,790. Sometimes, binding constraints are only slightly more severe than the nonbinding constraints that exist below them. Real added gains often require the consideration of a series of calculated changes.

6.2.2 Example #6: Lobo's Cantina

Lobo's Cantina is considering a redesign of its current layout with the interest of generating a higher profit margin while continuing to cater to the desires of its target market. It currently has a total area of 30 feet by 60 feet (1,800 square feet) to work with. The owner realizes that for everything to work, he will need to consider a variety of implied service and operating requirements when making a decision. The space needs to house its dining area, bar, kitchen, wash area, restrooms, storage, and host stations, which include both the greeting station and the rear cashiers.

Although the owner has considerable freedom in terms of how to specifically layout each area to provide for an aesthetic look, he does have to follow some rational rules in making the initial space division decisions. For example, if he plans to devote a large area of the floor to dining, he will want to make sure that he has enough kitchen and wash capacity to meet the

Microsoft Excel 12.0 Answer Report

Target Cell (Min)

Cell	Name	Original Value	Final Value
$B$23	Total Cost USA	$0	$44,290

Adjustable Cells

Cell	Name	Original Value	Final Value
$B$18	Cotton (yards) USA	0	300000
$C$18	Cotton (yards) Overseas	0	0
$B$19	Zipper (per unit) USA	0	50000
$C$19	Zipper (per unit) Overseas	0	50000
$B$20	Indigo Dye (ounces) USA	0	23500
$C$20	Indigo Dye (ounces) Overseas	0	1500

Constraints

Cell	Name	Cell Value	Formula	Status	Slack
$E$18	Cotton (yards) Materials	300000	$E$18>=$G$18	Binding	0
$E$19	Zipper (per unit) Materials	100000	$E$19>=$G$19	Binding	0
$E$20	Indigo Dye (ounces) Materials	25000	$E$20>=$G$20	Binding	0
$B$19	Zipper (per unit) USA	50000	$B$19=integer	Binding	0
$C$19	Zipper (per unit) Overseas	50000	$C$19=integer	Binding	0
$C$18	Cotton (yards) Overseas	0	$C$18<=$G$4	Binding	0
$C$19	Zipper (per unit) Overseas	50000	$C$19<=$G$5	Binding	0
$C$20	Indigo Dye (ounces) Overseas	1500	$C$20<=$G$6	Binding	0
$B$18	Cotton (yards) USA	300000	$B$18>=0	Not Binding	300000
$C$18	Cotton (yards) Overseas	0	$C$18>=0	Binding	0
$B$19	Zipper (per unit) USA	50000	$B$19>=0	Not Binding	50000
$C$19	Zipper (per unit) Overseas	50000	$C$19>=0	Not Binding	50000
$B$20	Indigo Dye (ounces) USA	23500	$B$20>=0	Not Binding	23500
$C$20	Indigo Dye (ounces) Overseas	1500	$C$20>=0	Not Binding	1500

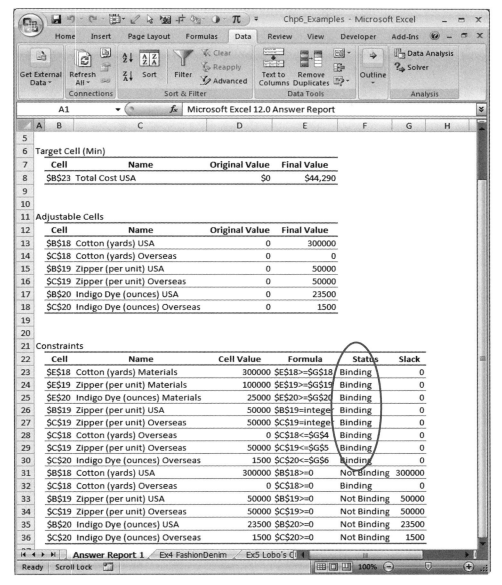

Figure 6.19. Sample output of the Answer Report.

	Purchase Allocation			Acquired		Production	
	USA	Overseas		Materials		Requirements	
Cotton (yards)	300000	0		300000	>=	300000	yards
Zipper (per unit)	0	100000		100000	>=	100000	zippers
Indigo Dye (ounces)	23500	1500		25000	>=	25000	ounces
Total Cost	$41,790						

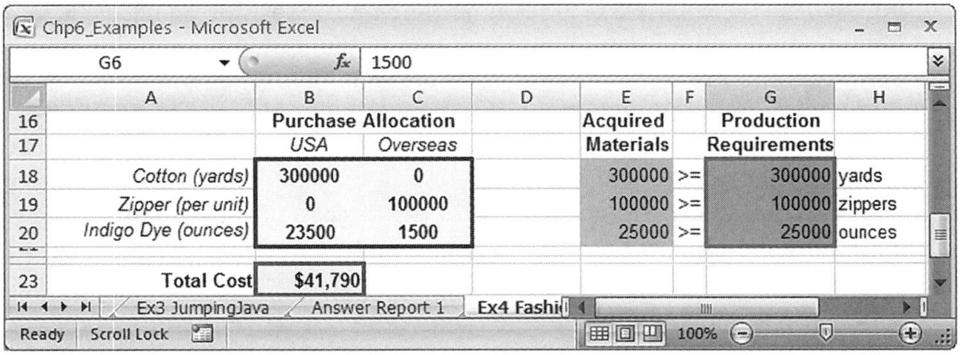

Figure 6.20. Alternate solution after eliminating a binding constraint.

implied demands of a population seated in that area. Demands for kitchen work (and, thus, requirements for kitchen space) will decrease as the size of the bar increases. Implied storage requirements (and storage space) will change depending on how much the restaurant is focused on bar service, as will restroom designs and the need for host stations. The following is a breakdown of the assumed restrictions with which the restaurant owner is dealing.

Fundamental Seating Dimensions:
Tables designed to seat four take up 24 square feet of space.
Tables designed to seat two take up 8 square feet of space.
Any seat at the bar (plus bar-counter space) takes up 5 square feet.

Additional Fixed Requirements:
There must be at least one greeting station that takes up a minimum of 20 square feet. Each host station is expected to provide enough capacity for handling 24 individual tables at most. Each additional host accommodation requires an additional 20 square feet of space.

There must be at least one rear cashier station (taking up 10 square feet of space) because bar customers pay at the bar and they don't need rear cashier service. In other words, the need for additional rear cashiers depends only on the amount of dining volume anticipated. Each rear cashier is thought to be able to handle work for up to twenty tables in use.

Minimum kitchen amenities begin with a required 40 square feet of space. Every additional twenty chairs in the dining area translate into another approximately 5 square feet in the kitchen. However, the current building and sewage code does not allow for a total kitchen capacity beyond 400 square feet.

Minimum cleaning amenities require a minimum of 20 square feet of space. Another 5 square feet of kitchen space is needed for every additional forty chairs in the dining area or the bar. Building and sewage codes limit this total space to 200 square feet.

Because of inventory management policies, the restaurant tends to buy alcohol less frequently than food, which it obtains throughout the day from neighboring markets; this means it generally stores more alcohol than other consumable inventories. Each additional seat at the bar increases the storage needs by 5 square feet. Each seat in the dining area increases storage needs by only 1 square foot.

Lastly, there must be one male and one female restroom. Each must have a total of 25 square feet to provide the minimal functionality (one sink and "chamber" per restroom). Each additional chamber adds another 15 square feet. The total number of chambers needed in each restroom should be based on expected average need at any given point in time. The forecast the restaurant will use to derive this total is: number of chambers per restroom must be equal to at least: (# bar seats)/30 + (# dining seats)/60. The sewage code allows for a maximum of five chambers for each restroom.

Profitability and Market Issues:

The owner believes that the average profit his restaurant can generate per dining seat over the course of a day is $340 for two-seat tables and $400 for four-seat tables, which are more likely to spend money on appetizers, and $560 per average bar seat. However, he is concerned that an excessive bar space might damage the image that the restaurant attempts to portray to its overall market segment (which consists of customers who might be attracted to either the bar or seated dining on any given day). With that in mind, the owner wants to make sure that the bar area never takes up more than half the area specific to dining. If we want Solver to help us, we'll have to translate those specifications into something more formulaic.

Interdependency Constraints in brief:

The number of greeting stations must be at least ((# of two- and four-seat tables combined)/24); total greeting station space will equal (# of greeting stations × 20).

The number of cashier stations must be at least ((# of two-and four-seat tables combined)/20); total cashier space will be equal to (# of cashier stations × 10).

The kitchen space should be at least (40 + (5 × ((two- seat tables × 2) + (four-seat tables × 4))/20)); total cannot exceed 400 square feet.

The cleaning space should be at least (20 + (5 × ((two-seat tables × 2) + (four-seat tables × 4)) + bar seats)/40)); total cannot exceed 200.

The storage space should be at least equal to (1 × ((two-seat tables × 2) + (four-seat tables × 4)) + (5 × bar seats)).

Total number of "chambers" should be at least ((bar seats/30) + ((two-seat tables × 2)/60) + ((four-seat tables × 4)/60))); total restroom space should be equal to ((25+25) + (15 × (number of chambers))).

Total area taken up by the bar can't be more than half the area taken up by dining.

Figure 6.21 shows an example of how we might structure the various decisions and their relationships to profitability and the functional requirements spelled out in this problem in spreadsheet form. (All constraints and relationships are built in as they were in previous examples.)

Again, if we're using Solver, we'll need to spell out which cells represent decisions and which cell relationships represent constraints. With the appropriate, meaningful cell labeling, we might have the results shown in Figure 6.22 in Solver (lots of constraints here; only a subset is shown in the figure).

And if we use this set of constraints, Figure 6.23 shows the results from Solver. Let's do this once again, omitting integer restrictions that can provide dubious solutions. (I doubt anyone would feel comfortable using a quarter side of a toilet.) So, we add appropriate integer specifications and get what's shown in Figure 6.24.

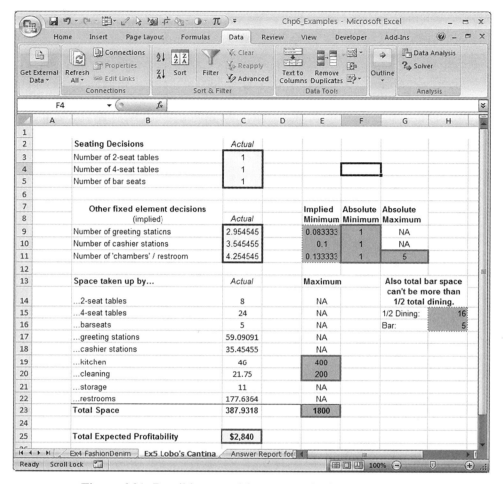

Figure 6.21. Possible spreadsheet setup for layout example.

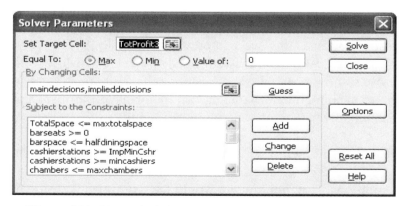

Figure 6.22. Example Solver specification for layout example.

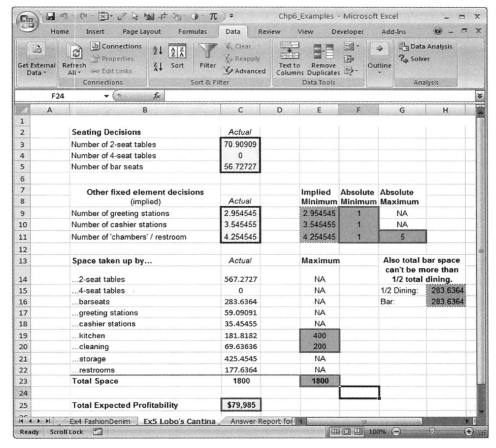

Figure 6.23. Initial solution to layout example.

That's more like it, but it's a very different solution seating-wise than what was previously suggested. Again, integer constraints can have a major impact on the general nature of a solution.

6.2.2.1 Interpreting Results

Take another look at the Answer Report generated in Figure 6.25. Again, Solver's labeling in these reports leaves something to be desired, but we get a general idea that we can make better sense of upon closer investigation. Rephrasing and omission of variables over which we don't have much control (for example, integer constraints) provides us with the results in Figure 6.26, in which the relative slackness of constraints are ranked from least to greatest. Now we have a better impression of what's holding us back from doing better, where our next greatest challenges exist, and where excessive slack might provide other implications on how we use resources.

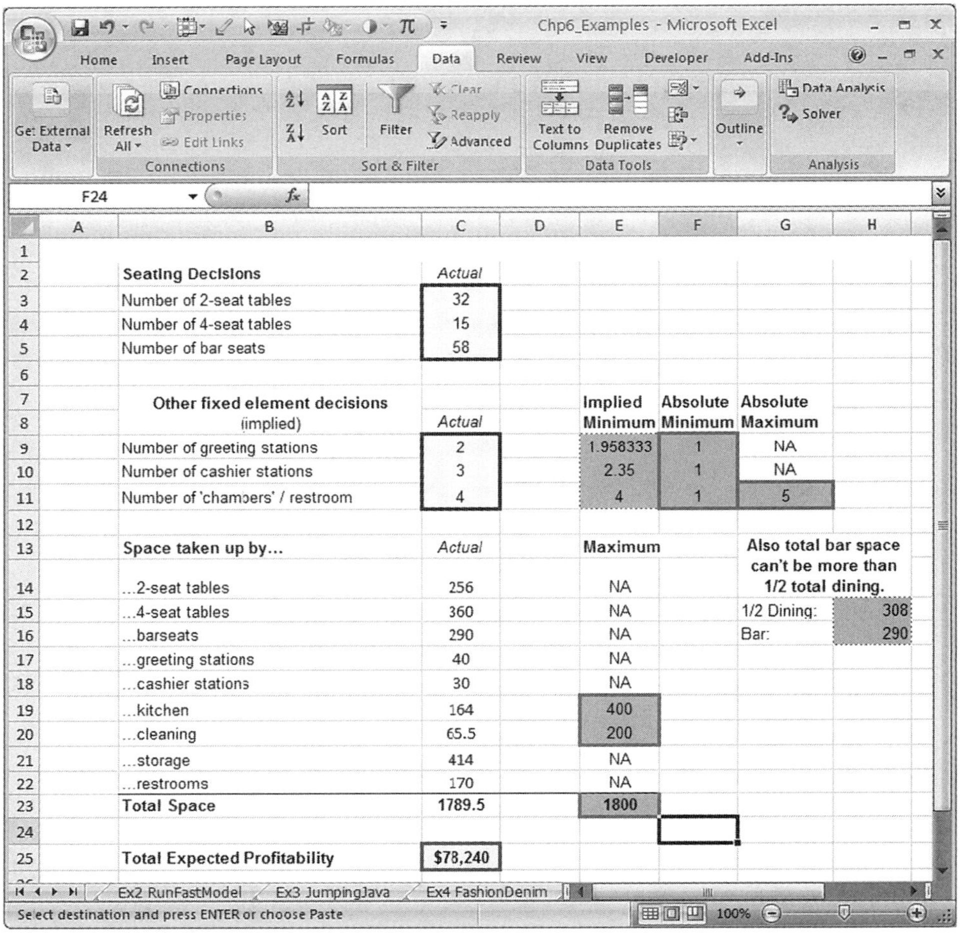

	Actual		Implied Minimum	Absolute Minimum	Absolute Maximum
Seating Decisions	*Actual*				
Number of 2-seat tables	32				
Number of 4-seat tables	15				
Number of bar seats	58				
Other fixed element decisions			**Implied**	**Absolute**	**Absolute**
(implied)	*Actual*		**Minimum**	**Minimum**	**Maximum**
Number of greeting stations	2		1.958333	1	NA
Number of cashier stations	3		2.35	1	NA
Number of 'chambers' / restroom	4		4	1	5

	Actual	Maximum	Also total bar space can't be more than 1/2 total dining.	
Space taken up by...	*Actual*	**Maximum**		
...2-seat tables	256	NA	1/2 Dining:	308
...4-seat tables	360	NA	Bar:	290
...barseats	290	NA		
...greeting stations	40	NA		
...cashier stations	30	NA		
...kitchen	164	400		
...cleaning	65.5	200		
...storage	414	NA		
...restrooms	170	NA		
Total Space	1789.5	1800		
Total Expected Profitability	$78,240			

Figure 6.24. Solution integrating meaningful integer constraints.

Interestingly, while we come close to the limits of several of the rules, the only one that is truly binding, aside from the integer limits, is the minimum chamber requirements. (We actually have a little slack on the use of cashier stations, too.) In reality, this constraint works in tandem with the total area requirement. We have additional space, but adding even one more seat would increase the restroom size requirements beyond the space available.

Oddly enough, coming up with some way of reducing the per-chamber size can impact our solution; reducing it to 14 square feet allows full use of our total space (now a binding constraint) with greater profit (about $500 more) and without major changes in our overall solution. A change to a chamber size of 12 square feet has a huge impact on our design (no more four-seat tables, but another $1,000 or so profit; and now the binding constraint is the sewage ordinance).

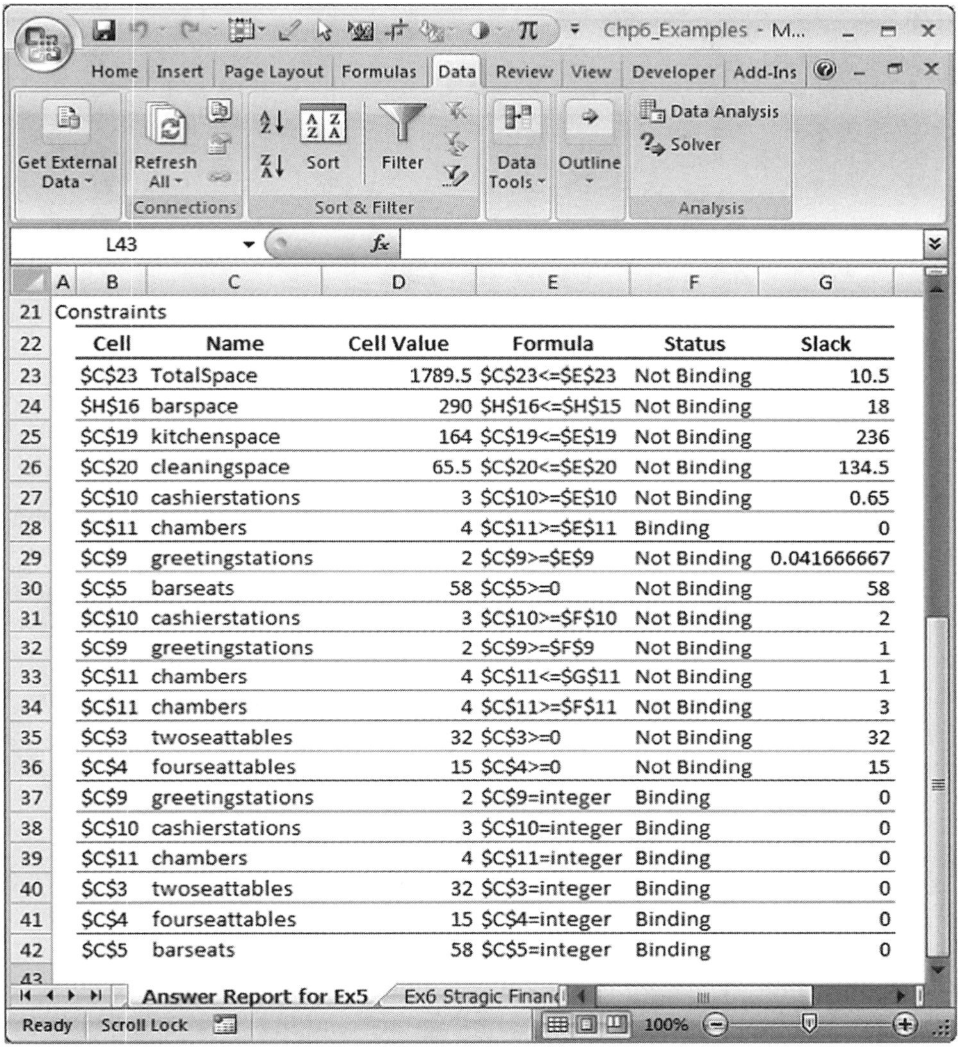

Constraints

Cell	Name	Cell Value	Formula	Status	Slack
$C$23	TotalSpace	1789.5	$C$23<=$E$23	Not Binding	10.5
$H$16	barspace	290	$H$16<=$H$15	Not Binding	18
$C$19	kitchenspace	164	$C$19<=$E$19	Not Binding	236
$C$20	cleaningspace	65.5	$C$20<=$E$20	Not Binding	134.5
$C$10	cashierstations	3	$C$10>=$E$10	Not Binding	0.65
$C$11	chambers	4	$C$11>=$E$11	Binding	0
$C$9	greetingstations	2	$C$9>=$E$9	Not Binding	0.041666667
$C$5	barseats	58	$C$5>=0	Not Binding	58
$C$10	cashierstations	3	$C$10>=$F$10	Not Binding	2
$C$9	greetingstations	2	$C$9>=$F$9	Not Binding	1
$C$11	chambers	4	$C$11<=$G$11	Not Binding	1
$C$11	chambers	4	$C$11>=$F$11	Not Binding	3
$C$3	twoseattables	32	$C$3>=0	Not Binding	32
$C$4	fourseattables	15	$C$4>=0	Not Binding	15
$C$9	greetingstations	2	$C$9=integer	Binding	0
$C$10	cashierstations	3	$C$10=integer	Binding	0
$C$11	chambers	4	$C$11=integer	Binding	0
$C$3	twoseattables	32	$C$3=integer	Binding	0
$C$4	fourseattables	15	$C$4=integer	Binding	0
$C$5	barseats	58	$C$5=integer	Binding	0

Figure 6.25. Answer Report for layout problem.

Another feature that the Answer Report provides is a summary of which constraints seem to be the least binding in a given scenario. The two most slack constraints in the original integer solution are those relating to the building code limits on the kitchen and cleaning spaces. A manager might ask, "If we're so far below our maximum allocations, could we sell the rights to such allocations to another neighboring firm?" – perhaps one that finds such limits to be currently restrictive. Furthermore, the implied requirements of the cashier station are more than fulfilled by the number of stations we have in the original integer solution. One implication might be that of underutilization.

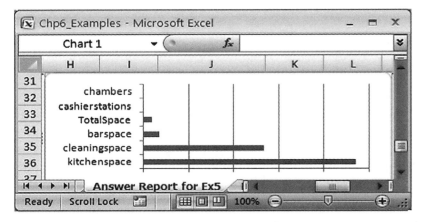

Figure 6.26. Pareto examination of constraints (binding and nonbinding).

A manager might then ask, "Could these stations be used for other activities, as well?" (This makes sense, particularly if they are multipurpose computers and not just mechanical cash registers.) The use of a Pareto chart in the last example shows how we can link the analysis provided by an automated decision generation engine (Solver) to a graphically meaningful depiction that a variety of managers might use in long-term planning. But there are still more striking examples of how one might present the findings drawn from the sensitivity analysis of optimized solutions.

6.2.3 Example #7: Strategic Focus for Investment Firms

A financial services firm currently provides six kinds of investment packages for its clientele: debt payment, college fund, small business, retirement, second home, and rapid growth. The development of any one of these investment packages involves some level of the following activities: needs assessment, asset specification, and analysis option construction consultation.

Based on the specializations of its workforces, number of hours needed to complete each of these activities differs for each package offered, as shown in Figure 6.26. Again, based on its workforce, the firm recognizes that realistically (at least in the midterm) it probably has a limited level of available hours for work in these various activities over the course of a year. These limits are also provided in Figure 6.27. At the same time, forecasts suggest that the profitability of each package could remain at the steady estimates shown during such a term. Due to changes in the market for these packages, the firm has decided to consolidate and focus on only a subset of these offerings. Given the numbers, how should the firm refocus its labor hours to maximize its total profit-generation capability? If it were to seek out additional labor-hour availability, what type of skill sets should it focus on?

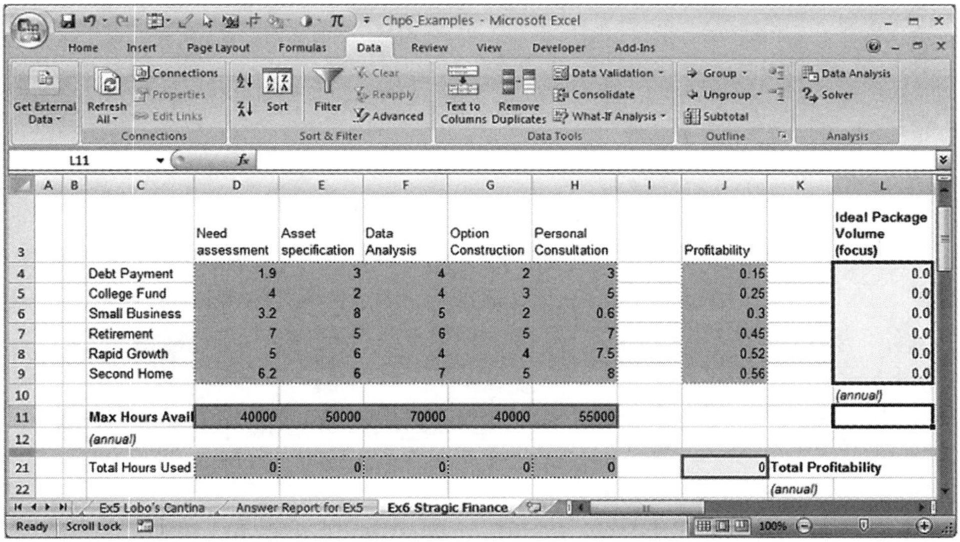

Figure 6.27. Spreadsheet set up for financial strategy example.

Let's start with Solver's initial solution to this problem, shown in Figure 6.28 (assuming at this point we can set it up appropriately in a spreadsheet). Looking at the total hours used, we can already get an impression of what labor constraints are truly binding here. But we can also ask for that information in Answer Report form (Figure 6.29).

I've shaded those constraints that we really have little hope of changing (that is, those that ensure we don't pursue "negative" volumes of certain service packages). Therefore, the three labor-hour constraints that seem to

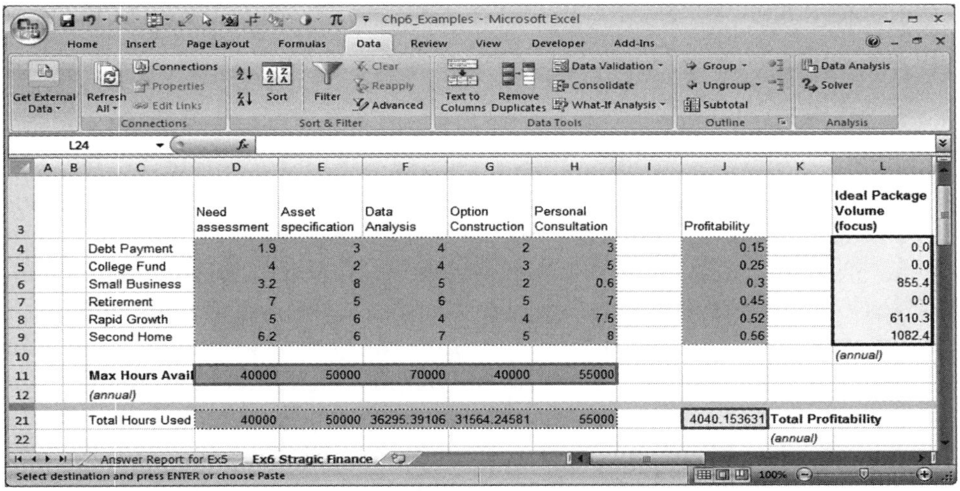

Figure 6.28. Solver's solution for financial strategy example.

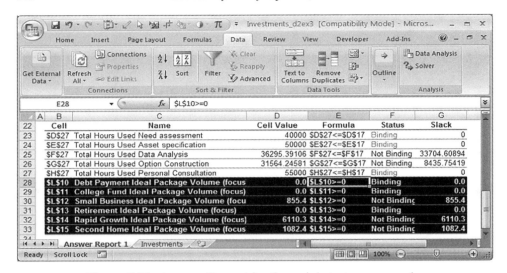

Figure 6.29. Answer Report for financial strategy example.

restrict our profitability relate to needs assessment, asset specification, and personal consultation activities.

Because the three packages that Solver suggests focusing on are small business, rapid growth, and second home, the firm might want to consider how sensitive its profitability is to various changes in volume (perhaps market driven), if it decides to focus on these three offerings, and what role the constraints play in this sensitivity. I've used an alternative approach to graphically depicting the critical impacts of constraints. Rather than demonstrating the areas of slack or underutilization as in the Pareto chart of the restaurant example, Figure 6.30 shows how profitability changes with different levels of labor devoted to two of the three suggested packages (keeping the volume of Second Home package work constant).

Ultimately, it's just a three-dimensional surface plot viewed from top-down with lighter shades of gray depicting greater profitability. Obviously, higher levels of work on both types of packages would generate greater total profit, but we are constrained by labor. We can't consider total workloads beyond certain limits (depicted by the black area in all but the lower left of the graph). The border between what's possible (or feasible) and what isn't essentially shows us the impact of multiple constraints on our decision all at the same time. Because I set up this graph so that you can turn off each constraint, we can see how individual constraints alone impact our decision making. Figure 6.31 shows the impact of only the needs assessment labor constraint. Figure 6.32 shows similar plots for the other two binding constraints, each in isolation. It is obvious that the presence of only one

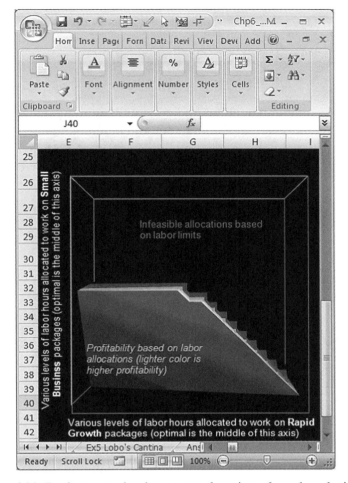

Figure 6.30. Performance landscape as a function of two key decisions.

of the constraints would allow for higher profit levels (and perhaps much higher).

One of the more important things that we might learn from this graphical depiction is that although the needs assessment labor constraint is officially binding at the optimal solution level, it doesn't have that much of an impact beyond what is created by the other two constraints. Figure 6.33 shows three constraint borders superimposed on the general constraints shown in Figure 6.30.

In this particular case, each of these frontiers intersects at the same point, which happens to be the point of profit maximization. As suggested by the previous plots, there are probably areas of higher profitability beyond this point, and all three constraints could independently limit such pursuits; however, the kinds of limitations imposed by the needs assessment constraint

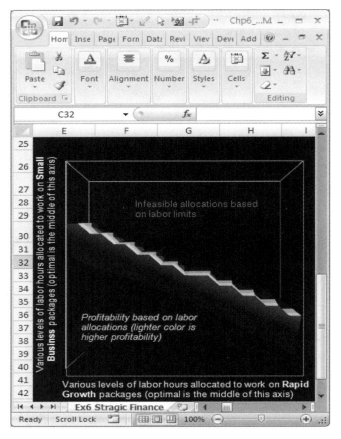

Figure 6.31. Impact of the Needs Assessment labor constraint.

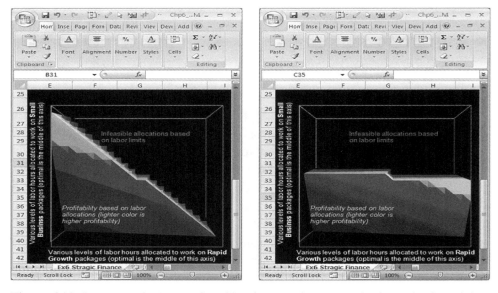

Figure 6.32. Impact of Asset Specification and Personal Consultation labor constraints.

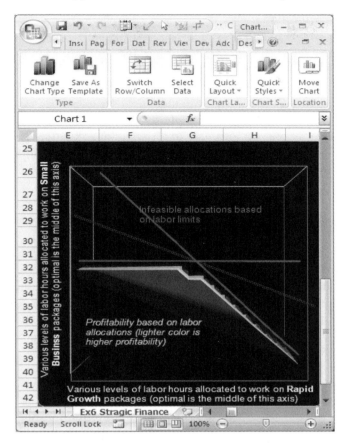

Figure 6.33. Compound impact of three constraints (feasibility frontiers).

are already defined if the other two constraints are active. Efforts to eliminate the needs assessment constraint after the suggested service consolidation (perhaps through additional training programs that allowed the firm's staff to conduct such activities in a more time-efficient manner), probably wouldn't have much of an impact on profitability. On the other hand, eliminating one of the other constraints might have a sizeable impact. This is exactly the kind of conclusion that's not easy to get at by simply viewing the nature of managerial prospects by initial reports alone.

Supplement: The OUtCoMES Roadmap

Sometimes, developing a strategy for tackling a problem with Solver can be daunting. The OUtCoMES roadmap has been developed to help and is especially for beginners. The following six steps outline the roadmap's process and serve as a general guide for all optimization problems.

1) **O**bjective specification.

   What is the final result you're aiming for? To maximize profit? Specify not only the measure of focus – for example, expected profit, level of risk – but also whether you are interested in either maximizing or minimizing that issue.

2) **Ut**ility factors (or decision variables) specification.

   List all factors that you (or decision makers in question) are in control of and can use in pursuit of the objective. Note that some of these factors may be indirectly relevant, or may serve simply to assist in the accounting process for your decision-making problem, but they are nevertheless worth outlining.

3) **Co**nstraints specification.

   List all factors that are fixed and limit the extent to which decision variables (utility factors) or even the objective may be modified. Note that some of these constraints may represent a limit (for example, can only spend up to $x on project #1), whereas others may represent relational limits (for example, project #1 and project #2 cannot both be pursued simultaneously). Note that "**Co**" also represents an implied attempt at this point to draw out a **Co**ncept map of how your objectives, decision variables, and constraints relate to one another. Continuing with the aforementioned example, the decision to pursue project #1 and to pursue project #2 are LINKED (they are not independent decisions). They may also be LINKED to maximum spends, as well as the objective. A simple concept map might therefore prove useful (see Figure 6.34).

4) **M**athematical equation generation.

   In part, this requires creating some notation for short reference to variables (for example, let "d1" be a 0,1 variable representing whether project #1 is pursued, let "x1" be the amount spent on project 1, let "m1" be the max spend on #1). Notation development is typically viewed as "simple," but it is not without its own pitfalls if done in a haphazard way. The more challenging task here is typically the *translation* of a concept map (suggesting linkages between the objectives, decision variables, and constraints) into specific mathematical forms using this notation. Again, building on the above example, the relationship between deciding to pursue project #1 and the "spend" on project #1 might take on the following mathematical form, given the stated notation: "x1 <= d1*m1." The requirement for either #1 or #2 being pursued might be stated as "d1 + d2 <= 1." For working with constraints that outline relationships between two binary variables (as in this last case) considering which areas of a 2x2 logic-matrix apply is often helpful. In such a matrix, if both variables can take on equal values (both 0 or both 1), part of the relationship must be an "=". If the first variable can also be greater than the second, but not less, the full relationship must be "d1>=d2" (see Figure 6.35).

5) **E**xcel model development.

   Actually code the equations you have developed into a model. Once you have an outline of what math applies, this is a fairly simple task. Usually, you just need to select cells for storing objectives, decision variable values, and cells for specifying other "facts" that are used in your math (for example, costs, returns,

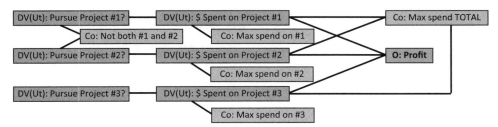

Figure 6.34. Example Concept Mapping of DV relationships and constraints.

Option1

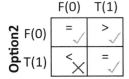

i.e. Option1>=Option2

Figure 6.35. Example use of an Inequality Matrix for developing math forms in constraints.

and limitations associated with specific variables). Additional cells are often used to contain intermediate calculations (you don't need to store all calculations in single cells, especially if calculations are complex). Experienced modelers often go directly to working in Excel for the earlier steps, hence this additional step becomes a given.

6) <u>S</u>earch for a solution (and <u>S</u>ensitivity Analysis)

Now that the problem is structured in Excel, it should be amenable to a host of automated solution procedures. Solver and RiskOptimizer are common tools for this task, although other tools also exist. In any case, the results of these searches should not be taken for granted. Any decent analysis must follow up with a critical examination of what the results mean and whether the actions suggested make sense. Are the model specifications correct? Can additional improvements be pursued further? How sensitive are solutions to the present assumptions?

PRACTICE PROBLEMS

Practice 6.1

A Fortune 500 company needs to hire a group of consultants from Just Right Consulting to assist with a large technology rollout that will require around-the-clock support. A day is divided into eight-hour shifts. The total number of consultants required during the day shift is shown in Table 6.4.

The client would like to minimize the labor costs associated with staffing the project. Consultants from Just Right work five days a week and are entitled to two

Table 6.4. *Details Associated with Consultant Staffing Example*

	Sunday	Monday	Tuesday	Wednesday	Thursday	Friday	Saturday
Consultants Needed	9	18	15	18	15	15	15

consecutive days off each week. We know there are only seven ways that each consultant can have two consecutive days off, with each break starting on a different day of the week (staggered approach). One straightforward way to structure the problem is to determine how many consultants of each break type to have staffed each day.

One twist in the problem is that any consultant required to work on Saturday receives an additional 5 percent overtime pay (think of their total weekday pay level as 100 percent; on Saturday it's 105 percent), whereas those that are required to work on Sunday receive an additional 7 percent of overtime pay (107 percent of typical weekday pay for Sunday). This will undoubtedly result in a tendency to avoid excess weekend scheduling whenever possible.

Determine how many consultants of each break type (that is, beginning their two-day break on a specific day) would be needed to at least cover the demand, while trying the keep the total cost as low as possible (again, accounting for weekend premiums).

Practice 6.2

Fun Viewing, Inc., is a new television network that has become extremely popular in recent months. Fun Viewing is trying to decide which TV shows to air during their fall lineup. The creative staff has worked tirelessly reviewing market research reports to give Fun Viewing an idea of how profitable each show will be (based on the number of viewers, ad sales, competing shows, and so on). Fun Viewing has allocated $28,000 for new TV shows. The objective is to generate the highest possible return on investment.

Eight scripts have been reviewed and deemed worthy to air on the network. Table 6.5 specifies the estimated return on investment (ROI) for each of these shows.

If a script is chosen, at least $700 must be allocated to developing the show. To maintain a variety of shows, the board of directors has stipulated that at most $7,000 can be invested in any project. A show's total return is the product of its ROI and the amount invested in the show.

Table 6.5. *Details Associated with TV Script Selection Example*

Show#	1	2	3	4	5	6	7	8
ROI	7%	9%	4%	25%	21%	14%	8%	16%

Table 6.6. *Constraints Associated with TV Script Selection Example*

Show 2 can't be pursued unless
   Show 1 is
	Show 4 can't be pursued unless
	   Show 3 is

Show 3 can't be pursued unless
   Show 1 is
	If Show 6 is funded, so MUST
	   Show 7 (and vice versa)

Show 4 can't be pursued unless
   Show 2 is
	Shows 5 and 6 cannot be funded
	   at the same time

The decision to finance some shows cannot be made independently of other funding decisions. The following must be met:

Determine which shows to invest in (1 = yes, 0 = no), and how much to invest in each, so as to maximize total returns for the resulting portfolio of TV shows (subject to the rules previously outlined).

Hint: The OUtCoMES roadmap (in this chapter's supplement) presents some examples that may be particularly useful in this problem. You should be able to solve this as an LP with Solver.

Practice 6.3

Football Fanatics, Inc., makes three types of footballs: the Pee Wee, the College Canon, and the Pro Player. The labor and materials requirements for each football are shown in Table 6.7 with information regarding the maximum amount of labor hours available (for a given activity) and the maximum amount of each material available.

The firm purchases only as much of the three materials (rubber, leather, and stitching) as it uses at the prices shown in the table. It wants the Pro Player to comprise at least 10 percent of all the footballs it produces and sells. In addition, the number of Pro Player and College Canon footballs (in total) must not be more than 50 percent of the total number of footballs produced and sold.

Table 6.7. *Details Associated with Football Fanatics Example*

	Revenue	Labor (hours/football)		Material Requirements (gram/football)		
		Cut	Assemble	Rubber	Leather	Stitching
Pro Player	55	0.3	0.5	250	200	60
College Canon	48	0.2	0.4	225	180	50
Pee Wee	30	0.1	0.3	150	100	40
	Max Available	40	100	35,000	28,000	5,000
	Cost issues	15	20	0.02	0.05	0.03
		[$/hour]		[$/gram]		

How many of each type of football should be produced to maximize its profits, subject to the availability and sales-planning constraints given? Which input constraint appears to be most limiting? How does this result differ when integer decisions (that is, whole numbers of footballs) are no longer assumed necessary for planning estimates? You should be able to solve this as an LP with Solver.

7

Complex Optimization

As an extension to the discussion in Chapter 6, it's relevant at this point to reconsider how a feature such as Solver can come up with a solution. Although it's not necessarily critical for developers to understand the detailed technicalities of these packaged programs, any developer worth his or her salt should understand at least the limitations of these algorithms.

7.1 How Solver "Solves"

Many people use Solver with the expectation that it can find the optimal solution for any kind of problem (of reasonable size). But even small problems can have their nuances that make the job extremely difficult for the standard Solver add-in, and the resulting solutions are prone to poor performance (substantially less-than-optimal managerial recommendations). Engines like Solver commonly use hill-climbing algorithms to search for optimal solutions. In reality, this is just another heuristic (see Chapter 5). It starts with a guess of what the solution might be and then it sees if small changes to any of the decision variables of that solution can result in better value for the objective function that is subject to constraints.

Hill-climbing algorithms typically look into only one solution at a time. For example, consider the following hypothetical performance surface (where performance along the z-axis is some function of the two decision variables x and y). In Figure 7.1, a shaded dot represents a possible solution, one that, at this point, appears to be less than ideal. From a local perspective, it certainly doesn't represent the apparent peak value of z attainable (shown by an ellipse).

7.1.1 Problems with Multimodality

From Figure 7.1, we get a visual impression of the objective landscape or terrain over which possible decision options may reside. Based on our

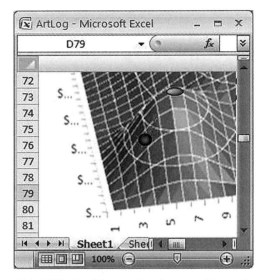

Figure 7.1. Hill-climbing active in a nonlinear frontier.

limited view of this landscape, we might immediately conclude that the best decision exists at the top of the hill. This immediacy is the result of the availability of the graphic visualization of this terrain, as well as our ability to interpret it. This does not typically represent the starting condition of a computer algorithm like Solver, which is charged with delivering an optimal solution. Instead, such algorithms are more or less restricted to information on the most recent solution considered (starting with the solution initially provided) and the nature of the terrain incrementally around it. It will pursue changes in the solution that improve upon the current objective (that is, to climb a hill) and then stop when it gets to a point where it can't make any more improvements (at the peak), but it doesn't recognize this as the best solution until it is actually there.

This seems simple enough; however, we can get into some pretty serious problems with this approach when performance landscapes are more complex. Depending on where our first guess is, we might essentially climb the wrong hill (one that's not the highest). Even we, as visual observers and integrators, might make such a mistake if we limit our overall view to the landscape shown in Figure 7.1, as opposed to the more global view shown in Figure 7.2.

In such cases, the algorithm provides us with what we call a local optimum, whereas the global optimum (best solution, represented by the shaded dot above the ellipse) eludes it. Because the standard Solver uses such an approach to handle nonlinear objective functions in optimization, problems with more than one peak may be impossible for Solver to solve – or at

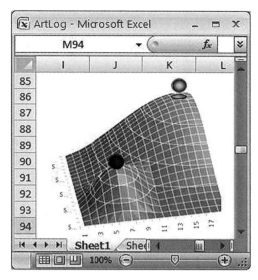

Figure 7.2. Hill-climbing stopped at a local peak, missing global optimum.

least impossible for Solver to guarantee that it has provided the best option available.

Is this something to be concerned with? Do difficult objectives and decision terrains really exist in practice that would make a reliance on hill-climbing algorithms alone problematic?

Marketing example: Demand is often dependent on price. If revenue is a multiplicative function of both demand and price, it's going to be nonlinearly related to the price decision. Beyond this, demand for one good often impacts demand for other goods that are either complements or alternatives. Therefore, when faced with multigood pricing decisions, the objective landscape for expected revenue may have many distinct peaks.

Finance example: Think about all the complex calculations financial planners have to deal with on a regular basis, beginning with even some of the simplest like NPV. Nonlinearity typically pervades their work. In cases where complex portfolio management decisions need to be made, particularly when the performance of options are thought to be interrelated, it is difficult to simply assume single-peak dynamics automatically apply. More to the point, making such an assumption and relying on a hill-climbing approach cannot only result in a suboptimal decision, but will also reduce the overall value provided by such analysts.

7.1.2 Problems with Discontinuity

Complex nonlinearities aren't the sole bane of simple optimization mechanisms. Solver's approach also expects that the objective function that you're

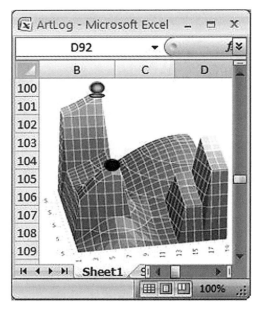

Figure 7.3. Hill-climbing efforts further complicated by discontinuity.

trying to develop a set of decisions for is a continuous one, not a choppy, subdivided, or staggered one (Figure 7.3). If your objective model includes elements such as IF statements or LOOKUP values – or if it relies on noisy, real-time data – Solver has its work cut out for it; however, don't bet on getting a great solution in these cases!

As a simple thought experiment, consider a firm that makes and ships a bunch of items over the course of a week (for example, 12,500 low-end wrist watches). Say that the total cost to run this operation is $28,125. Let's say we want to reduce how many watches we produce. If we produce only one watch, would we assume it would cost us just $2.25 ($28,125/12,500) to make? Of course, we wouldn't. We assume that there are fixed costs that don't diminish as a function of scale in most organizations. Furthermore, in many cases, organizations gain from nonlinear economies of scale due in part to efficiencies gained by processing (buying, assembling, shipping, and so on) in bulk.

Whenever decision variables (in this example, how much to produce) have a nonlinear impact on objectives (maximization of profit), the task of coming up with good solutions becomes more complex. With multiple and distinct nonlinearities, as well as conditional dependencies (for example, bulk purchase rates are adjusted not on a continuous scale but on a tiered scale such as $0.5/unit for 0–99 units of raw materials, $0.35/unit for 100–499 units), problems are even more complex and harder to solve.

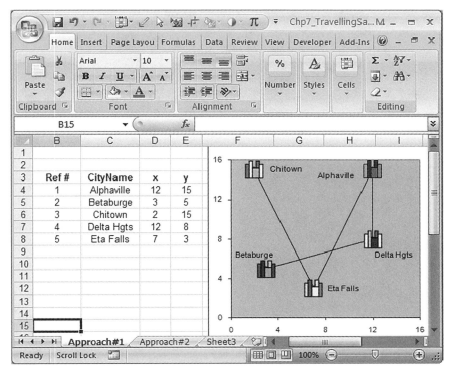

Figure 7.4. Five-city traveling salesman scenario.

7.2 The Benefit of Alternate Optimization Options

As a buildup to more effective approaches to complex optimization, let's further scrutinize the capabilities of the hill-climbing algorithm through a full-blown numerical example.

7.2.1 Problems with Vehicle Routing

The classic "traveling salesman/vehicle routing" problem is the same one we introduced when talking about heuristics in Chapter 5. It's a tough one to solve, especially when there are a large number of sites to visit. It's worth noting that this is essentially a "sequencing" problem, and although it is often applied to routing, it has similar applications in work scheduling (what to work on first), investment planning (where to transfer cash to next), training (what sequence of skills should be taught and in what order), marketing (what sequence of marketing activities will yield the best results), and so on.

Because we're already familiar with this setting, we'll stick to the routing case. Figure 7.4 shows five cities.

As with many problems, there are multiple ways to structure the decision-making framework. I have two approaches provided in the document

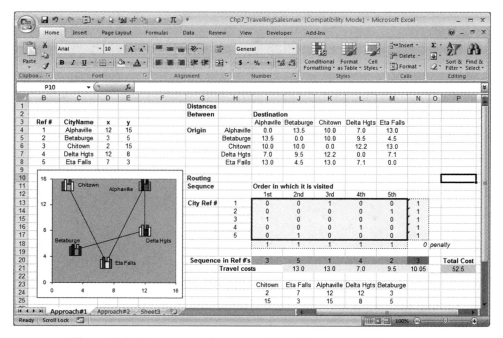

Figure 7.5. One approach to traveling salesman problem setup.

Chp7_TravelingSalesman.xls. Figure 7.5 shows an image of the first approach. I'm using both city names and reference numbers (Ref #'s) to refer to the sites along the route. I have a matrix that approximates travel distance based on straight-line distances (I could change this, but there's no reason to do so in this example). Although appearing in gray scale in this text, the available workbook in which this has been developed contains color demarcations for clarity.

For example, in the worksheet in blue (gray in text), I show the decision variables; in this case, they answer the following questions: "For a specific city will it appear in the route first? Second? Third? Fourth? Fifth?"

Those 1s and 0s basically represent true or false. The row below those decisions provides the sum of the (0,1) decisions above it. Because exactly one of the cities should be visited first, and only one should be visited second, that lower blue row should be all 1s. Similarly, the column to the right of that table is the sum of all (0,1) decisions to the left of it. Because each city must be visited exactly once, those sums should also be all 1s. Rather than create a formal constraint in this case, I'm going to create a heavy penalty for any attempted solution that breaks these rules (one that the computer will try to avoid in minimizing total travel cost).

The numbers in shaded gray depict the actual routing sequence based on all those (0,1) decisions. I could try to use Solver to come up with an optimal solution, trying to minimize total travel cost (which includes the

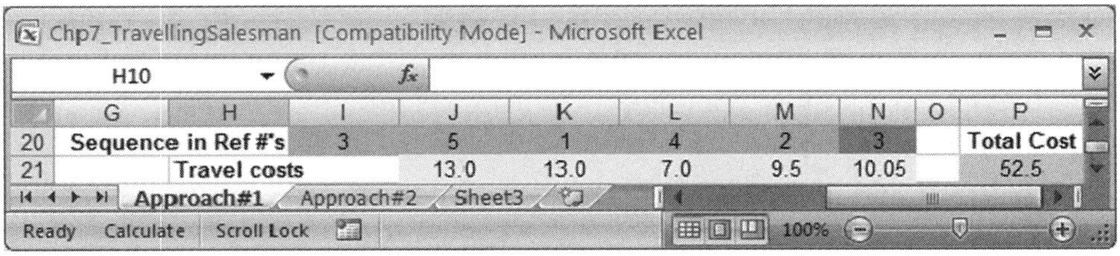

	G	H	I	J	K	L	M	N	O	P
20	Sequence in Ref #'s		3	5	1	4	2	3		Total Cost
21		Travel costs		13.0	13.0	7.0	9.5	10.05		52.5

Figure 7.6. Solution provided by Solver for traveling salesman problem (no change from original).

penalty function) by changing the decisions in the blue box. The necessary constraint is that these decisions must be (0,1) or binary in nature. Unfortunately, the relationship between the objective and the decision variables is far from a simple linear solution. If I try to use Solver (with target cell of $P$21, changing cells $I$13:$M$17, and subject to $I$13:$M$17=binary), Figure 7.6 demonstrates the result. In other words, Solver doesn't suggest a change in the solution, although we know visually that better solutions exist.

Perhaps the real issue was in the way I decided to set up the problem for Solver. Maybe I made it too complex for Solver. Another approach, although also problematic for Solver, is shown in Figure 7.7.

Here, the decision variables are more direct. They answer the question "What is the sequence of city reference numbers associated with the route?" It's just a sequenced list of city reference numbers. The only thing I have to ensure is that each city appears exactly once in this five-stop sequence, which is what I'm doing in the last column above using a COUNTIF statement.

Again, I'm going to use a penalty function to help avoid situations where any one city appears in the sequence more than once. What do I get from Solver using this approach? Same thing as before. Solver can't devise how to improve the current solution. With just five sites, this is not an extremely complex problem. Using a heuristic (for example, nearest next), or just by

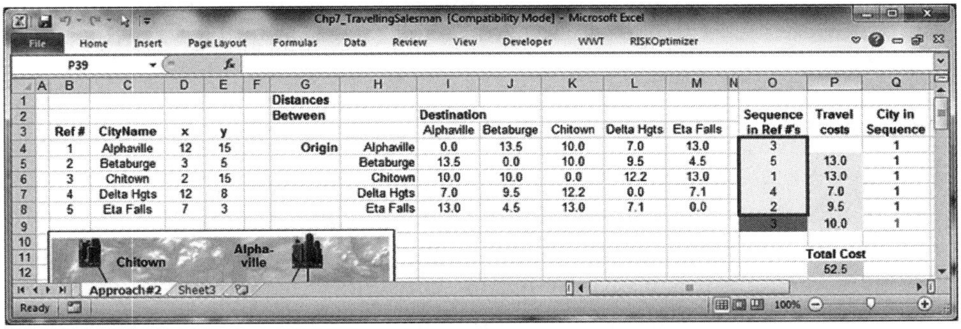

	B	C	D	E	G	H	I	J	K	L	M	O	P	Q
1					Distances									
2					Between		Destination					Sequence	Travel	City in
3	Ref #	CityName	x	y			Alphaville	Betaburge	Chitown	Delta Hgts	Eta Falls	in Ref #'s	costs	Sequence
4	1	Alphaville	12	15	Origin	Alphaville	0.0	13.5	10.0	7.0	13.0	3		1
5	2	Betaburge	3	5		Betaburge	13.5	0.0	10.0	9.5	4.5	5	13.0	1
6	3	Chitown	2	15		Chitown	10.0	10.0	0.0	12.2	13.0	1	13.0	1
7	4	Delta Hgts	12	8		Delta Hgts	7.0	9.5	12.2	0.0	7.1	4	7.0	1
8	5	Eta Falls	7	3		Eta Falls	13.0	4.5	13.0	7.1	0.0	2	9.5	1
9												3	10.0	1
11													Total Cost	
12													52.5	

Figure 7.7. Alternative approach to traveling salesman problem setup.

visual inspection, we'd be able to come up with good alternatives to the current solution. But Solver doesn't know how to think that way. When problems become much more complex – for instance, fifteen cities, thirty cities, or more – we're not going to want to figure things out by visual inspection. And we may like to have an alternative mechanism that is more sophisticated and possibly more effective than a heuristic to get to a good solution.

7.2.2 *RISKOptimizer on Vehicle Routing*

To get the job done, we'll be demonstrating the use of Palisade's RISKOptimizer package. As with XLStat, RISKOptimizer is a package that can function similarly to other standard add-ins in Excel. Its power, in this case, stems from its capability to tackle complex optimization problems and come up with good solutions by making use of what is referred to as a genetic algorithm (discussed at length in this chapter's supplement). Basically, a genetic algorithm starts by forming and considering a range of solutions to an optimization problem, and then step-by-step (that is, iteratively) it expands and discards sets of these solutions in an attempt to capitalize on the information they each provide. New solutions for consideration are based in part on the structure of good existing solutions (attempting to modify these toward improvement of the objective function) and in part on some random number pulls (to help investigate areas of the solution terrain that may not have been represented by earlier solutions). In this way, the best solution evolves from often less prospective beginnings that would otherwise render a simple hill-climbing algorithm useless.

First, ensure that the application has been installed. To make the most out of this application, open the program called @Risk followed by the associated program RISKOptimizer. (These are both Palisade products that come with an installation of the Palisade suite and can be found in the Palisade folder.) If you are asked about running macros, in this case, say Yes. When the program opens it should look similar to what you typically see in Excel, except for a variety of new tool icons under the Add-Ins tab (see Figure 7.8). Many of these tools provide statistical analysis that is similar to the capabilities of XLStat.

For now, however, we are interested only in approaches to solving complex nonlinear optimization problems, and there are only a few specific tools in which we're particularly interested.

To demonstrate the use of RISKOptimizer's genetic algorithm in optimization, we'll use the second traveling salesman and routing setup for illustration. Make sure this file is open and then select the RISKOptimizer settings icon (a double helix with a red distribution curve to its upper left). A dialog box should appear. As with Solver, we need to first say what we want

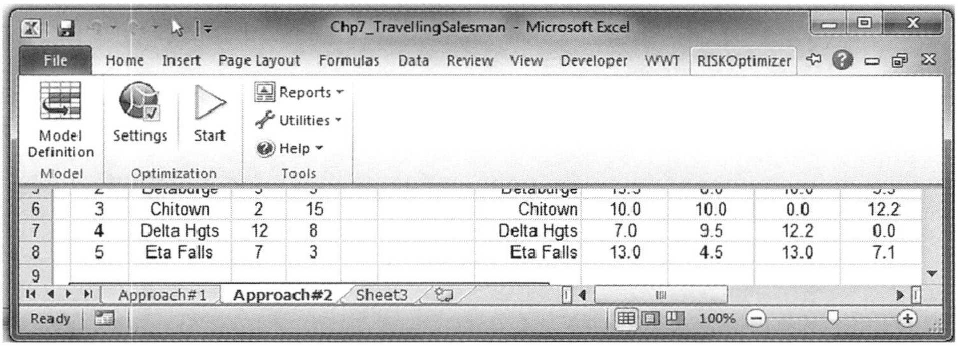

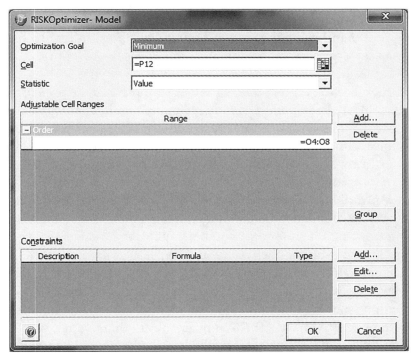

Figure 7.8. RISKOptimizer interface access.

to do. In this case, we want to minimize the total cost; located in P12. And, as with Solver, we also need to specify where the decision variables are (see Figure 7.9).

With RISKOptimizer, however, we're given a more sophisticated interface that allows us to help the computer approach the task we've assigned. In this interface, we can essentially describe the nature of the sets of decisions we want it to consider. In this case, we want the search to simply consider

Figure 7.9. Specifying objectives, decision variables, and constraints in RISK-Optimizer.

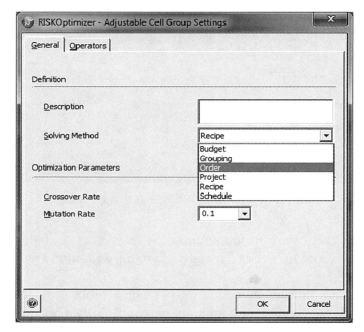

Figure 7.10. Selection of solving method when specifying decision variables.

alternative sequences or orderings of our nominal variable (city reference numbers). We can specify this by selecting the adjustable cells of interest (O4:O8) and then hitting the Group button (displayed in Figure 7.9). The result is a userform pop-up (Figure 7.10) that gives us the option to declare these variables be handled as a special type in the search.

The Order method for handling variables simply takes the preexisting values in the selected cells and mixes them up in an effort to search. In this case, such an approach guarantees feasibility (no city ever comes up twice, for example). Other available solution mechanisms are better suited to other kinds of problems. A summary of these methods is provided in Table 7.1.

With the appropriate solution-mechanism selected, we can now specify the decision variables – in this case, the cells in $O$4:$O$8. RISKOptimizer actually takes into account the possibility that our problem might have some uncertain (for example, random) numbers built into it. Unless we tell it otherwise, it'll try to evaluate each solution it comes up with numerous times, in order to create some typical performance level. We don't have random numbers in this case, so specify one iteration per evaluation (under RISKOptimizer Options shown in Figure 7.11). We'll revisit this option in Chapter 9.

We're now ready to let RISKOptimizer do its thing. Click on the Start RISKOptimizer button (a right-pointing blue triangle, akin to a Play button). RISKOptimizer shows the various solutions it develops (using its genetic algorithm), and that shows changes in our mapping of the route.

Table 7.1. *Types of Solutions Available through RISKOptimizer*

Method	Type of Decisions	Special Assumptions
Recipe	Typically for decisions that can take on a continuous or semicontinuous range of values. Common for decisions involving money invested, hours allocated, number of resources used, and so on.	None. Decisions may be varied independently (such that constraint feasibility/costs, for example, bounds on individual decisions)
Budget		Decisions may be varied independently provided the sum of all values is no greater than some specified value (and s.t. other constraint feasibility/costs).
Order	Typically for decisions that take on ordinal or nominal meaning. Order is common for vehicle routing tasks; Project would be common for project scheduling tasks.	Each of the initial decision values (e.g., 1, 2, 3, and 4; or even 3.14, 2.31, and 2.41) used exactly once in final solution (only order is manipulated)
Project		As with Order, with the additional assumption that some decisions must take on smaller values than (that is, "come before") others.
Grouping	Typically for decisions that take on nominal meaning. Grouping would be common to cluster analysis for example. Schedule would be common to appointment or independent course scheduling tasks.	Only the initial decision values (e.g., 1, 2, 3, and 4; or even 3.14, 2.31, and 2.41) can be assigned to the decision variables. Multiple variables will be assigned the same value.
Schedule		As with Grouping, with additional assumptions relating to the maximum number variables that can take on each value, and (similar to Project) any applicable precedent constraints.

RISKOptimizer quickly comes up with better solutions, which are shown in Figure 7.12.

The one limitation is that RISKOptimizer doesn't always know when to stop trying, but that's where that little red Stop button comes in. We could also have chosen an additional option to stop the search after, say, five minutes; we'll talk more about this in Chapter 9.

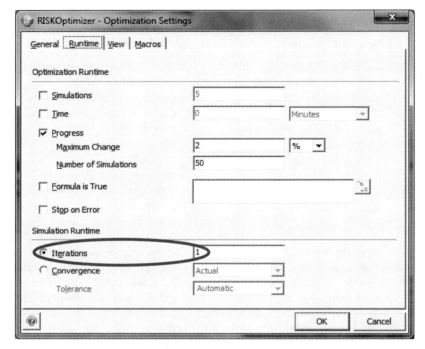

Figure 7.11. Specification of single iteration conditions on search.

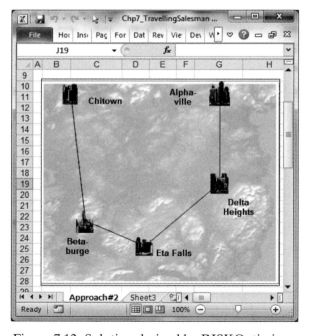

Figure 7.12. Solution derived by RISKOptimizer.

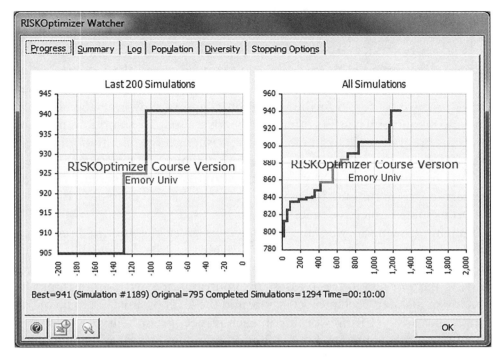

Figure 7.13. Progress graphs created by the RISKOptimizer Watcher during a search.

Another useful feature of RISKOptimizer worth noting at this point – particularly for those interested in getting a feel for how much progress is being made toward better solutions as time goes on – is the RISKOptimizer Watcher. When you start a search (large Play button on the RISKOptimizer ribbon), the lower left-hand corner will provide access to the search (allowing you to stop prematurely, if interested). It also has a small magnifying glass icon that opens up the RISKOptimizer Watcher. Figure 7.13 provides an example of the visual you might see applied to the next problem we'll look at. This presents a graphical mapping of the objective function as it evolves with alternative (and better) solutions encountered. Through such a visual representation, an analyst may be able to assess whether it's worth continuing the search for an appreciably greater length of time, or if a termination of the search can be made early on. We'll look at other ways to get visuals like this after the search is complete.

In a post-hoc sense, a similar capability is provided by the Log Simulation Data option, which triggers a prompt for the types of rich summaries that an analyst might be interested in after the search has terminated. A demonstration of the nature of these data summaries is provided in the next example.

7.2.3 *RISKOptimizer on Cluster and Group Development*

As suggested, RISKOptimizer is also capable of finding solutions for clustering and grouping problems. We've already discussed the potential value
of cluster analysis in the Chapter 5 Dodecha case (which is further discussed
in the practice set found further on in this chapter). However, the ability to
develop meaningful clusters often transcends standard assumptions made by
statistics programs (for example, that the best clustering solution minimizes
the ratio of within-group to between-group variance). In practice, the objective of our clustering may be much more idiosyncratic to our context and the
perceived interpretation of managers. Let's consider an example with a very
different sort of objective function.

Imagine a scenario wherein a manager is given the task of breaking a
workforce up into four groups, each of which will be responsible for one
of four projects. Before assigning workers to project groups, the manager
surveys the workers to try to assess the contribution each worker thinks he
or she can make to each project group, and the level of satisfaction he or she
thinks they will get from working in each project group. Surveys responses
range on a scale from 0 (low contribution/low satisfaction) to 10 (high con-
tribution/high satisfaction).

Given an interest in both high levels of contribution and satisfaction,
as well as an interest in keeping group sizes relatively equal (making
sure all groups are composed of between eighteen and twenty-two people), how should the manager assign the workers? The workbook Chp7_
WorkGroupSelection.xls sets up this problem for us.

We'll use RISKOptimizer on this one as we did previously. Unlike the
traveling salesman problem that simply required RISKOptimizer to consider several different sequences of numbers, this problem structure is
less defined. We're trying to maximize the sum of perceived contributions
and satisfaction levels, while limiting group sizes to between eighteen and
twenty-two people. All RISKOptimizer needs to do is assign workers to
group 1, 2, 3, or 4 (yielding eighty decision variables, each of which is an
integer from 1 to 4). Because this is not a sequencing problem, I'm going
to ask RISKOptimizer to use the Grouping approach to conduct a genetic
search for new solutions (Figure 7.14).

The potential use of a penalty function for group sizes outside the desired
range is an alternative approach and is also set up in the example workbook. These penalties become part of the objective function (negative con-
tributors). If the penalties are appropriately designed (that is, large enough
to ensure the desired group sizes), there shouldn't be a need to explicitly designate constraints. The approach often makes RISKOptimizer's

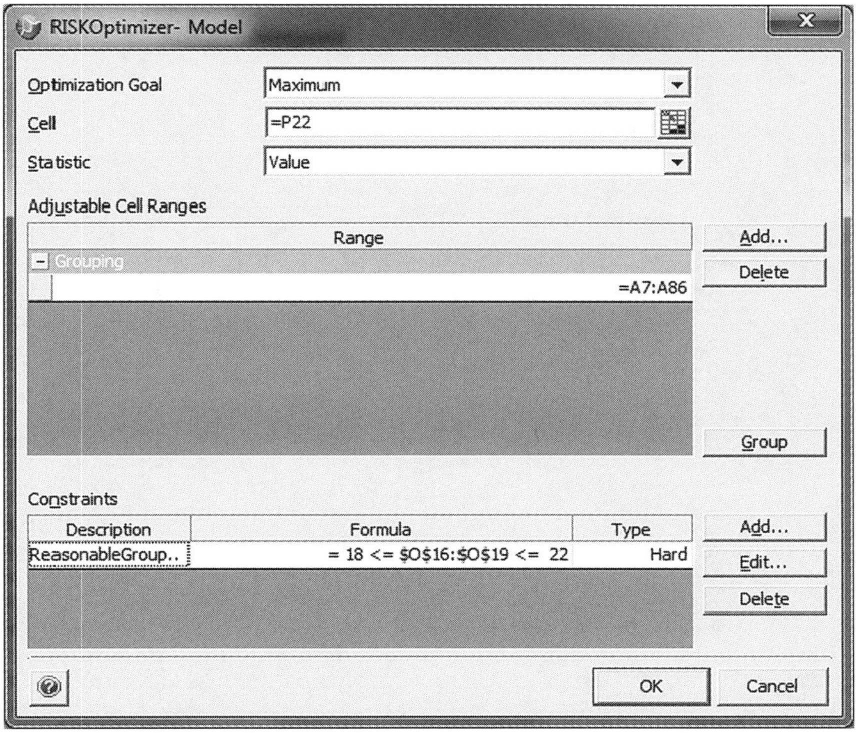

Figure 7.14. Specification of workgroup formation problem in RISKOptimizer.

search a little easier and is similar to designating constraints as soft in RISKOptimizer.

Allowing RISKOptimizer to run for about one minute, the algorithm is able to develop a grouping solution with an objective value of 1,024 (versus the original 795). After two and a half minutes, we're at 1,070. After ten minutes, we're at 1,087. Things don't change much after that point. We might manually stop the routine, or perhaps we could have been savvy enough to preset stopping conditions as an option of the run. For example, Figure 7.15 shows designating the amount of maximum search time in minutes or the degree to which the objective solution appears stable (here, the run is set to stop when very little, 2 percent, additional positive change is observed in the objective function over the last fifty solutions examined). Once again, the total number of iterations is set to "1" here because there is no point in reexamining each set of decision values multiple times – they will always have the same result. This would not be the case if some form of noise, or some computational dynamic, was introduced into the model.

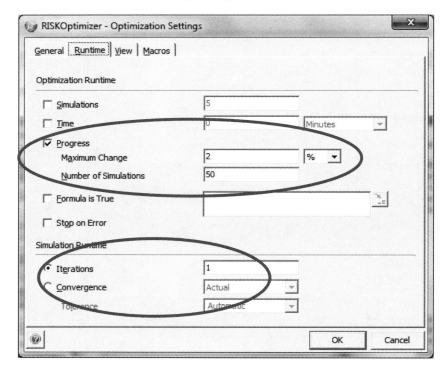

Figure 7.15. Specification of search-stopping conditions in RISKOptimizer.

One could also imagine including an additional stopping criteria of fifteen minutes. The search for better solutions occurs at whichever stopping criteria is met first.

After any search is stopped, RISKOptimizer provides the option of giving you a summary and a log of all solutions it has considered up until the point at which the search stops. This could be useful if you wanted to do further analysis on other solutions that are nearly as good. My recommendation to you is that you ask for reports only on best solutions (Figure 7.16), unless you have a very strong reason for otherwise. The number of solutions considered by RISKOptimizer over the course of ten minutes is enormous, and simply reporting all these solutions (both great ones and very poor ones) is going to take up a lot of time and space, often with little added value in analysis.

This is quite a bit of summary data. How could we use it to interpret the effectiveness of our investigation? At the bare minimum, we could use the log file to get a visual impression of how progress was being made on getting better solutions and to project how long it would take to get a solution that yielded a specific target objective (performance) level. For example, simply selecting the Elapsed time and Result columns, I could generate a connected scatter plot to show how much of an improvement we were getting

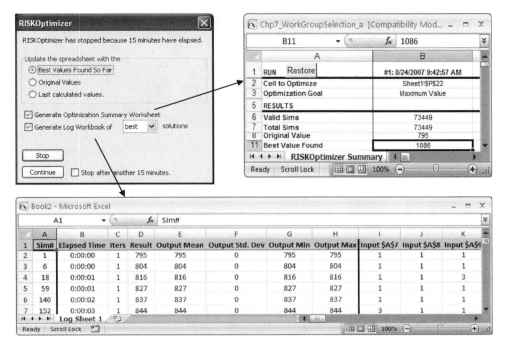

Figure 7.16. Sample output reports available from RISKOptimizer.

the last ten of the total fifteen minutes that elapsed (Figure 7.17), which isn't much.

Not to say that there isn't some fantastic solution we could have arrived at by waiting another hour, but such an improvement definitely doesn't appear promising at the fifteen-minute mark. Don't give up too early on a search process. Extending the length of the examination is ultimately the analyst's call, but there is virtue in knowing how best to use one's time.

7.2.4 RISKOptimizer on Schedule Development

As a last example of the type of complex problem for which RISKOptimizer might provide analysis strength, consider the task of developing a schedule that outlines the sequence and potential simultaneity of the work required for a large-scale project. Such projects typically consist of a series of discernable steps, many of which cannot be started before work on other steps has been completed. The availability of individual project workers is an added complexity. In many cases, some workers cannot easily handle more than one step at a time. However, because of the costs of transferring project experience from one worker to another, it is often beneficial (and sometimes necessary) to make sure that certain sets of steps are handled by the same

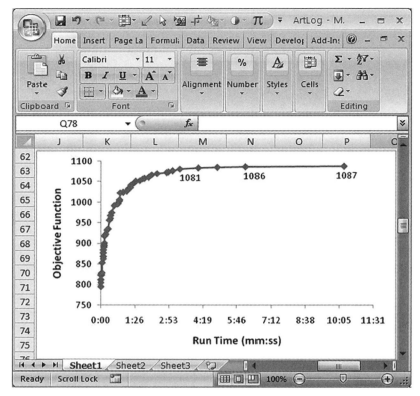

Figure 7.17. Improvements in search over time.

individual. The implied human resource and organizational issues, and complex constraints on the decision-making process coupled with potential non-linearities in the value of getting a project done quickly and with a high level of quality, make project management a complicated duty (see Figure 7.18).

The spreadsheet within which these facts are applied when developing relationships among the decision variables (to whom to assign project steps and when to start them) and the objective (how much total time should be expected for project completion) should also contain the mathematically codified forms of all relevant constraints (that is, both precedent and "no double-working" rules). An example workbook that captures this is provided in Chp7_ProjectScheduling. The main decision interface with a sample start solution is shown in Figure 7.18.

Keep in mind that even RISKOptimizer may be sensitive to the nature of starting solutions, especially when so many possible solutions and discontinuities exist. The more thought you put in your initial solution based on what you know as a planner, the better RISKOptimizer (and similar algorithms) will serve you.

	A	B	C	D	E	F	G	H	I
1	Estimated time, in days, on each step (assuming no information transfers are needed)								
2		Step	Worker1	Worker2	Worker3	Worker4	Worker5		
3		A	7	5	8	6	7		
4		B	8	8	8	7	7		
5		C	7	8	8	7	7		
6		D	7	7	5	8	7		
7		E	7	5	7	7	7		
8		F	8	6	8	8	6		
9		G	7	5	7	7	9		
10		H	6	7	8	7	6		
11		I	6	7	7	8	7		
12		J	5	5	8	7	5		
13		(above will be fed into the objective function to help estimate the total project time)							
15	Information transfer costs (existing when same worker isn't assigned to a set of steps)								
16		From Step-A to Step-D :			3	additional days on Step-D			
17		From Step-B to Step-E :			2	additional days on Step-E			
18		From Step-B to Step-H :			1	additional days on Step-H			
19		From Step-C to Step-G :			2	additional days on Step-G			
20		From Step-D to Step-J :			1	additional days on Step-J			
21		From Step-F to Step-J :			2	additional days on Step-J			
22		From Step-G to Step-I :			3	additional days on Step-I			
23		(above will serve as a kind of soft constraint incorporated into the objective)							
25		{implied is a project calendar starting at day "1" and lasting until							
26		at most day "94" (latest last start would be day 81)}							
28	Required precedence of steps								
29		Finish	Step-A before Step-C	begins					
30		Finish	Step-B before Step-F	begins					
31		Finish	Step-B before Step-G	begins					
32		Finish	Step-D before Step-F	begins					
33		Finish	Step-D before Step-I	begins					
34		Finish	Step-E before Step-G	begins					
35		Finish	Step-H before Step-J	begins					
36		Finish	Step-I before Step-J	begins					
37		(above will serve as hard constraints)							
39	Additional implied constraint:								
40		No one worker can be working on multiple steps at the same time							
41		(also a hard constraint)							

Figure 7.18. Facts and rules critical to the project scheduling problem.

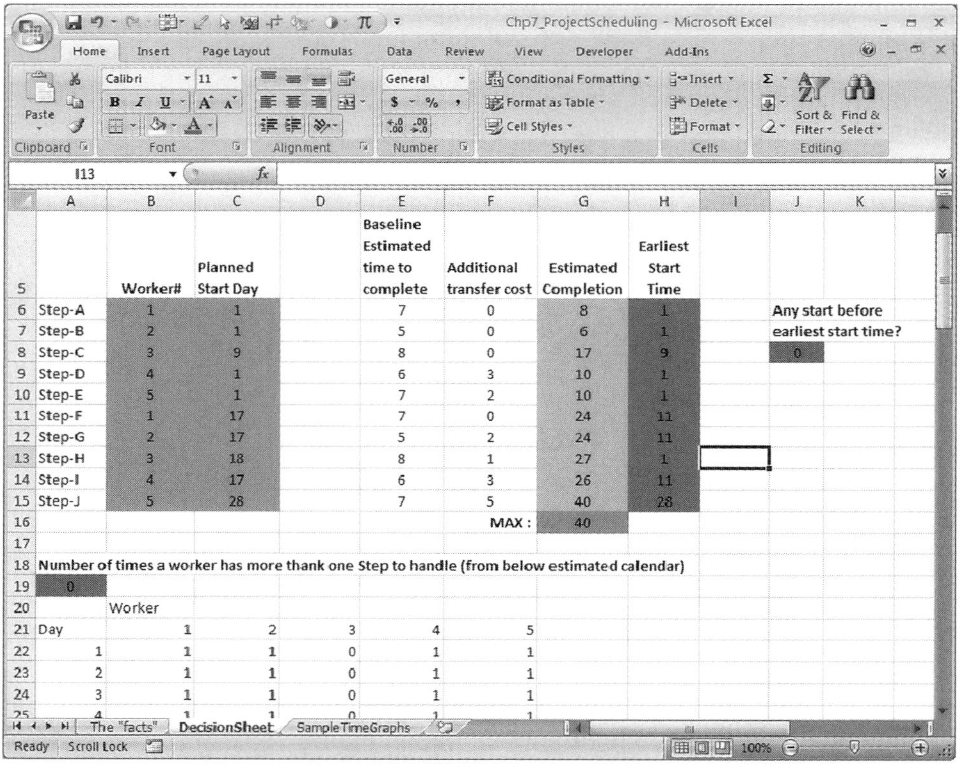

	A	B	C	D	E	F	G	H	I	J
5		Worker#	Planned Start Day		Baseline Estimated time to complete	Additional transfer cost	Estimated Completion	Earliest Start Time		
6	Step-A	1	1		7	0	8	1		Any start before
7	Step-B	2	1		5	0	6	1		earliest start time?
8	Step-C	3	9		8	0	17	9		0
9	Step-D	4	1		6	3	10	1		
10	Step-E	5	1		7	2	10	1		
11	Step-F	1	17		7	0	24	11		
12	Step-G	2	17		5	2	24	11		
13	Step-H	3	18		8	1	27	1		
14	Step-I	4	17		6	3	26	11		
15	Step-J	5	28		7	5	40	28		
16						MAX :	40			
17										
18	Number of times a worker has more thank one Step to handle (from below estimated calendar)									
19	0									
20		Worker								
21	Day	1	2	3	4	5				
22	1	1	1	0	1	1				
23	2	1	1	0	1	1				
24	3	1	1	0	1	1				

Figure 7.19. Setup for project scheduling optimization.

In this case, we're specifying two kinds of decision-variable search methods: recipe for the worker assignment, and schedule for the start dates. In truth, this isn't the best example of how the schedule was designed to work – it is actually more useful when all project steps take a fixed and equal amount of time. However, because this is a luxury not often found in the real world, it is probably more helpful for you to see a more realistic problem getting solved.

In any event, and even starting with a reasonably intelligent starting solution, RISKOptimizer is still able to provide an improvement – from a starting solution's project completion time of forty days to a project completion time of thirty-four days after about 6.5 minutes of search time. To help visualize any meaningful changes in the solution, I've also included in this workbook a couple of bar charts that have been customized to depict resulting solutions (as would Gantt charts common to project management). For contrast, Figure 7.20 shows what the initial solution in Figure 7.19 looks like in graphical form. Visually, the modifications to the initial schedule suggested by RISKOptimizer are clear and the benefit provided is

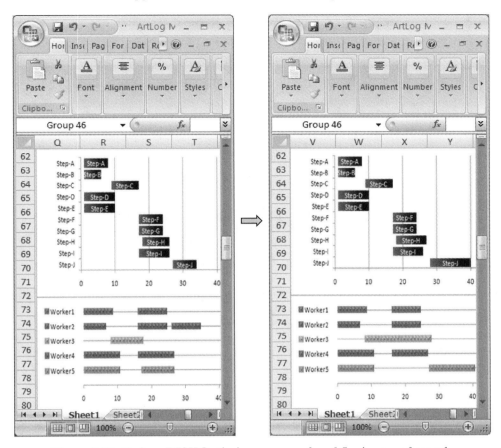

Figure 7.20. Before RISKOptimizer versus after 6.5 minutes of search.

rather striking: A 10 percent reduction in project completion time can provide significant cost savings while potentially freeing resources up for other work.

As a final reminder, as valuable as graphical depictions can be, they can appreciably increase processing time. If you want RISKOptimizer (or any other routine) to quickly run through a large number of solutions and calculations, you might consider postponing graphing until after every search has been conducted.

Supplement: A Primer on Genetic Algorithms

Genetic Algorithms in General

As mentioned, genetic algorithms represent an alternative to search tactics such as simple hill-climbing. They are based on at least two principles that are fundamental to biological science:

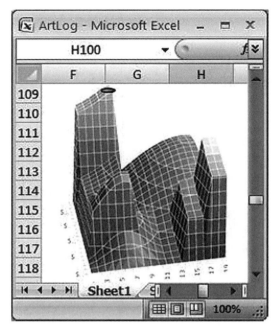

Figure 7.21. Reconsideration of complex objective terrains.

1) Entities, scenarios, and solutions that do well in nature also tend to be replicated in nature ("survival and progeneration of the fittest").
2) For improvements in nature to develop, there must be opportunity for diversity. Such diversity is typically the result of either the intermingling of sufficiently large populations, or the result of perturbations (mutations) that introduce novel changes.

These same principles can be used to help analysts develop high-performing solutions in the professional world.

Consider one of the more complex decision landscapes depicted in Figure 7.3 (here, as previously, the global optimum is designated by a gray oval; see Figure 7.21). This is certainly a difficult problem for a simple hill-climbing algorithm to solve alone. On the other hand, genetic approaches to solution searches, driven by the principles stated in the previously mentioned two points, operate very differently and are generally not impeded by false signals relating to local optima and complex nonlinearities (or certainly less prone to failure than hill-climbing in such cases).

For a genetic algorithm (GA) to start its work, it needs to begin with an initial pool of solution possibilities, an initial population in which traits are often random. Some of these solutions will certainly be better than others vis-à-vis the performance landscape. A starting population of eight example solutions (gray scale dots) is depicted in Figure 7.22.

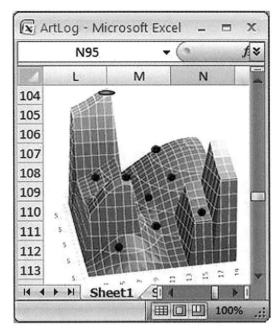

Figure 7.22. Possible initial solution set used by a GA.

The next step allows the survival-of-the-fittest concept to kick in by eliminating many of the poorer solutions (perhaps half of them). If our initial set consisted of eight solutions, this first cut would bring our solution set down to four. To reinforce the potential for future diversity and development, the algorithm would then temporarily duplicate each of the four remaining solutions, bringing the number of solutions back up to eight. I say temporarily because the nature of these solutions is about to change considerably.

Again, drawing on the first natural principle, a random pairing of each solution with another in that set of eight (four pairs of two) provides the foundation of a mechanism by which new solutions can be generated for consideration. The generation mechanism itself requires that some of the decision variable values get swapped with those of their partner. In the case illustrated in Figure 7.22, this might involve the x values only, with the y values retained. This swapping activity is referred to as crossover and is akin in nature to passing along a mix of genetic traits to offspring.

The result is not only new solutions with mixed traits (that is, x and y values in the graph), but also potentially novel performance characteristics (that is, z values) based on those traits (see Figure 7.23).

Overall, this process will give us a new population of possible solutions that may be very different from the initial set. Some of the new solutions may be much worse than their parents and some may be equivalent; however, some may be better – and that's the important point because we're going

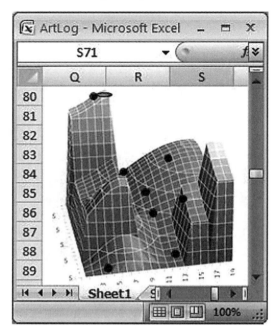

Figure 7.23. Possible first evolutionary iteration by a GA.

to repeat this procedure, cutting out worse performers and basing the next generation off the best. If we allow the population to evolve (eliminating the worst and then reproducing and swapping from the best) for yet another generation, we might find further improvements in our solution set, some of which may be very close to a globally optimal solution.

   With only a fixed initial population and the crossover mechanism, we're going to hit some limits in the extent to which we can find better solutions (for example, at this point, our gene pool is fairly limited). However, even small gene pools are capable of seeking out and attaining globally optimal solutions if we throw in the element of mutation. Along with the crossover mechanism, we could also pick a specific attribute (x or y) in a solution and randomly alter it in a way that creates something that crossover would never achieve by itself. The subsequent solution may put us in a position much closer to the global optimum, or further away, but in any case, it's different and its strengths and weaknesses as an alternate line of investigation will become apparent to use in future generations.

Genetic Algorithm Options in RISKOptimizer

RISKOptimizer uses both crossover and mutation in its search for globally optimal solutions to complex business problems. To make use of these mechanisms, and in accordance with the conceptual nature of genetic algorithms

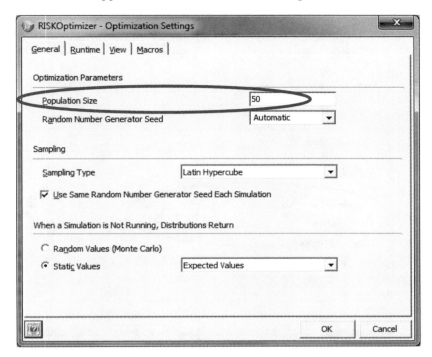

Figure 7.24. Specifying solution population size in RISKOptimizer.

just described, it will need to have a set of alternative solutions available from which to draw and develop next-generation solutions. Analysts can specify the size of this pool in the RISKOptimizer Options dialog box, as shown in Figure 7.24.

The specification of the size of the retained population (the gene pool) can have a significant impact on the effectiveness and efficiency of the search. Too small a pool can impair the development of novel superior solutions because only a limited set of existing ideas are available upon which to draw. Too large a pool can relate to the retention of too many inferior solutions that can similarly distract from effective searchers. So, what's a good population size? This is likely to differ for each and every problem type. The problem is that, early on, most analysts won't know what that size is and they learn only through the experience of running similar optimizations repeatedly. However, the makers of RISKOptimizer do suggest a population size of thirty to one hundred for most problems, with bigger populations relevant for bigger problems (that is, those with large numbers of variables and more complex relationships between those variables, constraints, and the objective function).

As for the nature by which the solutions in this population are used in the search for better solutions, RISKOptimizer also provides the means by

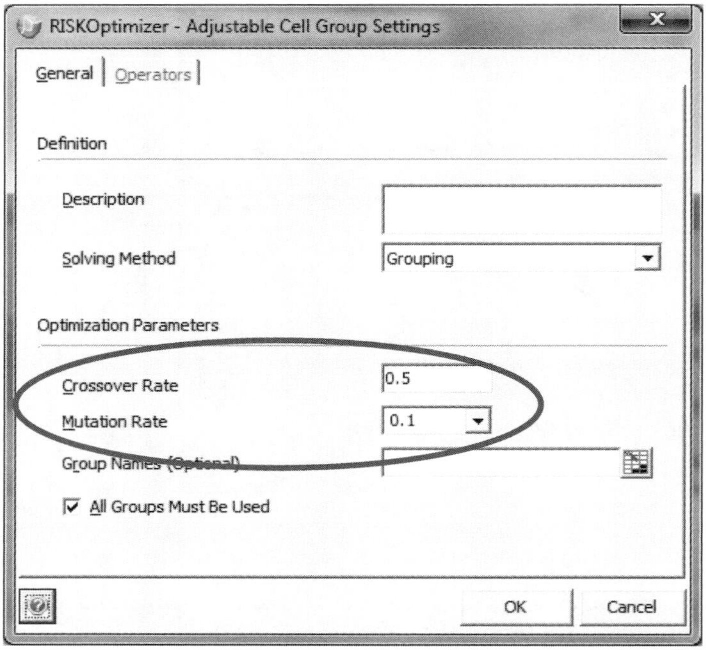

Figure 7.25. Specifying evolutionary dynamics in RISKOptimizer.

which to specify how certain decision variables are mixed and matched by the GA and then potentially subjected to mutation during the search. For any set of decision variables (the settings can differ for different decision variables), these options are available when the variable manipulation methods ("groups") are initially specified or when users elect to edit them in the RISKOptimizer interface (see Figure 7.25, and the discussion in Chapter 2, Section 2.2.2).

The crossover rate specified in RISKOptimizer can be anything between 0.01 and 1.0. For any two solutions being used in crossover to generate new offspring solutions, a crossover rate of 0.85 would mandate that 15 percent of all decision variables involved in a composite solution be substituted by other existing decision variable values (from the partnering parent solution) during crossover. In contrast, a crossover rate of 0.5 suggests that only half of the existing decision variable values will be retained. A crossover rate of 1 essentially equates to zero crossover (the generation of new solutions are supposedly handled predominantly through mutation instead).

Of course, the mutation rate is also modifiable and can be specified as anything between 0.0 and 1.0. A mutation rate of 1.0 specifies that any individual decision variable value in a composite solution involving multiple decisions be subject to random modification for the generation of new solutions. A mutation rate of 0.5 suggests that half of all decisions are subject to random mutation, while 0.0 relates to zero mutation in new solution development. The abundant use of a mutation rate also relates back to the specific selection of population size. If new solutions are being generated largely by mutation rather than by crossover, the need for large populations is reduced. (Random mutations allow even relatively small genetic pools to evolve.)

PRACTICE PROBLEMS

Practice 7.1

Recall the application of cluster analysis to the Dodecha Solutions case. The clustering algorithm used was a tool made available by XLStat. One of the implied goals of the clustering algorithm was to minimize the ratio of within-group to between-group variance, subject to the constraint that we were interested in distinguishing a total of four groups. The criteria for grouping (and the source of variation) included eight higher-level factors that were derived through Principle Components Analysis (PCA) conducted on an original set of thirty-two items.

Recognizing the semirandom nature of the grouping process (both in XLStat and through RiskOptimizer's genetic algorithm), attempt to replicate the groups derived in the XLStat example. Using the data set from the Chp5_DodechaSolutions workbook, compare how the resulting groups compare across the performance measures.

Can a similar story be told? Given our previous discussion in this chapter regarding the implications of random features in the grouping process, what might any significant differences imply for an analyst attempting to discriminate among project types?

Practice 7.2

Recall the issues of randomness brought up in the clustering discussions of Chapter 5; the same kind of randomness inherent to XLStat's search for groups applies here. RISKOptimizer isn't providing a complete search for more than $4^{80} = 1.46 \times 10^{48}$ solutions, just an evolving series of smart guesses.

Try to make a major manual modification to the initial solution while making sure that group sizes remain between eighteen and twenty-two. Look at the best solutions log and then compare it to that derived in the example solution presented in this chapter. Are similar objective function values obtained? Does convergence seem to occur much earlier for one-start solutions?

Try to develop a plot of best solutions at each of the ten-second intervals with your solutions on the y-axis and the example solutions on the x-axis (that is, organize the data so that best solutions at each ten-second interval are outlined for comparison purposes, then line up and plot the solutions corresponding to each interval). How could this depiction help to describe the relevance of starting solutions?

Regardless of group number, how similar are the group constituencies derived at the end of the two initial solution approaches? An example of how to depict this

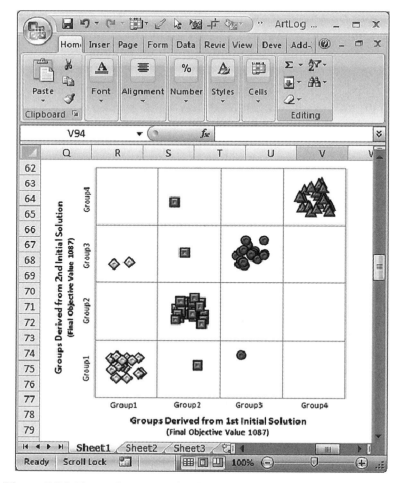

Figure 7.26. Example summarization of clustering result distinctions.

might involve the use of a scatter plot for four separate series of data (designated by the groups derived from the first best solution). Group membership from the first approach might be graphed against that from the second set of runs, with a little "jitter" added in (not graphing Person1's first group# versus Person1's second group#, but rather something more like x = first group# + (0.5-rand()), and y = second group# + (0.5-rand()). The result gives an impression of the population at each combination of result, something along the lines of that shown in Figure 7.26. Try it, and describe what you see.

Section 3

Leveraging Dynamic Analysis

8

Controlled Simulation Analysis

We've talked about how difficult it can be to find or construct an optimal solution to real-world management problems, in which we're faced with non-linear relationships and constraints that make it difficult to predict how specific decisions work together to impact performance. But in a certain way we've continued to simplify these real-world problems. There may be some shortcomings in the approaches we've taken in finding solutions, but what about the approaches we use to come up with the problems that we're trying to solve?

When we create a mathematical form to represent reality so that we can ultimately use analytics to provide an applicable real-world solution, are we missing something? And how much does this impact the real-world applicability and effectiveness of the solution we develop? These are critical questions for managers who want additional support in their decision making. Project managers don't want suggestions that come out of inappropriate assumptions.

What steps can we take to help ensure that we are, in fact, providing appropriate characterizations of reality when we structure problems and make sense of solutions? Although there are a lot of good places to start, one obvious place is an attempt to take into account the uncertainty associated with just about everything that takes place in the real world. In the problems we've examined in the previous few chapters, we haven't really dealt much with this issue; instead, we've assumed that certain elements of our decision context are relatively fixed or constant, such as:

- the amount of demand we need to cover in the next few days
- the amount of time it takes for a worker to serve a customer
- the nature of the transportation infrastructure (for example, traffic) on which we base cost and time estimates in routing
- the rate of return on stocks and other options in portfolio selection
- the actual cost to complete a project or new venture we may be considering (among a set of other options)

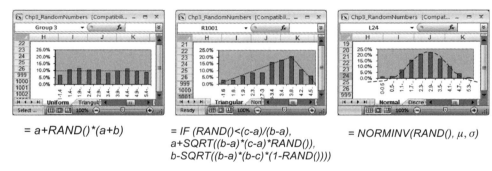

$$= a+RAND()*(a+b)$$

$$= IF\ (RAND()<(c-a)/(b-a),$$
$$a+SQRT((b-a)*(c-a)*RAND()),$$
$$b-SQRT((b-a)*(b-c)*(1-RAND())))$$

$$= NORMINV(RAND(), \mu, \sigma)$$

Figure 8.1. Pervasive role of the random number generation in simulation.

But in the back of our minds, do we really believe any of these are constant? If the answer is no, we should probably look into the potential impact that variation in these assumptions may have on the effectiveness of any given solution relative to other solutions from which we might be able to pick. If we want to incorporate variation into our models, how do we do it? We can start with the notion that most real-world data can be described not only by a characteristic value (a mean) but also by a measure of uncertainty (standard deviation). The ability to simply generate random numbers based on these two kinds of information is a critical first step toward formally incorporating variation in our decision-making process.

Remember that in Excel, we have a building block for generating just about any kind of random number that we can dream up – for example, the RAND() function, shown in Figure 8.1. All random numbers created within cells of a spreadsheet make use of this function.

8.1 Approaches to the Use of Simulation in Analysis

Simulation-based models can take on many forms, depending on how random numbers are used to construct various scenarios for evaluation. Two general categories that are worth distinguishing can be referred to as simulated variants and system simulations.

8.1.1 Simulated Variants

Simulated variants generally refer to a set of structured management problems or decision-making scenarios that are equivalent in structure but differ in the actual values of the parameters (for example, work rates, interest rates, and levels of demand) used to describe them. Simulated variants are useful in what managers call what-if analysis. For example, a manager might need to know how different the optimal solution to a problem would be if slightly different numbers (again, work rates, interest rates, and levels of demand) are applied; that is, would Solver or RISKOptimizer come up with a different solution if the numbers were slightly off? We call this a *preconstruction* approach to considering variation.

Alternatively, a manager might like to take a derived optimal solution (based on only best estimates; that is, mean values of demand) and test how well the resulting solution set of decisions would do if the numbers describing the problem changed; would it always ensure profitability? Would it always be technically feasible? We call this a *postconstruction* approach to considering variation. More sophisticated use of simulated variants would involve considering both issues in tandem. For example, a manager might need to come up with a set of potential of solutions based on slightly different initial problem parameters and then see how each does under a range of alternative parameters.

Perhaps the manager finds that one of the solutions (that does not appear to be the best based on the average values of the problem parameters) is much less sensitive to variation. As a result, this option might be much less likely to incur unacceptable costs or difficulties in applying it in an uncertain world. In turn, this would carry considerable more appeal than otherwise suggested, based on a simple average-driven assessment.

8.1.2 System Simulations

Many management problems require the consideration of decisions that impact not only one point in time, but actually have repercussions across time whereas later phenomena remain highly dependent on choices made earlier.

For example, the decision to put a specific inventory-ordering policy in place will impact the level of inventory available to a firm for the length of time during which the policy is in place. In fact, even the amount of inventory bought at a single point in time can have implications for performance in many subsequent periods. A decision to hire additional full-time staff or restructure the layout of a facility has similar long-term implications. In such cases, the impact of managerial decisions are still more difficult to assess because they involve numerous events that will take place in the future and about which we may know very little with any level of certainty. Impact can also be affected because these decisions may set into motion a series of events whose repercussions may be difficult to assess in a single closed-form calculation.

A system simulation is often used in such cases to provide a description of how a particular system operates, and how management decisions impact that operation. Variation is built into the activities of that system at each

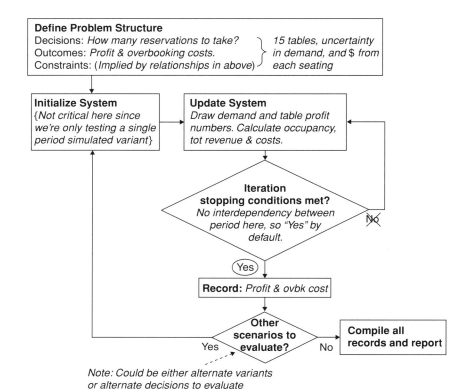

Figure 8.3. Design structure of the reservations simulation variants.

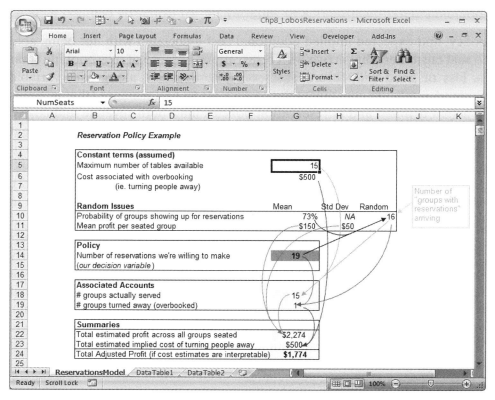

Figure 8.4. Example of the implemented simulation variant template.

Figure 8.5. Accessing Data Table functionality in Excel.

Although this spreadsheet structure is sufficient in providing an estimate of how well a specific policy might do given one set of random variable draws, a single variable draw can be misleading. It shouldn't form the basis for final consideration by decision makers. We'd like to be able to have stable estimates of policy performance that are representative of a full range of random draws, and we will want to be able to compare these results of various policies assessed the same way. A Data Table is a convenient tool that can be leveraged to this end. The Data Table tool is found by selecting Data > What-If Analysis > Data Table (Figure 8.5).

A Data Table is used to provide a series of permutations of a simulated variant structure (that is, a series of variants of outcomes based on the simulation design, each independent of one another). This tool is fairly straightforward after a spreadsheet structure is set up, such as the one demonstrated in this case. To clarify a couple of approaches to the leveraging of Data Tables, we'll start our work on a new worksheet.

Let's store our Number of Reservations decision variable in cell A1 of worksheet DataTable1 in Chp8_LobosReservationsBook. In cell A2, we can store the assumed cost associated with overbooking. To control the simulation outcomes from this sheet, go back to the ReservationsModel worksheet and replace the content of these respective cells (located in G14 and G6 of that first worksheet) with references to =DataTable1!A1 and =DataTable1!A2, respectively.

Now, we need to outline the structure of the Data Table. If we want a table of one hundred runs, we might enter the numbers 1 through 100 in the cells DataTable1!B6:B105, but this is mostly for our own reference. To designate the kinds of scenarios we want the Data Table to detail, we enter a variety of alternative reservation policies: for example, in this worksheet, fifteen to twenty-five reservation bookings in cells C5:M5. Finally, we need to designate what kind of outcome measure we want summarize in the table. For now, let's go with the Total Adjusted Profit figure (a merger of estimated profit across seated groups minus assumed costs due to overbooking). In the upper-left corner of our table outline, cell B5 in

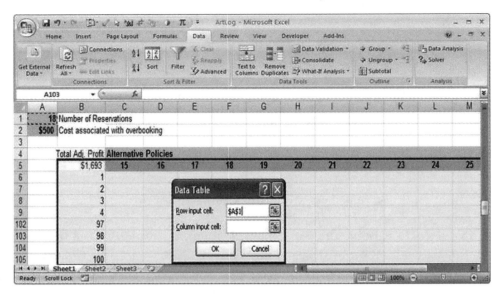

Figure 8.6. Developing a Data Table in Excel.

this case, we want a direct reference to the outcome measure (Reservations-Model!G24). This is often referred to as the *keystone cell* in this type of Data Table.

Now we're ready to let the Data Table tool do its work. Select the entire area of the table that contains the row labels (1–100), the calculation reference (cell B5), and the various scenario inputs (cells C5:M5). Select the Data Table tool to generate the Data Table dialog box, shown in Figure 8.6.

Now, before continuing, it's worth noting that one of the biggest barriers to the proliferation of Data Table use has been its generation interface (Figure 8.6). Most people don't find it immediately intuitive. However, there are some general rules to help guide us:

1) INPUTS: The fields in this pop-up userform are designed to allow the specification of inputs (values of variables) that impact the output(s) that will populate the Data Table (for example, simulated calculations).
   a. The "Row input cell" field is asking what to do with any values that might exist in the top row of the table. If these are inputs, then you will need to specify where in the worksheet those values should be substituted in order to derive a new calculated output. If the main calculation (for example, simulation) is actually on another sheet, circa Excel 2010, you're not going to be able to specify that location directly. Instead, select a cell on the Data Table sheet and have the corresponding cell on the modeling sheet reference that Data Table sheet's target cell.

b. The "Column input cell" field is used in the same way as the "Row input cell" field, except that it applies to the potential values contained in the left-most column of the Data Table.

Rule of thumb for INPUTS: Pick a place in the model.

2) LABELS: In some cases, the row or the column will be used to provide multiple calculations that are subject to the same input scenario. In simulation, this is useful because the relationship between inputs and outputs are not certain and are subject to some randomly modeled noise. Hence, repeated evaluations of the conditions in subsequent rows below the first top-row cell, for example, could provide the basis for generating statistics on the effects of that input (means, standard deviations, and so on), as well as for each of the other columns under the remaining top-row cells. In order to get this to work, the left-most column would contain some "dummy content" (for example, 1–100, representing replication 1 through 100), and the "Column input cell" would be some cell in the sheet that has no impact on the model's calculations. After all, these labels should not mean anything to the model itself. They're only meaningful in the sense of assessing variants of the models outputs. And that's exactly how they are used in this example.

Rule of thumb for LABELS: Send it somewhere harmless.

3) FORMULAE: In the current example, the kinds of calculations made throughout the Data Table are designated by the keystone cell in the upper-left cell (highlighted in the example). That's fine for this example. However, occasionally you'll want to assess multiple output calculations. We'll see this need in the second portion of this example. In order to do this, select either the top row or the left column to contain distinct formulae or references to different outputs calculated by the larger simulation model. In the example we'll see shortly, the top-row cells are used for this purpose. In order to tell the Data Table that you want to apply each of the top-row formulations in populating the cells below them, you'll need to keep the field "Row input cell" blank. After all, you don't have inputs of any kind in that top row by such a design, not even "dummy inputs." Incidentally, you'll never have both the row and column headers contain formulae. In part, this would prevent the possibility for inputs, but more important, the Data Table mechanism won't know whether to fill its bulk with calculations down from the top, or across from the side.

Rule of thumb for FORMULAE: Keep it blank.

So, in the present example, here's how we would go about specifying the table. First, in the field labeled "Row input cell," select A1, which is the cell we are using to store our decision variable and which we are using now to control the nature of the simulation. This tells the table generator that you will want to substitute the various alternative policies you've designated at the top of the table into this input field to generate your results. In the "Column input cell" field, select any blank cell to the left or above the table

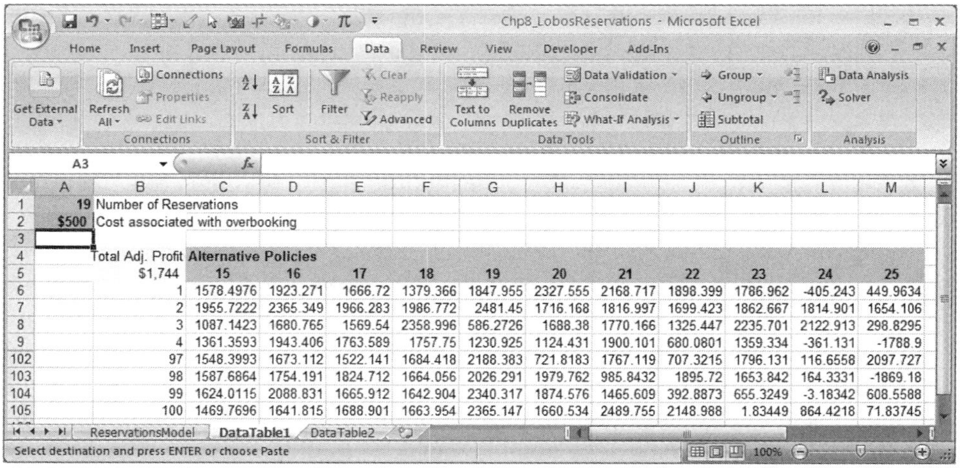

	A	B	C	D	E	F	G	H	I	J	K	L	M
1	19	Number of Reservations											
2	$500	Cost associated with overbooking											
3													
4		Total Adj. Profit	Alternative Policies										
5		$1,744	15	16	17	18	19	20	21	22	23	24	25
6		1	1578.4976	1923.271	1666.72	1379.366	1847.955	2327.555	2168.717	1898.399	1786.962	-405.243	449.9634
7		2	1955.7222	2365.349	1966.283	1986.772	2481.45	1716.168	1816.997	1699.423	1862.667	1814.901	1654.106
8		3	1087.1423	1680.765	1569.54	2358.996	586.2726	1688.38	1770.166	1325.447	2235.701	2122.913	298.8295
9		4	1361.3593	1943.406	1763.589	1757.75	1230.925	1124.431	1900.101	680.0801	1359.334	-361.131	-1788.9
102		97	1548.3993	1673.112	1522.141	1684.418	2188.383	721.8183	1767.119	707.3215	1796.131	116.6558	2097.727
103		98	1587.6864	1754.191	1824.712	1664.056	2026.291	1979.762	985.8432	1895.72	1653.842	164.3331	-1869.18
104		99	1624.0115	2088.831	1665.912	1642.904	2340.317	1874.576	1465.609	392.8873	655.3249	-3.18342	608.5588
105		100	1469.7696	1641.815	1688.901	1663.954	2365.147	1660.534	2489.755	2148.988	1.83449	864.4218	71.83745

Figure 8.7. Data Table content for multiscenario runs on a single outcome.

area (a blank cell must be designated here for the syntax to work). The result should be a table populated with outcome data for a hundred variants of the simulation, for each of the scenarios represented in the top row of the table, which is shown in Figure 8.7.

The nice thing about this table is that you can change just about any of the features of the simulation, including both constants such as cost figures and the nature of relationships (that is, formulae), and the Data Table should provide updated information more or less instantly in response to these changes. For example, try changing the cost figure in cell A2 or replacing the reference in cell B5 (currently pointing to Total Adjusted Profit) with a reference to ReservationsModel!G23 (the implied cost of turning people away).

Somewhat less convenient is the Data Table's general dedication to a single outcome measure. Here, we can select any one outcome measure to generate variants, but only one at a time. We could create an entirely separate table for another outcome, but those measures would not be linked to the values in this table – the outcome in the first data cell of this table would be based on entirely different random number pulls.

Similarly, we could try to generate a single Data Table that generates variant outcomes for a set of different measures under a specific decision (policy) scenario. The worksheet DataTable2 actually does this. The table was developed by starting with a structure similar to Figure 8.8 in which the top row references each of the three outcomes stored in the cells on the main simulation worksheet.

After selecting the table area that includes the left-most column and all three subsequent columns for which calculations are provided, and again

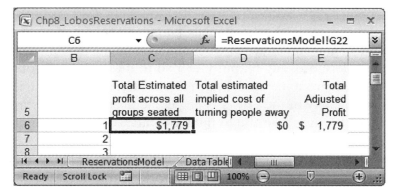

Figure 8.8. Setting up a Data Table for multiple outcome use.

calling on the Data Table tool, the Data Table dialog box will ask for information. This time the only information we want to provide is a reference in the "Column input cell" field to a blank cell outside of the table such as cell A4. This indicates to Excel that we want to use the default calculations in the top row to build the rest of the table, and we don't want to use any information for separate calculations. The result is shown in Figure 8.9.

The values in each individual row of this table are related, as evidenced by the fact that the Total Adjusted Profit values really do represent the difference between the values in the first two columns, even though they are generated by the Data Table, as opposed to a post-hoc calculation. In this case, because we're evaluating only a single-policy scenario, each row essentially represents a single variant (a single random number pull). This means that complex relationships between any two outcomes (for example, covariance structures) can be assessed and visualized. In some cases, the ability to visualize possible interdependencies in this way proves critical in meaningful and intelligent approaches to trade-off analysis.

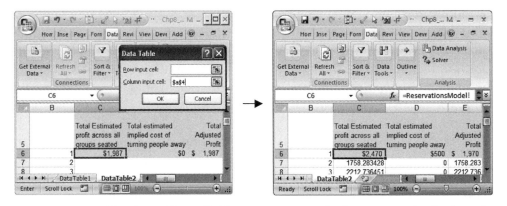

Figure 8.9. Specification of Data Table parameters and subsequent refreshed result.

At this point, it is worth reiterating that the Data Table is both an input and an output mechanism. Any nonlabel inputs (designated on the top row or left column) must go where the main computational model can make use of them. Furthermore, any output intended to fill the interior of the Data Table must come from the model calculations affected. This is an important point, because many of the errors I see people making stem from errors in "connection." It's always useful to think of Data Tables as being the beginning and end points of a closed-loop system of calculations.

In the examples just examined, the Data Tables were on worksheets other than the main model. They were feeding data into a particular cell in their own sheets, which the model was looking at (for example, feeding into A1 on the DataTable1 sheet, a cell that the model was pulling data from). The model had to contain some reference to cell A1. In terms of overall flow that allowed the following to take place: Data Table Row data→A1→Model (to use in its calculations). I've seen people do the equivalent of having a Data Table send input into A1, and then have A1 reference the model – in terms of flow that's more like Data Table Row data→A1←Model (whatever default input exists). The result would be both the model and the Data Table sending information to A1, and the model not being affected by Data Table inputs at all. Any outputs pulled into the Data Table would not be meaningful in terms of input effects. Therefore, be careful with how you design the flow of information with these tools.

8.2.2 Perfumery at Phipps: Uncertain Cost and Pricing Effects

Clearly, Data Tables provide multiple approaches to looking at the effects of things that may or may not be under the control of the decision maker. We'll look at another example to drive this point home. Consider a local entrepreneur thinking about opening a store that sells customized perfumes in Phipps Plaza in Atlanta. Before moving forward, she would like to determine estimates (averages) of the total profit level she can expect depending on (1) the price per bottle sold, which she has discretion over, and (2) potential variable unit costs, which she's unclear about at this point and which may be subject to uncontrolled variation. Basically, she would like to construct a table (or tables) that outlines a range of possible profit scenarios based on per unit price and cost.

Now, along with realizing that variable unit costs may be subject to change (beyond her control), she also realizes that even the best estimates of demand are subject to error. In general, the demand models she's working with are based on existing models from industry and are driven in a large part by her choice of price. Price drives demand, and together both price

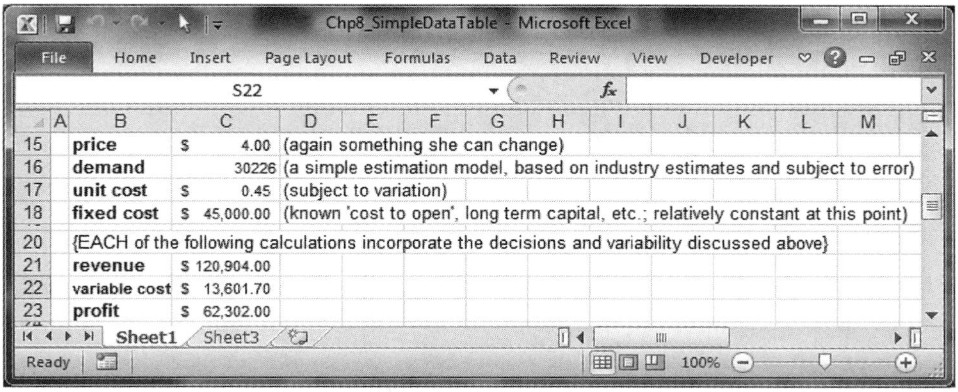

Figure 8.10. Averages confronted in revenue and profit estimation.

and demand impact revenues and profit, once those uncertain costs are considered. However, like all estimates, there's a certain amount of uncertainty inherent. Therefore, she wants these tables to provide a picture of how much variability she may face in any given price and cost scenario. Figure 8.10 presents the known data and the uncertain unit price- and cost-based model outputs she is currently working with (see Chp8_SimpleDataTable).

At least a couple of Data Table structures might be considered to depict the effects of price and cost along with the variability she's facing in demand. The first, presented in Figure 8.11, is a Data Table that simulates ten possible outcomes (profit levels) resulting from each of twelve distinct price points ($2.50 to $5.25 per unit at $0.25 intervals). Similar to the example in Section 8.2.1, this table is generated by specifying where the row data should go, and in this case the "Row input cell" should be specified as C15 in the userform. A cell not related to any calculations (A33, for example) is used as a dump for the labels in the left column, and the upper-left keystone cell points to the profit calculation. Note that any one of the resulting simulated demand levels within the Data Table isn't very informative. Rather, summary statistics on the distribution of outcomes associated with each price point are critical for interpretation and decision making (for example, the average anticipated demand at $2.50 and the standard deviation around that average).

An alternative Data Table structure that might be considered here, because the effects of both price (yet to be selected) and cost (yet to be fully determined) clearly have an impact on profit, would consider the joint impacts on various levels of these two issues. In order to do so, it might seem like the best option would be to continue to use the top row of the Data Table to designate possible price points while using the left-most column to contain alternate cost points. The only difference in the creation of

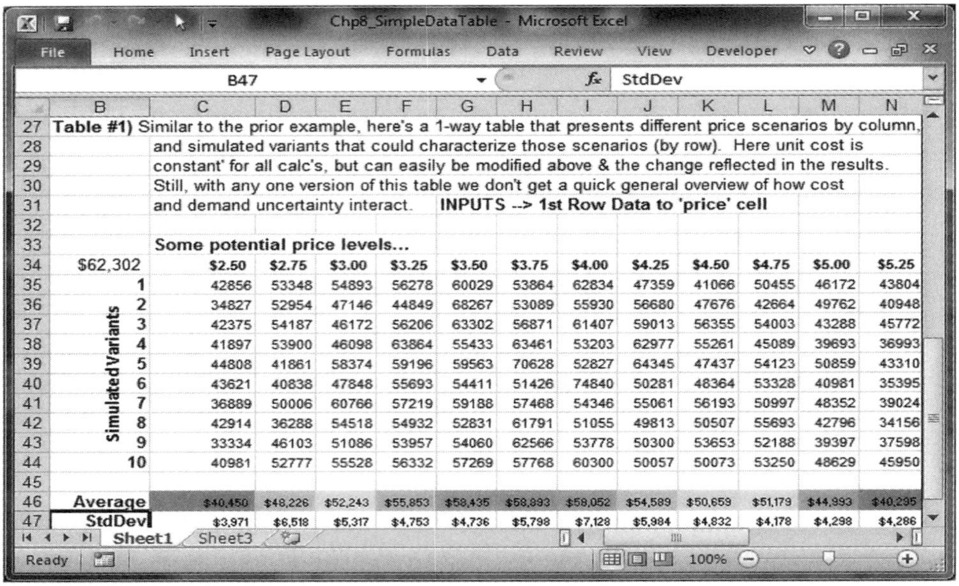

Figure 8.11. One-way (one input) Data Table for considering demand-price sensitivity.

such a Data Table, aside from ensuring that cost points were actually listed in the left-most column, would be in specifying the column input data as the location where the profit model is expecting to see costs (in this case, C17). The result is what is commonly referred to as a two-way (two inputs) Data Table and this is presented in Figure 8.12.

One might be tempted at this point to calculate averages and standard deviations for each of the levels of price and cost (also shown in Figure 8.12). In this particular case, these results could be informative; however, there are some caveats. Specifically, there are always possibilities in complex models (as in reality) that two issues have joint effects that cannot be accounted for strictly through the addition of their separate effects. These so-called inter-action effects are the focus of a great deal of research across disciplines. Their existence tends to make prescriptions to practice more nuanced and occasionally more complicated. Nevertheless, without their appropriate con-sideration, decision makers run the risk of extremely shortsighted and costly outcomes.

If the joint impact of price and cost was something that couldn't easily be estimated by additive effects, any single simulation of a combined price and cost point (Figure 8.12 Data Table interior cells) would be fairly difficult to interpret. Moreover, the general nature of trends in the joint impact of these factors could not be discerned. As it is, the trends in joint impacts depicted in Figure 8.12 apparently have various inconsistencies (for example, at a price

Chp8_SimpleDataTable - Microsoft Excel

| File | Home | Insert | Page Layout | Formulas | Data | Review | View | Developer |

B47 f_x StdDev

	P	Q	R	S	T	U	V	W	X	Y	Z	AA	AB	AC	A	AE	AF
27	Table #2) Here we're looking at how profit varies based on both price and cost (on the rows).																
28		We're only generating a single simulated variant for each price-cost combination.															
29		So although we get a 'broader' view of possible variability, we loose some of the finer details															
30		on each specific price-cost combination we might be able to gather from Table #1.															
31		*In this case, both tables can be indispensable to the entrepreneur's decision…*															
32								INPUTS --> Row to 'price' cell, Column to 'cost' cell									
33			Price levels…														
34	$62,302	$2.50	$2.75	$3.00	$3.25	$3.50	$3.75	$4.00	$4.25	$4.50	$4.75	$5.00	$5.25		Avg	SD
35	$0.38	47973	44770	50988	57571	60421	57110	60172	55893	63598	60450	52180	41682		$54,401	$6,894
36	$0.40	42145	47117	51870	63650	57734	59700	55994	60890	56835	44544	51305	35388		$52,264	$8,520
37	$0.43	41191	54419	52638	53035	60106	56951	55975	57364	56866	47961	44688	35046		$51,353	$7,597
38	$0.45	43756	44925	61220	63119	55296	50317	49980	62274	57132	54454	40512	39696		$51,890	$8,342
39	$0.48	38399	46935	46450	51786	51288	59695	56847	51673	60692	54487	44309	41589		$50,346	$7,015
40	$0.50	36604	48820	49562	39485	54510	57953	60192	54172	53000	49005	36571	32453		$47,694	$9,199
41	$0.53	42792	43214	58883	49737	57616	56897	58026	55195	47514	51283	50116	40153		$50,952	$6,522
42	$0.55	43450	44806	51449	50415	53441	56168	53017	50889	46928	45627	49037	38725		$48,663	$4,927
43	$0.58	40073	44477	46737	50213	62856	58041	54297	55198	49541	46474	32357	31973		$47,686	$9,534
44	$0.60	38529	50419	49956	53187	46292	58972	58472	51097	50054	47590	35907	40671		$48,429	$7,205
45																
46	Avg	$41,491	$46,990	$51,975	$53,220	$55,956	$57,180	$56,297	$55,465	$54,216	$50,188	$43,698	$37,738			
47	SD	$3,290	$3,413	$4,746	$7,036	$4,884	$2,697	$3,216	$3,884	$5,687	$4,975	$7,080	$3,705			

(Left side vertical label: Possible unit costs)

Sheet1 / Sheet3

Ready   100%

Figure 8.12. Two-way (two input) Data Table for considering combined price and cost effects.

point of $3.25, profits seem to increase as cost moves from $0.43 to $0.45). Of course, these inconsistencies are artifacts of the random nature of simulation, but they leave the observer wondering what really is going on.

What we would like is to have multiple iterations of each of those price-cost point combined effects so that we essentially have averages at each interior cell (rather than a single random trial). There are numerous ways we can accomplish this, including using an Excel capability and method introduced earlier in Chapter 3: Living Records.

The workbook Chp8_SimpleDatatable_wlivingrecord.xls provides an example of how we could iteratively evolve a solid estimate of a combined effects map for price-cost joint impacts on profit. This structure effectively takes previous information developed in a Data Table and creates a living record of the same size on a separate sheet. The living record sums all the outputs that the Data Table simulates and develops, and creates averages that can be clearly visualized (either in tabular form or using a surface plot – see Figure 8.13).

The introduction of iterative calculations to provide an averaging method for assessing combined effects in this simulation foreshadows the use of iterative mode in the more complex systems simulations, which will be discussed in Section 8.3. It also raises the question as to whether there are alternative automated ways to derive solid estimates of combined effects that might expand beyond two dimensions (that is, the ostensibly complex

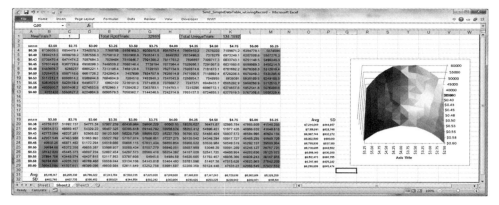

Figure 8.13. Living record methods in robust estimate of joint effects in a two-way Data Table.

effects of three or more variables combined simultaneously). We'll consider this in our third and final simulate variant example before moving on to more complex system simulations.

8.2.3 Acquiring a Diamond in the Rough: ROI Windows Given Yearly Variation

A major Internet company is thinking of purchasing another online retailer. The retailer's current annual revenues are $100 million, with expenses of $150 million. Current projections indicate that the retailer's revenues are growing at 15 percent per year and its expenses are growing at 5 percent per year. However, we know that projections might be in error and that even with a relatively good estimate of growth, yearly fluctuations will exist. What we would like to know, for a variety of assumptions about average annual revenue and expense growth, is an impression of the number of years before the retailer will show a profit.

The setup for this example can be found in the workbook Chp8_DT_DOE. For now, we'll start with the assumption that there is little significant within year variation in growth (SDs = 0.01 percent) and that we just aren't aware of what those stable rates of growth will be. As shown in Figure 8.14, there are a series of calculations needed to assess what these growth rates will translate to in terms of the potential appeal of the acquisition (and how much the acquiring firm might be willing to purchase it for). First, we'll need to calculate the expected annual revenues and expenses for each future year (starting from acquisition), to try to figure out when the firm would start to see a positive annual return.

The final calculation of "when" a within-year breakeven takes place requires both the underlying financial calculations as well as some logic

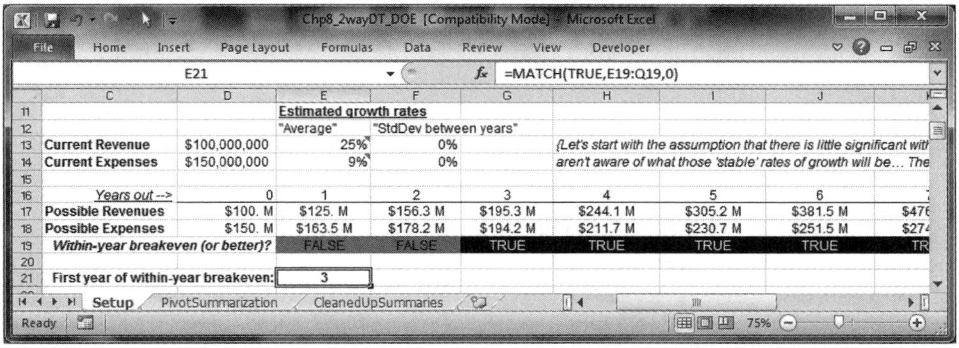

E21 =MATCH(TRUE,E19:Q19,0)

	C	D	E	F	G	H	I	J
11			Estimated growth rates					
12			"Average"	"StdDev between years"				
13	Current Revenue	$100,000,000	25%	0%		{Let's start with the assumption that there is little significant wit		
14	Current Expenses	$150,000,000	9%	0%		aren't aware of what those 'stable' rates of growth will be… The		
15								
16	Years out -->	0	1	2	3	4	5	6
17	Possible Revenues	$100. M	$125. M	$156.3 M	$195.3 M	$244.1 M	$305.2 M	$381.5 M
18	Possible Expenses	$150. M	$163.5 M	$178.2 M	$194.2 M	$211.7 M	$230.7 M	$251.5 M
19	Within-year breakeven (or better)?		FALSE	FALSE	TRUE	TRUE	TRUE	TRUE
20								
21	First year of within-year breakeven:		3					

Figure 8.14. Setup for estimates of return on investment and breakeven calculations.

statements, and, in this case, the use of a MATCH function to find the first year in which breakeven or better occurs (see cell E21). This result ("first year of within-year breakeven") could ostensibly be the key output calculation for a two-way Data Table (an example is provided in Figure 8.15; #N/A indicates that over the period examined, no breakeven year is identified).

The trends in the results appear to be fairly regular and internally consistent in Figure 8.15. Of course, if we change the levels of within-year growth variance to something other than insubstantial (to better reflect real-world scenarios), we are presented with the same problem we faced in Section 8.2.2: unclear joint effects. Next, we'll address this problem in a way that is distinct from the previous approach.

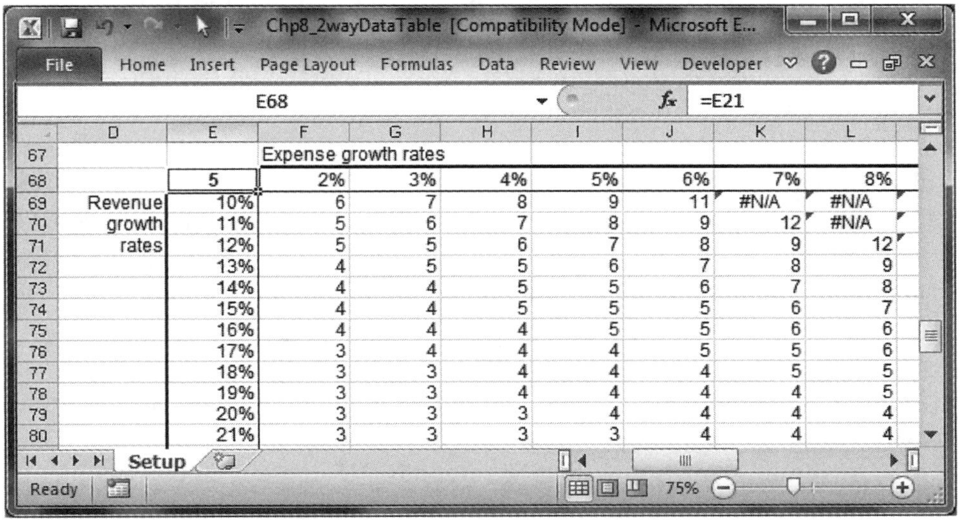

E68 =E21

	D	E	F	G	H	I	J	K	L
67			Expense growth rates						
68		5	2%	3%	4%	5%	6%	7%	8%
69	Revenue	10%	6	7	8	9	11	#N/A	#N/A
70	growth	11%	5	6	7	8	9	12	#N/A
71	rates	12%	5	5	6	7	8	9	12
72		13%	4	5	5	6	7	8	9
73		14%	4	4	5	5	6	7	8
74		15%	4	4	5	5	5	6	7
75		16%	4	4	4	5	5	6	6
76		17%	3	4	4	4	5	5	6
77		18%	3	3	4	4	4	5	5
78		19%	3	3	4	4	4	4	5
79		20%	3	3	3	4	4	4	4
80		21%	3	3	3	3	4	4	4

Figure 8.15. Data Table for combined expense and revenue growth rates without within-year variation.

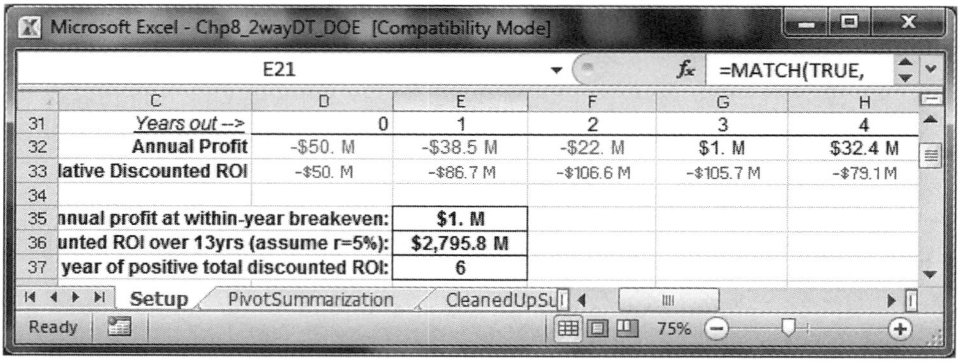

	C	D	E	F	G	H
31	Years out -->	0	1	2	3	4
32	Annual Profit	-$50. M	-$38.5 M	-$22. M	$1. M	$32.4 M
33	lative Discounted ROI	-$50. M	-$86.7 M	-$106.6 M	-$105.7 M	-$79.1 M
34						
35	nnual profit at within-year breakeven:		$1. M			
36	unted ROI over 13yrs (assume r=5%):		$2,795.8 M			
37	year of positive total discounted ROI:		6			

Figure 8.16. Additional calculations of interest as outputs in Data Table simulations.

8.2.4 Design-of-Experiment Approaches to Data Table Use

Let's say we'd like to avoid the iterative averaging method used in Section 8.2.2, but would nevertheless like to look at solid estimates of joint effects. Let's further say we'd like to look at multiple outputs generated simultaneously (as in Section 8.2.1) and consider more than two changing factors as inputs (akin to an *n*-way Data Table if such a thing existed). Doing all this with a single Data Table might seem daunting to those new to these methods, but a general approach to aid us does exist. It involves encoding combinations of multiple inputs into a single meta-input, using that meta-input as the lone Data Table source of input to a model, and disentangling the various input levels represented by that meta-input for use in the model calculation. The approach, borrowing from the research community, is referred to as the Design-of-Experiments (DOE) method to Data Table development.

Before we get into structuring a Data Table using the DOE approach, let's outline the other performance measure we might be interested in. Perhaps we'd like to know for each growth rate scenario: (1) what the year's profit will be if or when we actually "hit the black"; (2) what the discounted total ROI over thirteen years might be; and (3) the year in which a positive ROI is realized (if ever). These issues, along with the within-year breakeven year, would constitute four separate performance indicators (outputs).

Now, let's specifically spell out what types of average rate scenarios we're actually interested in getting simulated results for. Let's say we'll get sufficient appreciation for the joint impacts of expense growth and revenue growth rates, in the presence of within-year variation, if we examine five overall revenue growth percentage rates (10, 15, 20, 25, and 30 percent), jointly with four overall expense growth percentage rates (3, 5, 7, and 9 percent). This gives us a total of twenty (5×4) combinations to investigate. Figure 8.17 provides a summary of these factor-level combinations.

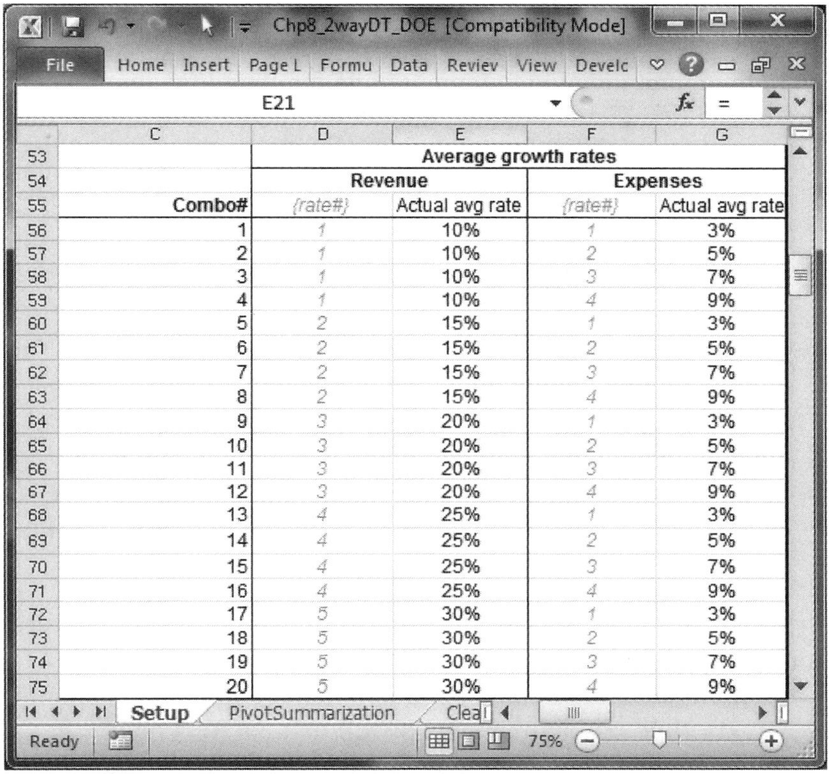

	Average growth rates			
	Revenue		Expenses	
Combo#	{rate#}	Actual avg rate	{rate#}	Actual avg rate
1	1	10%	1	3%
2	1	10%	2	5%
3	1	10%	3	7%
4	1	10%	4	9%
5	2	15%	1	3%
6	2	15%	2	5%
7	2	15%	3	7%
8	2	15%	4	9%
9	3	20%	1	3%
10	3	20%	2	5%
11	3	20%	3	7%
12	3	20%	4	9%
13	4	25%	1	3%
14	4	25%	2	5%
15	4	25%	3	7%
16	4	25%	4	9%
17	5	30%	1	3%
18	5	30%	2	5%
19	5	30%	3	7%
20	5	30%	4	9%

Figure 8.17. Design of Experiment (DOE) to be executed by a Data Table simulation approach.

Essentially, this is the experimental design we would like a Data Table (of some kind) to evaluate multiple times across the various outputs of interest.

Notice that in this table (also part of Chp8_DOE) I'm making ample use of reference numbers to help give a label to each of the combinations (which will make the development of the new EVERYTHING Data Table a whole lot easier, not to mention simplifying any future changes in the average rates I've chosen to study).

Now, consider the critical step that emphasizes why I've put that DOE table together to begin with. Instead of directly specifying the growth rates that are needed in the calculations of the table, I'm going to enter into the original calculation cells, where overall revenue and expense growth rate averages exist, a couple of VLOOKUP functions that figure out "what rates to calculate with" based on the DOE combination being examined. For example, let's store some combination number (1–20 as in Figure 8.16) in cell I69 of our sheet. In order to translate that combination number into the revenue growth rate average it represents, I could enter "=VLOOKUP(I69,C56:G75,3,0)" into cell E13 (where the model expects

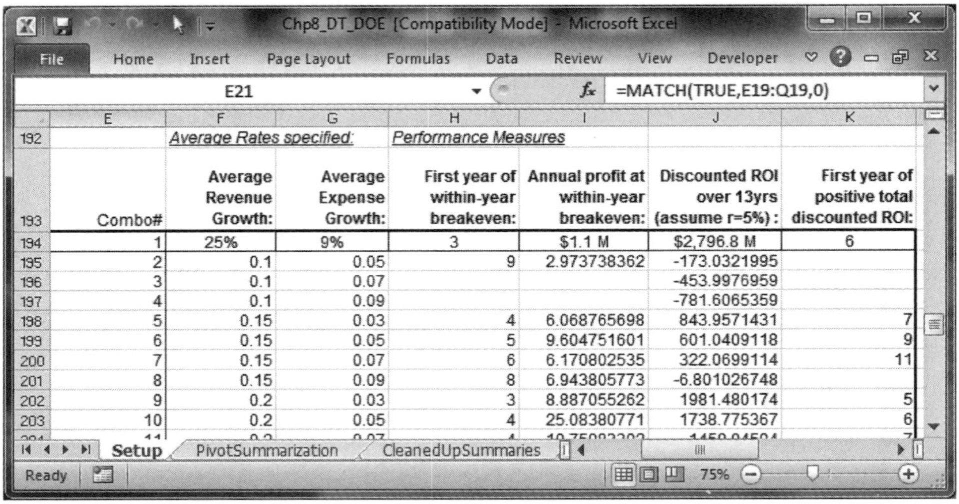

	E	F	G	H	I	J	K
192		Average Rates specified:		Performance Measures			
193	Combo#	Average Revenue Growth:	Average Expense Growth:	First year of within-year breakeven:	Annual profit at within-year breakeven:	Discounted ROI over 13yrs (assume r=5%) :	First year of positive total discounted ROI:
194	1	25%	9%	3	$1.1 M	$2,796.8 M	6
195	2	0.1	0.05	9	2.973738362	-173.0321995	
196	3	0.1	0.07			-453.9976959	
197	4	0.1	0.09			-781.6065359	
198	5	0.15	0.03	4	6.068765698	843.9571431	7
199	6	0.15	0.05	5	9.604751601	601.0409118	9
200	7	0.15	0.07	6	6.170802535	322.0699114	11
201	8	0.15	0.09	8	6.943805773	-6.801026748	
202	9	0.2	0.03	3	8.887055262	1981.480174	5
203	10	0.2	0.05	4	25.08380771	1738.775367	6

Figure 8.18. DOE applied to generate multiple input and multiple output responses.

to see expense growth rate averages). This returns a value of 25 percent to that cell if a combo number of 13, 14, 15, or 16 is being examined (again see Figure 8.16). A similar tactic is used in cell E14 for the expense growth rate average. Every time a new number between 1 and 20 is placed in cell I69, these numbers can change. This combination number, impacting multiple inputs simultaneously, is exactly the kind of thing we want our Data Table to be feeding to the spreadsheet through its left-most column of inputs. In fact, we'll want to include the numbers 1 through 20 several times in order to avoid the $N = 1$ errors from before, so we can ultimately develop some solid estimates that are not driven by outliers.

At this point, we can use a Data Table structure for multiple outputs, except that instead of the left column numbers serving solely as labels, they're representing multiple combined inputs. I've included the decoded inputs as "outcomes" in the Data Table depicted in Figure 8.18 because they will be useful in subsequent data summaries. Ratcheting up the within-year variation, you might now be able to see results similar to those (by general nature, not precise numbers) presented in Data Table interior in Figure 8.18.

Note that the table appears to be incomplete here – this is because I've started to clean it up a bit, replacing things like "#N/A" with "blanks." This is a useful step for the more advanced cleanup I'm about to do using a tool we've seen before: a PivotTable (see Figure 8.19 and the PivotSummarization sheet in the Ch8_DT_DOE workbook). In such a PivotTable, the multiple simulated runs of each combination can be averaged and the standard deviation calculated for each of the performance measures. These summaries can be organized by the two factors the DOE combination numbers

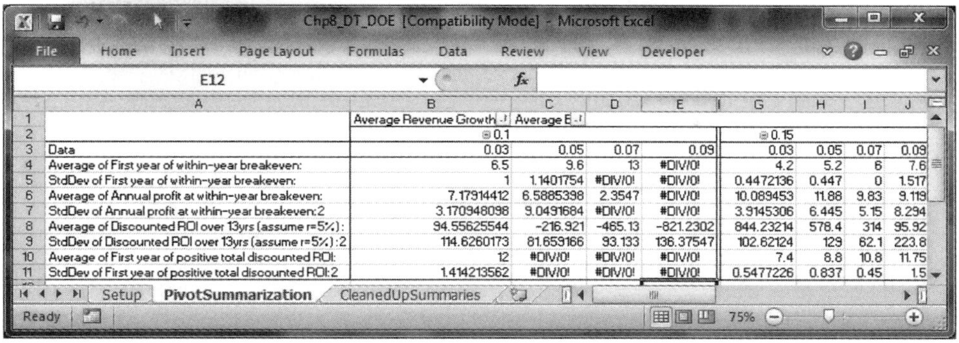

Figure 8.19. Using a PivotTable to summarize a complex Data Table.

were depicting only because they were also included as outputs in the Data Table structure.

Of course, we can develop still cleaner versions of the PivotTable Summaries to make what we want to demonstrate more transparent to another user. For example, we could create a mirror of the pivot summary on a separate sheet and then modify the formatting (see Figure 8.20 and the CleanedUpSummaries sheet in the Ch8_DT_DOE workbook).

8.3 Assessing System Simulations

Although Data Tables can be extremely useful in providing quick results for a variety of simulated variants, they can be hard to apply (on their own) to cases where iterations of calculations need to be conducted. In such cases, more sophisticated approaches to assessment must be used.

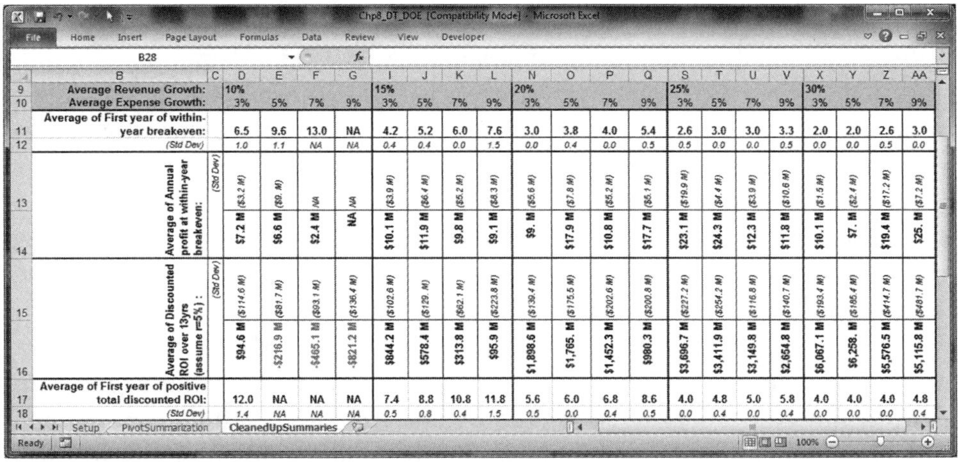

Figure 8.20. Results cleaned for presentation purposes and interpretation.

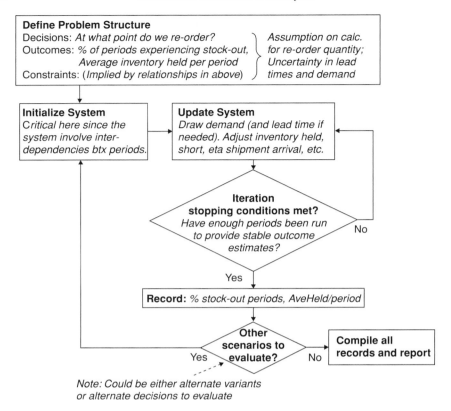

Figure 8.21. Design Structure of the Inventory System Simulation.

As an illustration of the need for iterative calculation that builds on established values, consider another decision policy that Lobo's needs to make: inventory reordering. Inventory policies critically impact the availability of certain stocked items (liquor and dry goods, in particular), but are also highly dependent on uncertain issues such as periodic demand and fulfillment lead times. For some complex policies, or those subject to complex forms of uncertainty, the use of system simulations may be the only mechanism for assessing their overall effectiveness.

The flowchart shown in Figure 8.21 presents a fairly simplified inventory system that nevertheless is sufficiently complex to warrant a demonstration of the shortcomings of Data Tables and the value of alternate approaches to assessment.

The primary decision variable in this case is the reorder point, or the specific level of current inventory that triggers a call to our suppliers for a shipment of new supply. Ostensibly, the quantity of the resulting new order is also a policy decision but one that we'll put aside for now in the interest of simplicity. For now, we'll assume that the size of each reorder is designed

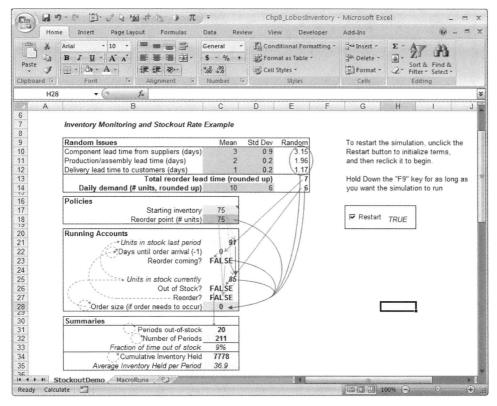

Figure 8.22. Example of the implemented system simulation.

to cover average expected demand over average expected lead times, and it will recuperate the deficit between reorder point and most recent supply level (that is, the one that triggered the reorder). This can all be built formulaically into the spreadsheet.

As in the simulated variants example, we could have multiple outcome measures worth noting. One would certainly be the average amount of inventory held per period. This outcome would be implicitly traded-off against some measure of stock-out costs and would become the basis for decision making (policy selection). Another outcome measure might be the percentage of periods during which we could anticipate experience stock-out conditions.

A related valuable outcome might be the average level of inventory short, either for the timeline as a whole or specific to those stock-out periods. We'll keep things simple here and just focus on the first two of these – percentage of periods experiencing stock-outs and average per-period inventory holdings. The workbook Chp8_LobosInventory provides an example of how this design might be implemented (see Figure 8.22).

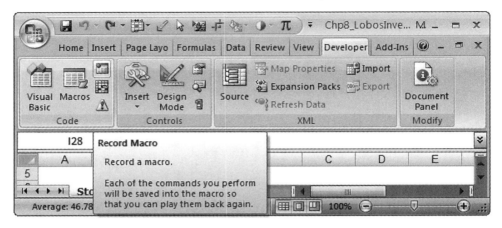

Figure 8.23. Accessing macro recording capabilities in Excel.

As mentioned in previous chapters, F9 provides a mechanism for iteration, although, admittedly, F9 only progresses the simulation through a single iteration of the simulation. But realistically, overall summaries of the effectiveness of any policy need a much larger set of iterations for true representation. Furthermore, decision makers are likely to be interested in the comparison of multiple policies. What are the implications of all this?

Let's think about it. Say we want to slightly change the policy under consideration so that the reorder point is 75 units. To record the summary results for this policy we would have to first change the policy we wanted to evaluate by typing in 75 for the reorder point value. Then, we would have to carry out the following steps, at minimum:

1) Reset the spreadsheet's summaries (type False and True for Reset).
2) Press F9 as many times as you think is necessary; some logical stopping rule could be applied here.
3) Pick a clear spot in the workbook to save these summaries.
4) Copy and "paste-special" the values of those summaries.

We could do all these steps manually, but that would add up to a lot of work if we want to generate and store summary measures for many different management policies. We can use the Macro function to record a set of actions so that we could get Excel to repeat that same set of actions on command (and in one click). Macro functionality is found under the Developer tab, as seen in Figure 8.23.

For now, we'll start with a demonstration of one of the simplest forms of macro recording – simulation data recordkeeping. To keep things organized, we'll store this data in an additional sheet called MacroRuns. I've set up a duplication of some of the data relevant to our assessment of this system in another area (cells K32:K35) of the main worksheet to make all subsequent

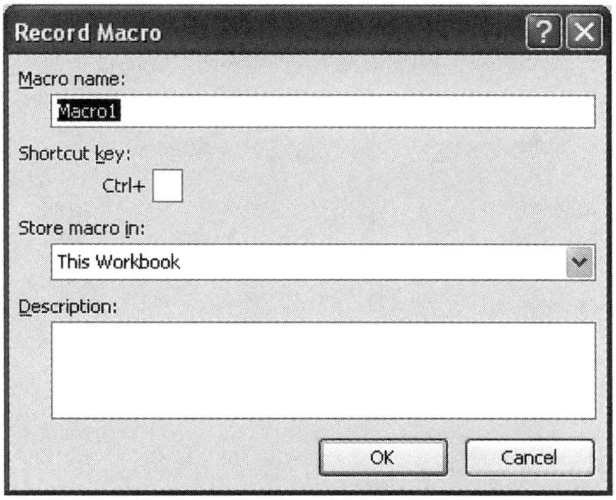

Figure 8.24. Initial specification interface presented for macro recording.

copying easier. Select the Record Macro option in the Developer tab to open the Record Macro dialog box, as shown in Figure 8.24.

In this dialog box, we can name our macro, describe it in depth, and even create a shortcut key for later execution. The default name Macro1 has been selected by the system. If we don't want to specify any information of our own, we can simply click OK and the macro will start recording the actions we take (within certain limitations, which we'll discuss in more depth in Chapter 11).

The following are the actions that the macro will record:

1) Again, as stated, I've got to reinitialize this system simulation to get clean results, so I'm going to reset the spreadsheet's summaries by typing "False" and return, then "True" and return for the Reset value in H18. For now, we'll just type these things in, rather than use the check-box shortcut I've included (Excel circa June 2007 doesn't record actions on an object, which is a devolution from the Excel 2003 version).

2) To generate the kinds of summary outcomes I want, I'll hold down F9 until I cover 200 periods worth of iterations. This is tedious, but further on we'll talk about better ways to get this done. I've already picked a clear spot in my workbook to save those summaries (the MacroRuns worksheet), and I've consolidated the critical system parameters and outcomes I want to build my record from (cells K32:K35 on the main sheet). So, at this point, I can simply copy those cells, go to the MacroRuns spreadsheet (for instance, cell B2) and right click to perform a "paste-special operation." Specifically, I don't want to paste formulas or references. Instead, I want to paste fixed "values." Although they are organized vertically in the main sheet, I'd like to paste them horizontally in the MacroRuns sheet, so I'll be selecting both the "values" and "transpose" options in my paste (Figures 8.25 and 8.26).

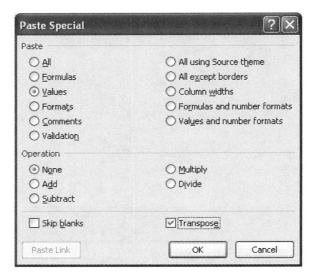

Figure 8.25. Using the Paste Special option during a simple macro recording.

And that's it. Now, I'm going to hit the Stop Recording button (small square at the bottom of the screen). The square icon shown in Figure 8.27 will change at this point to represent the record button. These buttons are usually more convenient than the menu-driven system.

The macro is now saved and available for future use. There are several ways to activate a recorded macro, and the first is menu driven. Select the Macros option on the Developer tab to open the Macro dialog box. Choose the macro you want (in this case, Macro1) and then click Run (Figure 8.28). Another way to open and run a macro is through the use of the shortcut key that you specified when you created the macro.

There is also an object-based approach available for any developed macro called Make a Button. The easiest way to use this is to draw your own button: Choose Insert Shapes to open the Shapes drop-down menu (see Figure 8.29). For any object, such as a drawn circle or an inserted .jpg, right-click on that object to see a number of property options including Assign Macro (shown

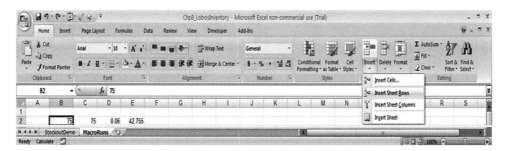

Figure 8.26. Inserting rows during a simple macro recording.

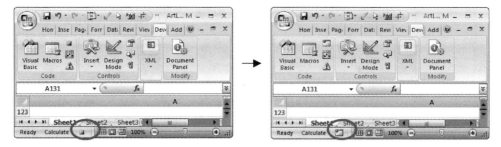

Figure 8.27. Quick stop to a macro recording.

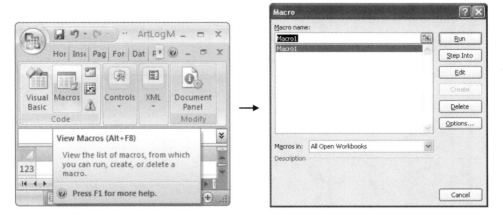

Figure 8.28. Menu-driven activation of a macro.

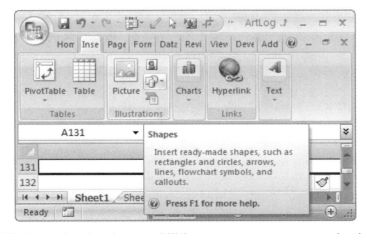

Figure 8.29. Accessing drawing capabilities to generate a macro activation button.

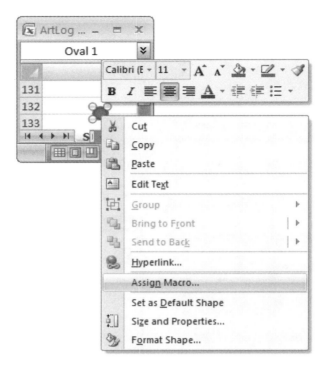

Figure 8.30. Assigning a macro to a drawn button.

in Figure 8.30). Selecting that option then allows you to specify what macro will be associated with that object.

After a macro is assigned, place the cursor over the object to change the cursor icon from that of an arrow to that of a pointing finger (indicating that the object can now be clicked to run the assigned macro). The use of text to add immediate clarity regarding the role of that new button adds to its usefulness as an intuitive and readily accessed means of executing macros (for you, as well as others using your workbook). And there's no limit to the number of macros and buttons you can place within a workbook.

As we will discover in Chapter 13, there is a range of related button approaches to interfacing with macros, although having introduced three different approaches, it's worth emphasizing that any one of these should work to replicate the system simulation recording procedure that we set out to perform (provided we are recording our actions correctly). The macro currently recorded in the Chp8_LobosInventory workbook works as expected.

We could run this for any number of scenarios to try to assess which one works best for our interests; however, if we wanted to be still more sophisticated in our simulation development, we could (if we knew how) consider making this whole process even more automated not just by recording our actions in a macro, but also by editing the recorded actions. That's going to require some knowledge of how to access how Excel recorded those actions in the first place (that is, in VisualBasic code), and this will be the focus of discussion in Chapter 11.

8.4 An Introduction to Stochastic System Structures

As valuable as the approaches to simulation presented thus far may seem, it is worth noting that most real-world systems are more complex with uncertainty built into not only the characteristics of events (for example, how many customers arrive) but also whether or not certain subsequent events take place (for example, upon arrival which customers will request comparable services, which will require payment by credit, and how many who are paying by credit will want to split the bill). Of course, all of this is important to those trying to manage the types and amounts of resources needed to fill all these different needs at any given point in time.

Stochastic is a key term used to describe the complexity associated with these real-world systems in which uncertain events are followed by still other uncertain events. Stochastic processes can be thought of as a series of specific steps, stages, or states where the transition from one step to another is characterized by some amount of uncertainty. For example, although loan processing at a bank may involve a preestablished series of steps, and although one might be able to describe the progress through this process by a specific and typical ordering of these steps, mistakes – or simply variations – in requirements may require that certain steps be repeated before the process is successfully completed. Sometimes, these alternative sequences through the process cannot be predetermined prior to entry into the processes and are subject to issues that are uncertain or only made apparent during a process. This is a common representation of the probabilistic tendency for such sequence variation often adopted by analysts and is referred to as a transition matrix.

In a slightly simpler process example, let's consider a three-state process. Specifically, assume we have a prototype development process that can be meaningfully broken into three steps. At each step, a different worker takes possession of the work, and at each step, a decision is made whether to advance the prototype for further development and testing or to send it back to a previous stage of consideration and rework.

The workbook Chp8_TransitionMatrices depicts how the information relevant to capturing the uncertain and interdependent nature of this system is used. Specifically, the boxed area of cells labeled Transition Matrix provides a set of probabilities that describes how likely it is for a job in one state (1, 2, or 3) to transition (move) into another state. In this table, the probability

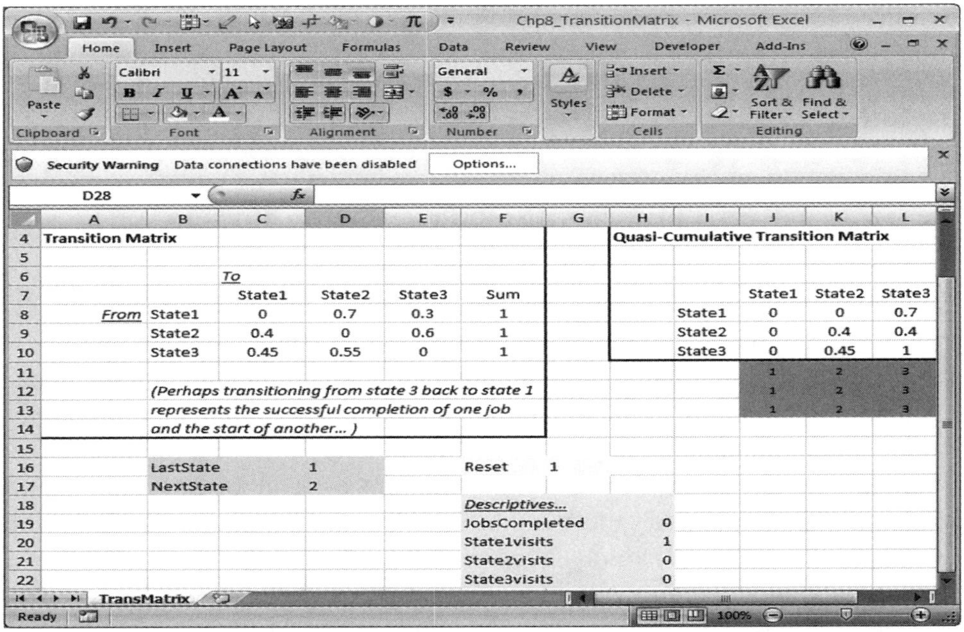

Figure 8.31. Example of transition matrix as a possible component of a system simulation.

of transitioning from State 1 into State 2 is 0.7, or 70 percent. Because any job in State 1 must go somewhere, the sum of transition probabilities in each row should sum up to 1, as demonstrated in the column labeled Sum shown in Figure 8.31.

In the adjacent table labeled Quasi-Cumulative Transition Matrix, I've used some simple addition to help indicate probability thresholds, which are useful in getting a random transition between discrete states to actually work. It's a bit sloppier than necessary, but it's fairly transparent for the purpose of introducing how these random transitions might be generated. Specifically, I've developed this adjacent table with the sole intention of using it with the conveniently provided HLOOKUP function. As discussed in Chapter 2, HLOOKUP can be used to search for a specific term in the top row of a table and return information from a lower row of the same column in which the entry was found. However, provided that entries in that top row are sorted, VLOOKUP can also conduct a search for the last closest entry that doesn't exceed what's being looked for (for example, 3 if 3.14 is being looked for in a sorted array of integers, or perhaps Michael in a sorted list of first names). To ensure such a search takes place, simply make sure that the last term in the HLOOKUP is a 1 (for example, HLOOKUP(RAND(),J8:L13,3,1) to indicate a sorted search).

In this case, where the next state is in part determined by a random decimal ranging from 0 to 1, the use of HLOOKUP with a table that contains both these quasi-cumulative probabilities and some indication of the associated next state works well, provided we are able to consistently indicate where those next-state references are. This consistency is provided by the deliberate indication of state references (1, 2, 3) in the three rows (rows 11–13) below each of the quasi-cumulative probability rows (rows 8–10). Think of rows 8 through 13 as constituting the template from which appropriate subtables for lookup will be formed. The use of the OFFSET function allows us to specify which subtable should be focused on, and therefore which starting row to use in a lookup.

As an example, if a job is currently in State 3, we would use an OFFSET function to shift our focus from the subtable J8:L11 to J10:L13 (that is, offsetting our focus by two rows from the start of the template table to make sure the quasi-cumulative probabilities are in the top row of the subtable considered).

We could then use the HLOOKUP function on that OFFSET subtable and the RAND() function to randomly determine which state to transition to after State 3. If the random value searched for is 0.21, based on the numbers in this case, HLOOKUP will see the first value in the offset subtable (0.0) as adequate but will view the second value (0.45) as excessive; therefore, looking three rows below the last adequate value will return a 1. Similarly, in this case, a random value of 0.48 would return a 2. In this way, as used in the sample spreadsheet, the transition matrix description of a 45 percent chance of 3 to 1, and 55 percent chance of 3 to 2, is fully captured. This is a nice example of the compound use of multiple functions in Excel, and although it's effective and fairly straightforward, it's not the most elegant.

As a final note, there's nothing stopping us from adding in complexity that accounts for unique costs (and variation in costs) for being in each state, or for having a single job stay in progress for some excessive total amount of state visits. These structures are often commonplace in complex system simulations that evolve over time. The same macro-based approaches to iteration and recordkeeping apply with simulations where such stochastic processes are embedded.

Supplement: Simulation Control Made Friendly

Excel provides two sets of mechanisms by which to develop visually appealing and user-friendly interfaces. One set is referred to as ActiveX controls; the other is referred to as Form controls. Often, you can get the same task accomplished with both. These controls allow developers to add elements

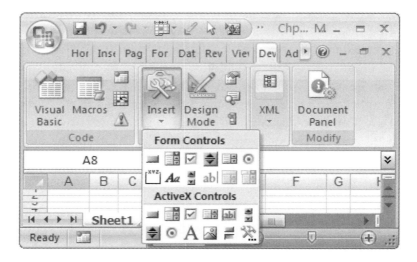

Figure 8.32. Controls available through the Excel menu interface.

such as check boxes, option buttons, and drop-down menus to their spreadsheet as alternatives to changing values in cells. Form controls often provide a simpler interface for developers, but I find that ActiveX controls ultimately provide more versatility and a greater range of options for development. We'll stick to the ActiveX controls for this discussion (functioning examples found in Chp8_SampleControls), starting with the basic text box.

Text boxes duplicate the contents of any individual cell in a workbook, but because it's an object unto itself, it can be positioned anywhere in a workbook. This can be valuable because although cells in complex decision-support environments may be difficult to relocate meaningfully (without messing up other parts of the design), the locations of these text boxes has no impact on what's going on behind the scenes. You could even group the text box with other objects, such as graphs, so that when you move a set of objects in your spreadsheet, the text box moves along with that group. To create a new text box (or any other control for that matter), under the Developer tab, select Insert from the Developer tab, as shown in Figure 8.32.

Click the Text Box icon in the toolbox to generate a new text box at any point in the spreadsheet. When created, you will automatically enter Design Mode where you have a wide range of control properties that you can edit. Right-click on the new box and select Properties to open the Properties dialog box, shown in Figure 8.33.

The Linked Cell property is the most important of your new control properties. This indicates the value shared by both the text box (in this case) and a particular reference cell on the spreadsheet (that is, if the linked cell is A1, whatever value A1 takes on will show up in the text box). Keep in mind this

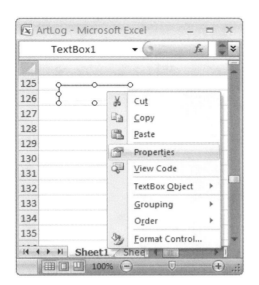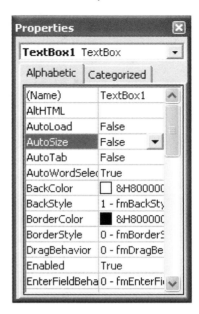

Figure 8.33. Modifying the properties of a text box ActiveX control.

important point: Any formatting in the linked cell will not transfer to the text box; only the value contained.

Consider the example of setting the value in cell E9 to =NOW() – that is, the current date and time signature – and formatting that cell to show hours:minutes:seconds. Linking a new text box to that cell will copy the value of that date and time signature to the text box. In Excel, this value is a numeric string that, although useful from a system perspective, doesn't mean much to a typical user. In the case of 11:56:42 on January 4, 2006, the string is 38721.49771 (see Figure 8.34). Again, the same value is contained in both the cell and the text box and the only difference is in the format by which the value is presented.

On the other hand, if we completely convert the date and time signature to a string of characters (no longer a numeric value) whose construction is

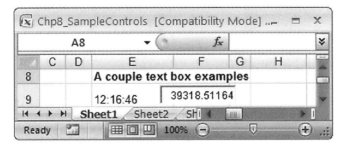

Figure 8.34. Numerical value translation of a date entry by a text box.

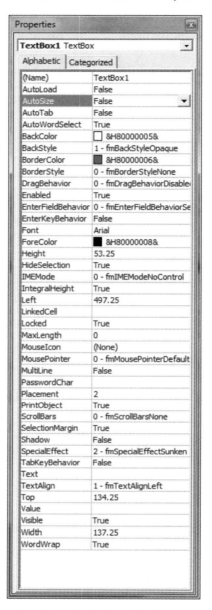

Figure 8.35. Specified text depiction of a date entry by a text box.

based on a certain formatting rule (for example, using the TEXT function, "=TEXT(NOW(),hh:mm:ss)", the text within both the cell and the text box should be consistent. They both contain the same text, as shown in Figure 8.35. Incidentally, cell linkage with controls works in both directions. If you change the content of that cell in the spreadsheet, that change will appear in the text box. If you type different content into the text box, that cell will take on that value. Keep in mind, however, that this will also erase any formulae that might have been in the cell previously, if that's the nature of how the cell was used.

It is also worth noting the variety of other properties that you could use in configuring your text box, including (refer back to Figure 8.33):

Background and font color and types
If you want the control to take on a three-dimensional appearance
What aspect the cursor takes on when it runs over the control
Whether the text within the box should wrap
Whether scrolling the text content is available for the box

As with cells and other objects, you can also change the label of the control for more intuitive reference. In this example, call it CurrentTime rather that TextBox1.

Having a basic familiarity with TextBox creation, we can now discuss other controls that can come in handy when interfacing in Excel. Buttons (under the rubric of controls) are really no more than that – imagine that you can click to start an existing automated set of events. You can get the same functionality from any object to which you assign a macro in Excel.

Buttons created through the Controls menu just give you the convenience of something that already looks like a button that should be clicked (something you might have to work with to create an aesthetic image using the standard drawing tools).

Check boxes, which you've already seen applied in previous examples, are also a nice convenience control that allows users to toggle between two settings (for example, 1,0; Yes, No; On, Off; Restart, Stop). As with text boxes, a number of the same standard control properties can be modified (for example, colors and labels). One unique difference is that check boxes also allow you to add fixed text labels that accompany them on a page, such as Restart or StandardCheckBox.

Another unique feature of check boxes is the ability to use them in a *triple state*. In this case, each click on the box will move the user through the states of True, False, and #N/A (other). This could be useful if, for example, you had three alternative settings that you would like to make available through this kind of object-oriented interface (Figure 8.36).

Option, or radio, buttons add an additional level of complexity that is not present with check boxes. Whereas check boxes typically react independently of one another, radio buttons (see Figure 8.37) are designed to be used as one of a set; in other words, each radio button is used to represent specific alternatives, only one of which may be active or relevant at a specific time. An example would be the selection of a single candidate for a specific position during voting, the selection of a specific shipping option for an

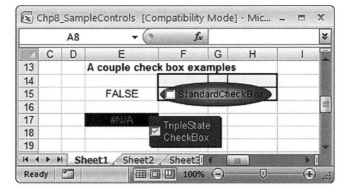

Figure 8.36. Examples of check boxes active in a spreadsheet.

order, or the selection of a specific accounting classification for filing an item on an expense report.

A critical property is the group name. The group name represents the set of alternative radio buttons that each individual button works in conjunction with. By default, new radio buttons created on a worksheet will receive the name of that worksheet as their group name. But similar to all other properties, you can (and usually should) change this. For example, for one set of buttons that represent interchangeable options, you might use the group name Radios1; for another set of buttons that are not dependent on the choice made in the first set, you might use the label Radios2. Specifying different groups for independent sets of radio buttons will ensure that they don't interfere with one another's functionality.

Another point to note here is that the various buttons in a group should be assigned to their own individual cells to avoid confusion. Therefore, for a set of three radio buttons, three cells in a spreadsheet should be used to capture the state of the buttons (such as, the second button was clicked and the others were not). IF statements are typically used to convert

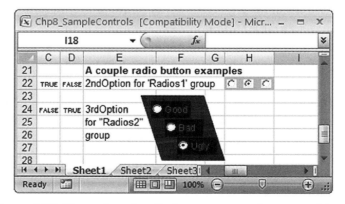

Figure 8.37. Examples of radio-button groups in a spreadsheet.

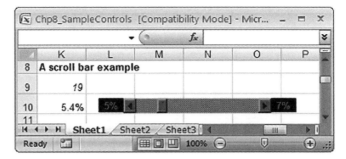

Figure 8.38. Example of the scroll bar in a spreadsheet.

this information into a single result: for example, =IF(B24,"1stOption",IF (C24,"2ndOption","3rdOption")).

Scroll bars, as shown in Figure 8.38, provide mechanisms by which to select a continuous range of values bound by upper and lower limits (rather than by a discrete set of options described by check boxes and radio buttons). For example, you might want to allow a user to specify an interest rate between 5 and 7 percent, a minimum average labor force IQ between 900 and 1,100 (e.g., on the SAT), or a maximal budgetary allowance between $10,000 and $35,000. A scroll bar might be a nice choice for an interface on such a decision.

However, Excel currently has some annoying limitations. For example, you can specify upper and lower bounds but they have to be integers. In fact, all values represented by the scroll bar have to be integers. If you specify a range between zero and one hundred and you don't mind the fairly simple task of rescaling to fit the range you are interested in (for example, 5 to 7 percent), this isn't really an issue. It's just annoying that this limitation is something you need to work around.

Drop-down menus are another nice interface control for situations in which a wide range of options might exist (for example, list boxes or combo boxes). One of the additional properties of these controls requires the specification of a list of alternative options, which can be presented as a sequence of cells in a column of a worksheet as shown in Figure 8.28. A combo box with such a reference list specification provides a compact form that can be expanded by the user for item-selection purposes. An alternative to adding a list box embedded control is to use the Data Validation resource under Data>DataTools. This provides some listing options that are limited but fairly easy to implement and modify. Essentially, it allows you to restrict the content of a cell to match only one of the elements in a range on that same sheet. However, we'll find that mastering the use of similar noncell structures will be more effective and come in much more handy when developing more sophisticated user interfaces (Chapter 13).

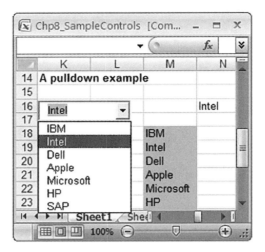

Figure 8.39. Example of a drop-down menu in a spreadsheet.

PRACTICE PROBLEMS

Practice 8.1

Using the approach demonstrated in Section 8.3, build a report that shows not only the average, but also the best (MIN) and worst (MAX) cases for the cost (holding) and stock-out rates (as before, across 200 iterations or trials). Run this three times for each of eleven reorder point policies ranging from sixty to seventy. The end result should be a table with eleven records, each describing the average, best, and worst cases of cost and stock-out rates. Comment on how average performance might not be completely informative with regard to "best policy" selection.

Practice 8.2

Reconsider the Lobo's Reservations example simulation from the previous practice section. We selected random numbers based on a specific level of variation, and we limited ourselves to a few specifically structured scenarios. But we might want to find out how different the performance of this system might be given alternative overbooking charges and alternative levels of variation (more or less) in customer dollar contributions.

Use three option buttons to depict different possible levels of variation characteristic of the random numbers involved in the simulation (with standard deviations of 10, 15, and 20). Use drop-down menus to allow individuals to choose among the application of three distinct overbooking charges ($220, $250, and $280). Using a report format similar to that of the previous practice problem, summarize the results of these $3 \times 3 = 9$ possible combinations. To simplify the work, limit your consideration to the case in which twenty-eight reservations are made.

9

Simulation Search, Optimization, and Reporting

A natural extension of a discussion of simulation, given our existing understanding of optimization, is how the two methods can be used together. The basic question behind simulation optimization is:

What decision (if any) tends to provide relatively superior results regardless of the uncertainty associated with the real-world problems they are designed to resolve?

Simulation provides the means by which to incorporate uncertainty into the evaluation of a specific decision or a predetermined handful of such decisions; however, this question implies a much greater scope. It suggests a formal search for the best decision across a vast range of possible alternative decisions. For simulated variants, the term *best* takes into account not just the average or expected value of parameters describing the setting (as would be common in discrete optimization), but also the potentially extreme performance of outliers, be that good or bad. For system simulations, the best would necessarily need to further relate to performance as the result of a sequence of events where the interplay of initial guiding decisions, complicated by uncertainty, might be extremely difficult to assess without sufficient simulation runs. The follow-up question then is:

How can we integrate the techniques associated with simulation and optimization into a single solid mechanism for meaningful decision support?

Here again, we gain from the robustness of Excel and the availability of additional applications that capitalize on Excel's computational strengths. Specifically, we can return to a more in-depth and nuanced discussion of the various features of RISKOptimizer that, along with Excel, make all of this possible. Although other packages exist that might provide similar simulation optimization capabilities, we'll focus on RISKOptimizer, given our familiarity with its usefulness in assisting in difficult optimization problems (see Chapter 7).

9.1 Basic Simulation Optimization Capabilities

There are a number of characteristics of simulation optimization procedures that are available to users of RISKOptimizer. In particular, two are worth mentioning here in detail (others have been described previously in the Chapter 7 Supplement).

9.1.1 Optimization Stopping Conditions

As suggested in Chapter 7, RISKOptimizer's search for an ideal solution (a decision policy that meets the objective subject to any relevant constraints) can be terminated manually by clicking the Stop button at any point during evaluation. However, users are also given the opportunity to pre-specify under what conditions the application can stop its search: for example, if an individual doesn't have the time to continue to monitor progress and would at the same time like to free up system resources for doing other work on their computer when ideal solutions are discovered. This automatic termination is made possible through a variety of tactics that are available through RISKOptimizer.

These can be found under Options when the RISKOptimizer interface is being used to specify the particulars of an optimization procedure. The RISKOptimizer Options dialog box is shown in Figure 9.1.

As shown in Figure 9.1, an optimization search can stop after a given set of decision policies have been examined. In Figure 9.1, if the analyst felt that the assessment of fifty alternate solutions (a fairly small number in actuality) was sufficient to draw conclusions, they might click the box marked Simulations = 50 or change the amount to a more appropriate number. Note that the term *Simulations* in this dialog box is used somewhat misleadingly to represent the "number of alternative solutions" considered in the simulation optimization.

If an analyst wanted the search to stop after two minutes, she could specify that under Minutes. Other stopping conditions include other measures of finality in a search that might otherwise continue for a very long period of time. Change in Last allows the search to terminate when the changes in the performance of subsequent solutions considered becomes less than practically significant (in the current example, if the average performance of the last one hundred decision policies doesn't differ by more than 0.01 percent among those solutions that are valid, or, in other words, meet all required constraints). The Formula is True option provides a mechanism through which the user can reference any customized calculation aimed at assessing the convergence of the search upon a desired solution. This may

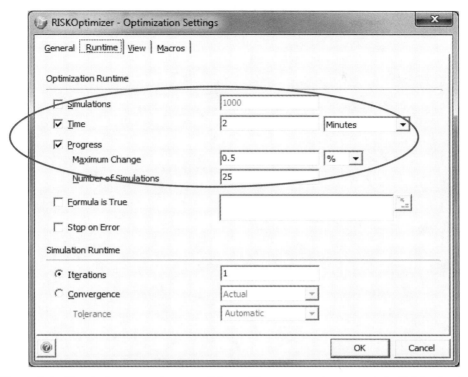

Figure 9.1. Simulation stopping conditions: How many times each individual solution is examined.

be used much like a goal seek option in Excel, or may be more nuanced to the needs of the analyst.

It is also worth noting that users need not rely on any one of these stopping conditions alone and can have as many simultaneously active as they want. For example, the analyst might want to make sure that the simulation search stops at the ten-minute mark or before, if little practical change has taken place in the previously assessed one hundred solutions. The check box nature of the interface allows for multiple stopping conditions to be applied simultaneously toward this end.

9.1.2 Simulation Stopping Conditions

Recall from Chapter 7 (where we first introduced RISKOptimizer) that we had specified a single iteration to be run for each solution considered (see Figure 9.2). This, of course, made a great deal of sense because there was no uncertainty built directly into our optimization models at the time.

However, in the case of simulations, the benefit of generating a wide range of simulated variants as part of the complete assessment of potential policies is clear. Any one random number pull can provide a misleading picture of

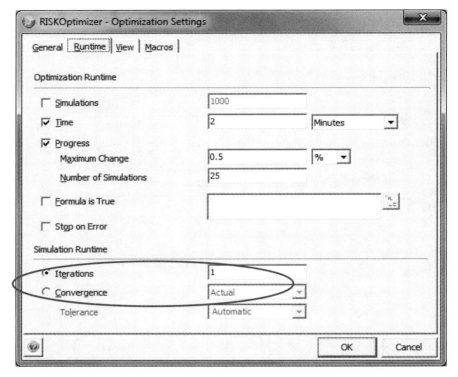

Figure 9.2. Optimization stopping conditions: How long the search is conducted for alternate solutions.

the effectiveness of a policy, particularly in the case of simulated variants where single-period performance can be easily impacted by an unusual random draw. Therefore, it is useful to be able to require RISKOptimizer to consider a set of possible outcomes in its assessments and overall search for optimal solutions. In the case of simulated variants, increasing the number of iterations specified provides exactly this kind of capability.

In the case of system simulations, the use of iterations needs to be thought out much more carefully, as will be discussed further on in this chapter. Nevertheless, specification of multiple iterations can be useful for system evaluation as well.

As a side note on the use of multiple iterations for evaluating policy performance that includes uncertainty, one convenient mechanism to ensure policy comparability across even a small set of iterations is that of the Random Number Seed field (also found in the RISKOptimizer dialog box). An analyst can specify that the same set of random numbers is ostensibly drawn in evaluating each new policy decision under consideration during the search (see Figure 9.3).

By specifying the Use Same Seed Each Sim check box, the analyst can be better assured that RISKOptimizer will be making apples-to-apples comparisons with regard to the conditions under which each possible policy solution

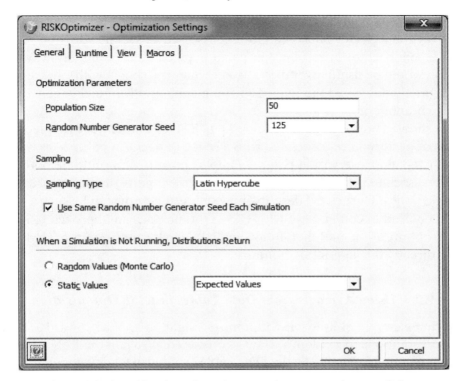

Figure 9.3. Specification of random number generation conditions.

is being judged. Typically, this is a default setting, but it's one worth paying attention to, particularly when a relatively small set of random number draws are being specified during solution assessments.

Alternatives to specifying a discrete number of iterations for the evaluation of each policy considered (for example, generate one hundred possible outcomes associated with each decision considered) include the Stop on Actual Convergence and Stop on Projected Convergence options. In cases where you might not know how many iterations to run to get a stable characterization (average) of performance, you can actually let RISKOptimizer try to figure it out on its own. This takes a little control out of the hands of the analyst, but it can be helpful if the number of iterations needed to assess certain policies is appreciable greater (and unknown) relative to some more simplistic policies.

9.2 Optimization of Simulated Variants

For simulated variants, iterations relate to new random number draws that, in turn, provide alternative performance results for a specific decision. This is valuable particularly in cases where average performance may not be sufficiently informative for decision comparisons (that is, high average performance may also equate to high variance and therefore high risk), or when average performance cannot be assessed based the distribution or interdependence of uncertainty in performance (which is largely why simulation would be useful over discrete assessments to begin with). In Chapter 8, we briefly described the Data Table, a mechanism for quickly generating a large number of iterations.

We showed how we could develop Data Tables that either provided estimates of performance associated with a range of decision policies, as well as (in our second Reservation policy example) how to view multiple potential results associated with multiple related yet distinct performance measures of a single policy. Here, we'll describe how the results provided by such a table could be used in conjunction with RISKOptimizer as an approach to simulation optimization, and then follow up with an alternative approach driven more directly through RISKOptimizer.

9.2.1 *Using Averages from Data Tables in RISKOptimization*

As a first example of how RISKOptimizer might be applied toward seeking out best solutions to random variants, consider once again the Lobos Reservations example, specifically the DataTable2 spreadsheet developed for that problem. In that second Data Table, performance is tabulated for a single overbooking policy in terms of both earned direct profit and implied costs of ill-will from overbooking. These are broken out and summarized in Data Table form for one hundred random scenarios. If we were interested in finding only a policy to maximize expected profit, subject to a service constraint (on average, only overbooking at most by one table 80 percent of the time and incurring an average overbooking cost of $400 maximum), we might specify the optimization search in RISKOptimizer as shown in Figure 9.4.

Under Options in RISKOptimizer, we'll also request a log of the progress of the solution so we can monitor development over time. Because our iterations are basically being covered by the DataTable, we won't request any more than a single RISKOptimizer-based iteration per decision policy evaluated. After a few minutes the performance appears to have leveled off. And the best result seems to be a reservation policy of around twenty bookings, although the there does seem to be considerable variation among best solution performance and other acceptable solutions (this is worth noting because there's only one decision variable being modified in this case).

A closer inspection of the optimization summary log (at least those solutions that met the service constraint) shows that the solution of twenty bookings along with neighboring solutions – for example, seventeen and eighteen bookings – are fairly comparable, and the standard deviation of twenty is relatively high. In some cases, analysts might look at results such as these and

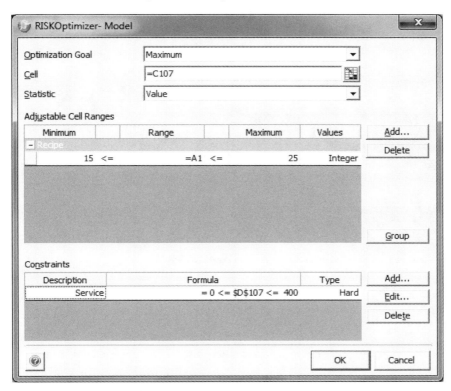

Figure 9.4. Problem specifications for simulation optimization of reservation problem.

consider implementing options that perform second-best, simply to avoid high levels of performance risk.

9.2.2 Using RISKOptimizer Iterations for the Same Result (without a Data Table)

An alternative approach to generating the same result is to capitalize not on Data Table functionality for developing simulated variants (that is, iterations in RISKOptimizer lingo), but instead on RISKOptimizer's built-in iteration mechanism. To accomplish this, we need to modify only the source of the performance and constraint results in RISKOptimizer (the single calculations of profit and cost from the main model sheet) and to specify to RISKOptimizer that we would like for it to run one hundred iterations for each solution considered, just as the Data Table had been providing (see Figure 9.5). Because DataTables won't be necessary in this approach, those associated sheets could also be deleted from the workbook, and may actually save the processor a lot of trouble and allow the search to proceed more swiftly.

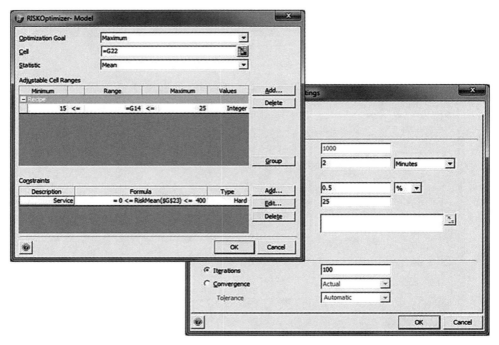

Figure 9.5. Alternative specification leveraging RISKOptimizer iteration capabilities.

It is worth noting that to get the constraints to apply equally in this case, we will need to specify that we are interested only in meeting the service constraint "on average" (that is, across all iterations of each policy assessed). We could be more stringent, but our search might yield different results and wouldn't be a fair comparison given that the Data Table approach was basically just looking at satisfying the constraint, on average, across its one hundred trials. We can make this modification to the service constraint by asking that the mean service level for each policy (across all iterations) be considered, rather that the final value (of each iteration, or the last one viewed).

Ultimately, the result of an otherwise preferred policy of around twenty bookings is comparable to that derived by the other method; A close inspection of neighboring results show them to be similar as well. However, the RISKOptimizer handling of iterations tends to converge upon this conclusion much faster than the Data Table approach.

9.3 Optimization of System Simulations

Before getting into the use of RISKOptimizer with system simulations, it is worth taking a moment to consider the potential for complications associated with relying on iterations for the simultaneous generation of multiple

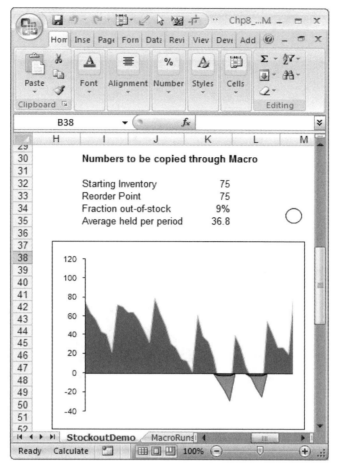

Figure 9.6. Anticipated history generated in single iteration mode.

pulls of random numbers and development of evolving systems based on circular loop calculations.

Let's reconsider the Lobos Inventory example from Chapter 8. The demonstration file for this example was Chp8_LobosInventory. We've already shown that we can use the F9 key to run through a series of calculations. We've also demonstrated how we can record a macro for repeating a large set of such recalculations to ultimately build a rich and valuable history of the performance of decisions (that is, reorder point policies) made for the system. For 200 periods, Figure 9.6 shows the kind of result we might generate using the macro we considered in the last chapter (which was designed to effectively recalculate things 200 times).

For richness of description, I've also chosen to track the last forty periods (following the same method from the Web data acquisition discussion in Chapter 3), and provide a graph showing the inventory positions for those

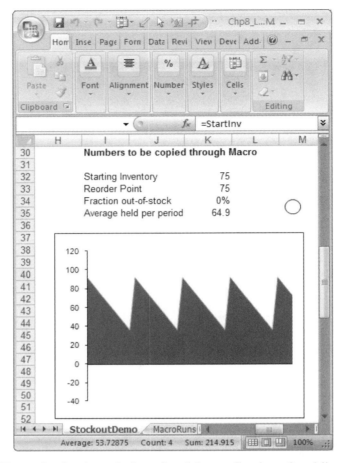

Figure 9.7. Example of unintended results of the application of multiiteration mode.

last forty periods. The presence and impact of variations in demand and delivery lead times is certainly apparent.

Attempting to simply increase the number of iterations conducted in quick succession doesn't give us what we might expect. Adjusting the number of iterations to 200 rather than 1 gives us results similar to Figure 9.7.

Not only are the performance results vastly different than those provided by our macro (64.9 versus 36.8 inventory held, and 0 percent versus 9 percent stock-out rates), but so is the overall character of the inventory level depiction recorded and graphed. What happened? I have to honestly say that the first time I encountered something like this, I was a little thrown. Partly because I didn't expect it, and partly because I didn't have any immediate intuition as to why it was happening. Looking carefully at the graph, it would seem as if a uniform set of calculations was taking place in repetition without the impact of newly (periodically) drawn random numbers. It seems as

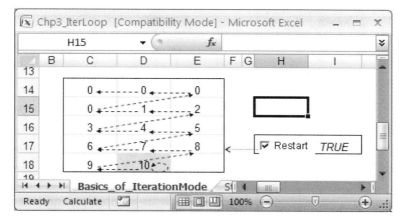

Figure 9.8. Previously depicted results of multiple iterations in a linked system.

if any random number generation that we may have started with simply did not continue as iterations were being calculated.

But why would that happen? The answer lies with the way Excel views the application of iteration mode. Iteration mode largely exists to update cell calculations that are codependent on previous values contained within those same cells (or on other self-referencing cells that they in turn reference). In other words, iteration mode exists to allow for the iterative calculation of cells that are dependent on circular loops. Other cells that are not dependent on the system of circular referencing are simply not going to be updated multiple times when multiiteration settings are on.

To illustrate, let's consider a much more simplified scenario where we want to simultaneously make use of both random number generation and some sort of system evolution (and recordkeeping). To keep things simple, we'll look at a variant of the first example we used back in Chapter 3 when introducing iteration mode. Recall the following table shown in Figure 9.8 used to illustrate how a simple one-point self-increment could be developed and propagated across a set of cells above or in the same row left of a self-referencing cell (again, only when iteration mode is active).

First, let's substitute the former contents of D18 that formerly contained =D18+1 with something that makes use of the random number generator (for example, $= D18 + RANDBETWEEN(1,5)$). By doing so, we retain the circularity that is so critical to the use of iteration mode in developing living records, while simultaneously allowing for a random-numbers generating mechanism. At a single iteration setting, new random numbers are pulled and the record is updated. A multiiteration setting (ten iterations in quick succession) will update ten cells in the remainder of an otherwise empty table upon Restart, based on those ten random pulls. The result is shown in Figure 9.9.

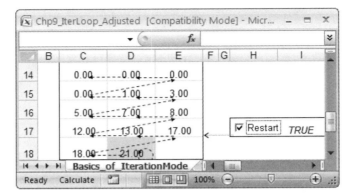

Figure 9.9. Demonstration of integrating random number generation into a circular loop system.

Close investigation of Figure 9.9 shows that the differences between the cells in the order of their tabulation differ in magnitude as would be expected with new random number draws (for example, 21−18=3, 18−17=1, 17−13=4). So, everything seems to be working as planned. But imagine that instead of generating the random number within the self-reference call itself, we used =D18+K14 and placed =RANDBETWEEN(1,5) in cell K14. If we weren't considering the use of a multiiteration setting and instead we elected to use something like F9 to generate random numbers and propagate our living record, there would be no real difference observed in our results (ten hits of F9 in a single iteration setting would provide a table with similar variation between cells as that provided in Figure 9.9).

However, under a multiiteration setting, this structure only generates a single random number. It will make use of that same number throughout all cell updates in the table but will lack the kind of variation we would otherwise anticipate. We'd get the results shown in Figure 9.10.

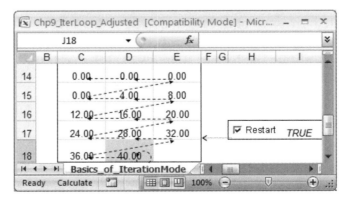

Figure 9.10. Propagation of random number whose generation is not part of a circular loop.

Close inspection of Figure 9.10, using the external random number generation and reference and a multiiteration setting, creates a table where the cells tabulated in order differ throughout by exactly four (a single random pull between one and five).

Why? Certainly, cell D18 is still referencing itself, and all related cells depending on D18 would also be part of that circular dependency and thus subject to consideration during Excel's iteration-mode-based updates. However, as stated previously, random number generation (in cell K14, in this case) is not taking place in a cell that is dependent on a self-reference. It is being used by a cell that contains a self-reference, but that doesn't matter to Excel. As far as the application is concerned, there is no obvious need to update this cell in accordance with the settings of iteration mode – the multiiteration settings don't apply. Pressing F9 once forces ten iterations of the cells in the table dependent on D18, but K14 is not dependent on any self-reference whatsoever and is updated only once (only one random number is pulled).

In part, this is a nice way to distinguish the nuances of iterations (as specified in iteration mode, for example) from that of recalculations in Excel (as activated by F9, for example). At the same time, the issue encountered is something that can easily be adjusted for. Here, if we need to make sure K14 contains a self-reference to be included in the activities of iteration mode, why not just add a self-reference to that cell? Something as simple as throwing in a +K14*0 (yes, itself times zero) would do the trick, without having any impact whatsoever on the output of that cell. It's a simple tricking of the application, and may seem pointless from a purely mathematical perspective, but it is meaningful from an Excel logic perspective, and the bottom line is that it gets the job done.

Using this minor addition in multiiteration mode will, in fact, give us exactly the kind of result we saw when the random number generation was embedded in cell D18. Because this is precisely the kind of problem that the original version of the Lobos Inventory model faced when we attempted to use it in under a multiiteration setting, the same kind of solution should apply. It is worth noting that because several calculations are dependent on the same randomly generated set of numbers, it makes sense that they are generated external to other calculations, such that if in a given period multiple calculations rely on a randomly generated lead time, they should all be referencing the same randomly generated lead time for that period. If an appropriate dummy self-reference term (such as K14*0 in the simpler example) is introduced into each random-number generating cell, then the Inventory model will act exactly as we'd want it to under a multiiteration setting. Chp9_LobosInventory Adjusted includes this change (and it's the only change). The results under a 200-iteration setting are now comparable to the

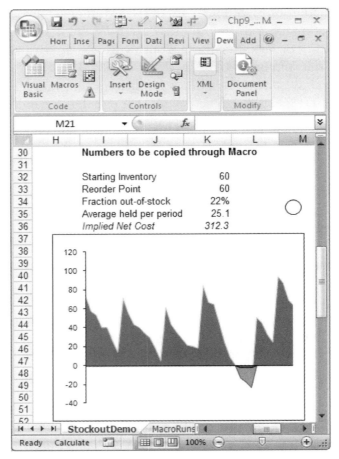

Figure 9.11. Possible spreadsheet setup for inventory system simulation optimization.

results provided by the macro (running in single iteration mode), shown in Figure 9.11.

The only challenge left in using RISKOptimizer for system simulations is in ensuring that the system is reset on the evaluation of each decision scenario (in this case, each combination of order-up-to point and other terms that might be viewed as potentially adjustable decisions, such as order quantity and even lead time averages if alternate carrier options exist at cost).

Note that what we've done to capitalize on the multiiteration setting has implications beyond a single simulation of this system. As we are about to discuss, such a capability can be useful in a search for optimal policy characteristics, but it can also be useful in the comparison of a specific performance measure across a small discrete set of policies. Similar to the first example used on the Lobos reservations case in Chapter 8, the adjusted Inventory workbook can be modified to allow for proper Data Table tabulation across a discrete set of order-up-to levels. We would have to add an additional and somewhat awkward conditional statement to reset the system whenever iterations reached their limit (200 here), but otherwise we could use a similar procedure to that first discussed when introducing the Data Table tool to provide end-of-simulation values for comparison. Chp9_LIwDT Adjusted provides an example of how this might be accomplished.

9.3.1 RISKOptimizer with Calls to a Reset Macro

To demonstrate how a Reset macro could be used in conjunction with RISKOptimizer for simulation optimization, let's first consider how we might actually develop such a macro. Basically, we'll use the same approach we took when recording a macro in Chapter 8. All we want here is a macro that will set the value of the reset (or Restart) cell in the workbook (cell H18 in the inventory workbook) equal to False, let the spreadsheet recalculate the numbers, and then set the cell equal to True.

That's all. Because of this, all we need to do to make such a macro is to start recording a new one, enter False into cell H18, press Enter, press F9, and then enter True into H18, again followed by pressing Enter and another F9 (just to get things started right). Those F9 hits are critical to ensuring these changes register when RISKOptimizer runs this macro.

Stopping the recording at that point will give us what we need to initialize each new investigation – this is basically the initialize-system step denoted in the simulation flow charts in Chapter 8. In the following discussion, we'll assume we haven't been creative in naming the macro and that we've gone with the default label of Macro2 for this simple automation. (Note that this macro is already available in the Chp9_LobosInventory Adjusted file.)

9.3.1.1 Use under Excel's Multiiteration Setting

To make the setup in RISKOptimizer as simple as possible, let's define a single objective that integrates the two costs represented in this system: holding costs and shortage costs. Let's just assume for now that every unit of inventory held per period, on average, costs twice the amount as the goodwill lost from each day that we are out of stock. This is because we assume all customers will ultimately be served, albeit not instantaneously, via backorder. That is, let's create a Net Implied cost in cell K36 equal to 2*C35+C31. We'll use that sum as the objective function we're aiming to minimize. Because these two components of the cost function trade off against one another and are nonlinear functions of our policy, it is likely that the combined objective function will be nonlinear, as well, with considerably high costs appearing at both ends of the reorder-point policy spectrum (another trait well suited to the use of RISKOptimizer).

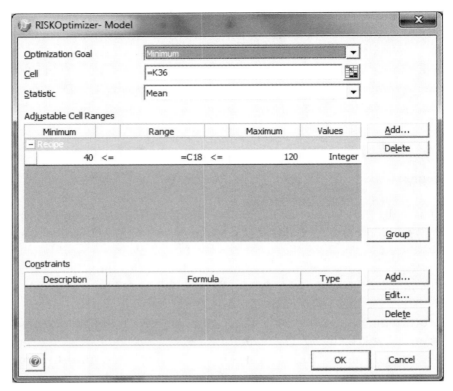

Figure 9.12. Specifying a macro call in RISKOptimizer before each solution is considered.

What we specify to RISKOptimizer as far as the objective, decision variables, and constraints might be something as simple as shown in Figure 9.12, assuming we have reason to suspect the best policy exists somewhere between a reorder point of 40 and 120, and the existing automatic calculation of reorder quantity in cell (C28) doesn't need reconsidering.

As far as making use of the Reset macro before simulating each alternative policy, we'll want to specify additional information under the Macros button in the RISKOptimizer Settings dialog box (Figure 9.12). Click this button to open the RISKOptimizer Macros dialog box, shown in Figure 9.13. We want the system to be reset before each new system simulation is run, so we'll specify exactly what is shown in the figure.

Before we run this, we'll want to make sure of one more thing. We'll want to make sure Excel is going to evaluate our system simulation across 200 periods each time RISKOptimizer gives it a new solution (a new reorder point) to consider. We make this change in Excel (File>Options>Formulas>Enable Iterations, 200). Automatic recalculation should be specified.

Now, we should be ready to run the RISKOptimizer search for an ideal solution. After one minute, given the objective and everything else specified

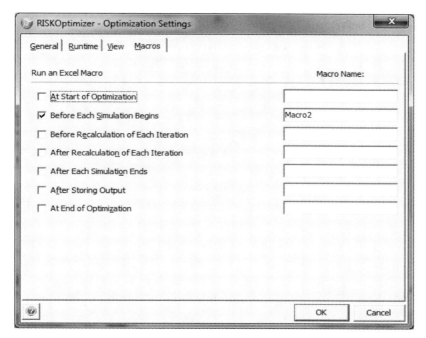

Figure 9.13. Specifying a macro call in RISKOptimizer before each solution is evaluated.

in the system model, the best reorder-point solution found should be around sixty (that is, inventory reorders placed whenever the inventory level reaches or goes below sixty units). A graphical inspection of the simulation output log shown in Figure 9.14 provides the same overall observation.

A caveat at this point is worth recognizing with regard to the use of Excel's multiiteration mode in the way we just described. RISKOptimizer is notorious for taking additional actions in the spreadsheet that would otherwise trigger a multiiteration run in Excel. If you aren't aware of all the activities RISKOptimizer is triggering, this can generate somewhat muddied results. Having said this, we'll now consider an alternative to the use of Excel's multiiteration mode approach.

9.3.1.2 Using RISKOptimizer's Built-In Multiiteration Mechanism

RISKOptimizer also provides an alternative mechanism for iterating us through the 200 periods with which we're interested. To demonstrate, our setup will involve making sure we are running Excel in single iteration mode (as opposed to multiiteration mode). Instead, we'll specify these 200 iterations by clicking the RISKOptimizer Options button to open the RISKOptimizer Options dialog box (Figure 9.15). As shown in the figure, we'll specify 200 iterations in the Simulation Stopping Conditions section of the dialog box.

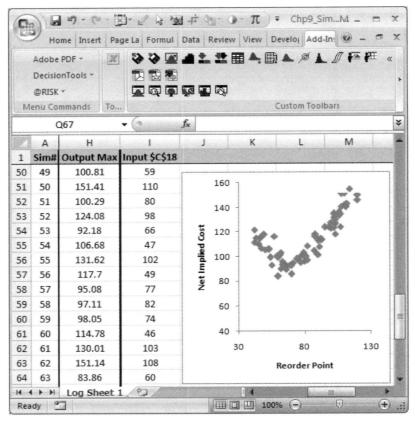

Figure 9.14. Reviewing nonlinearities inherent to the solution space encountered.

This essentially tells RISKOptimizer to recalculate the spreadsheet (pull random numbers, refresh totals, reassess conditional statements, generate a new period's worth of data) 200 times before moving on to the consideration of an alternative solution.

At this point, our analysis approach needs to be a little tricky because RISKOptimizer is going to view every single iteration it generates as a possible policy outcome. This isn't exactly what we want because we know that, in reality, each iteration represents a single period, and performance in any one period may be extremely misleading (and highly variable). What we're interested in is average performance across the 200 periods. The average inventory held early on (for example, periods one through five) will tend to be very high compared to the average account after 200 periods. Furthermore, the number of periods of stock-out can never be more than the number of periods considered; thus, early iterations by RISKOptimizer will also have much fewer of these than the final total after 200 iterations. RISKOptimizer's averages of the numbers it sees across all 200 of its

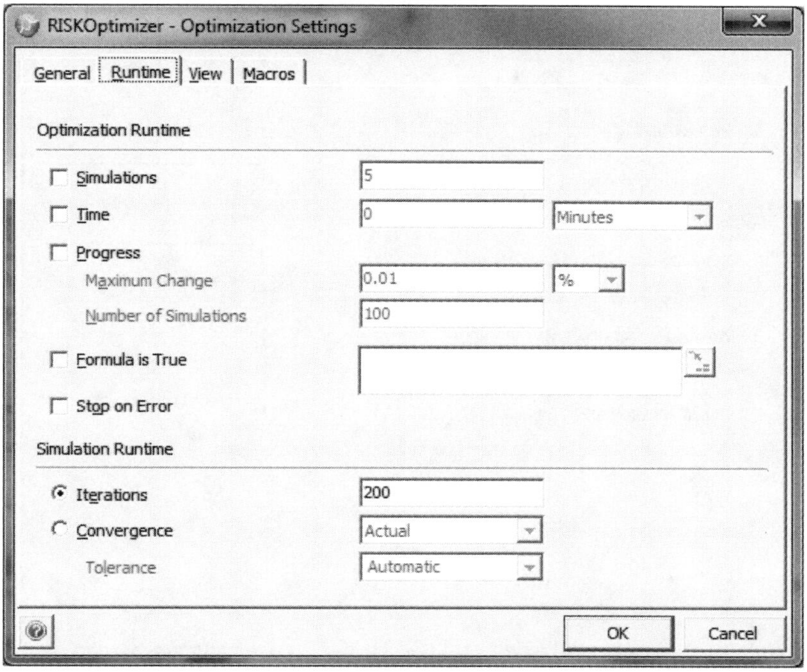

Figure 9.15. Specifying the use of RISKOptimizer iteration for a system simulation.

iterations will therefore not reflect the ending values we would otherwise be recording for this system and neither would the minimum or maximum values.

Although there's no easy way to cut out the earlier iterations of RISKOptimizer (as is fairly common practice in simulation analysis where starting conditions are misleading), there are ways to cut out early numbers through directly modifying Excel calculations. In this case, we could capitalize on our knowledge of how we're calculating our objective function to modify the averaging calculation in cell C35. We know the number of out-of-stock periods must be a nondecreasing function of time such that that number can only increase as subsequent periods are iterated. We could, for example, substitute into cell C5 =IF(C32>=199,C34/C32,0) to make sure that the positive cost contributions of holding inventory are taken into account only in the objective function at the end of the 200 iterations. The Maximum (not the Average) values provided by the RISKOptimizer log will then be most representative of the kind of system summaries we're looking for. This doesn't help RISKOptimizer find best solutions for us, per se, but it does help us make sense of the RISKOptimizer log for visual inspection of where best solutions may reside.

Note that structuring objective functions differently from this example could bypass a less-than-ideal approach to capitalizing on RISKOptimizer's

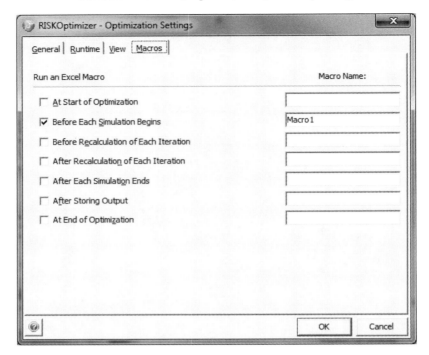

Figure 9.16. Alternate preevaluation macro call in RISKOptimizer.

built-in iteration capabilities. However, because we are mainly interested in demonstrating the nuances of RISKOptimizer, we'll leave such consideration up to the intrepid reader.

9.3.2 *RISKOptimizer with Calls to a Recalculation Macro*

RISKOptimizer's macro calls can also be used to prompt the Visual Basic driven iteration of the system across 200 periods, as made possible by the macro written in Chapter 8. To reillustrate, we should make sure that we are:

1) Running in single-iteration mode in Excel Options
2) Evaluating each solution only once (simulation runtime iterations = 1 in RISKOptimizer)

Otherwise, our setup in RISKOptimizer will be the same as in the previous example, as far as objective, decision variables, and constraints are concerned.

The nature of our macro calls will change. We'll want to initialize at the start, call our Macro1 from Chapter 8 (Figure 9.16) every time a new policy is considered, and then call our new reset function every time a simulation ends.

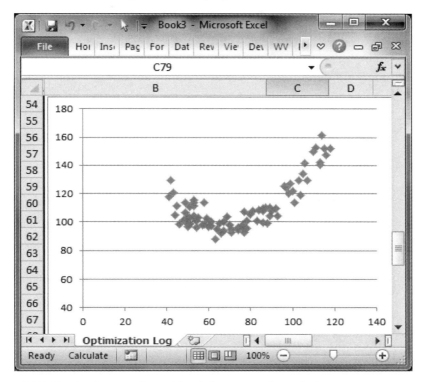

Figure 9.17. Reviewing nonlinearities inherent to the solution space encountered.

We might stop the optimization after one minute to see how we're doing. Figure 9.17 shows an example of the log of solutions considered during that one-minute period, along with a graph describing the nature and variability of the relationship between the reorder-point policies considered and the objective function (Net Implied Cost). Given the objective and everything else specified in the system model, the best reorder-point solution found was around sixty-one (that is, inventory reorders placed whenever the inventory level reaches or goes below sixty-one units). Note again that this is essentially the same answer we got in the past two approaches.

The only criticism that one might voice would be with regard to the amount of noise around what seems to be the central trend. That noise is actually meaningful. It depicts the uncertainty around the average performance of each reorder point. However, there are ways to neaten things if the goal is to minimize based on more robust estimates of cost.

What's needed for this goal is a repeated consideration of each of the possible reorder-point solutions, not by simply looking at each solution over 200 periods, but looking at each solution multiple times (each time over 200 periods). In other words, we want (1) a search that will consider multiple alternative solutions to our decision-making problem, or multiple simulations in the terminology of RISKOptimizer; (2) multiple reexaminations

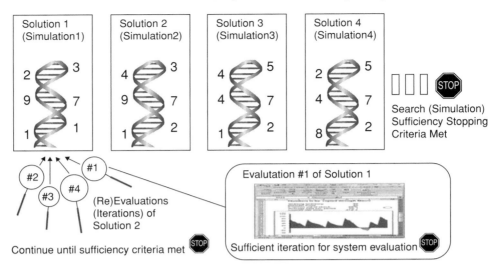

Figure 9.18. Conceptual structure of a system simulation solution search with repeated evaluation.

of each of these solutions (as was accomplished in Section 9.2 either with RISKOptimizer's internal iterations or a Data Table); and (3) a multiperiod examination of each solution to allow for system dynamics to play out (as we've demonstrated through the use of macros or multiiteration options). Conceptually, this kind of search for good solutions is depicted for a six-variable decision problem in Figure 9.18.

Fortunately, we've already seen the availability of iterative techniques for generating new and separate evaluations of solutions. We used one in Section 9.3.1.2 to evolve some performance estimates for a single solution over 200 periods. But we don't need that here, because the macro we've recorded (Macro1) does that for us. That has freed up RISKOptimizer's reevaluation capabilities so that they can be leveraged now in the way they were in Section 9.2.2. Let's say we do this, and tell RISKOptimizer to consider each solution five or ten times (to generate averages that might be enough to significantly increase the robustness of assessments), and we run Macro1 to evaluate each solution across 200 periods to generate those five or ten estimates.

To get this to work, we may need a slight addition to our macro call specification in RISKOptimizer. As in Figure 9.19, we need to think both in terms of the initialization that takes place the first time each new solution is considered (before each simulation, in the terminology of RISKOptimizer) as well as after each subsequent consideration of that solution (all of those iterations beyond the first that are still part of the simulation solution consideration).

The result of this setup, in Excel's single iteration mode, should look a bit leaner in terms of variance than the previous results. It might look a bit like the depiction in Figure 9.19.

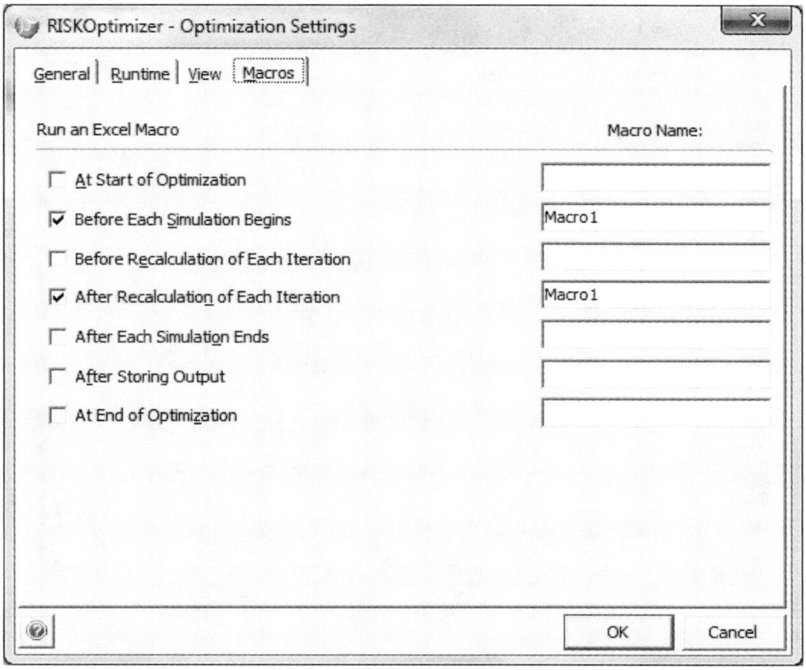

Figure 9.19. Calls for a multievaluation search calling a multiperiod system simulation macro.

This brings us to a final note on reporting the results of a simulation analysis and solution search. Although the nature of these searches cannot guarantee that "optimal solutions" are pinpointed, we can gain insights into the goodness of the best solutions encountered, relative to others encountered. Graphical illustrations of the relative strength of solutions based on search logs (for example, Figure 9.20) can be compelling exhibits in reports to higher-level decision makers. They emphasize the salience (or lack thereof) of differences between alternative competing policies.

However, with all of the emphasis on the importance of capturing uncertainty, graphs of "typical performance" may not be sufficient. Risk is also relevant. Many managers would give up a little expected performance for a sizeable reduction in downside risk. To that extent, an exhibit like that of Figure 9.20 might actually be misleading because the variance associated with each policy performance has been more or less washed away. Fortunately, RISKOptimizer can also capture standard deviations, minimums, and maximums as it tabulates averages. This allows for the potential of depicting general risk in an associated graph. If anything more complex than these are needed, we may need to rely on a more flexible reporting tool.

We can develop that flexibility through tools we've already seen: Data Tables and macros. Imagine recording in a macro the actions involved in developing a Data Table that described numerous intermediate and final

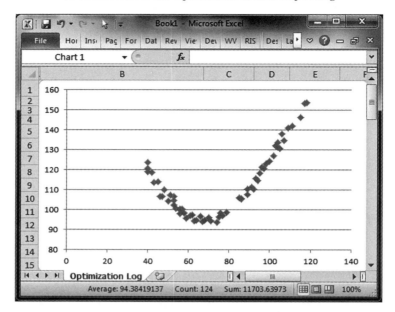

Figure 9.20. Variance reduction in a multievaluation, multiperiod system simulation search.

performance measures associated with a policy (RISKOptimizer will generally only provide summary measures on the Objective). We might have a table similar to that in Figure 8.9. We might not need to have such a table active in each step of the search (it might slow down run-time), but it might be something nice to have as one of the final artifacts describing the best policy reached (such a macro might be called "At End of Optimization" by RISKOptimizer). With a table like this, any variety of descriptive details can be presented with regard to the option, including its upside and downside, as well as the dynamics of intermediate performance measures.

PRACTICE PROBLEM

Recall the project scheduling problem from Chp7_ProjectScheduling. In reality, the time to complete specific tasks can only be truly estimated and is automatically viewed as associated with some level of uncertainty. In each of the cells where estimated completion times are being tabulated (E6:E15), introduce an additional term +RANDBETWEEN(1,4) to allow for the simulation of such uncertainty. Use a RISKOptimizer procedure similar to that originally applied in Chapter 7 for this problem, but additionally specify that ten iterations (ten simulated variants) are considered for every solution considered. After five minutes of run time, use the RISKOptimizer log to comment on the nature of the performance variability of the final solution suggested relative to other best solutions encountered along the way.

10

Visualizing Complex Analytical Dynamics

The visualization of analytical dynamics comes naturally to the tools developed in Excel. This is largely due to the dynamic nature of graphs constructed in Excel. For example, if we wanted to depict the range of possible outcomes associated with specific decisions for which outcomes had a describable level of uncertainty or variation, it would be simple enough to introduce a random term into tabular forms and then graph the result. As always, pressing the F9 key would simply draw another random number from the built-in generator and augment the associated data tables and plots to represent the volatility of those outcomes.

For example, based on the Data Table generated in the Lobo's Reservations case, we could graphically depict the variable nature of our results using the high-low-close plot (although tricked out a bit) provided in that workbook. Every time F9 is pressed, we would see how much the variability in outcomes across policy types was subject to change (simply based on different separate and independent sets of random data draws). The result, shown in Figure 10.1, would depict an alternative array of outcomes that could be associated with a set of decisions. Another example is shown with the second Data Table example, shown in Figure 10.2.

This, in itself, might be entirely adequate in providing insights regarding the sufficiency of the number of variants examined. If the results don't change much, the best policy, or any possible relationship between the associated outcomes, is probably well represented.

In this case, the system being visualized is assumed to follow dynamics that are essentially devoid of memory; that is, systems where future conditions are independent of past conditions. But most systems in practice do have a memory of some kind. For this reason, it is worth going over a few mechanisms through which to build memory into system visualizations. There are many forms of such memory, and the complexity of these forms ultimately impacts the complexity and richness of the visualization to be designed. We'll start out with the simplest form and work our way up to more complex forms.

269

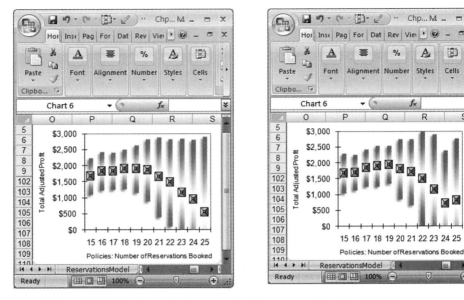

Figure 10.1. Profit variation graphed in two randomized (F9) instances.

10.1 Random Walks

One form of memory concerns position, or what we might call the state of an element within a system. Upon a single iteration, the state (or graphical position) of the element might change slightly. Even if the magnitude of the

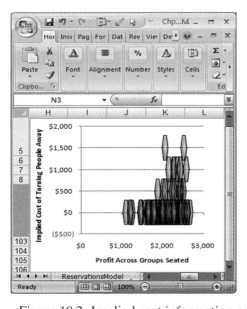 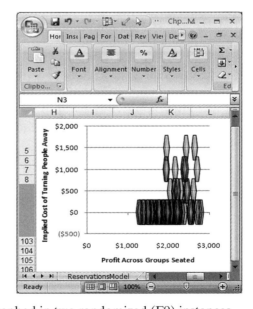

Figure 10.2. Implied cost information graphed in two randomized (F9) instances.

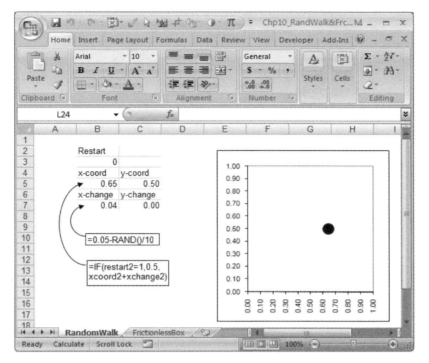

Figure 10.3. Example of RandomWalk dynamics graphed.

change is entirely independent of state, the new state represents a new starting point for any other change to follow. When changes are entirely random and independent but subsequent states are clearly linked to prior conditions, a random walk occurs. This is illustrated in Chp10_RandWalk&FrctnlessBox (Figure 10.3).

Although seemingly uncharacteristic of common experience, there are many cases in which such models provide shockingly sufficient descriptions of the kind of dynamics we might observe in the real world – feeding patterns of pigeons, the physical meanderings of a drunken college student, the socioethical meanderings of sober financial professionals, and so on.

10.2 Frictionless Boxes

Some systems involve much more defined mechanisms for changes in the state of an element. This could be called directional or trajectory memory. In such cases, both the current state and directional tendencies are critical in determining future states and trajectories. The simplest example of this is a frictionless box where an element set in transitional motion maintains its trajectory until certain boundary conditions are met. It then partially reverses its trajectory (that is, it ricochets), based on what boundary condition is met.

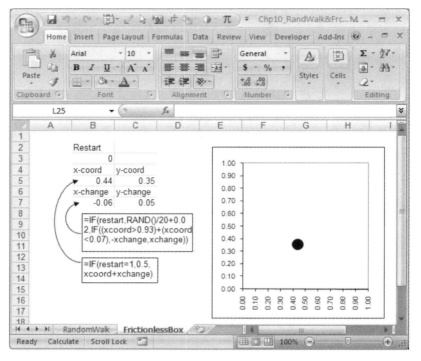

Figure 10.4. Example of FrictionlessBox dynamics graphed.

An illustration of this is provided in Chp10_RandWalk&FrctnlessBox and shown in Figure 10.4.

Once again, although a zero loss of energy or momentum seems unlikely as characteristic of mechanical systems, prior trajectory dependency and deflection responses, in general, are common characteristics of many physical, social, and economic systems. It wouldn't take much to incorporate features such as loss of momentum or additional, more complex boundaries (for deflection) into this kind of a model.

10.3 Dynamics in Google Documents Visualization

Because we covered both the extraction of data from Google documents and the writing of Excel data to Google documents in Chapter 3, it seems only natural to discuss some of the impressive graphical capabilities made possible through Google, based on imported Excel data. For example, let's reconsider the data we were first introduced to in Section 4.1. We discussed the difficulty of depicting the trajectories of firm performance in terms of EPS as a function of changing levels of relative holding costs (inventory per sales). At one extreme, we had a jumble of data depicted on a graph with little hope of making sense of it. At the other extreme, we had a pruned

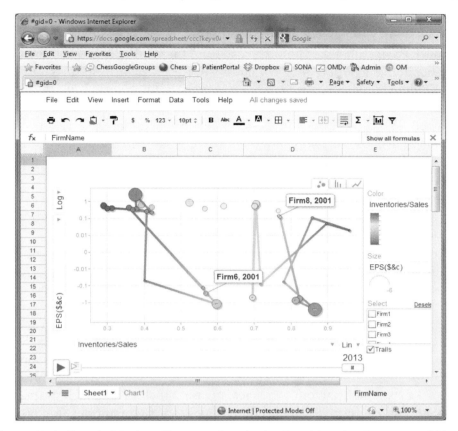

Figure 10.5. Google Motion Chart used to depict firm histories from posted Excel data.

version of that data, which was appreciably more useful but still lacked the ability to fully depict the complex trends for each given firm.

A more nuanced approach to pruning and depicting the history of individual firms would be easily developed if the data were arranged in Firm, Year, EPS, and Inventories/Sales format in a Google document. Let's say I rearranged my data in that workbook to accommodate this data structure, and used the GoogleWriter add-in to post the data to an available Google worksheet (or I simply cut-and-pasted it, if this is a one-time posting event). The Motion Chart option, under the Insert command tab and the Chart>Trend charting option in Google not only allows data to be depicted but also highlights any number of the firms in the set. Figure 10.5 provides an example of the Motion Chart in action.

The timeline Play button allows the history of the data set to develop from the earliest time point to the latest. With the Trails option active, any selected entity (Firm, in this case) will not only show the changes its attributes encounter over time, but it will also depict the path taken through time to get there. In Figure 10.5, Firm8 starts out with a high level of holding costs and high EPS, it eventually loses EPS while increasing holding costs, it regains EPS at still higher holding costs, and then it finally drops those costs and encounters a period of high volatility in EPS. One firm starts out at mid-land holding costs and experiences a period of holding cost reduction simultaneous with EPS increases. It eventually returns to a point close to where it started. Were there specific policies put in place that gave rise to these dynamics? Almost certainly, although there is most likely a fair amount of variance that cannot be easily tied to policy. The trajectory of Firm6 appears much more "controlled" (EPS trends well with relative holding costs, which are certainly subject to managerial influence). Firm8 has a much more seemingly volatile and harder to explain history. Does that in itself say anything about management?

How much easier is speculation on this data, now that we've imbued it with some life? This is exactly the kind of visualization that can come in handy in developing concrete hypotheses and targeted analytical tests. Although a very smooth mechanism for time-panning, the Google spreadsheet's capabilities here are not entirely unique. Keep in mind that we can create scroll bars in Excel as well (see the supplement in Chapter 8 and more advanced interfacing forms in Chapter 13). Because we've already demonstrated in this chapter that we can create visually dynamic graphics in Excel based on "random" changes, it's not much of a stretch to imagine generating much more "structured" changes that we might develop around a historical panning mechanism in Excel.

10.4 Path-Directed Flows

The notion of systems that retain memories of both state and direction opens the door to still more complex and potentially meaningful graphical visualizations, including those that retain memories of progress between states along much more nuanced trajectories. For example, consider the visual simulation provided in the Chp10_LobosFloorPlan workbook (see Figure 10.6).

As in the previous examples presented in this book, opening this workbook and holding down the F9 key will allow the visual simulation to cycle through. Seeing this in action, an initial reaction might be to view this as far beyond the skill of someone just getting the hang of developing tools in Excel. But the building block and ideas on which this visualization are based are straightforward. We've actually covered them all in one form or another already.

Pasting images in place of scatter plot points (the images of the waiters and mariachis in Figure 10.6 are just points in a scatter plot).

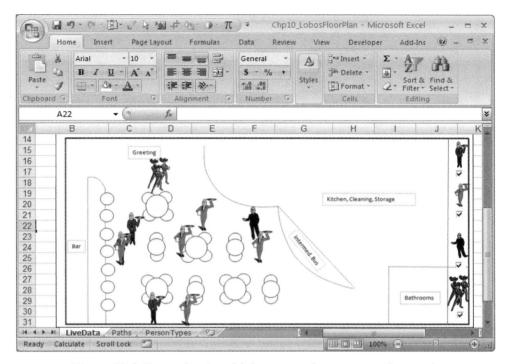

Figure 10.6. Example of multielement path-movement by graph.

Pasting a background for a plot (that's the restaurant backdrop).

The apparent motion of the points along paths; there's the iteration mode at work, again used in the evolution of a living record, in conjunction with the transition matrix concept introduced in Chapter 8 and a little bit of careful graphical design.

Easier said than done? There is some complexity in this last point, but like all processes, it's not something that can't be broken up into a set of logical steps.

10.4.1 An Introduction to Visualizing Path-Directed Flows

Let's take a look at a more simple illustration of how these tools are used together. (We'll get back to the specifics of this particular example in a bit.) At this point, let's not attempt to take into consideration physical proximity in the graphics. To keep it simple, let's just represent the three steps of a process as three points plotted to a graph. For structure, we'll make use of the same transition matrix example introduced in Chapter 8. In the Chp10_TransMatrixRvstd workbook, the worksheet labeled TransMatrix+ StateChangePlot (Figure 10.7) provides the same structure as discussed in Chapter 8 with the addition of only a few new elements.

The additions include three sets of x–y coordinates (in various shades of gray) to spatially distinguish the three states on a scatter plot, as well as a

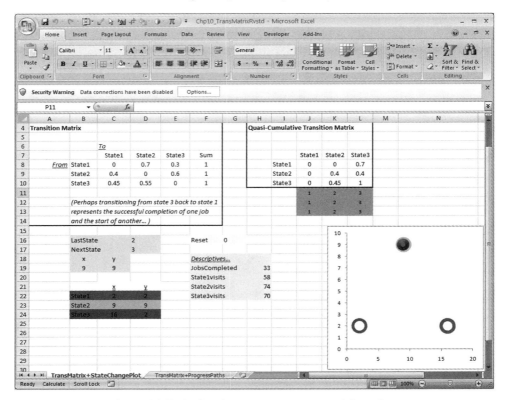

Figure 10.7. A simple state-to-state transition plot.

pair of x–y coordinates based on that set of three, which specifically captures what state a job resides in at any point in time. Holding down the F9 key updates the tabular data as before, but now it also provides a visual representation of job progress between these states.

Although informative, such a visual is still somewhat limiting in its capability to depict flow. Instantaneous movement between states is generally difficult to keep track of visually in this manner, particularly in cases where multiple jobs may be transitioning among the same states at the same time. More gradual progress between transitional states often proves more useful in these kinds of system simulations.

10.4.2 Visualizing Progress along Paths

To provide a visualization of transitional progress over much more visually complex paths, we can fall back on the kinds of capabilities discussed when we introduced scatter plots in Chapter 4. These plots are constructed based on a series of data points. In many cases, the ordering of these points are irrelevant to analysis; in other cases, such as those associated with

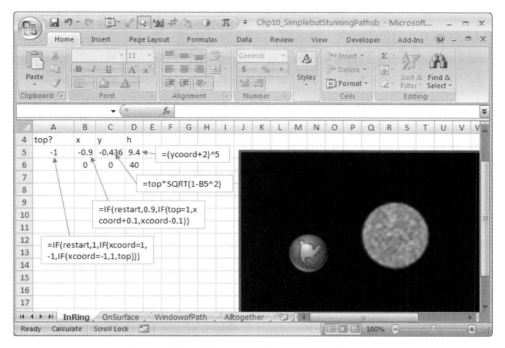

Figure 10.8. Simple nonlinear path dynamics.

transitions between states within a process, their ordering is critical to intuitive understanding.

Let's start by considering a single path structure described by a set of x-y coordinates. We'll pick a simple path structure to begin with – for example, that of a circular or oval path. For aesthetic purposes, we'll illustrate this with a depiction of the Earth moving in orbit around the sun (see workbook Chp10_SimplebutStunningPaths). In this case, the illustration is constructed through the use of a bubble plot and is further augmented through the manipulation of size of bubble Earth as it moves along the path.

As shown in Figure 10.8, the path itself is nothing more than an application of the equation of a unit circle ($y=+/-\text{sqrt}(1-x2)$) in iteration mode, with the value of x changing in small increments, either positively or negatively depending on whether the right or left boundaries of the circular path have been reached. The squashed appearance of the circular path is nothing more than an artifact of the squashed nature of the vertical scale. As you can see by opening the workbook example and holding down the F9 key, subsequent iterations provide the appearance of the Earth moving in front of the sun and then dipping into the background as it travels to lower and lower y coordinates in the plot (see Figure 10.9). Although this may be a decent illustration of technical capabilities, it is still a fairly limited example as far as practical application is concerned.

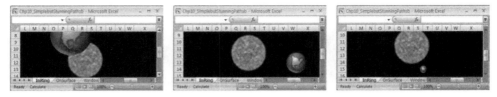

Figure 10.9. Several phases of a nonlinear path dynamic graph.

To get more practical, we could capitalize on our knowledge of transition matrices to merge multiple paths into a system depiction over which progress between states can be monitored. Referring once again to the three-state transition matrix example, the TransMatrix+ProgressPaths worksheet (Figure 10.10) provides a further extension in which individual points between the spatially represented states are specified. These points outline straight-line paths between these states – that is, positions of jobs along the paths represent progress in the transition between any two states. Because progress may be either forward (for example, 1 to 2) or backward (2 to 1) we have six sets of x–y coordinates (three of which are simply reversals of the other three). Additional features include cells that keep track of

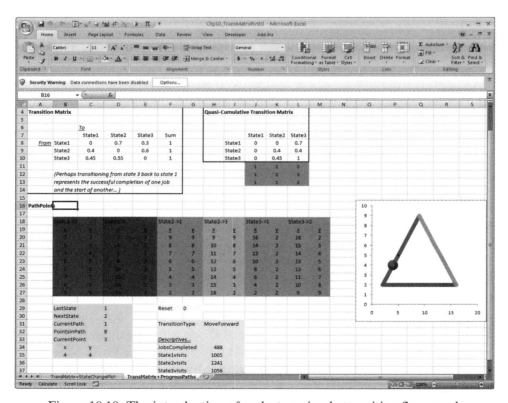

Figure 10.10. The introduction of paths to a simple transition flow graph.

which of six paths a job is on, how many total points of progress exist along each path (eight in all cases here), as well as how far the job has progressed along its path (referenced here as CurrentPoint).

Here, the x–y location of the job is dependent directly on path information: specifically, a column (path) and row (progress on path) OFFSET reference (see associated worksheet). On each iteration, a job progresses along the current path until it reaches the last point on that path. At that point, the same lookup mechanism used for determining what next state will be transitioned into is used. In iteration mode, this is followed immediately by the designation of the next appropriate path and a resetting of the path progress (CurrentPoint record) to 1. F9 demonstrates the iterative progress in this example.

10.4.3 Custom Path Visualizations: Lobo's Floor Plan Revisited

In some cases, the graphical specification of path structures may be preestablished or extremely straightforward, in terms of laying out *x* and *y* coordinates within a table. For example, perhaps changes in performance follow the arc of a production possibilities frontier or some set of conceptually and practically meaningful mathematical constraints. However, in many real-world simulations, the kind of dynamic path movement that is most telling relates to much more complex forms that aren't easily described by a series of formulations. Some of these are based on spatial considerations such as internal or external physical infrastructures of facilities. Others may be designed to represent transitions that are conceptually diverse and complex, such as representing the processing of new design ideas as opposed to the assembly of prototypes by design, or the retooling of staff in preparation for new work deployment). For example, let's consider an example from earlier in this chapter (Figure 10.11).

Ultimately, this is really nothing more than a more complex variant of the path types we've discussed. In this particular example, to organize what would otherwise be a difficult-to-manage set of spreadsheet calculations, we are making use of three sheets in a single workbook. One of these sheets simply contains the set of x-y coordinates that specify the pathways that elements can move along in the graph (Figure 10.12).

The visual shown in Figure 10.11 is nothing more than a scatter plot graph containing a line-linked presentation of that tabular data, superimposed on a graphic of a restaurant blueprint. (Approaches to massaging this set of coordinates to fit neatly with the natural paths of a scanned blueprint are discussed in the Chapter 10 Supplement.)

On the PersonTypes worksheet shown in Figure 10.13, I specify the transition matrices relevant to this graphical simulation. In this case, these

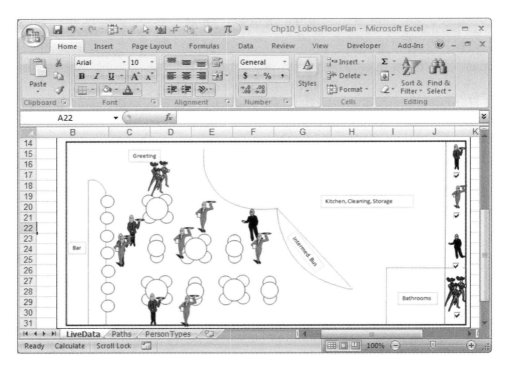

Figure 10.11. Revisiting the multielement path-movement example.

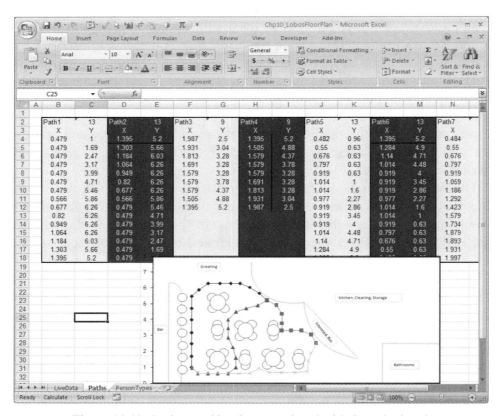

Figure 10.12. Paths specification associated with flow depicted.

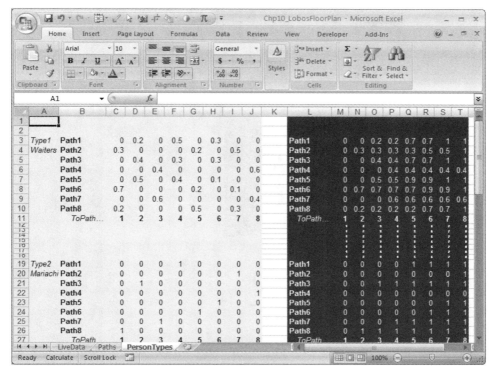

Figure 10.13. Transitions specification associated with flow depicted.

matrices specify the probability of an individual shifting onto an alternate path upon completion of the one they are currently on. The same lookup mechanism that was used to determine where to go next based on a random number pull in the three-state example is used here with eight states. Hence, we're drawing on the concept of stochastic processes introduced at the end of Chapter 8.

Different people may be described by different types of movement, and so the transition matrices of busboys are not the same as the manager's or the mariachi band's. Along with these transition matrices are cumulative matrices that are used when Excel actually needs to determine which next random path the person will embark upon.

The main page (LiveData, shown in Figure 10.14) is the most complex, and is therefore fully annotated, complete with red triangles on the column headers. Ultimately, the logic used here is no more complex than the structures discussed in the examples of the iteration mode. The complexity comes into play only when you consider how all of these elements and techniques come together to form a single integrated system. Of course, the caveat is that even the coolest (or simplest) graphics can get messy at times. When complete graphical depictions limit the capability to get a point across or

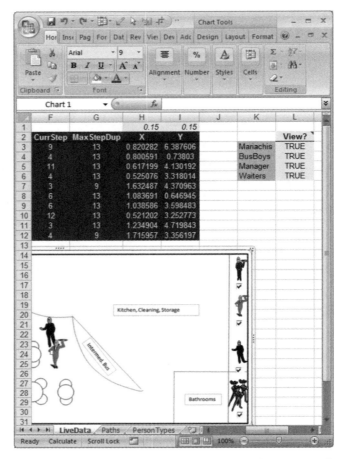

Figure 10.14. Pruning visuals through leveraging the ranges of graphs.

come to an understanding, partial depictions of representative or critical data are more useful.

Along these lines, another handy feature of this example is the use of controls to help provide a graphical pruning mechanism, again with the intent of focusing on only specific elements of the dynamic visualization. Here, we see the addition of a toggle associated with each type of entity class (that is, the waiters, the busboys) that can be set to TRUE or FALSE (that is, 1 or 0). If TRUE, the entities in that class show up somewhere along their associated paths; If FALSE, their x–y coordinates are set to (−1, −1) and are out of range for the graph (they don't appear on the portion of the graph that we view). It's a bit of a fake-out, but it gets the job done. Plus, this allows for the development of more sophisticated pruning interfaces, such as the control-based check boxes that were introduced in Chapter 8 Supplement.

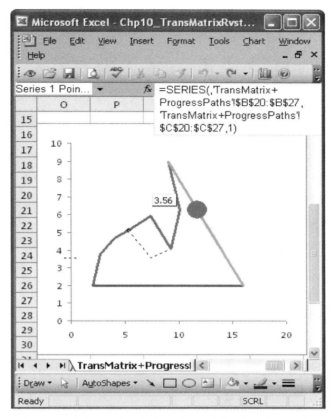

Figure 10.15. Manipulating plotted fixed-value points.

Supplement: Visually Derived Paths

Rather than trying to change the visual depiction of these paths through modifying the coordinates in tables, we could rely on alternative visual techniques for path adjustments and design.

Plot-Pulled Extractions

One way to do this involves making use of the graphed-data manipulation discussed in Chapter 4. Depending on your version of Excel, this approach may or may not be available; it is certainly available in the 2003 version. Once again, using the three-state example for illustration, all you need is to select a specific path (set of data) within the graph, select a specific point to adjust, and pull either horizontally or vertically on that point (assuming it relates to fixed data rather than a function) until it is in more visually representative location (see Figure 10.15).

System visualizations set up the way we have outlined in this chapter don't need any more changes for these plot-pulled manipulations to become

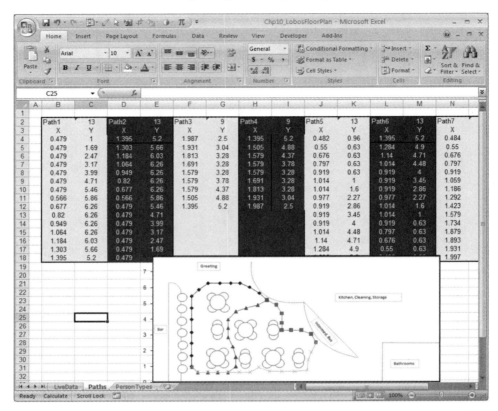

Figure 10.16. Revisiting the point-structure used in the floor plan example.

effective. In the case of the Lobo's floor plan example, I actually used this very technique. I started with a set of points (0,0), (1,1), (2,2), and then plotted them in a scatter chart. At that point, they're just a single straight line. After choosing the restaurant layout as a background picture for the plot, I started selecting each of those points and pulling them into positions that roughly corresponded to what might be commonly traveled paths within the restaurant layout; for example, note that people don't appear to be passing through walls or over tables in Figure 10.16.

In truth, it takes time to make things seem well spaced. As with the three-state example, some paths on the page are simply the same points of existing paths placed in the opposite sequence (representing travel in the opposite direction of a given path). To save time when creating these reverse paths, I simply set the first point on the reverse path equal to the cell reference for the last point on the forward path, the second point equal to the cell reference for the second last point on the forward path, and so on. This soft referencing allowed for any later changes to the original path without having to make subsequent changes to the reverse version.

Working without Excel 2003's in-graph manipulation capability makes this a bit tougher, and it is a shame that that capability was lost in subsequent

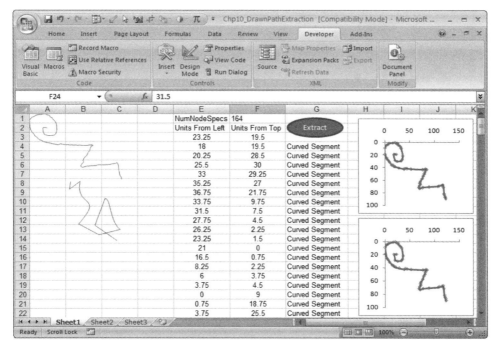

Figure 10.17. Path-point data extracted from a scribble.

versions. Fortunately, the ClickPlot add-in mentioned in Chapter 4 provides a handy alternative, regardless of which version of Excel you have.

Drawn-Path Extractions

A very different and alternative approach is to simply draw a path using the drawing objects available through Excel and then extracting coordinate information from the drawn lines. If you have a rough idea of what you want the path to look like, you can use the freeform, curve, or scribble options in the Shapes drop-down menu (Insert>Shapes). If you want the path to approximate a designated blueprint of some sort, there's no need to first insert that blueprint into a graph. When available in Excel, you can simply draw your path over the inserted picture.

Regardless, the real trick is to get the structure of those drawn paths into a tabular form of which your visual simulation can make use. Unlike plot-pulling approaches, which require a tabular structure, no coordinate data associated with drawn lines is automatically linked to the spreadsheet.

Fortunately, there are some simple Visual Basic codes that can be used to get the data you'll need. The workbook labeled Chp10_VisuallyDerived-Paths also contains a worksheet that demonstrates how coordinate data can be extracted from a variety of drawn paths. Figures 10.17 and 10.18

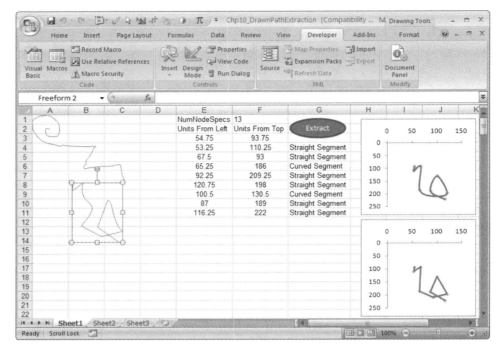

Figure 10.18. Path-point data extracted from a freeform with added curvature.

provide two examples of tabular sets of coordinates extracted from two very
differently drawn paths, along with subsequent scatter plots that validate the
extraction process.

The following code provides a mostly foolproof approach to extracting
path-point data from either of these kinds of drawn paths.

```
Sub ExtractPoints from DrawnLine()
  Columns("A:I").ClearContents
  Range("E1") = "NumNodeSpecs"
  Range("F1") = Selection.ShapeRange.Nodes.Count 'Number of
    'node records in in freeform record. Includes curvature
    'data if any.
  Range("E2") = "Units From Left"
  Range("F2") = "Units From Top"
  NumTruNodes = 0
  For Count = 1 To Selection.ShapeRange.Nodes.Count
    NumTrueNodes = NumTrueNodes + 1
    If NumTrueNodes > 1 Then
        If Selection.ShapeRange.Nodes.Item(Count)._
            SegmentType = 0 Then
            'Check whether node starts a straight line segment
            Range("G3").Offset(NumTrueNodes - 1) =_
              "Straight Segment"
```

```
        Else 'Otherwise, "jump over" curvature data built into
            'freeform record
            Count = Count + 2 'Note: Not typical within a For
                'loop, but an easy solution in this case
            Range("G3").Offset(NumTrueNodes - 1) =_
                "Curved Segment"
        End If
    End If
    Range("E3:F3").Offset(NumTrueNodes - 1) = Selection._
        ShapeRange.Nodes.Item(Count).Points
  Next
End Sub
```

If you'd like to see this code in action with a polygon you've drawn, the program is available for use in the Chp10_DrawnPathExtraction workbook and can be executed on any line drawn in that workbook. It will be looking for a "selected polygon" for point extraction, so make sure one is selected prior to running the program. If you need some meaningful polygons, but don't want to draw one yourself, you can find a number of possible resources online that offer free vector drawings that can be converted (with VISIO) into importable drawn polygons in Excel. There's also the freely available HeatmapDeveloper add-in discussed in Chapter 4. The images it generates are drawn polygons. Any one of those could be applied here.

For those who are intrigued by this automation and are further interested in leveraging the full capabilities of Excel, keep reading! As we are about to see in our discussion of the VB Editor environment (Chapter 11), this code (and any VBA code you have access to) can also be copied and pasted into other workbooks, manipulated, and expanded upon for more advanced applications.

Section 4

Advanced Automation and Interfacing

11

Visual Basic Editing and Code Development

Many effective decision support systems rely not only on the ability of a manager to present information, analysis, and meaningful dynamics (for example, through graphics), but also on enabling users to realize the intended use of those elements by themselves (without the developer holding their hand). This is often going to mean providing sufficient documentation that might go beyond cell labeling and embedded comments. It may mean coming up with some kind of a customized user-driven help or wizard component as part of the DSS that makes use of not only automated numerical and graphical demos, but also other objects, such as images and .wav files, which could be incorporated into the workbook. This is often going to mean a level of automation that stretches the limits of the kind of work that can happen at the spreadsheet interface alone. In fact, it may be impossible to achieve by using only the top layer of an Excel workbook. Let's see how macros and the Visual Basic (VB) Editor might provide us with some new options in this regard.

11.1 The Visual Basic Editor

Let's take a deeper look into one of the first macros I introduced. Opening the Chp8_LobosInventory workbook provides us with an opportunity. To see the code associated with this macro, select the Developer tab on the main menu bar and then select Visual Basic (which will open the general VB Editor screen) or click Macros (see Figure 11.1), and from the associated dialog box select the specific name of the program code you are interested in viewing (in this case, generically called Macro1) and then Edit.

The VB Editor in Excel has its own distinct structure (fairly distinct from that of the Excel spreadsheets). Because any given macro may be specific to a single workbook, worksheet, or even refer to an included add-in (such as

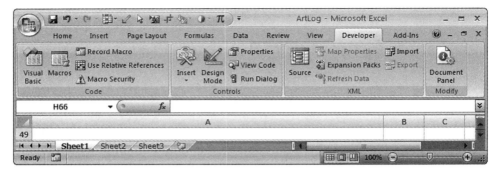

Figure 11.1. The Developer tab and associated elements.

Solver), the VB Editor provides a mechanism to categorize the macros that are associated with any workbook currently open in Excel. That mechanism is the Project window that appears to the left of the VB Editor interface (shown in Figure 11.2).

Figure 11.2. Basic elements of the VB Editor environment.

11.1.1 Confronting Code

The critical feature of the VB Editor is the code window (shown to the right of the Project window in Figure 11.2). In this and all cases discussed in this text, the code we're interested in will be stored in the Modules folder in the VBA Project window. If you don't see any code at this point, open that folder and double-click on Module1. The code associated with the Chapter 8 workbook should appear. When you record a macro, this is precisely the kind of stuff Excel writes for future reference (that is, for repeating or editing the actions you've recorded). This is also where all ground-up code development takes place (in lieu of macro recording). This is a useful point, in part because not all useful code can simply be generated through macro recording alone. Admittedly, it's probably one of the most intimidating areas for new developers, particularly those without computer programming backgrounds. But don't give up yet. As an experiment, let's try to interpret the language Excel and the VB Editor use to keep track of some of the actions we may have recorded. Table 11.1 shows an abridged and annotated version of the code written and used in the Chapter 8 example.

Again, I've fully annotated the code (the text in Table 11.1 is not actually present in the code itself), but even if you didn't have this annotation, do you think you could have guessed what some of these lines did? Some are fairly obvious, or at least suggestive (for example, Range("H18").Select, Selection.Copy, or Selection.EntireRow.Insert). VB capitalizes on simple elements of the English language, making it easy for even laypersons to navigate. Some code is more cryptic, but in general we could get a sense of what's happening here by attempting to read through the code as if it were steps in a set of cooking instructions. As with any good cookbook, we also have tools in Visual Basic for Application (VBA) that will help us read the code. Here, we see for example the use of "_" to denote a line continuation, sort of like a hyphen breaking a word up. In the next subsection, we'll see some more sophisticated tools for better understanding code (and where problems may exist). The bottom line is this – you'll find that recording and editing macros is one of the best ways for noncomputer-programmers to learn to do some amazing things with code.

11.1.2 Walking through Code and Checking for Bugs

There are resources available to help pinpoint where things go wrong in code, and believe me, they will – again and again and again. For every minute that beginner (and even advanced) developers spend on coding, they may find themselves spending that same amount of time (and often much more)

Table 11.1. *Annotation and Code for Chapter 8 Example*

Annotation	Actual Code
Name/Start of macro	Sub Macro1()
	'
Notes	' Macro1 Macro
	'
Selection of active cell	Range("H18").Select
Specifying "reset/reinitialize"	ActiveCell.FormulaR1C1 = "FALSE"
Call to Recalc (eg. F9) to reset	Calculate
Reselection of active cell	Range("H18").Select
Specifying "start simulation"	ActiveCell.FormulaR1C1 = "TRUE"
Call to Recalc to iterate	Calculate
	Calculate
	Calculate
~200 of the same lines (for 200 periods iterated	:
	Calculate
	Calculate
Select key cells	Range("K32:K35").Select
Copy them as a set	Selection.Copy
Select the "record" sheet	Sheets("MacroRuns").Select
Select a starting cell there	Range("B2").Select
Paste the copied cells there (note that the "_" is used to denote code statement continuation on next line)	Selection.PasteSpecial Paste:=xlPasteValues, Operation:=xlNone, _ SkipBlanks:=False, Transpose:=True
	Application.CutCopyMode = False
Insert new row in anticipation of next record paste	Selection.EntireRow.Insert
	Sheets("StockoutDemo").Select
End of macro	End Sub

figuring out where they went wrong with the coding and what they can do to resolve it. There are a few features available to help in this process.

The first feature is the ability to "step-through" a macro line by line, as opposed to just letting a macro run until it ends (or breaks down). In VB Editor, after a specific macro is selected and the blinking line cursor appears in the code (as for editing), pressing the F8 key will step the developer through the code line by line. Each line will be highlighted in yellow, signifying that the particular line of code has just been or is being processed. A yellow arrow also appears at the side bar of the code window to emphasize the current line (see Figure 11.3).

As an alternative to using F8, some developers prefer to allow larger macros to run for a longer segment of code and stop only for checking when

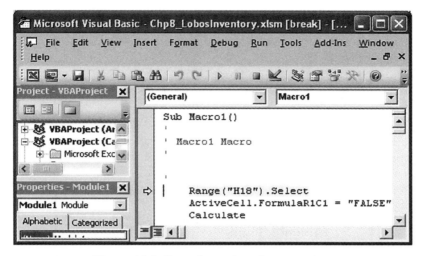

Figure 11.3. Step-through code execution.

specific points of interest are reached. Those specific points are often chosen by developers because there is some intuitive feeling that something around that point is likely to cause some problem, such as something has either just recently had the possibility of going wrong, or it is about to. To insert these breakpoints, the developer can select the line of code of interest, right-click, and select Toggle>Breakpoint (see Figure 11.4). The line then gets shaded maroon and a maroon circle appears to the left of the code. Another fast way is to select a line of code and press F9 in the VB Editor, or, more simply, toggle breakpoints on and off by clicking on the bar area immediately to the left of the code.

There can be as many breakpoints as there are lines to a code (although there would be little point in adding so many). When added, the developer can start a macro run in the VB Editor (using the Play button). The macro will run up until each breakpoint and then stop until the next breakpoint is reached, the macro ends, or the macro breaks down because of a processing error. At each break, the developer has the opportunity to check what the spreadsheet looks like, and even check on the status of some data maintained by the macro, which can provide a wealth of insights that we'll discuss further on in this chapter.

11.2 Additional VBA Capabilities: Object Manipulations

Before devling into in the syntax and logic of VBA code structures, let's preview some of the many activities that VBA makes possible, in coordination with Excel. At this point, it should be clear that there are many other objects you might encounter, construct, or manipulate aside from cells in a

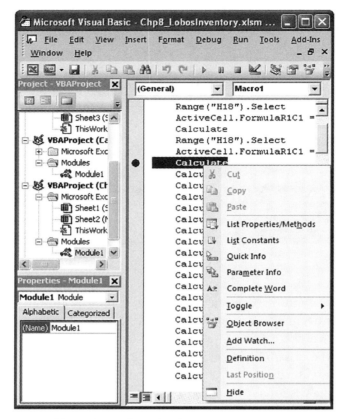

Figure 11.4. Toggling breakpoints in code.

workbook. Objects such as graphs, buttons, and clips of various types can reside within a workbook, and may ultimately serve as the primary vehicles for users to interface with a DSS. Yet, as with cells, there's often much more to these objects than you might first expect.

Similar to cells, all objects have a certain set of properties that can be manipulated. Many developers refer to the full set of properties of any object as a record, although the structure and content of those records may be very different depending on the objects. For example, objects such as check boxes are specifically designed to possess properties that a simple circle drawing would not. Check boxes contain a property that describes the cell to which they are linked, and whether they are checked or not checked, for instance.

At the same time, simple circle drawings possess other attributes like line-type, which check boxes don't (at least not in an identical form). Regardless of these nuances, there are some properties that all these objects share:

Name/Label: What the object can be referenced as
Location (x,y): Where the object is located in a spreadsheet
Visualization (size, color, and shading): What it looks like

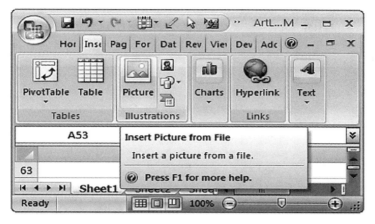

Figure 11.5. Importing pictures into Excel.

11.2.1 Incorporating External Objects into Workbooks

Let's see what we can expect if we decide to import a picture into our work-book. Start by going to Insert>Picture and then browsing for an image to import (see Figure 11.5). For my own reference, I'm going to rename this object SampleImage (using the same labeling/naming field I would use to name cells and cell ranges). In doing so, I'm essentially updating the name attribute of that image. The image is shown in Figure 11.6.

Note that when the picture is selected in Excel, the Picture toolbar displays at the top of Excel. The items on that toolbar represent other attributes

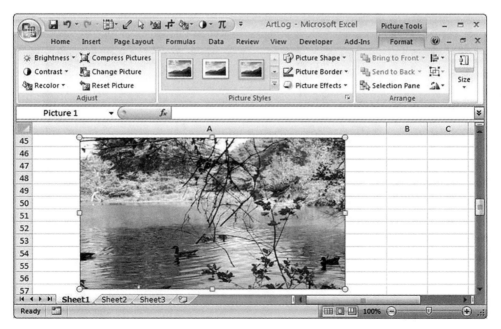

Figure 11.6. Example of picture import and available editing tools.

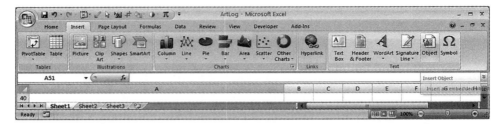

Figure 11.7. Access to general object importation.

of that object's data record (for example, color, brightness, orientation, size, line thickness).

Aside from static images, you can also insert other kinds of audio-visual objects, such as sound and video clips (generally found under the Object button through the Insert tab in Excel 2007; see Figure 11.7).

We can edit elements of a sound clip, such as where we want it to start or stop, in the same way that we could edit different attributes of imported images. Figures 11.8 and 11.9 display the subsequent object selection and specification steps associated with inserting a wave sound object, for example.

For future reference, I'm going to use the labeling/naming field to rename this object as SoundClip. At this point, it might also be worth inserting an actual sound file into the newly created template, using the Edit>Insert File option in the dialog box depicted in Figure 11.9 (to reaccess the dialog box just right-click on the newly imported object and select Open from the short-cut menu).

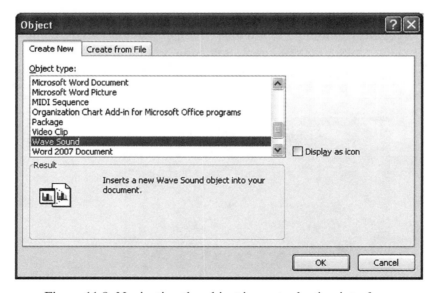

Figure 11.8. Navigating the object import selection interface.

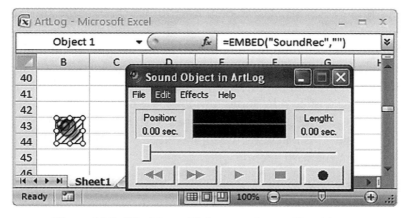

Figure 11.9. Working with imported .wav file objects.

11.2.2 Object Macros

Given our existing discussions on the development of macros for repeating common actions, let's use one of the new objects we've imported to see what Excel will allow us to record on objects rather than just cells. Pick any random cell on the spreadsheet. To make sure that the object is not yet selected, we want to record the selection as well. Then start recording by selecting Macros>Record Macro to open the Record Macro dialog box. Enter a name for your macro, such as ImageMacro, and then click OK.

While we're recording, let's try some simple manipulations of the imported image. For example, we might select the image and drag it to the right. We might then pull on one of the corners of the image to expand it a little. Then, click the Brightness button in the Picture toolbar a few times to lighten things up. The results are shown in Figure 11.10.

Now, let's stop the recording. Try to play your macro by going to the Developer tab (in Excel 2007) and selecting Macros as you did before. This time, select the macro of choice and hit Run. If the actions are repeated perfectly, you're probably using either Excel 2003 or a patched version of Excel

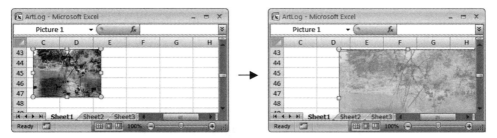

Figure 11.10. Editing a picture object while recording a macro.

2007. If nothing happens, it may be a function of the version of Excel 2007 you are using.

Here is some good news for Excel 2007 users. If you create a macro that manipulates objects (such as pictures) in a previous version of Excel (such as Excel 2003) and then use that file in Excel 2007, it should work. Alternatively, if you know the code enough to create a macro that manipulates an object from the ground up using the built-in Visual Basic Editor, you should still be able to get those actions to run in Excel 2007. We will take a look at how to do this in the next section.

In any case, if the recording mechanism does work, the code recorded should look something like this:

```
Sub Macro1()
  ActiveSheet.Shapes("SampleImage").Select
  Selection.ShapeRange.IncrementLeft 120#
  Selection.ShapeRange.ScaleWidth 2.35, msoFalse,_
    msoScaleFromTopLeft
  Selection.ShapeRange.ScaleHeight 2.34, msoFalse,_
    msoScaleFromTopLeft
  Selection.ShapeRange.PictureFormat.IncrementBrightness 0.03
  Selection.ShapeRange.PictureFormat.IncrementBrightness 0.03
  Selection.ShapeRange.PictureFormat.IncrementBrightness 0.03
End Sub
```

No annotation here, and I'm not going to spend much time walking through this code because it's fairly clear what each line is getting at if you just spend a just few seconds reading through it. For example, some lines clearly have to do with the selection of the object in question (in this case, the image); other lines clearly pertain to manipulations of the location of the object, the size of the object, and the brightness of the object.

Nevertheless, it's worth pointing out at least one less-intuitive structure. Specifically, VB actually has a range of Location(x,y) change commands for objects, although, in this particular case, the VB Editor has defaulted to the use of the command IncrementLeft for the horizontal movement recorded (IncrementTop would be the associated command for vertical movement). When the IncrementLeft command is used, it means that the left edge of the object will be moved a certain horizontal distance.When moved to the right, that distance will be positive (+); when moved to the left, it will be negative (−). So, in this case, the code would actually move the object to the right, just as I did during the original recording in Excel 2003. This is a case where the designed use of language-rich syntax doesn't hit home as intuitively as one might have hoped. It's just something to get used to.

Table 11.2. *Annotation and Code for Basic Clip Play Macro*

Annotation	Actual Code
Name/Start of macro	Sub Macro2() '
Notes	' Macro1 Macro '
Selection of wave object	ActiveSheet.Shapes("SoundClip").Select
Play sound clip	Selection.Verb Verb:=xlPrimary
Call to Recalc (e.g., F9) to reset	End Sub

Perhaps surprisingly, in contrast, the code representing the activation and playing of the sound clip is much simpler than the graphic manipulation. Table 11.2 shows the annotated the code clip. It's nice to see that only two lines are really relevant here.

It's worth pointing out that in both the image-movement case and the sound-clip case, there is considerable reference to something called selection. The IncrementLeft 120# action seems to be just a feature of the selection in the first case, while the Verb Verb:=xlPrimary seems to be a feature associated with the selection in the second case. Both are functional attributes that apply to only certain objects. We know that they are associated with selected objects because of the use of a dot (.), which links their use to the key term selection in all cases. The use of this dot notation will become increasingly familiar to you as a developer as you encounter more advanced codes (ones that you've recorded, been given, or wrote from scratch). This serves a little like the period in the Dewey decimal system used at libraries to get into increasingly more specific features of a larger category of attributes (or, drawing on our Principal Components Analysis discussion, it's like specifying how each individual item relates to a higher-level factor). This notation can be used in both constructing data storage mechanisms in VBA (records) and in other functionality that comes standard with selections.

11.2.3 Turning on Embedded Browsers

As nice as it might be to embed an image, sound clip, or video in a workbook, these things take up a great deal of space and make sharing the document difficult. Fortunately, there's a nice alternative to storing media content: the Internet. And there's already a special object in Excel that allows us to access media within the spreadsheet environment: Microsoft Web Browser, found under Developer>Insert>More ActiveX Controls. Once selected, what you will see is an empty object. Leaving developer mode you might see a rectangle with a black background displaying a Microsoft logo. To activate the embedded browser and have it point to a desired Web site, say, Google, you'll need to modify the properties of that new object. The following is example code that might be used, assuming you don't change the default name "WebBrowser1":

```
ActiveSheet.Shapes("Webbrowser1").OLEFormat.Object.Object._
    Navigate2 "www.google.com"
```

Running this code in a macro would provide a presentation of the Google main page, or whatever page you pointed to in the code. For example, you might navigate the object to a YouTube video of choice. Getting back into developer mode, you could also resize the object in the spreadsheet (there's also VBA code that could do this automatically). Basically, this opens up infinite options for media placement in the workbook environment and the impact on file size is minimal.

11.2.4 A Final Example: Regression Revisited

In Chapter 2, we introduced two mechanisms for developing best-fit model estimates in data (regression). Formulaically, we have the LINEST function available in Excel. We also have the Data Analysis tool that can present a fixed report of the same type. In Chapter 4, we were introduced to yet another mechanism for developing best fits within scatter plots. However, the numerical results of these best fits were only presented in the graphs themselves and appeared inaccessible to the spreadsheet (where they could be used in additional analysis). Fortunately, these best-fit equations in the scatter plots are simply another attribute of those plots, and, as such, they can be accessed through the same dot notation we've been seeing applied to the media objects we've just seen.

For example, the VBA code from Chp11_BestFitData would take the text associated with a trendline (the R-square and estimated fit equation) and store it in a cell labeled "TrendlineData." The assumption here is that the scatter plot is called "Chart 1" and exists on the sheet "OriginalData&Plot." There is also an assumption that a trend line (and data series it is based on) already exists. The "_" denotes a line continuation. We'll see this in VBA code again later.

```
Sub PullTrendLineData()
  Range("TrendlineData").Value = Sheets("OriginalData&Plot")._
    ChartObjects("Chart1").Chart.SeriesCollection(1)._
    Trendlines(1).DataLabel.Text
End Sub
```

If you want to change from a linear fit to a logarithmic one, no problem:

```
Sub ChngtoLogarthmic()
  Sheets("OriginalData&Plot").ChartObjects("Chart1").Chart._
    SeriesCollection(1).Trendlines(1).Type = xlLogarithmic
End Sub
```

Changing back to a linear fit:

```
Sub ChngtoLinear()
  Sheets("OriginalData&Plot").ChartObjects("Chart1").Chart._
    SeriesCollection(1).Trendlines(1).Type = xlLinear
End Sub
```

Deleting the trend line all together:

```
Sub DeleteTrendLine()
 Sheets("OriginalData&Plot").SeriesCollection(1)._
   Trendlines(2).Delete
End Sub
```

11.3 Syntax and Storage

Now that you've gotten a taste of what you can accomplish using Excel macros and VBA code, we're ready to talk about the basic standards in VB. Literally, all macros, subroutines, and programs typically start with the following in the VB Editor:

```
Sub SubroutineName () 'whatever name you want to use
```

And end with the following:

```
End Sub 'always the same regardless of the macro
```

Everything between those two lines represents what will take place (or could take place, as we'll see in a moment) when the macro/subroutine is run. Remember that we can start the run of any macro directly from the Excel workbook interface by going to Macros>View Macros>Run or by assigning a macro to an object such as a control button or image that we've created or imported.

11.3.1 Introduction to VB Data Storage: Variables and Types

One of the first things you might want to do in developing a new subroutine to run in Excel is define any variables that you want the VB Editor to keep track of outside the spreadsheets of the workbook. In other words, we're talking about data that isn't actually stored in any of the cells of the workbook. There are a number of reasons why you might want to temporarily store data this way.

Referencing and modifying data that's present in the cells of spreadsheets actually takes a little longer than doing the same with data stored only by the VB Editor during run-time. Think about it this way. The computer has a large block of memory it makes available for storing content. When Excel is running, part of the computer's resources performs regular checks for changes in open workbook spreadsheets. Recall from Chapter 2 the variety of attributes associated with each cell in a spreadsheet (fix or formulaic content, visual size, fixed or conditional formatting, comments, links to externals, and so on). Whether they are used or not, these attributes come default with each cell, so they are already fairly complex things. Data stored behind the scenes in VBA, on the other hand, can be stored in much simpler structures, without a need to define all the bells and whistles that come with cells. Accessing this doesn't need to involve the additional step of asking the Excel environment to access the data-content portion of something more complex. Changes to data stored behind the scenes in VBA also doesn't risk a full-blown recalculation of the formulae contained in other cells in a spreadsheet, which happens if cell content is changed (unless certain precautions are taken such as "manual updating" in Excel options).

If you have a lot of data that you plan to access and base multiple, repeated calculations on, this data simplicity can really make a difference in the amount of time it takes for the program to run. You may not want to do this for all the data you use in the workbook; it makes sense to have some of it stored in spreadsheet form if, for example, you want to make sure it's retained when you save the workbook. But during long and exhaustive data cleaning, manipulation, and calculation exercises, this kind of virtual storage comes in handy – I don't expect many to be able to make this "efficiency" distinction in the smaller tools developed up to this point. However, it is a large enough distinction to spur discussion by analysts on the topic of how to streamline Excel–VBA integration in large Excel-based applications.

Also, some data take on structures that may be difficult or cumbersome to meaningfully store in spreadsheet format. For example, let's say we want to run a simulation that takes into account all the restaurant franchises in a niche market that exist in each of the forty-eight contiguous states. Based on historical data, some franchises open whereas others close over time. Imagine that for the ease of certain calculations we want to make sure our data remain sorted by state and restaurant chain. Storing and changing this data in a spreadsheet over the time window of the simulation would mean either inserting and deleting rows of data (and knowing where to do such deletions and insertions based on state and chain), or adding data at the end of a list and then re-sorting that list every time new data is added.

This can be a lot of work, even if fully automated. A better way to do this might be to store that data in some kind of an array format in the VB Editor, something that automatically indexes data the way you want (for example, by state, chain, and franchise number) while keeping track of which franchises are open and which are closed. In particular, certain forms of these variables (called dynamically linked lists) are used extensively by DSS developers. We'll focus on the simpler forms of arrays here. Let's start by outlining some of the most basic kinds of data structures in VB: single-value variables and single-variable data types. Common types include:

Integer: For whole numbers ranging from $-32,768$ to $+32,767$
Long: For whole numbers ranging from $2,147,483,648$ to $2,147,483,647$
Single: For all numbers ranging from as small as $\pm 1.4 \times 10^{-45}$ to as large as $\pm 3.4 \times 10^{38}$
Boolean: For variables that take on the value of either True or False
String: For variables that take on text values (such as someone's name)

Note that each of these single-variable types can be used to construct a variety of more complex data types. For example, they could be used to build a record or combination of different variables, each of a potentially different type: for example, the name {String}, student ID {Long}, and class grade {Single} for an individual student. Alternately, they could form variable arrays, which are lists of values for multiple instances of the same kind of variable, such as a list consisting solely of individual students' names {An array of Strings}.

They could also be used to construct *variable record arrays*, or lists whose entries are each a record that includes a student name, ID, and class grade. To ensure that the VB Editor is handling data the way you want, define the variables you want it to keep track of right at the beginning of your macro/subroutine. All declarations start with the term *Dim* and are followed by the name you want for your VB variable and a description of the type of variable it is.

For example, we could create a new subroutine called Subroutine Name in which two variables are defined – one called NewInteger that is designed to hold integer-type values, and another called NewStudentName that is designed to hold text type values fifty characters in length (max). The "*50" designation specifies this, although is often not a requirement for String declaration.

```
Sub SubroutineName ()
   Dim NewInteger As Integer
   Dim NewStudentName As String*50
End sub
```

After declaration, you can use these variables within your subroutine without any doubt regarding how the VB Editor will interpret them. You can now develop additional code that assigns and changes values for these variables. Here's the kind of syntax you might use to assign a value to the NewStudentName variable.

```
NewStudentName = "Dorian McAnderstein"
```

The general rule when using the "=" sign in VBA to make one thing take on the value of another is that the item on the left side (in this case, a VBA-declared variable) always takes on the content on the right side of the equal sign. This will always be the case. Because of this, you can't place a constant on the left side, only VBA variables or spreadsheet cell locations such as Range("A1").

It's valuable to note that the name you give a variable in VB Editor has absolutely nothing to do with any labels or names you've applied in the spreadsheets of the workbook. Regardless, you can easily copy and paste values from VB variables to cells in a spreadsheet, or the other way around. For example:

```
Range("Sheet1!A2") = VBvariable1
VBvariable2 = Range("RateofReturn")
```

This would place the value that is currently in your VB variable called VBvariable1 into the cell A2 in Sheet1 of your workbook, while setting VBvariable2 to whatever value is currently in the workbook cell labeled RateofReturn.

11.3.2 Declaring and Using More Complex Variables

To create a variable array (list) of strings for storing multiple (say, twenty-five, maximum) student names, we would use a declaration like this:

```
Dim NewStudentNames(25) As String*50
```

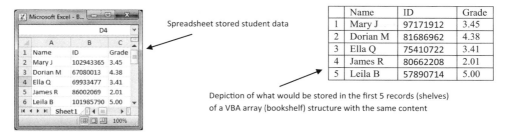

	Name	ID	Grade
1	Mary J	97171912	3.45
2	Dorian M	81686962	4.38
3	Ella Q	75410722	3.41
4	James R	80662208	2.01
5	Leila B	57890714	5.00

Spreadsheet stored student data

Depiction of what would be stored in the first 5 records (shelves) of a VBA array (bookshelf) structure with the same content

Figure 11.11. Comparison of data stored in a spreadsheet versus the same structure in an array of records.

You can think of this as a bookshelf with twenty-five shelves. Every shelf is exactly the same size and is able to accommodate the same kind of thing – here, a string of up to fifty characters in length.

After such a declaration, to set the third name in that list (third shelf in the bookshelf) to a name in your workbook, such as a name you know is in cell B30 of Sheet1, you'd use:

```
NewStudentNames(3) = Range("Sheet1!B30")
```

However, analysts often have more complex data structures to work with. Rather than just having a list of names, we might have a list of students – each characterized by a name, a student ID, a grade in a class, and so on. The kind of bookshelf we'll need to accommodate this data may still have identical shelves, except each shelf will have various compartments, each designed to store different content. Comparing this structure to that of the cell structure of a spreadsheet, you'll find striking similarity, as in Figure 11.11. That's good. In using VBA behind the scenes of Excel, you usually want to be able to pull in data from the sheets and push it back out. When the data is of the same dimensions both in the sheet and in the VBA code, the task of pulling in and pushing out that data is trivial.

To create a variable record like that of Figure 11.11, accommodating multiple entries of grouping of numerous different variable types, you could use the following syntax.

```
Type StudentInforRecord
  Name As String * 50
  ID As Long
  Grade As Single
End Type
Sub Macro1()
  Dim NewRecords(50) As StudentInfoRecord
End Sub
```

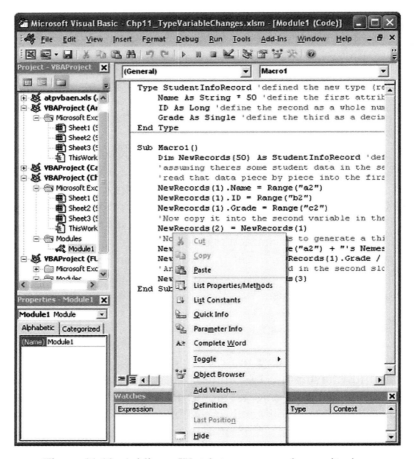

Figure 11.12. Adding a Watch to macro code monitoring.

Obviously, this is a much more complex declaration than the one presented previously, but it's still something we can get our hands around. The first thing that's happening here is the definition of a new type of variable, one that contains three components of Name, ID, and Grade. This must be typed at the top of the VB Editor code before the subroutine starts. The second is a declaration of a variable base on that new type. This is how we might assign values to two fields of the first element (shelf) of this new variable:

```
NewRecords(1).Name = "Dorian McAnderstein"
NewRecords(1).ID = 555442727
```

Note that each field of the record is designated by a dot (.) followed by the name of the field to be used. This dot-notation is used to specify an aspect of the larger record element (which compartment of a selected bookshelf) we want to make use of. The nice thing is that we've already seen this dot-notation in action in our Section 11.2 teasers. This same notation will be encountered throughout your experience with VBA to allow you to drill down to more and more specifics of control.

As a quick example to pull all of these ideas together, consider the following macro code:

```
Type StudentInfoRecord 'defined the new type (record)
  Name As String * 50 'define the first attribute as a string
  ID As Long 'define the second as a whole number
  Grade As Single 'define the third as a decimal number
End Type
Sub Macro1()
  Dim NewRecords(50) As StudentInfoRecord 'define the variable
    'array assuming theres some student data in the second
    'row...read that data piece by piece into the first
    'variable in the array
  NewRecords(1).Name = Range("a2")
  NewRecords(1).ID = Range("b2")
  NewRecords(1).Grade = Range("c2")
    'Now copy it into the second variable in the array
  NewRecords(2) = NewRecords(1)
    'Now use those two records to generate a third
  NewRecords(3).Name = Range("a2") + "'s Nemesis"
  NewRecords(3).Grade = NewRecords(1). Grade / NewRecords(2).ID
    'And now modify the record in the second slot once again
  NewRecords(2) = NewRecords(3)
End Sub
```

Ultimately, the code outline is a bunch of seemingly random manipulations of information storage devices, but hopefully it allows a little more familiarity with the nature of variables and how different kinds of variable structures interact with one another.

11.3.3 Watching for Changes in Stored Information

All the variables and types just described are helpful because they provide the means of storing information outside the spreadsheet proper and the means of storing information in forms other than the piecemeal structure typically associated with spreadsheet records. However, the storage of information in VB-based variables does leave one particular issue to be desired: visibility. Generally speaking, it often appears to those starting out that what happens behind the scenes in VB is a bit clouded in mystery, or at least much

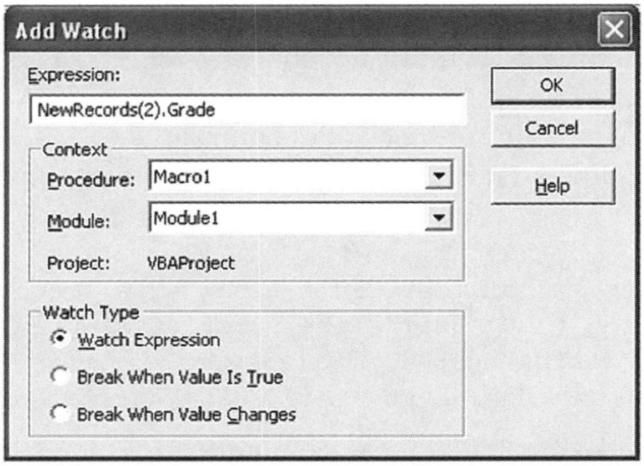

Figure 11.13. Specifying the nature of a Watch.

more difficult to get a handle on than the kinds of calculations that take place in a spreadsheet.

In reality, this may have more to do with the roots of those developers transitioning from spreadsheet environments where data storage units (for example, cells) are ever present, to VB environments where only specific data storage units (for example, variables) exist on a need-to-exist basis (that is, when associated macros are being run). Even when macros are being run and variables are called into existence for the use of storage and calculation, the changes to the contents of these variables may not appear immediately obvious. Fortunately, the VB Editor does provide the means of making the values stored and changed within these variables crystal clear to developers who are interested in monitoring their change throughout a macro run. The tool provided to accomplish this is called a *Watch* and it is generated by right-clicking anywhere on your code to open a shortcut menu. From there, select Add Watch (shown in Figure 11.13). This process is facilitated if you select the variable of interest and right-click directly on it.

Selecting Add Watch opens the Add Watch dialog box (Figure 11.13), which enables you to specify exactly what you want to watch as you step through the macro (for example, using F8, or running the macro with break-points active). The Watch then appears at the bottom of the screen (Figure 11.14), which is what you'll want to keep your eyes on for changes in the variables selected. After stepping through to the end of this particular macro run (in Chp11_TypeVariableUse), theWatch screen should appear as shown in the lower panel of Figure 11.14.

11.3.4 Facilitating VBA Interaction in Complex Spreadsheets

Although we can accomplish a great deal of heavy lifting behind the scenes in VBA through the use of data stored in VBA variables, we still often have a need to interact with the spreadsheet (often, the original source of data as

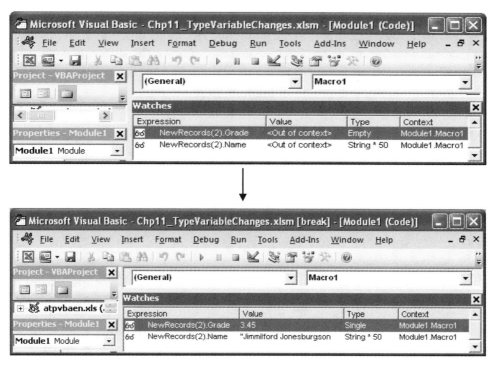

Figure 11.14. The initial and changed displays of variable Watches before values are assigned.

well as the reporting interface for data work conducted in VBA). To avoid delays that otherwise might come from regular spreadsheet usage, we can take the following precautions in our VBA–Excel interactions:

1) When Running VBA script, unless regular spreadsheet calculation and data updates are needed, run Excel in "manual update" mode in Excel Options. If you'd like to make that specification in VBA, the following code can be used:

    Application.Calculation = xlCalculationManual

2) To toggle back to automatic updates, the following line of VBA code can be used:

    Application.Calculation = xlCalculationAutomatic

3) If you want to only perform a recalculation over a very specific set of cells while in manual mode, the following code can apply (for example, over the range B10-C15):

    Range("B10:C15").Calculate

11.4 Common Operations in VBA

With all of these variable declarations, the nagging question remains: How can we complete tasks with data stored in VBA variables? Like the long list of functions already built into Excel, a comprehensive coverage of what we can do in VBA is certainly beyond the scope of this text; however, it is useful to cover at least a few examples to illustrate some of the differences and, in particular, some of the advantages of doing work in the VB Editor.

11.4.1. Syntax for Basic Operators

Many basic arithmetic functions are the same in VB Editor because they are in the Excel spreadsheets. Others, such as MOD, work a little differently. In a spreadsheet, we use MOD(12,5) to find 2 (the remainder of 12 divided by 5). In VB code, we use 12 MOD 5. Why does the spreadsheet use syntax different from the VB Editor in case like this? There's no good reason, suffice to say that Microsoft has a large workforce. Some employees develop spreadsheet functions whereas others work on VB. Sometimes, their approaches differ.

This can be a bit annoying, but here's something to consider: If you really need to know how to calculate something that you can figure out in the spreadsheet but can't figure it out with code, you might save yourself some trouble and just do the calculation in the spreadsheet and then simply reference the calculated cell in the VB Editor. This can save you a lot of frustration (the help available on VB functions is less useful than the help provided with functions in the spreadsheet).

11.4.1.1 Random Numbers

In spreadsheets, we can use Rand() to generate a decimal value between 0 and 1. In VB, we use Rnd. There's no real difference here, aside from a loss of a vowel and the lack of parentheses.

11.4.1.2 OFFSET

In Excel spreadsheets, we use OFFSET(C5,2,4) to access the cell two rows below and four columns to the right of C5. In VB, we use Range(C5) and Offset(2,4) to access the same spreadsheet data in the VB Editor.

11.4.1.3 IF Statements

In the spreadsheet, we type the following into a cell, for instance, cell D5, to set its value to 4 when C5=1, and 3 otherwise: = IF(C5=1,4,3). In VB, we would use:

```
IF Range("C5")=1 Then
    Range("D5")=4
Else
    Range("D5")=3
End if
```

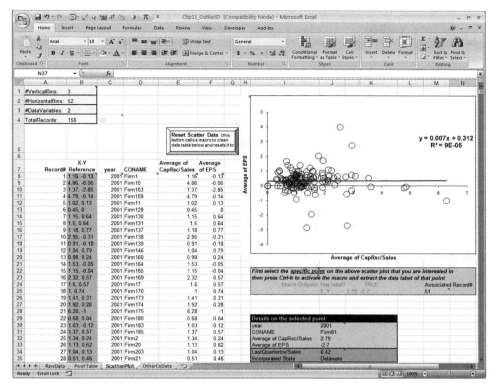

Figure 11.15. Example of graph-point interaction and macro use.

At first, this may seem more complex than what we're familiar with in the spreadsheet, but it actually represents a fairly robust structure into which a wide variety of actions can conditionally take place. For instance, if C5=1, I might also want to run Solver and a sound clip to start. I can do this by entering more code into the framework. I couldn't do this by just using a spreadsheet's IF statement.

Now, let's consider a more complex application in which the IF statement proves useful. We've already taken several looks as the dot-notation structure common to what the VB Editor writes when macros are recorded, as well as common to the use of user-defined records for information storage and reference in VB. It's worth taking an additional look at these structures just to reinforce some familiarity. The Chp11_OutlierID workbook provides an example of some fairly simple code in which both functional and descriptive attributes are being used to do some powerful things. We'll focus on the ScatterPlot sheet in this workbook, shown in Figure 11.15, which, incidentally, also contains examples of the integrated use of a pivot table.

Opening the VB Editor and the associated Modules folder in this case reveals the following two macros:

```
Sub CreateDatatoPlot()
'Activated by a button assigned to the macro in this case
  Dim Rangetext As String 'need to define a storage
   'place for a line of text to be created below
  Rangetext = "B8:F" + Range("TotRecords_p_7") 'This term
   'and all it contains must be treated entirely as text
   'to work below
  Range("B9:G2007").Clear 'just clearing out the region of
   'the worksheet where we're gettin the data to be plotted
  Range("B8:F8").Select 'now I'm selecting the range of
   'formulae to copy
  Selection.AutoFill Destination:=Range(Rangetext),_
    Type:=xlFillDefault
   'using the range specified above to only fill in the
   'necessary rows with the copied formulae
End Sub
Sub GetDataLabel()
'Shortcut Ctrl-k to activate
  Range("HasDataLabel") = Selection.HasDataLabel 'Just for our
    'infor
  If Selection.HasDataLabel Then 'and as a failsafe
   Range("DataLabel") = Selection.DataLabel.Text 'output the
    'point's label
  End If
End Sub
```

The first of these routines selects a range of cells, which happens to be a set of cells in row 8. It then conducts an autofill using the formula content of that selection to fill in a larger range of cells below it (defined by the string variable Rangetext and based on some specifications described in the associated spreadsheet).

The second routine assumes the user has first selected something and then has attempted to access information on that object to return to the spreadsheet. In this case, the assumed object is a graphical point on a scatter plot, and the information returned is the label data the point has associated with it. This is particularly useful in this case to identify outliers in a graph and subsequently exclude them from visualization and analysis such as line-fitting.

In both cases, we are making use of selections of some sort, and drilling down to capitalize on their attributes. The first is a selection of cells; the second is a graphical object. In the first case, we are drawing on a functional attribute of a selection (autofill, a verb essentially). In the second case, we are drawing on a descriptive attribute (datalabel.text, an adjective essentially).

Regardless, VB is able to recognize the appropriateness of our drill down based on the starting point – that is, based on what exactly the selection happens to be, just in the same way that it is able to make sense of the attributes of a record based on how we've defined the nature of the record type definition.

11.4.2 Date/Time Functionality

In the spreadsheet, there are a number of ways to get and make use of date/time information maintained by the system clock. For example, the Now() command provides the date/time signature at any given moment. Like the Rand() function, every recalculation in a sheet containing Now() updates the value returned by that function to reflect the passage of time. What is returned by Now() is a composite of the current data and time.

If it's formatted correctly, then it should be easy to understand, but ultimately it's just a long decimal number. If formatted like a long decimal number, it will look like one – and one that wouldn't at first glance seem to have a lot of immediate intuitive meaning. Another function, TimeValue, serves in a related capacity by translating a recognizable time text string such as 3:30:15 into a long decimal value of the kind that Now() and other time functions actually work with. DateValue serves a similar role with arguments such as Jan 4, 1982.

In VB, multiple tools for accessing and utilizing system clock data are also available. For example, the term Now (without the parentheses) can similarly be used to generate a consolidated decimal value that incorporates today's date and time. Also, the TimeValue function works just as it does in the spreadsheet. However, in VB, the combined use of these two functions take on particular relevance because of still more advanced functionality that does not exist directly in the spreadsheet. The Application.Wait function, a mechanism for generating delays during macro runs, is a prime example of how these two can be used together.

Why would someone want to intentionally add a delay to a macro? Sometimes, macros run too fast, at least too fast to allow for a meaningful visual demonstration of dynamics. Sometimes, it's even desirable to make users wait for calculations because we may need to wait for certain online updates. In any event, Application.Wait serves this purpose. As an extremely simple example, if at any point you want to force a one-minute delay in the middle of a macro, just insert the line: Application.Wait (Now + TimeValue("0:01:00")). That's it. Easy to customize, easy to interpret – and it works.

11.4.3 Iteration Structures: Loops

Given a little insight into how these common elements are dealt with differently in the VB Editor, we might assume that there are different, possibly better, ways of dealing with other tasks we've performed in the spreadsheet. And we'd be right. A case in point is the use of Excel's iteration mode as a mechanism for getting us through a series of sequential events. This is often done better in the VB Editor through what are called *loops*.

11.4.3.1 For-Loops (Fixed-Finite Iteration Structures)

When we know how many times we want some action repeated, or we know how many items we want the same or similar action applied, no matter what that action is, For-Loops can get the job done quickly. Here's an example of what the Chapter 8 code might look like if all 200 or so of those Calculate lines were condensed using a simple For-Loop:

```
Sub Macro1()
'
'Macro1 Macro
  Range("H18").Select
  ActiveCell.FormulaR1C1 = "FALSE"
  Calculate
  Range("H18").Select
  ActiveCell.FormulaR1C1 = "TRUE"
  For Count = 1 To 200
    Calculate
  Next
  Range("K32:K35").Select
  Selection.Copy
  Sheets("MacroRuns").Select
  Range("B2").Select
  Selection.PasteSpecial Paste:=xlPasteValues,_
    Operation:=xlNone, SkipBlanks:=False, Transpose:=True
  Application.CutCopyMode = False
  Selection.EntireRow.Insert
  Sheets("StockoutDemo").
  Select
End Sub
```

A few more than 200 periods seem to get recorded, but that's purely a result of the rest of what's going on in the code and is fairly easy to fix. The main point is that the code has been greatly reduced and becomes much easier to read, manage, and edit. Furthermore, there are plenty of other actions that could take place within each iteration of that loop, such as complex calculations or even multiple calls to add-ins like Solver or external applications like MapPoint.

Let's go over another simple example before moving on to an alternate approach to replication (and iteration) in VBA code. Consider the following code:

```
Sub WriteText1()
Dim count As Integer
  For count = 1 To 20
    Range("a1").Offset(count, 0) = count
    Range("a1").Offset(count, 0).Interior.Color = _
     count * 12 + 900100
  Next
End Sub
```

When this code runs, the numbers 1 through 20 (literally, the values of the count variable used in the loop) will be written to subsequent cells in the active worksheet, starting at cell A1. The color of each subsequent cell's interior will also get modified based on a numeric color code. Each cell will have a slightly different fill color as a result, starting from green and approaching yellow. The result of the run is shown in gray scale in Figure 11.16.

This example is nice in that it demonstrates how the count variable in the loop can be used as much more than just an iteration mechanism. In the related code, it is used to specify an output value, an offset level as well as a formatting modification.

11.4.3.2 While-Loops (Open-Ended Iterations)

In contrast, While-Loops are useful when we don't know how many times we want some action repeated, or we don't know how many things we want the same or similar action applied to, no matter what that action is. These loops end when specific conditions are met, similar to the stopping logic used as part of RISKOptimizer's functionality. Consider the following code as an alternative to the For-Loop code that generate the changes in Figure 11.16.

```
Sub WriteText1()
Dim count As Integer
  count = 1
  Do While count <= 20
    Range("a1").Offset(count, 0) = count
    Range("a1").Offset(count, 0).Interior.Color = _
      count * 12 + 900100
    count = count + 1
  Loop
End Sub
```

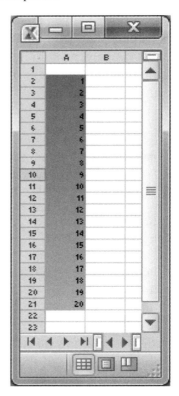

Figure 11.16. Resulting spreadsheet changes associated with a loop code.

Here, the count variable isn't the driving mechanism of the loop. Rather, it serves only to help specify the stopping criteria of loop repetition (end the loop repetition as soon as count is NOT less than or equal to 20). In order for this to work, count first has to be initialized to 0, as in the code. Within the loop, count has to be incremented (count=count+1). If this didn't take place, the loop would continue to repeat itself forever – after all, the count would always stay $< = 20$. This is an important point we'll mention again in a moment. Other than that, the same result as that presented in Figure 11.16 is generated. As in the previous example, count plays multiple roles in the output generation.

As a more complex example that combines the use of some of the date/time functions as well as GetEvents, consider a While-Loop used to simulate a simple count-down timer. The Chp11_BasicClock workbook provides such functionality. The main sheet appears in Figure 11.17, allowing individuals to enter in the number of minutes to be counted down from and a button that activates the looped count-down macro.

Before getting into the code for this one, it's probably worth making a general warning statement regarding the use of While-Loops: They are notorious for causing headaches for developers. Although For-Loops has a fixed

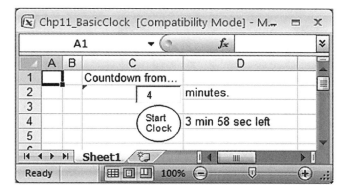

Figure 11.17. Interface for example of use of a While-Loop.

and certain end, While-Loops may never find the condition needed for stopping. This results in an *infinite loop* that might stop only if the user presses Ctrl-Alt-Delete, or when the computer dies – whichever comes first.

Of course, there are other ways to build in mechanisms that allow users to force exits from loops of any kind or at least maintain control during the running of long loop processes. Generally speaking, when macros are running, users are not given much of an opportunity to do other work in the workbook containing these macros. This shouldn't be a problem in many cases where macros get their work done quickly. But when macros take a long time to run, for example when they involve a long series of repetitions of the kind that is common to the use of loop structures, the cursor appearance in the spreadsheet environment will take on the characteristic hourglass icon until the macro has come to an end.

This can be a bit frustrating for some individuals who would like to maintain greater control over specific aspects of a DSS during these runs. Fortunately, certain clauses can be added to code to allow for such control. One of the most common of these clauses is DoEvents. Much like Calculate, it is typically used by itself within a program. Functionally, it allows items such as forms and controls on the spreadsheet to respond to actions taken by users while running macros that contain this line of code.

Let's take a look at the code working behind the scenes of the BasicClock example. The following is a clip of the code, as fully annotated in the file.

```
Sub EfficientClockSub()
  MaxTime = TimeValue("0:01:00") * Range("CountdownFrom")
  TimeSpent = 0 'Initialize this time keeping record
  StartTime = Now 'Note that 'Now' is a predefined term in
          'VB and provides the current system time
  Do While TimeSpent < MaxTime 'Do as long as MaxTime isn't
          'reached
```

```
    DoEvents 'Allows forms/controls on the spreadsheet to
        'respond to actions taken by user while clock runs.
        'Allows general access of cells but stops code upon
        'deliberate entry of new data directly into cells
    '**Below this point you might code in things that need to
        'be calculated or
    '**refreshed via VB...
    TimeSpent = Now - StartTime 'Update the time keeping
        'record
    Range("TimeLeft") = MaxTime - TimeSpent 'Here we're just
        'displaying the amount of time left
  Loop
End Sub
```

Leveraging a DoWhile loop structure, the macro essentially continues to update the amount of time left in the countdown on the main spreadsheet until the system time reaches a point equal to or greater than the initial system time plus the length of time originally requested to be counted down from. However, notice that along with all of the date/time elements being used, there is a continued reference to DoEvents within the main While-Loop.

As stated, the DoEvents clause allows for certain cursor activity that would otherwise be disabled in its absence. Another interesting feature of DoEvents is the fact that direct data entry into a spreadsheet cell while running a macro (which it ostensibly allows) can actually offer or force a direct exit from the running of that macro (that is, typing into the spreadsheet with DoEvent can shut down the macro).

This can serve as a convenient exit, but it can also prove inconvenient if the shutdown takes place accidentally. As a word of caution – if you want to allow interfacing with forms or controls (as introduced in Chapter 8) during a macro run, and if you want to use DoEvents to give you that functionality, you might want to make sure that users are not able to accidentally shut down the program halfway through a run. One way to prevent this is to protect the interfacing worksheet against any types of potentially inadvertent selections and sheet modifications (we'll get into the specifics of sheet protection in Chapter 13). We'll find that we can do this while keeping any cells unlocked for which you want to allow changes through VB or in forms or controls (hence, allowing the specific kind of control desired during macro runs while avoiding errors).

11.5 User-Defined Functions

A natural extension of the discussion we've had so far regarding the values, capabilities, and structures of macros is to spend some time on functions, another development mechanism made available through the VB Editor.

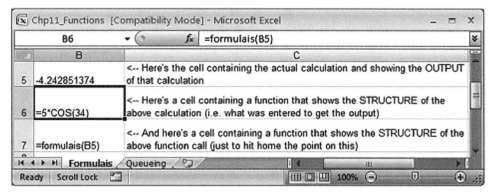

Figure 11.18. Interface for example of user-defined function.

11.5.1 An Introduction to Functions

Figure 11.18 shows an incredibly simple example of a function that writes out the formula content of another cell, something you would typically have to go into a cell directly to see. You will not find this function automatically built into Excel; it is not listed under Formulas>Insert Function under a typical install. Instead, I created it to provide a simple example of a user-defined function that anyone could create. After a function is created or a workbook containing its code is opened, it will appear in function listings or at least be recognized in some form by Excel. However, for the time being let's just see what this function is all about. Here's a clip from the Chp11_Functions workbook in which it was coded.

Table 11.3 shows the VB code that makes it possible to use the function formulais in the spreadsheet. Note the structure here, one that is distinct from that of a macro. This distinction has to do with the purpose behind user-defined functions. The main purpose is to take inputs and kick out individual outputs to the cell that references them. Although what happens within the code of a function may be as complex as what takes place in the code of a macro, the role of a macro is, in contrast, to execute a set of actions that results in something other than a single value getting returned to a single cell (although that can take place, it's usually not the main objective). User-defined functions are just like any other function in Excel, except they don't

Table 11.3. *Code and Annotation for Basic Function Structure*

Annotation	Actual Code
Name/Start of function *and* arguments (or "inputs") to the function	Function formulais(cell as Range)
Actions/Calculations taken by the function	formulais = cell.Range("a1").Formula
End of function	End Function

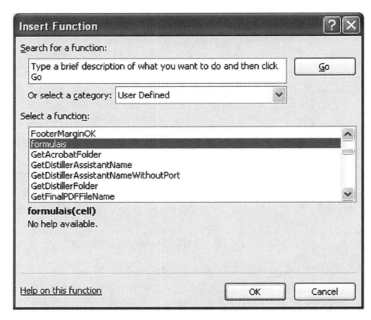

Figure 11.19. Recognition of user-defined functions by Excel.

come standard – they need to be built by users. In contrast to being activated by a button or a selection from a "macro list," they are called directly from cells within a spreadsheet or other programs in VB Editor, with the assumption that a sufficient specification of inputs is provided for them to do the number crunching they were designed to do.

And as for making sure that the right kinds of inputs are fed into a user-defined function when being used in a spreadsheet, recall that Excel will recognize the function when defined. In other words, you should be able to locate it in the Insert Function dialog box shown in Figure 11.19 (note the formulais section of this dialog box) when the workbook that contains the function is open. Furthermore, Excel will attempt to provide assistance with the inputs required for a user-defined function in the same way that it attempts to provide assistance for all other functions. Note specifically that in Figure 11.19, Excel is suggesting that the key input to formulais is a cell reference. No more help is provided, but perhaps additional help is not needed.

You could always provide more help in the comments of the function code, but this would require users to open VB. If you were determined to make sure something other than No help available appeared below your function in the Insert Function dialog box, there are still some options. One way is to start creating a new macro recording in the spreadsheet and designating the kind of descriptive help you might want to appear for your existing function. Copy and paste all of the content of that function (aside from the function header and footer) into that macro, delete the original function, and then change the header and footer information on the macro to convert it into a function instead. That description should appear whenever the function is selected in the Insert Function dialog box. It seems like a backward approach, but it's fairly foolproof and ultimatley gets the job done.

11.5.2 More Complex Examples

Now, let's consider some more complex user-defined functions (UDFs) to really emphasize what we can do.

11.5.2.1 Data Access and Presentation: Online Stock Data

Recall in Chapter 3 the discussion of linking Excel to external data sources. One of those data sources was an "existing connection" referred to as MSN Money Central. We can actually open up one of these existing connections using VBA. Consider the following code in Chp11_TickerPFunction :

```
Sub NewQuery(Ticker As String) 'This subroutine creates a
    'query for data on the TICKER specified in its argument;
    'something that would be sent in with a call
    'to this macro
  Sheets.Add After:=Sheets(Sheets.Count) 'actually not
    ' 'adding' but rather a means of 'selecting' a sheet by
    'a function
    With Worksheets(Sheets (Sheets.Count).Name)._
      QueryTables.Add(Connection:= _
      "URL;http://moneycentral.msn.com/investor/external/ _
      excel/quotes.asp?SYMBOL=" + Ticker,_
      Destination:=Range("$A$1")) 'Above code changes the
        'online source of data based on a stem URL and a
        'specification -- in this case a TICKER
        'The WITH in this statement also starts a reference
        'to other attributes of the query used in the data pull
    .RefreshStyle = xlOverwriteCells 'let's just overwrite,
        'don't need past info stored in this case
    .RefreshPeriod = 0 'let's not allow autorefresh
    .WebFormatting = xlWebFormattingNone 'no need to use web
        'formatting, too complex
    .Refresh BackgroundQuery:=False 'Action: Now pull that data
        'in to the sheet
  End With
  Sheets.Add Before:=Sheets(1) 'again not actually adding;
      'rather selecting first main sheet
End Sub
```

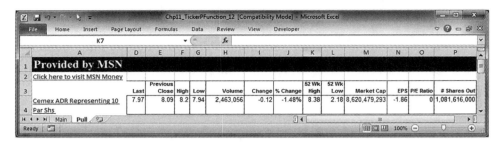

Figure 11.20. New worksheet with MSN data pull generated by a macro.

The assumption in this code is that the direct destination for the data pull will be the last sheet of the workbook. If this macro was called somehow such that a text value for Ticker was provided (for example, "BA", "MMM", and so on), then on the final workbook sheet we would generate a pull with data relating to the specified stock from the MSN Money Central site (similar to that presented in Figure 11.20).

Of course, we need that "other code" to call this macro in the first place. In this case, a UDF can supply that need. The following code is an example of a UDF designed to receive a ticker symbol as input with specifications on the nature of the output desired and work with the NewQuery Macro:

```
Function StockData(Ticker2 As String, Optional Other As _
  String, Optional num As Single)
  'sends back specified info [Optional specification] associated
  'with ticker the additional parameter (a single); allows
  'users to insert Rand() so that the function keeps updating
  'on F9
  If Not Range(Sheets(Sheets.Count).Name + "!b1") = Empty Then
    'if a query already exists...
      ModQuery (Ticker2) '...just call the macro that updates it
  Else
      NewQuery (Ticker2) 'Otherwise create that page and query
  End If
    'Application.Wait (Now + TimeValue("00:00:01"))
    'Need if longer delay
  If (Other = "") Or (Other = "Price") Then 'Checks whether
    'optional parameter has value
    StockData = Range(Sheets(Sheets.Count).Name + "!d4")
    'returns Price to function
  ElseIf Other = "EPS" Then
    StockData = Range(Sheets(Sheets.Count).Name + "!n4")
    'returns EPS value to function
  ElseIf Other = "P/E" Then
    StockData = Range(Sheets(Sheets.Count).Name + "!o4")
    'returns E/P value to function
```

```
  ElseIf Other = "All" Then
    StockData = CStr(Range(Sheets(Sheets.Count).Name + "!d4"))_
    + " ; " + CStr(Range(Sheets(Sheets.Count).Name + "!n4")) _
    + " ; " + CStr(Range(Sheets(Sheets.Count).Name + "!o4"))
      'returns ALL values as one string
  Else
    StockData = "UnknownRequest" 'One of the above three options
    'hasn't been entered
  End If
End Function
```

Therefore, the inputs to this UDF include a ticker symbol (of type string), and two optional parameters. The first is a string specifying the kind of output: Other as String, containing such text from the user as "EPS", "All", and so on. The second allows for live updatability. Specifically, it takes in a numerical parameter that can include a random term, hence triggering a recalculation (requery) of stock data upon F9 hits or other spreadsheet changes.

The alternate ModQuery macro referenced here is used if a query on the last sheet exists but simply needs modification.

```
Sub ModQuery(Ticker As String) 'Just edits the query given a
    'ticker and refreshes it (pulls in new data)
  Worksheets(Sheets(Sheets.Count).Name).QueryTables(1). _
    Connection = "URL;http://moneycentral.msn.com/investor/ _
    external/excel/quotes.asp?SYMBOL=" + Ticker
  Worksheets(Sheets(Sheets.Count).Name).QueryTables(1)._
    Refresh BackgroundQuery:=False
End Sub
```

A result of the multiple application of this UDF to four separate tickers is presented in Figure 11.21. In this case, cell B1, named RefreshToggle, contains a random number. That is fed into the UDFs in cells B5 through B8 as the third parameter. Pressing F9 will thus trigger a refresh of the data put and data presentation.

11.5.2.2 Complex Math Made Easy: Queuing Equations

For those who remember the queuing equations from any Operations coursework you may have taken, you'll recall that they are pretty hairy. For those not familiar with these equations, consider yourselves lucky – they aren't exactly fun to work with. As an example, the following are some of the formulae needed for estimating associated calculations, such as line-length probabilities and average wait times for situations where you have multiple

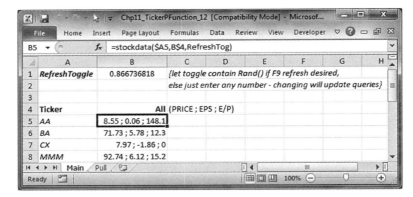

Figure 11.21. UDF for pulling stock data from the Internet.

servers (*c* could equal cashiers, clinicians, accountants, and so on) but only limited space (*N*) to accommodate people waiting.

Finite-Queue M/M/c Model:

$$P_0 = \frac{1}{\left(\sum_{i=0}^{c} \frac{\rho^i}{i!}\right) + \left(\frac{1}{c!}\right)\left(\sum_{i=c+1}^{N} \frac{\rho^i}{c^{i-c}}\right)} \qquad P_n = \begin{cases} \frac{\rho^n}{n!}P_0 & for\ 0 \le n \le c \\ \frac{\rho^n}{c!c^{n-c}}P_0 & for\ c \le n \le N \end{cases}$$

$$L_s = \frac{P_0\rho^{c+1}}{(c-1)!(c-\rho)^2}\left[1 - \left(\frac{\rho}{c}\right)^{N-c} - (N-c)\left(\frac{\rho}{c}\right)^{N-c}\left(1-\frac{\rho}{c}\right)\right] + \rho(1-P_N)$$

$$W_s = \frac{L_s - \rho(1-P_N)}{\lambda(1-P_N)} + \frac{1}{\mu}$$

Here, λ is the average number of people arriving per time (minute), μ is the average time needed by a server to complete a customer's request, and ρ is the ratio of λ/μ. The first function, P_0, then, represents the probability of having no one in the system (in line plus those being served) at any given moment in time, while P_n represents the probability of having exactly *n* people in the system. The terms L_s and W_s, respectively, represent the average anticipated number of individuals in the system, and the average amount of time an individual can expect to spend in the system (again, in line and at the counter) before their needs are filled.

The calculations of these estimation terms are not trivial. In particular, the summations over a range of values are not particularly fun to do by hand. In a spreadsheet, we could do all the required summations by setting up a table

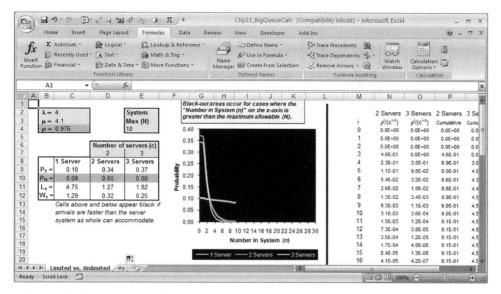

Figure 11.22. Example of extensive calculation space occupied on a spreadsheet.

and calculating a sum of all appropriate cells in that table, as shown in Figure 11.22. But this takes up a lot of space even in the spreadsheet – space that we could be using for something else. The Chp11_BigQueueCalc workbook contains the extensive spreadsheet usage in Figure 11.22.

Fortunately, we can easily create a sum of sequential terms in VB through using loop structures such as For...Next. Not only does this eliminate the need to take up space in the spreadsheet, it's actually more concisely developed in VB. In contrast to spelling all this out in the spreadsheet alone, the associated function codes (for all four functions) take up space only behind the scenes. The second spreadsheet in the Chp11_Functions workbook, shown in Figure 11.23, gives an example of how functions are being leveraged to provide a much more spreadsheet-frugal approach to this model.

Additional notes on the newly crafted functions and their arguments are displayed in this sheet in columns M through P, but notice that they are there only for clarity purposes. The big thing is that absolutely no calculations need to be made in these columns to let the calculations of interest take place.

Instead, we have the following functions working behind the scenes in VB:

```
Function P0(c_ref, rho_ref, N_ref As Range)
   firstsum = 0
   secondsum = 0
   c = c_ref.Range("a1").Value
   rho = rho_ref.Range("a1").Value
```

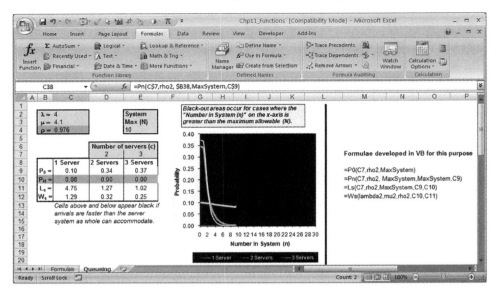

Figure 11.23. Example of function-enabled frugality in the use of spreadsheet.

```
N = N_ref.Range("a1").Value
cfact = WorksheetFunction.Fact(c)
For i = 0 To c
  firstsum = firstsum + (rho ^ i) / WorksheetFunction.Fact(i)
Next
For i = (c + 1) To N
  secondsum = secondsum + (rho ^ i) / WorksheetFunction._
    Power(c, i - c)
Next
P0 = 1 / (firstsum + (1 / cfact) * (secondsum))
End Function
Function PN(c_ref, rho_ref, littlen_ref, bigN_ref, P0_ref _
        As Range)
  c = c_ref.Range("a1").Value
  rho = rho_ref.Range("a1").Value
  littlen = littlen_ref.Range("a1").Value
  bigN = bigN_ref.Range("a1").Value
  Pnot = P0_ref.Range("a1").Value
  cfact = WorksheetFunction.Fact(c)
  littlenfact = WorksheetFunction.Fact(littlen)
  If (littlen >= 0) And (littlen <= c) Then
    PN = Pnot * WorksheetFunction.Power(rho, littlen) _
        / littlenfact
  ElseIf (littlen > c) And (littlen <= bigN) Then
    PN = Pnot * WorksheetFunction.Power(rho, littlen) _
        / (cfact * WorksheetFunction.Power(c, littlen - c))
```

```
  Else
     PN = " "
  End If
End Function
Function Ls(c_ref, rho_ref, N_ref, P0_ref, PN_ref As Range)
  c = c_ref.Range("a1").Value
  rho = rho_ref.Range("a1").Value
  N = N_ref.Range("a1").Value
  Pnot = P0_ref.Range("a1").Value
  PbigN = PN_ref.Range("a1").Value
  cless1fact = WorksheetFunction.Fact(c - 1)
  rhocpow = WorksheetFunction.Power((rho / c), N - c)
  product1 = Pnot * WorksheetFunction.Power(rho, c + 1) _
          / (cless1fact * ((c - rho) ^ 2))
  product2 = (N - c) * rhocpow * (1 - (rho / c))
  Ls = product1 * (1 - rhocpow - product2) + rho * (1 - PbigN)
End Function

Function Ws(lambda_ref, mu_ref, rho_ref, PN_ref, Ls_Ref _
         As Range)
  Lambda = lambda_ref.Range("a1").Value
  Mu = mu_ref.Range("a1").Value
  rho = rho_ref.Range("a1").Value
  PbigN = PN_ref.Range("a1").Value
  Lsubs = Ls_Ref.Range("a1").Value
  Ws = (Lsubs - rho * (1 - PbigN)) / _
    (Lambda * (1 - PbigN)) + 1 / Mu
End Function
```

You might think this looks complex and are not sure you want to take this route. It's no more complex than cranking out the calculations within the cells of a spreadsheet. Many of the lines of code here are just referencing cells from which to draw information. Others are absolutely critical calculations that would be present in the spreadsheet otherwise.

And there's still another benefit to developing functions in VB rather than within spreadsheet cells. Building user-defined functions for complex calculations tends to be less prone to errors than a pure spreadsheet approach, particularly when the calculations are bound to be repeatedly used in many ways within a spreadsheet.

11.6 Error Handling

Regardless of how careful we are in coding and how much time we invest in debugging, there is always some risk that the person we hand our macros and UDFs to won't use them as intended or will perhaps encounter scenarios

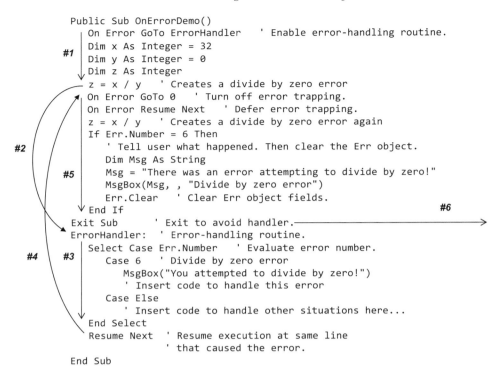

Figure 11.24. Error handlers effecting the flow of code when triggered.

we couldn't have dreamed, which results in failure on the part of our code. There are several approaches we can take to minimize this. On the front end, there are fool-proofing tactics we can apply to help guide users down the path of "correct use." We'll discuss these in Chapter 13. However, at the back end, there are also some nice capabilities available. They generally fall under the header of Error Handling.

These are the most common forms of error handling using "On Error":

Syntax setup (pre-error)	What it does when an error is detected
On Error GoTo Handler	Code advances to the "Handler" line and executes any code immediately following it. "Handler" can be any term you want that hasn't already been used or defined elsewhere (except 0, -1)
On Error Resume Next	Simply advances code to the line immediately following wherever an error takes place (ignores the error line)
On Error GoTo 0	Disables error trapping/handling in the subroutine

Let's look at an example of these error handlers at work. Figure 11.24 shows the sequence and direction of flow as a result of various error handling rules. Note in particular how the GoTo and Resume Next create deviations from a standard top-down code read.

As demonstrated in the example, when errors take place, information about them is temporarily recorded by the system and is therefore accessible by code. Here are some examples of common operations and data available to error-handling procedures.

Err.Clear is called solely to clear the most recent error from the error structure. In the event you fail to clear the error, it would persist and be called again (syntax:Err.Clear).

Err.Number is the "ID" number for the event itself (syntax: If Err.Number = 6 then....).

Err.Description is a string expression describing the error raised [syntax: Msg-Box("Uh oh!! : " & Err.Description)].

Err.Source is a string displaying the name of the object or application that generated the error raised [syntax: MsgBox(Err.Source & " friggin' messed up again")].

Err.HelpFile is the fully qualified path to an MS Windows *.hlp file used by your application

Err.Raise is called to force an error of the specified, optional properties to occur. Therefore, you can call up the reference to an error at run time to generate a list of all errors, display a specific help context ID, or display a help file for specific errors to the user (syntax: Err.Raise 6).

It is also worth knowing what specific kind of errors (Err.Number codes) are most frequently encountered by new developers. Here are leading ones:

0: No Error

6: Overflow Program error (when calculations of numbers that can't be stored are attempted; for example, 1/0, or sqrt of -1, and so on)

7: Out of memory (when in a code run, the total amount of available memory for temporary storage is exhausted)

9: Subscript out of range (when you try to reference a slot outside of the range of an array)

13: Type Mismatch (for example, when you try to assign a text value to a variable defined as integer)

35: Sub or Function not defined (when it looks like your code is trying to call a function or subroutine that doesn't exist)

438: No such property or method (for example, when trying to access the "funk-level" property of a cell ... or using the command "Range("A1").chillout")

11.7 Making Functions and Macros Available to Other Workbooks: Creating Add-Ins

If at the end of all of your VBA macro or UDF development, you feel they would be useful across various workbooks that you and others will use in the future, you have an additional way to save your work. You can save what you've developed in VBA as an add-in. All you need to do after saving the

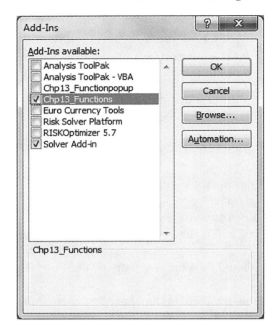

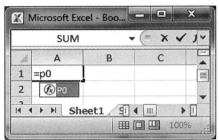

Figure 11.25. Excel's recognition of add-ins and UDFs included in add-in files.

file as a regular workbook (so you can easily edit it later), is go to Save As under the File tab (or, Office Button in 2007). Save the file as an add-in. The typical location for add-in saves will be a subfolder in the user folder of your computer. If that's not where the file ended up, you might want to put it there manually. To locate any add-ins in that folder, simply go to Options – Add-Ins and "Excel Add-Ins." Yours should appear on the list, as demonstrated in Figure 11.25.

If your add-in involves a user-defined function, it should now be recognized by the spreadsheet (as per the spreadsheet panel in Figure 11.25 with the P_0 function). If your add-in is a macro that is Ctrl-key activated, that same Ctrl-key activation can be used if the add-in is selected as active. In Chapter 13, we'll see how to develop strong front-ends in these applications. Stronger user interfaces can also be saved as part of an add-in, making for a very nice packaging of otherwise complex work.

PRACTICE PROBLEMS

Practice 11.1

Import both an image and a .wav file of your choice into Excel. Create a macro that activates the .wav clip and then use the time functions in Excel to make the image slowly fade away over a fifteen-second period. Then, make the image slowly reappear, again over a fifteen-second period. Do this either by building the macro

Table 11.4. *Example Structure for Tabular Output*

	Total	Total	Total
Now	Hours	Minutes	Seconds
2/10/2008 13:26	13	806	48,387

from the ground up, based on code similar to that showed in the example of this chapter, or through using a version of Excel that allows for object macro recording.

Here's a hint on how to make your image appear to fade away: You can use several approaches, but one approach is to increase the amount of lighting provided to an image. This is one of the options on the Picture toolbar.

Here's another hint: For the time functions, use whichever you think are appropriate, but it's actually good practice to do a little snooping around because there are multiple approaches to getting this information (see the functions under the category Data & Time). You may find, for example, the NOW() function to be useful, as well as the HOUR, MINUTE, and SECOND calculations. Use Excel's function help to learn how these may help. Table 11.4 shows an example of how you might set up your tabular output in a spreadsheet.

The one point to reiterate here is that the NOW() function will update only if you ask it to, such as by pressing F9 or making some other change in the spreadsheet. In this way, it acts a little like the RAND() function. In the VB Editor, you can also do this using the one-line command Calculate. Anytime that is used, the workbook is updated.

Practice 11.2

Create a function for calculating the y coordinate associated with the x coordinate of a circle. Your input should be the value of x, the radius of the circle, and some binary input that designates whether you want the lower or upper half of the circle to be referred to for your value of y. The standard formula for a circle is:

$$R^2 = X^2 + Y^2 \text{ or } Y = +/ - \text{sqrt}(R^2 - X^2)$$

12

Automating Application Calls

Many applications such as Microsoft MapPoint and RISKOptimizer can be leveraged through the primary interfaces with which they were designed, but they can also be called from behind the scenes through the same Visual Basic (VB) developer environment discussed in Chapter 11. From a decision support development perspective, there are several advantages to making such calls from behind the scenes. First and foremost, behind the scenes control can eliminate the need for users to become acquainted with alternative interfaces in the course of using a DSS that leverages their capabilities. Another advantage is the potential avoidance of outputs that automatically accompany the use of these applications, but are nevertheless visual and information distractions from the main point of the DSS design. The appearance of seamlessness in a designed DSS is also facilitated by VB-driven automated calls to applications. This has the potential for engendering greater confidence in the developed DSS, as well as in the developers. This chapter covers several approaches to working with such applications in roughly the order in which they have been introduced throughout this book.

12.1 Calls to MapPoint

The Chp12_MapPointCall workbook provides a template through which we can demonstrate how Excel, through VB, can leverage some of the functionality of MapPoint. As with all other demonstrations in this chapter, we'll present only a smattering of what can actually be done. To start, let's consider a hypothetical need to get information regarding a route that starts in Seattle and passes through four additional cities before returning to Seattle. The workbook outlines these stops (shown in Figure 12.1).

Clicking on the "Click to route" button activates a macro that:

- Activates the MapPoint application
- Adds the specified cities to a new route

Figure 12.1. Front end for activating macro call to MapPoint.

- Asks MapPoint to map and calculate the distance for that route
- Gives feedback on the covered distance and sequence of the route
- Takes a snapshot of the MapPoint window for pasting
- Pastes, crops, and shifts the copied picture

The result is shown in Figure 12.2.

The VB code used to deliver this result is:

```
Private Declare Sub keybd_event Lib "user32" _
  (ByVal bVk As Byte, ByVal bScan As Byte, _
   ByVal dwFlags As Long, ByVal dwExtraInfo As Long)

Sub Route_calc()

  Dim objApp As MapPoint.Application
```

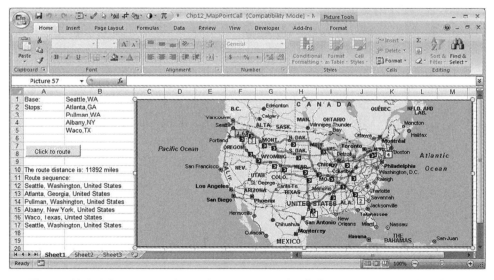

Figure 12.2. Map generation using macro and existing sequence of site visits.

```
Dim objMap As MapPoint.Map
Dim objRoute As MapPoint.Route

Set objApp = CreateObject("MapPoint.Application") 'Set up the
    'Mappoint application
Set objMap = objApp.ActiveMap 'Get the active map
Set objRoute = objMap.ActiveRoute 'Select the active route

'Clear, then add route stops
objRoute.Clear
objRoute.Waypoints.Add objMap.FindResults(CStr(Range("B1")))._
  Item(1)
For stopnumber = 1 To 4
 objRoute.Waypoints.Add objMap.FindResults(CStr(Range("B1")._
  Offset(stopnumber, 0))).Item(1)
Next
objRoute.Waypoints.Add objMap.FindResults(CStr(Range("B1")))._
  Item(1)
objRoute.Calculate 'calculate route distance covered
objApp.Visible = True 'Make the mappoint object visible

'***** Make this code active to optimize the route,
'if desired and if not already optimized
'objRoute.Waypoints.Optimize
'objMap.ActiveRoute.Calculate 'calculate NEW route distance
                            'covered
Range("A11") = "Route sequence:" 'Outputs
For i = 1 To objRoute.Waypoints.Count
  Range("A11").Offset(i, 0) = objRoute.Waypoints.Item(i).Name
Next
Range("A10") = "The route distance is: "_
      + CStr(Round(objRoute.Distance)) + " miles"
    'Here's just a little extra code to implant a
    'screen capture of the
    keybd_event &H12, 0, 0, 0 'Plant "Alt" key
    keybd_event &H2C, 1, 0, 0
    keybd_event &H12, 0, &H2, 0 'Release "Alt" key
    CaptureDesktop = True
    objMap.Saved = True'Trick MapPoint into thinking
                      'we've saved it (allowing auto-close)
    Sheets("Sheet1").Range("C1").Select
    ActiveSheet.Paste

    'And just to do a little cropping
    Selection.ShapeRange.PictureFormat.CropLeft = 182
    Selection.ShapeRange.PictureFormat.CropTop = 277
    Selection.ShapeRange.PictureFormat.CropRight = 4
```

```
            Selection.ShapeRange.PictureFormat.CropBottom = 22
            Selection.ShapeRange.IncrementLeft -180
            Selection.ShapeRange.IncrementTop -270
End Sub
```

This is possibly a bit overwhelming for a novice, but for those who have read through Chapter 11, there's a lot of material here that should seem familiar. For example, references to cell contents using the Range syntax shouldn't be new, nor should the use of an offset with a For-Loop and reference to any of the picture manipulations in the later portion of this code. The two novel areas of code involve the various calls to MapPoint and the calls associated with screen captures of the mapped result (the first three lines of code preceding the subroutine and the four lines of code following the output of the route distance).

Unfortunately, most of these codes are outside standard macro recording, particularly Excel 2007's approach to macro generation. One could rightly ask, "So, how in the world would I learn how to use this code?" For starters, there's nothing stopping someone from editing or copying this code to another workbook toward a similar end. Much of this arcane material, if not available in an advanced programming text, is also available online through various blogs and help sites. For those interested in learning how to get more done in MapPoint (or with screen captures) through VB, one of the best and cheapest ways is to simply pick some of the code from this example as search terms and see what comes up. We'll leave that to the intrepid reader.

At this point, to advance the discussion of interfacing between Excel and MapPoint given the present code, let's reconsider the result provided. Arguably, the route depicted here seems to be a poor design from a time management (and total distance covered) perspective. Certainly, there are better sequences that MapPoint could come up with; however, the macro in its current form isn't asking for MapPoint to perform any optimization. The portion of the code that would make such a request has been commented out by preceding it with apostrophe. It's simple enough to activate it; just remove the apostrophe and click on the Macro button once again.

As the augmented algorithm runs (unfortunately, the optimization through an indirect call to MapPoint is not as fast as would be desired), the MapPoint interface refreshes and suggests that the optimization protocol has provided a more ideal solution, again based solely on time management and total distance covered. Depending on how much time it takes, Excel may provide the message shown in Figure 12.3.

This designates that Excel recognizes there is still more to be done in the macro, but before any additional actions take place, it will need to wait for the work to be completed in MapPoint. Again, given the length of time

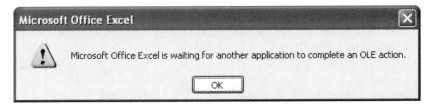

Figure 12.3. Message relating delay associated with simultaneous application activity.

MapPoint needs to develop optimal routes, this could take a while. But eventually MapPoint should be able to do its work. If all goes well, the final product in this case appears as shown in Figure 12.4.

Note the updated distance and route sequence, as well as the updated mapping of the route. This is certainly something on which a developer could spend more time to make appear more aesthetically pleasing, but it's not bad in terms of a rough cut at functionality with fairly limited VB code.

12.2 Calls to Solver

In contrast to MapPoint (a potentially stand-alone application), Solver is an add-in and is almost always used only within the context of Excel. Not all add-ins work well with macros, particularly those that are acquired from third parties that did not develop these applications with VB developers in mind. Fortunately for us, Solver is a gleaming exception. In Solver's case, we just need to make sure we have our specifications set up the right way (for

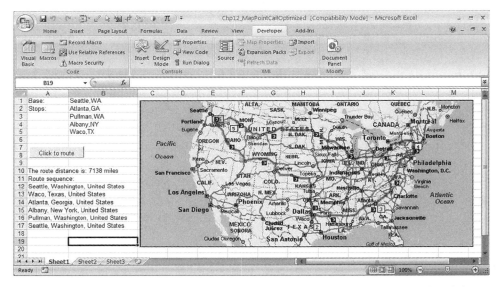

Figure 12.4. Map generation using macro and optimized sequence of site visits.

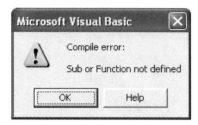

Figure 12.5. Message due to nonreferencing.

example, we need Solver to actually be active in our version of Excel) and know just a little more syntax to get Solver to actually do things by itself.

The following is the kind of code we would get if we simply took a workbook that contained an existing math-programming problem structure and started recording a macro right before we asked Solver to come up with a solution (at least in Excel 2003).

```
Sub Macro1()
  SolverOK SetCell:="$D$4", MaxMinVal:=1, ValueOf:="0",_
    ByChange:="$b$2:$c$2"
  SolverSolve
End Sub
```

Even though the VB Editor created this code, it is not likely to be able to repeat this procedure without us giving it a little more information. In fact, oddly enough, it may not even seem to recognize elements of the code it has just written. If you're able to record the same action into code comparable to that just presented, the results might look like Figure 12.5 when you try to run the newly recorded macro.

The problem here is that although the VB Editor was told how to turn those actions into code, it wasn't told what to use when executing that code. The Editor needs to know that it should be referencing Solver in running this code. To make the VB Editor aware of this, we need to formally add Solver as a reference, similar to how we added in Solver as a tool for the Excel workbook the first place. In the VB Editor, go to Tools>References to open the References-VBAProject dialog box shown in Figure 12.6.

Check the SOLVER box in the Available References list and then click OK. Solver is now formally a reference for the VB Editor, and we should be able to run a macro that uses Solver. Note that adding code similar to the following may provide a mechanism to forego adding the reference manually:

```
ThisWorkbook.VBProject.References.AddFromFile
Application.LibraryPath ... "\solver\solver.xla ...
```

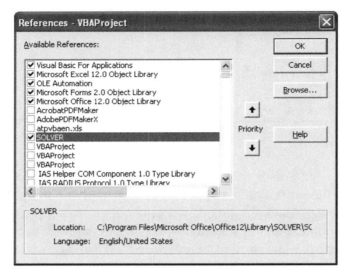

Figure 12.6. Referencing associated applications in VB Editor.

However, depending on how your applications are set up, this may not work for all developers, so don't place all bets on it. The list of Solver-related commands that can be called through VB is as extensive as the number of options made available by Solver. The following is a subset of the more useful commands from a standard DSS standpoint:

SolverSolve UserFinish:=True: This command allows Solver to accept the final solution it comes up with and save the associated values of the solution decisions in the associated cells. This way you don't have to click OK every time a macro running Solver comes up with a solution.

SolverReset: This command clears all Solver contents (for example, it deletes all constraints, objectives, and decision variable references that would typically be retained after each Solver run). This could be useful if you decide to create a program that uses different kinds of constraints in alternative iterations.

SolverDelete CellRef:="$B$2:$C$2", Relation:=4: This command deletes a specific constraint; in this example, one that constrains two cells to be integers (that's what Relation:=4 refers to).

SolverAdd commands: In general, Solver allows for five kinds of relationships to be depicted by constraints as shown in Figure 12.7.

As a result, the following two commands can be used to add individual constraint for the <= (Relation:=1) or integer (Relation:=4) types.

```
SolverAdd CellRef:="$B$2", Relation:=1, FormulaText:="10"
SolverAdd CellRef:="$B$2:$C$2", Relation:=4,_
  FormulaText:="integer"
```

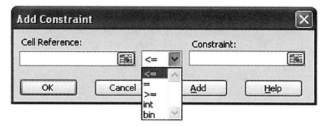

Figure 12.7. Menu interface for editing constraints.

12.3 Calls to RiskOptimizer

For problems with more complex structures, or those that involve forms of uncertainty that don't lend themselves to the kind of closed-form analysis with which basic Solver's hill-climbing algorithm works well, we've seen that other approaches may be necessary. The use of genetic algorithms, as made available through additional tools such as RISKOptimizer, has already been discussed as an option. It can also be called from behind the scenes using VB code, again perhaps as one of many steps involved in a larger analysis around which a decision support tool is designed. Let's consider a couple of the past examples discussed in the book and how we might more seamlessly automate their interface with Excel.

12.3.1 Work-Group Selection Revisited

Let's again consider the form of the work-group selection problem last formally discussed in Chapter 7. We showed how RISKOptimizer could be used to derive group constituencies subject to criteria that might be outside the bounds of a typical XLStat clustering. (We'll get back to calling XLStat in VB shortly.) To call RISKOptimizer to run its routine behind the scenes, we'll want to have RISKOptimizer formally loaded (much in the same way that we might preload Solver, if not already present, before running macros that call it). In addition, as with Solver, a formal reference to RISKOptimizer needs to be made through the VB Editor before the Editor can recognize the code being referenced in any macro calling the application. Here, you're looking for something like RiskOpt.xla to be added in as a reference.

When this is done, we can start to develop some simple code to get RISKOptimizer to do its thing. Assuming we're using the original Chapter 7 version, perhaps with an additional stipulation that the search stops after one minute (again, just to illustrate how this works), the following code would be more than sufficient (taken from Chp12_WorkGroupSelection_VB1).

```
Sub AutoCluster()
  EvOptimize ActiveWorkbook, "myStopRoutine"
    'Note that EvOptimize is a function that expects a
    'string for its second argument...that string entry
    'itself may be another user defined function
End Sub
Public Function myStopRoutine(stopReason As Integer) As Integer
 myStopRoutine = EvBest + EvLogWorkbook + _
  EvLogWorkbookShowOnlyNewBest
    'added specification that states we would like to have:
    ' 1) The Best solution found to be saved to the workbook
        'In contrast to EvBest, EvOriginal keeps the original
        'solution
    ' 2) The a log of the search presented in a new workbook
    ' 3) The log should contain ONLY the best solutions
        'discovered during the search
End Function
```

In actuality, the code could be still more simplified, but the structure presented, in which a function is used to specify the nature of the results provided, is a particularly convenient means of suggesting possible extensions
of its use. For example, there's nothing stopping a developer from further
specifying whether the best solution found should overwrite the original,
based on inputs provided by their users in a customized interface or whether
all solutions encountered should be saved in the logbook (even poor ones
or those that might fundamentally violate assumed constraints). Here, a
few references to designated cells in a workbook interface (or, a dialog box
along with the use of IF-THEN structures within the function) would do the
trick.

Aside from manipulating the nature of the output, developers also have
the option of manipulating the nature of the problem to be solved by
RISKOptimizer as well as the approach taken in doing so. Rather than taking a piecemeal approach to explaining each of the various items that are
useful in developing code that can build optimization problems in RISKOptimizer from the ground up, at this point, we'll simply consider a complete
set of integrated code. Rich annotation will serve in place of a formalized
discussion of the role of each element of code.

Ultimately, the kinds of specifications made here are comparable to those
that would be made with Solver specifications. To assist in understanding,
the following code (from Chp12_WorkGroupSelection_VB2) has been organized in the way we discussed problem structures. It starts with a specification of the problem's objective and approach to optimization (for example,
GA stopping rules), the nature of the decision variables, and the potential
nature of constraints (if not otherwise built into the objective and/or bounds

on decision variables). It concludes with the specification of output interfaces desired and finally the commencement of the optimization protocol
(as introduced in the earlier example).

```
Sub RunIt()
  Dim returnCode%

  If SetupModel() Then
  'if setup takes place without error...
    EvOptimize ActiveWorkbook, "myStopRoutine" 'Note that
    'EvOptimize is a function that expects a string for
    'its second argument...that string entry
    'itself may be another user defined function
  End If
End Sub
Function SetupModel()
  Dim mySettings As EvSettingsType
  Dim returnCode%

  returnCode = EvReadSettingsDefaults(ThisWorkbook,_
    mySettings) 'creates blank template

  With mySettings 'A statement letting VB editor know that much
    'of the following will provide specifications to the
    'existing RISKOptimizer settings everything to follow
    'that is preceded by a "." describes an attribute
    'of "mySettings"

  .CellToOptimize = "sheet1!$P$22" '
  .OutputFunction = EvRiskFuncMean 'What is the nature of the
    'output to be maximized. In optimizations that don't
    'involve simulation, using the parameter EvRiskFuncMean
    '(ie. focusin on the mean performance of a decision policy
    'option) is sufficient. It's usually also the statistic of
    'performance used in simulation optimization. However in
    'simulation optimization, other measures of performance
    'will be different. These include but are not limited to:
    '    EvRiskFuncStdDev : The std. dev. of performance
    '       across variants
    '    EvRiskFuncRange : The range of performance across
    '       variants
    '    EvRiskFuncPercentile : The value of the approximated
    '       P-percentile of variants seen. Here the
    '       P-percentile would also need to be specified
    '       in code such as mySettings.OutputFunction
    '       Parameter=0.13
```

```
.OptimizationGoal = EvMaximize 'What kind of optimization on
   'above EvMinimize and EvTargetValue are other options. In
   'the latter case the target would also need specification -
   '.TargetValue=412 for eg.

.PopulationSize = 10 'This relates to how the genetic
   'algorithm works...ie. how many past solutions are
   'considered in constructing new solutions moving
   'forward. Relevant for both non-simulation and simulation
   'optimization. See earlier notes from Chapter 7
   'supplement on GA population size

.StopOnMinutes = True 'Should the search stop after some
   'amount of time?
   'Additive so could simultaneously use
   'mySettings.StopOnTrials=True for eg.
   'or .StopOnChange=True
   'or .StopOnFormula=True
.StopMinutes = 1 'For trials - .StopTrials=40 for eg.
   'or .StopChangeTrials=100, .StopChangeMagnitude=5,
   '    .StopChangeIsPercent=True would all need to be
   '    specified if you wanted to stop the search after
   '    no changes by >=5% in last 100 trials
   'For "StopOnFormula" - .StopFormula = "sheet1!$P$32>1200"
   'for example.
.SimStopMode = EvSimStopIterations 'Combined with below...
.SimMaxIters = 5 'For non-simulation optimization, should be
   ' as small as possible (ie. 5) since nothing is
   ' essentially being simulated. For either the
   ' optimization of simulation variants or system
   ' simulations, depending on the approach taken this
   ' number may be much larger.
   ' See the detailed discussion of iterations in Chapter 9
   ' to get a better feeling for how this might need to be
   ' set for different approaches.

.numAdjustableGroups = 1 'Here we outline our decision
    'variables
ReDim .AdjustableGroups(1 To 1) 'Need to define how many
   'variable 'groups' exist
With .AdjustableGroups(1)
   .crossoverRate = 0.5 'As noted in Chp7, this and the
      'mutation rate need to be
   .mutationRate = 0.1 'specified, otherwise new/better
      'solutions can't be found
   .solvingMethod = "GROUPING" 'or "RECIPE", "ORDER" etc.
```

```
       'depending on need
     .numInputRanges = 1 'see below
   ReDim .InputRanges(1 To 1) 'Need to define how many
       'variable cell-ranges feed in
   .InputRanges(1).Reference = "sheet1!$a7:$a86"
       ' "WorkerAssignments"
       ' or something like "sheet1!$a7:$a86"
   .InputRanges(1).IsInteger = True
   .InputRanges(1).MinValue = 1
   .InputRanges(1).MaxValue = 4
  End With

'Hard constraints can also be specified for example:
  '.numConstraints = 3 'if 3 hard constraints applied
  'ReDim .Constraints(1 To 3)
  '.Constraints(1).ConstrainType = EvConstraintHard
  '.Constraints(1).EntryMode = EvEtryModeFormula
  '.Constraints(1).Formula = "ActualSize=20"
  '...contraints 2 and 3 would then also need specification

  .GraphProgress = True 'Activate the RISKOptimizer watcher
       'during the search
  .GenerateLog = True 'Make sure a log of the search is
       'being kept

'Other possible settings for embedded Macro Calls DURING
'RISKOptimizer search
' .RunBeforeSimMacro = True
' .BeforeSimMacro = "SomeSuperMacro"
'    The above lines would call "SomeSuperMacro" before each
'    new decision policy is evaluated. Particularly useful
'    for simulation optimization (again see Chp9)
' Related timing variants include BeforeRecalcMacro,
'    AfterRecalcMacro, AfterSimMacro,
'    AfterStorageMacro, StartMacro and FinishMacro...all
'    associated with the standard RISKOptimizer Macro call
'    interface discussed earlier

End With 'Needed to tell VB editor you are done specifying
     'attributes of mySettings in general
returnCode = EvWriteSettings(mySettings) 'Need to "write"
     'the specifics to RISKOptimizer
SetupModel = True 'More relevant if we had been checking for
     'errors along the way here

End Function
```

Used in conjunction with code that initiates and stops the actual optimization process, these kinds of specification protocols provide the convenience of switching between various optimization problem structures without going through the hassle of restructuring them manually (see example Chp12_WorkGroupSelection_VB2 for the full implementation).

12.3.2 Inventory System Simulation Revisited

Because RISKOptimizer is useful in simulation optimization settings, it is worth reviewing how the code for building and executing an example of such optimization might be structured. For illustration, consider again the Lobos Inventory optimization example from Chapter 9. The same kinds of elements used in the annotated code in Section 12.3.1 apply here. With this in mind, and with the interest of providing a contrast in implementation, it is both sufficient and appropriate to present the code that would apply to this case in a similar fashion. A copy of the workbook containing this code is provided in Chp12_LobosInventory_VB. The following is the structure of the setup function (consolidated and free of annotation that has already been provided in the previous examples).

```
Function SetupModel()
  Dim mySettings As EvSettingsType
  Dim returnCode%
  returnCode = EvReadSettingsDefaults(ThisWorkbook,_
   mySettings)
  With mySettings
    .CellToOptimize = "StockoutDemo!$K$36"
    .OutputFunction = EvRiskFuncMean
    .OptimizationGoal = EvMinimize
    .PopulationSize = 10
    .StopOnMinutes = True
    .StopMinutes = 5
    .SimStopMode = EvSimStopIterations
    .SimMaxIters = 5
    .numAdjustableGroups = 1
    ReDim .AdjustableGroups(1 To 1)
    With .AdjustableGroups(1)
      .crossoverRate = 0.5
      .mutationRate = 0.1
      .solvingMethod = "RECIPE"
      .numInputRanges = 1
      ReDim .InputRanges(1 To 1)
      .InputRanges(1).Reference = "StockoutDemo!$c18"
      .InputRanges(1).IsInteger = True
```

```
    .InputRanges(1).MinValue = 40
    .InputRanges(1).MaxValue = 120
  End With
  .GraphProgress = True
  .GenerateLog = True
  .RunBeforeSimMacro = True 'NOTE that as in Chapter 9 we
    'need to sim
  .BeforeSimMacro = "Macro1" 'several periods to truly assess
    'a "trial"
 End With
returnCode = EvWriteSettings(mySettings)
SetupModel = True
End Function

Public Function myStopRoutine(stopReason As Integer) As Integer
 myStopRoutine = EvBest + EvLogWorkbook +_
  EvLogWorkbookShowOnlyNewBest
End Function
```

Although the previous examples are designed to illustrate how various VB commands can be used to suit the needs of DSS developers, it is far from comprehensive. Other references – including Palisade's guide to RISKOptimizer, which accompanies a purchase of their software – provide decent coverage of the various syntax options available for manipulating the optimization protocols through VB. The alternative references are often in dictionary format, but if you plan to be spending a great deal of time automating RISKOptimizer behind the scenes, they may be helpful down the road.

Note that if you encounter unexpected error messages relating to references to outdated versions of RISKOptimizer or other older settings after you've saved a workbook that references Palisade's applications, simply unload all such add-ins and VB Editor references and save the document as reference free. Reopening and reloading the add-ins and references should restore functionality.

12.4 Calls to XLStat

As we've seen in the previous discussion of XLStat's capabilities, many of the kinds of analysis it provides naturally work very well together. Notably, it is not uncommon for analysis to begin with variable reduction techniques such as PCA, use developed factors as a part of subsequent cluster analysis, and then a follow up with discriminant analysis. Although the reexamination of a specific set of data through these methods may not be needed in many contexts, firms that regularly make it their business to do this kind of sequential analysis with a wide variety of incoming data sets (for example, information intermediaries and marketing research firms) could find the ability to glean the takeaways from a consistent, combined approach – all at the click of a single button that is extremely convenient and perhaps less prone to errors in data management that can be made between steps.

Fortunately, to accommodate such applications, the developers of XLStat have made it compatible with calls from VB macros, and with fairly straight-forward scripting. The following are examples, applicable to the Dodecha case from Chapter 5, for each of the three data consolidation approaches we've discussed.

Principal Components

```
Sub Run_PCA()
 'Must have reference to XLStat-MCA.dll to run
 Call LoadRunPCA(Range("FullData!$B1:$AG116"), 1, True,_
    Range("FullData!$A1:$A116"), NoScreenupdating:=True)
  'The first term above outlines where your data is located
  'The second term, "1", specifies that the data is arranged in
  ' attribute columns and observation rows
  'The third term, "True", specifies that the first row
  ' contains attribute labels
  'The fourth specifies where observation labels (eg. ref #s)
  ' can be found
  'The last specifies that you want to skip additional prompts
  ' and only want to see the final results
  'Additional optional specifications include PCA Type (eg.
  ' other than Peason(n-1), etc.)
End Sub
```

Cluster Analysis

```
Sub Run_Kmeans()
 'Must have reference to XLStat-CLU.dll to run
 Call LoadRunKMN(Range("PCA!$C943:$J1058"), False, 4,_
  WithColLabels:=True, ObsRange:=Range("FullData!$A1:$A116"),_
    NoScreenupdating:=True)
  'The first term above outlines where your data is located
  ' (recall it is on PCA sheet) .
  'The second term, "False", specifies that the columns of data
  ' do not represent observations but rather represent factors
  ' (hence observations are by row)
  'The third term, "4", specifies the "K" or number of
  ' groups to be derived .
  'The fourth "True", specifies that the first row contains
  ' attribute labels
  'The fifth specifies where observation labels (eg. ref #s)
  ' can be found
```

```
'Additional optional specs include Clustering criteria (eg.
' other than Determinant(W), etc.)
End Sub
```

Discriminant Analysis

```
Sub Run_Discriminant()
'Must have reference to XLStat-LOG.dll to run
Call LoadRunDisc(Range("FullData+Clusters!$b1:$b116"), _
    Range("FullData+Clusters!$c1:$ah116"),_
    Range("FullData+Clusters!$a1:$a116"), _
NoScreenupdating:=True)
  'The first term above outlines where your "group" data is
  ' located
  'The second term outlines where your predictive data (ie.
  ' attribute data here) is located
  'The third term specifies where observation labels (eg.
  ' ref #s) can be found
End Sub
```

As suggested by the comments, the code must be run with XLStat loaded and the associated library files referenced as needed (for example, XLStat-CLU, XLStat-KMN, and XLStat-LOG). Functioning code can be found in the Chp12_Dodecha_VB file under the CodeforRuns module. Additional specifications that are not outlined here but may be of interest to developers can be made through the menu-driven interface. When specified there, they should be remembered by the application and should exist along with any other specifications made in the code.

As a note on automated calls to Discriminant Analysis, errors in execution may be caused by the presence of the Form19.txt file (typically founding the Addinsoft/XLStat folder). Removing that file prior to run should resolve the issue. Other run-time issues may also occur in workbooks where multiple runs of these tools have taken place. For general assistance with XLStat calls, refer to http://forum.xlstat.com.

12.5 A Final Note on the Value of Linguistics

As a closing personal comment, it is necessary to reinforce that although knowledge of the specific syntax needed to automate via VB is obviously useful, an understanding of why it should be used will always be more critical. Any well-trained syntax expert doesn't have a ghost of a chance developing something useful in practice unless he understands what's needed in practice and is able to distinguish that from the superfluous. Expert programmers can be found. Work can be delegated to them. The most effective professional analysts aren't those that know all of the code that exists, but rather they know what can be done (by hired programmers, if need be), what needs to get done (to benefit real-world practice), and how to integrate and delegate abilities toward that end. It's this general awareness of "the possible," and a specific understanding of how integration can deliver novel, meaningful, and practical results that is the real message here.

Supplement: Setups for Embedded MapPoint Controls

Written by Denys Lu, Blackbelt Student, Emory University

In 12.1, we demonstrated the use of an already embedded MapPoint control in Excel. In this section, we'll go over how we developed that connection to begin with. We'll then set up a sheet and associated VB code that takes an address and searches for it in the MapPoint control. The map will then show that address in the center. We'll also take the additional steps to add buttons to zoom in and out of the map and to recenter the address.

Part A: The MapPoint Control

The key to this functionality is the MapPoint control. Like other controls you've used in previous examples, the MapPoint control is a programmatic object that can be placed (and then used) on your Excel spreadsheet. This control is included with MapPoint. Importantly, the developer *and* the users must have MapPoint installed in addition to Excel.

1) In Excel, go to the Developer tab of the ribbon.
2) In the Controls section, click Insert (Figure 12.8).
3) At the bottom of the menu that pops up, click the *More Controls...* button.
4) You will now be presented with the More Controls dialog box; scroll down to *Microsoft MapPoint Control 18.0* (this number will be smaller if you're using a version of MapPoint before 2011). Click OK (Figure 12.9).
5) Your cursor will now change to cross hairs so you can "draw" the control. Go ahead and make a decent-sized rectangle. You will now see your embedded control (Figure 12.10).
6) Notice the namebox. The name of this instance of the MapPoint control is *MappointControl1*. For more advanced applications of these techniques, you could create numerous instances of MapPoint in your spreadsheet showing different places on the map (for example, maps of the European, American, and Asian sales regions).

Part B: Setting Up the Input Cells

In Excel, set up the input cells for the user to specify the address he is searching for.

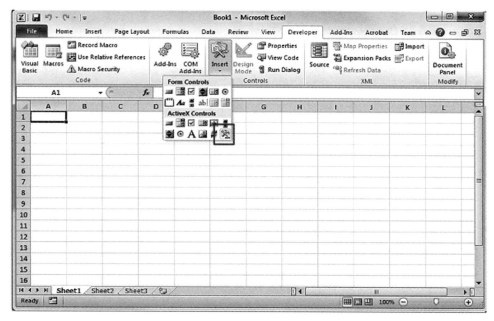

Figure 12.8. Locating additional embedded controls available in Excel.

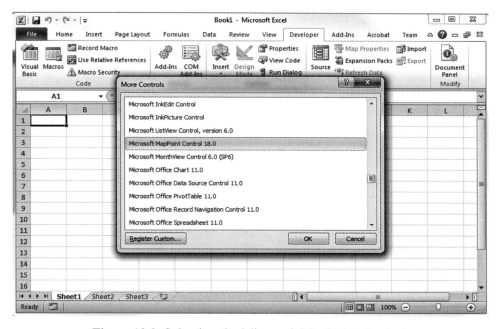

Figure 12.9. Selecting the Microsoft MapPoint Control.

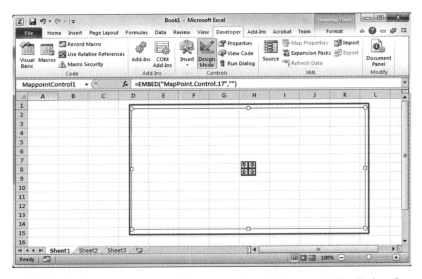

Figure 12.10. Initial appearance of the embedded Microsoft MapPoint Control.

Create Labels:

- Cell A4: **Address:**
- Cell A5: **City:**
- Cell A6: **State:**

Input Cells (name these cells, the names will make it easier to get the inputs programmatically):

- Cell B4: *StreetAddress*
- Cell B5: *City*
- Cell B6: *State*

Part C: The MapPoint Code

In the Developer tab of the ribbon, click Visual Basic. Use the following code:

```
Sub ShowAddress(streetAddress As String, city As String, _
   state As String)
 Dim oMap As MapPoint.Map
 Dim oFindResults As FindResults
 Dim oLocation As Location
 oMap = MappointControl1.ActiveMap
 'Search for the address that the user inputted
 oFindResults = oMap.FindAddressResults(streetAddress,_
  city, , state)
 'If no address is found, show a message box
```

```
    'else put a push pin on the map and center the map to it
    If (oFindResults.Count < 1) Then
      Call MsgBox("Couldn't find any addresses", vbOKOnly,_
                "No addresses")
    Else
      oLocation = oFindResults.Item(1) 'Use the first found
        'address
      Call AddPushPin(oMap, "Found Address", oLocation)

      Call oLocation.GoTo()        'Center the map on the location
    End If
    oMap = Nothing
    oFindResults = Nothing
    oLocation = Nothing
  End Sub

Sub AddPushPin(oMap As MapPoint.Map, name As String,_
                oLocation As MapPoint.Location)
  Dim newPin As MapPoint.Pushpin
  newPin = oMap.AddPushPin(oLocation, name)
  'MapPoint has a library of different pins, each pin is
  'identified by a number
  newPin.Symbol = 343
  newPin = Nothing
End Sub
```

Part D: The Search Button

Now, we must create a button that will tell Excel to have the MapPoint control search for the inputted address. Create an ActiveX button and give it a name of *FindAddressButton*. Change its caption to "Find Address" as well.

After these steps, your input area should look something like Figure 12.11.

Double-click the Find Address button. Excel will show the VB Editor and automatically create an event handler that will get called when the user clicks the button. Use the following code:

```
Private Sub FindAddressButton_Click()
  Dim streetAddress As String
  Dim city As String
  Dim state As String
  streetAddress = Range("StreetAddress")  'Get the input data
  city = Range("City")
  state = Range("State")
  'Pass the input data to MapPoint
  Call ShowAddress(streetAddress, city, state)
End Sub
```

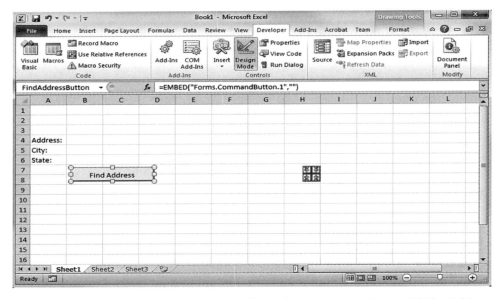

Figure 12.11. Setup of search button, address input cells, and preinitialized Map-
Point control.

Part E: Initializing the MapPoint Control

When you open the MapPoint application, it performs a number of initialization functions. For example, it opens a blank map of North America so
you can begin searching for addresses and navigating around the map as well
as setting what units you'll be using (here, miles versus kilometers). We will
also need to perform some of these initialization steps to prepare the map
for use in our spreadsheet.

1) In the VB Editor, add the following subroutine:

```
Public Sub InitializeMap()
  Dim oMap As MapPoint.Map
  'Load the North American map
  Call MappointControl1.NewMap(geoMapNorthAmerica)
  oMap = MappointControl1.ActiveMap
  'Configure the control so the drawing toolbar is visible
  ' and set the units to miles
  oMap.Application.Toolbars.Item("Drawing").
  Visible = True
  oMap.Application.Units = geoMiles
  oMap = Nothing
End Sub
```

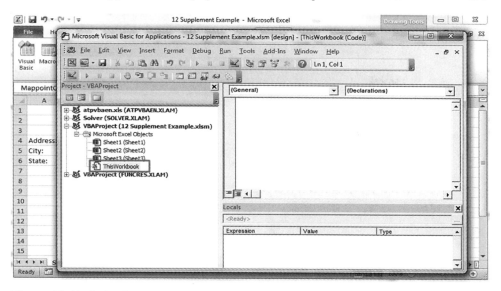

Figure 12.12. Selection of the ThisWorkbook Object for coding in the VB Developer.

2) Now, we need Excel to run the InitializeMap() subroutine whenever it loads the spreadsheet. To do this, we will create an event handler for the Workbook Open event. In the project tree, double-click *ThisWorkbook* (Figure 12.12).
3) You will now be in the code page for the workbook (in contrast to the Sheet1 code page). In the selectors at the top, choose *Workbook* in the left selector.
4) This will automatically select the *Open* event in the right selector. The Visual Basic editor will automatically create an event handler that will run whenever the workbook first opens. Use the following code within this object programming window:

```
Private Sub Workbook_Open()
   'Notice we need to specify where to find the code
   'The InitializeMap subroutine is in Sheet1
   Call Sheet1.InitializeMap()
End Sub
```

Part F: Test Run

Now save the workbook as a macro-enabled Excel file and close Excel. Then, open the workbook again. When it opens, Excel will see the event handler and Initialize the map. Note that this may take a little bit of time because MapPoint is also being started up (in the background; Figure 12.13).

Now, enter an address into the spreadsheet and click Find Address. This should activate the macro written earlier and locate (if recognized) the address specified (Figure 12.14).

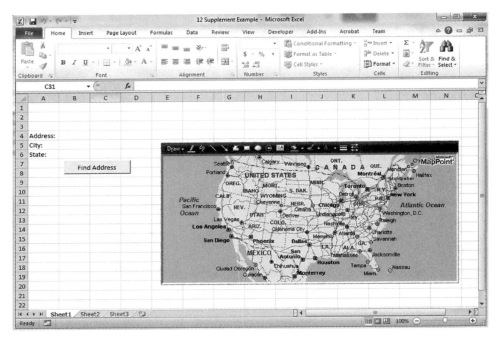

Figure 12.13. Updated MapPoint object after initialization.

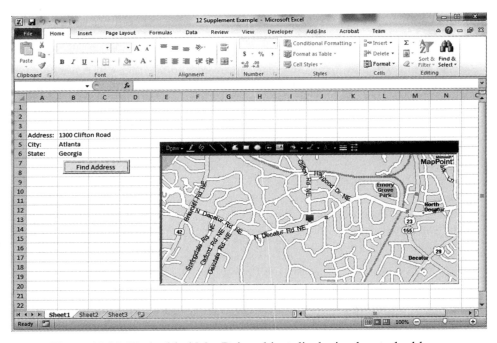

Figure 12.14. Embedded MapPoint object displaying located address.

Table 12.1. *Scenarios for Automated Analysis and Summary*

Revenue Maximizing Enrollments		Total # of Communication Training Hours for "Geeks"		
		7	11	13
Total # of Analytic Hours for "Geeks"	2	{#Geeks} {#Beatniks} {$Revenue}		
	6			
	10			

PRACTICE PROBLEMS

Practice 12.1

Recall the Atlanta Professional Training example we first introduced in Chapter 6. We used Solver to find an optimal solution to this problem given a single set of parameters such as revenue numbers and hours required per student per curriculum for both the geek and beatnik types.

Now, imagine that APT was reconsidering the number of hours the geek students should be required to take in the two categories of Etiquette and Analytics. The director would like to see how much his revenue-maximizing enrollment would vary under nine different scenarios. Each scenario is represented in Table 12.1.

Set up a table similar to this in Excel. It doesn't need to be exact; I've used the Merge cell option under Home>Alignment to combine some cells and make the table look neat.

Now, create a macro that does the following:

1) Copy a new set of Geek curriculum parameters (hours needed) outlined by one of the row and column combinations in the table (for example, six hours of analytics and eleven hours of tact/diplomacy) into the template we originally used when solving this problem.
2) Run Solver to generate the revenue-maximizing enrollment (assuming integer constraints on the number of students).
3) Record the revenue-maximizing enrollment (that is, the number of geek and beatnik students) and the associated revenue level generated by Solver for that set of parameters in the associated cells of your table.
4) Design your macro so that it does this for all nine scenarios, one after another, so that you generate a completely filled table with only one activation (for example, one click) of the macro.

Practice 12.2

Use VB calls to MapPoint to get every point-to-point distance between five locations (of your choosing) in the United States. Use that data as you did the straight line data in the Chapter 7 routing example, and use VB calls to RISKOptimizer to find the minimum total roundtrip sequence. Assume a single excursion that hits each point in turn. Choose a fixed starting and ending point if you desire to facilitate the search. Limit RISKOptimizer search time to five minutes.

13

Guided and User-Friendly Interfaces

As you've probably guessed by now, decisions can become increasingly complex as we increase the number of variables and constraints to maintain reality and practicality in our decision-making process. Similarly, the ability to concisely provide visualizations of what is possible and what is ideal (and, conversely, what isn't) becomes increasingly challenging. Given this complexity and the perceived need in industry to nevertheless pursue means of assisting people in decision making, the concept of the dashboard has come into being and continues to gain popularity.

A dashboard, from a general decision-making perspective, is basically a computer interface that allows individual users to simultaneously view various depictions (that is, presented structures) of data and information, as well as various subsets of data (that is, content) relevant to a particular task and user context. For example, Figure 13.1 shows four dashboards that I've personally put into use for research and consulting purposes in the recent past.

Two of these are highly oriented toward geographic (specifically, logistics) tasks; the other two are designed with project management tasks in mind. You'll notice that each of these consists of multiple frames and multiple control- and form-based interfaces. Some make use of parameterization forms more so than others. Some make use of graphs and charts predominantly, whereas others make rich use of tables with key indices summarized. All of them were designed as applications that could function through the use of Excel alone, and are highly mobile from a distributional perspective.

Of course, there are obvious advantages to integrating the wide range of capabilities made available through associated packages such as MapPoint, XLStat, and RISKOptimizer into DSS designs. In reality, high mobility is not often a key requirement of decision support systems and can easily be overshadowed by the need for advanced application integration. The most critical issue, of course, is practical usability paired with honest and ethical rigor on the part of developers. A detailed understanding of user needs from both a strategic-value perspective (driven by real business goals and

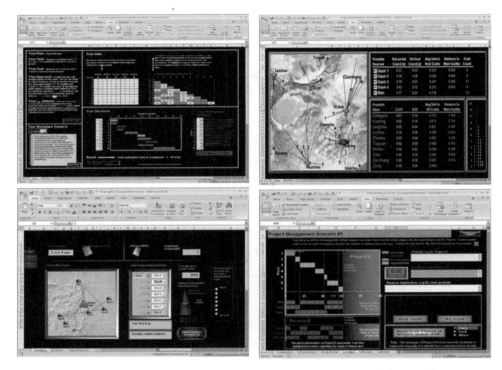

Figure 13.1. Several examples of dashboard developed in Excel.

decision requirements) and from a tactical-use perspective (appropriate context-specific metric depiction and user-oriented visualization/control) is essential to ensuring these attributes.

Unfortunately, in many cases, it may be impractical to assume that one dashboard design applies to the myriad of users that a DSS is designed to assist. For this reason, still more advanced dashboard designs are increasingly the mark of excellence, allowing individual users to independently choose and alter these depictions and subsets. PivotTables and the use of check-box triggered pruning mechanisms can be instrumental in providing flexibility to users. Recall the examples in Chp10_LobosFloorPlan (making use of check boxes) and Chp11_OutlierID (making use of PivotTable capabilities), each of which were designed with such pruning capabilities in mind (see Figure 13.2).

Excel's Change Chart Type and QuickLayout options are a rough approximation of the kind of user customization possible in the structuring of graphical depictions, but nevertheless may be extremely helpful in at least thinking about dashboard flexibility opportunities. Similarly, the ability to simply adjust the scale of axes in graphs, built and easily accessed through Excel, are also valid avenues of consideration in designing customizable depictions.

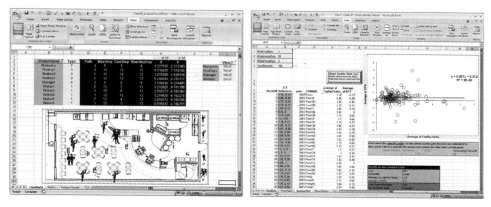

Figure 13.2. Two examples of visualization customization via pruning.

Ultimately, even greater flexibility comes into play through the full leveraging of macros to reveal customized visualizations on an as-needed basis.
The avenues made available through the leveraging of behind-the-scenes
VB coding provide the ability to avoid superfluous data, graphics, and controls that, presented in an untimely fashion, can lend to confusion, misuse,
and disasterous professional decision making. Granted, the art of managing access is often one of the last issues considered in DSS design, particularly for those just starting to hone their skills in development; however, it
remains a critical element of DSS excellence overall. With this in mind, the
following final sections outline approaches to augmenting DSS interfacing.

13.1 Interface Locking and Protecting

Under the Home tab of the main Excel menu, you'll find the general Format
drop-down menu (Figure 13.3) that includes various options that are meaningful to security measures you might want to capitalize on in your DSS
design.

One of the elements subject to consideration when adding protection to
workbooks is which cells, if any, should be locked. Locking cells can have
multiple implications when the spreadsheets and workbooks within which
they reside are protected. One consequence is the inability to make modifications to cells that are locked, either manually or through VB, without
first unlocking or unprotecting through the code. At the same time, calculations and functions present within locked cells can still be updated automatically when sheets are protected, as can graphs based on these calculations.
Cells can be toggled between locked and unlocked states through either
right-clicking and modifying their properties, or through the Format drop-
down menu shown in Figure 13.3. The same drop-down menu allows for the

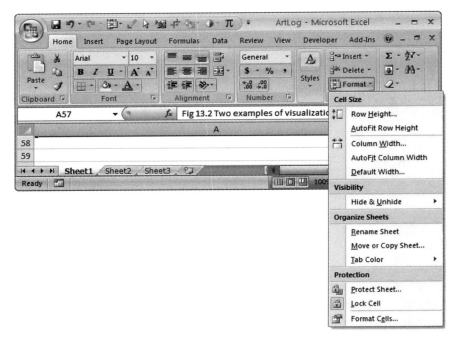

Figure 13.3. Access to interface locking and protecting mechanisms.

protection of a spreadsheet in Excel 2007. The Protect Sheet dialog box generated for detailing sheet protection is shown in Figure 13.4.

Note the variety of options that are contained in this dialog box. In general, the option to protect (that is, prevent changes) to locked cells should seem a natural one; however, developers are also given the option to assign

Figure 13.4. Customized specifications for sheet protection.

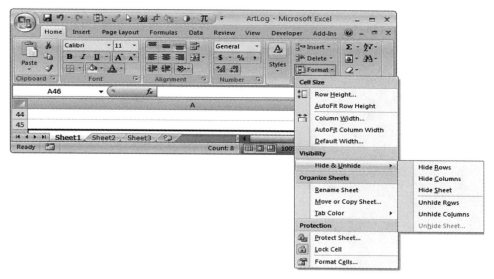

Figure 13.5. Hiding and unhiding interface.

a password to the protection mechanism so that the sheet cannot be unprotected by those who don't know the password. Developers are also given a slate of check boxes to customize the nature of the protection. These are basically aimed at lessening the severity of the protection, such as allowing unlocked cells to be selected, or allowing objects to be edited while blocking most other activities. Chp13_BasicClockProtected provides a follow-up to our previous discussion of the benefits and caveats to the DoEvents syntax in VB. Another mechanism by which to indirectly protect sheets of your DSS from tampering is simply by hiding them, as shown in Figure 13.5.

The hide and unhide options for rows, columns, and entire sheets are found in the Format drop-down menu. After a sheet is protected, all rows or columns that had been hidden prior (but nevertheless might hold vital data and calculations) cannot be unhidden or expanded. It's a way to quickly hide spreadsheet structure without going overboard on interface refinement activities.

If developers are seriously interested in ensuring that hidden sheets remain hidden, an additional level of protection needs to be applied. This can be found under Review>Protect Workbook, as seen in Figure 13.6. Protecting the structure of the workbook with or without a password prevents hidden sheets from being manually unhidden.

13.2 Dynamic Interfacing: Pop-Ups and Dialogs

The ability to call up forms and controls on an as-needed basis can be highly effective in the structuring of a DSS interface. It ensures that these controls

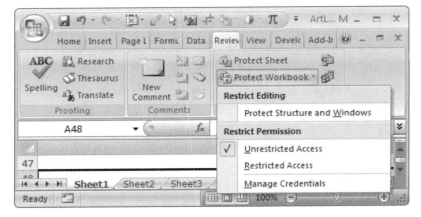

Figure 13.6. Workbook protection options.

don't get in the way of more critical elements of your interface when they are not needed. Also, the ability to withdraw access to these controls can be critical in fool-proofing your DSS against inadvertent changes that these controls could generate. To start the development of a user-defined pop-up or dialog, enter the VB Editor and select Insert>UserForm. This will generate a new user form. The form toolbox may also appear; if it doesn't, select View>Toolbox from the main header (see Figure 13.7). You'll use this toolbox for a variety of tasks.

13.2.1 Constructing and Linking a Userform: An Example

In Chp13_FunctionPopup, I provide an example where I've designed a dialog box using a number of basic forms you've already seen in Chapter 8. Figure 13.8 outlines and summarizes how most of the various controls were

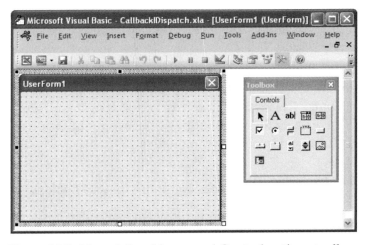

Figure 13.7. User-defined forms and Control options toolbox.

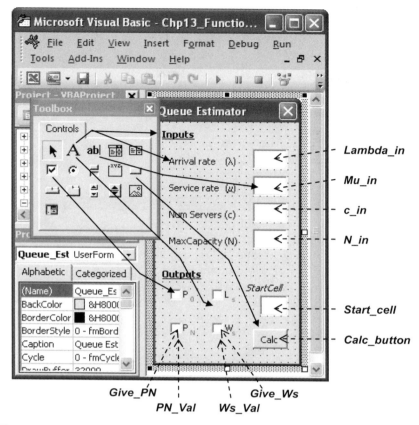

Figure 13.8. In-form control applications and labels used for VB reference.

dragged and dropped onto the newly generated user form, as well as how incidental changes such as name-property changes were made to fit the existing terminology of the QueueEstimator function developed in Chapter 11.

With the dialog box form showing in the VB Editor, double-click on any form component of choice to get access to specifying code for that particular item. Specifically, double-clicking on the Calc button would create a new private subroutine for you to edit to your needs (its privacy refers to its designed use specifically in reference to the dialog box interface).

```
Private Sub Calc button Click()
End Sub
```

Thankfully, these subroutines are coded the same as anything else in VB. The following is what I've developed as a subroutine for the Calc button (the functioning code is available in Chp13_FunctionPopup):

```
Private Sub Calc_button_Click()
  Dim Lambda, mu As Double
```

```
  Dim rho, c, N As Double
  Dim Pnot As Double
  Dim Pn As Double
  Dim Ls As Double
  Dim Ws As Double
  Lambda = Lambda_in.Value
  mu = Mu_in.Value
  If Lambda <> 0 And mu <> 0 Then
    rho = Lambda_in.Value / Mu_in.Value
    N = N_in.Value
    c = c_in.Value
    Pnot = Calc_P0(c, rho, N)
    Pn = Calc_Pn(c, rho, N, N, Pnot)
    Ls = Calc_Ls(c, rho, N, Pnot, Pn)
    Ws = Calc_Ws(Lambda, mu, rho, Pn, Ls)
    P0_val.Caption = WorksheetFunction.Round(Pnot, 3)
    PN_val.Caption = WorksheetFunction.Round(Pn, 3)
    Ls_val.Caption = WorksheetFunction.Round(Ls, 3)
    Ws_val.Caption = WorksheetFunction.Round(Ws, 3)
    Cellposition = Start_cell.Value
    If Cellposition <> "" Then
      If Give_P0.Value Then
        Range(Cellposition) = Pnot
        Cellposition = _Range(Cellposition). _
            Offset(1, 0).Address
      End If
      If Give_PN.Value Then
        Range(Cellposition) = Pn
        Cellposition = Range(Cellposition). _
            Offset(1, 0).Address
      End If
      If Give_Ls.Value Then
        Range(Cellposition) = Ls
        Cellposition = Range(Cellposition). _
            Offset(1, 0).Address
      End If
      If Give_Ws.Value Then
        Range(Cellposition) = Ws
      End If
    End If
  End If
 'Unload Queue_Estimator
 'If active, the above line would hide the dialogue after a
 'one time use
End Sub
```

Close inspection reveals that I've intended to use this single button to activate the full array of calculations specified in the original QueueEstimator (from Chapter 11), but in this case you should output only the calculations requested by the user and the results specifically where the user has indicated with the StartCell entry form.

To activate this form (that is, to actually get it to display on request from someone working through the Excel interface), I'll need something to call it into existence. Specifically, I'll need another macro defined under Modules, structured such as the following.

```
Sub Call Estimator()
  Queue Estimator.Show vbModeless
End Sub
```

If I assign that macro to a simple image I've created or imported (to serve as an activation button), the clean version of the interactive dialog box will appear. Entering the appropriate parameters into the text fields and clicking Calc should give me exactly the kind of output I designed for. And it does. I'll get some summaries of results built into this version of the dialog box and their values written to the spreadsheet depending on what outputs I asked to be copied.

One note on syntax: The vbModeless term used in the dialog box call is an addition that allows a little more mobility by the user while the dialog box is showing: For example, it allows the user to view other sheets and interact to some extent through the main Excel toolbars. Another interesting feature of vbModeless is that I can move the entire Excel interface out of site while still interacting with the interface. Figure 13.9 shows a clip of the dialog box on my computer desktop. To this extent, dialog boxes can serve as handy and compact specialty calculators when you may want to deal with numerous applications at the same time (aside from Excel).

13.2.2 More Sophisticated Userform Options

Aside from the standard textboxes, checkboxes, and fixed-list boxes that we've encountered here and in our discussion of sheet-embedded controls (see the Chapter 8 Supplement), in the realm of userforms we have many more options, particularly when paired with the setup capabilities of VBA. For example, list boxes in a userform setting can leverage additional properties allowing multiple items in the list box to get meaningfully selected. This is the multiselect setting of list boxes in userforms, and can be accessed under the list form's properties in the VB Developer. An image of this selection is presented in Figure 13.10. However, once selected, you won't see any immediate changes in the appearance of the list box under development. Like so many other objects, this is because you haven't specified the content of that list box yet. In the embedded list boxes we've seen in the

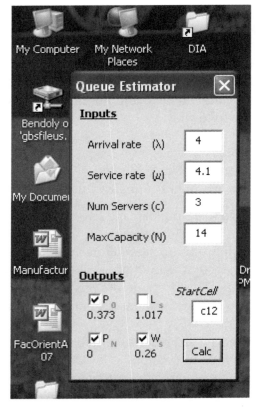

Figure 13.9. User-defined dialog box called.

Figure 13.10. The MultiSelect option of userform listboxes.

Chapter 8 Supplement, as well as in the use of the data validation tool, the lists that fed these controls resided somewhere in the same spreadsheet. The same option exists here by the property name RowSource. Of course, with VBA, you also have the option to automatically change this as needed (see the example of HeatMapDeveloper add-in, where the contents of both a single-select and a multiselect list box are populated in VBA based on earlier selections).

In the case of a multiselect list box, the process of figuring out which selections a user has made in this list involves a little more work than what you might encounter with a single-select list. First of all, it's useful to talk about how we might initialize this list so that when the form pops up, it contains items that you might want checked by "default." The following code in the userform's private subroutines (accessed by double-clicking on the form) should do the trick, provided you have a listbox called ListBox1 in multiselect mode, and a list of default selections in Sheet1 (text of items in column A, TRUE or FALSE representing selections in column B).

```
Private Sub UserForm_Activate() 'this is what happens when the
    'form is activated (the name _Activate is a 'reserved' term)
    For count = 0 To (ListBox1.ListCount - 1) 'so if there are
    'five items they would be indexed 0,1,2,3,4
        ListBox1.Selected(count) = Range("Sheet1!b1").Offset(count)
    Next
End Sub
```

Once again, we see the criticality and versatility of loop structures in getting this setup accomplished. Similar use of loop structures can then be applied when you are interested in outputting which of the items have been selected – say, following a click of a command button (CommandButton1) on that same form:

```
Private Sub CommandButton1_Click()
    Dim count As Integer
    For count = 0 To (ListBox1.ListCount - 1)
        Range("b1").Offset(count) = ListBox1.Selected(count)
    Next
End Sub
```

This use of spreadsheet content (perhaps on a hidden worksheet) as a default establishing and resetting mechanism is a nice, easy way to increase usability. An example is provided in the GoogleWriter add-in introduced in the Chapter 3 Supplement.

Figure 13.11. Embedded macro button versus macro buttons integrated with control/menu interface.

Further additions that can increase the ease of use in complex userforms include the leveraging of multipage controls and control locking and unlocking mechanisms. Multipage controls essentially multiply the space available on userforms, and allow users to perform tab-based navigation to access specific utilities made possible by those forms. A nice open example of this is provided in the ClickPlot add-in introduced in Chapter 3. Of course, in some cases, you don't want users to be able to "skip ahead." Sometimes, you need them to make earlier specifications before attempting to make later ones. To that end, VB manipulation of "enabled" property of objects comes in particularly handy. For example, if you don't want an individual to be able to access one of the pages in your multipage form, simply change the form's enabled property to FALSE. Change it back to TRUE when you're ready to give them access.

13.3 Customizing Primary Excel Interfaces

Along with being able to generate pop-up control panels on an as-needed basis, there is also the potential for actually customizing the primary interfaces and hovering off workbook – with which Excel users otherwise normally interact. In other words, instead of having a button (which activates a macro or dialog box) residing somewhere among the cells of a spreadsheet, you could place that button where all other buttons already built into Excel reside, such as within the command bar, Quick Access bar, or among the drop-down menus (see Figure 13.11).

It's yet another tactic for keeping work and other items out of the way of the premium space available in the spreadsheet environment. And, frankly, we can create these kinds of customized additions to the Excel command button and menu environment fairly quickly, both through manual and automated approaches.

13.3.1 Manual Additions in Excel 2007 and Later Versions

If the primary development environment is Excel 2007 or later, there is a fairly straightforward approach to adding customized buttons. You can

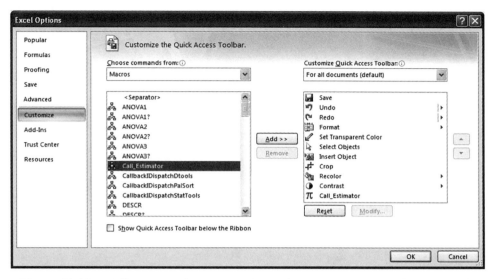

Figure 13.12. Adding macro buttons to the Quick Access Toolbar (Excel 2007).

use the Office button to access the Customize screen where any exist-
ing tool (including user-developed macros) can be added to the Quick
Access Toolbar. The Modify Button dialog box, accessed upon select-
ing the "Modify..." option shown faded next to the Reset button in
Figure 13.12, enables you select a button picture that suits your needs (see
Figure 13.13).

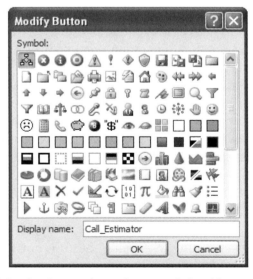

Figure 13.13. Selecting button icons for user-defined buttons in Excel 2007.

Figure 13.14. Adding user-defined buttons in Excel 2003.

13.3.2 Manual Additions in Excel 2003

Menu bar customization in Excel 2003 is different from later versions of Excel, in part because users seem to have more flexibility in how added elements will appear. The approach involves right-clicking anywhere on the existing command bar and then selecting Customize from the shortcut menu to open the Customize dialog box (Figure 13.14). Choose the Commands tab, and then select Macros from the Categories section. Custom Menu Item and Custom Button display in the Commands section of the dialog box, both of which can be utilized to generate changes to the existing toolbar interface; for example, the Custom Button option allows you to place a new button within that interface.

The button doesn't do anything when first added, unlike the manual Quick Access approach in Excel 2007; similar to any button we create in the spreadsheet, we'll need to assign it to a macro or subroutine that we've developed in VB. Not only can we change the icon for this new button, but we can also change its name. To make these kinds of changes, you'll need to be in the CommandBar Edit mode. Start in the Customize dialog box. In this CommandBar Edit mode, right-click on the newly placed button (in this mode) to access to a range of options, including Assign Macro, Change Button Image, and Name.

It's critical to note that all newly minted buttons must have a name starting with an ampersand (&). The & won't appear to users, but is critical in ensuring that Excel recognizes the new object. Forgetting or erasing the &

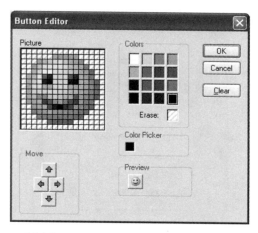

Figure 13.15. Pasting in button icons in Excel 2003.

can eliminate any work you've done in editing the button, which can be frustrating.

Another feature present in Excel 2003 but *not* in Excel 2007 is the ability to edit the appearance of the button icon at the pixel level in the Button Editor dialog box (Figure 13.16). If you don't have time to be a pixel artist, the Paste Button Image option (shown in Figure 13.15) allows you to take any image or graphic item available and then copy and paste it into that 16-by-16 square area. You lose some resolution, but the work is quick.

13.3.3 Fully Automating Button and Menu Setups

Aside from their presence in the menu bar, user-designed buttons have a particular nuance to them that distinguishes them from buttons that would otherwise be embedded in a spreadsheet. When created, these command bar buttons become registered in a file called Excel.xlb (or something similar, depending on your system configuration), which is usually in your C:\Windows directory. This allows the buttons to appear in your command bar no matter what workbook you open in the future as long as that workbook is on the same computer. For example, if I reboot my computer and then open a fresh workbook in Excel, that command button should be there. It should have all the properties I assigned it when I last edited it. It'll even know enough to find the macro to which it was assigned, unless the workbook containing the code for the macro has been moved.

The downside is that because the button is defined in that Excel.xlb file and not in a workbook, simply transferring the workbook file (for example, via e-mail) won't bring that button along for the ride. There are

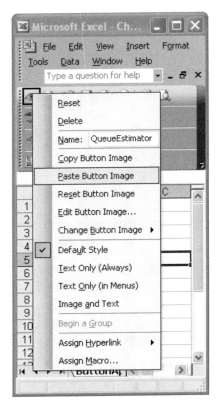

Figure 13.16. Editing button icons in Excel 2003.

at least two ways around this. You could insist that clients use the specific Excel.xlb file that you use (which seems an unlikely option in most situations), or you could write a macro that creates a set of menu command buttons for your specific DSS (and maybe handles updates in cases where code files are moved around). For illustration, I'll use a variant of the dialog box generator file discussed earlier in this chapter. The following is how you might structure that kind of installation code in that particular case (functional in Chp13_CustomSetup).

```
Sub AddNewMenuItem()
  Dim CmdBar As CommandBar
  Dim CmdBarMenu As CommandBarControl
  Dim CmdBarMenuItem As CommandBarControl
  Set CmdBar = Application.CommandBars("Worksheet Menu Bar")
     'Point to the Worksheet Menu Bar
    Set CmdBarMenu = CmdBar.Controls("Tools")
     'Point to the Tools menu on the menu bar
  Set CmdBarMenuItem = CmdBarMenu.Controls.Add
     'Add a new menu item to the Tools menu
```

Figure 13.17. The final result when this code is run in Excel 2003.

```
  CmdBarMenuItem.Caption = "QueueEstimator"
     'Set the properties for the new control
  CmdBarMenuItem.OnAction = "'" & ThisWorkbook.Name _
    & "'!Call_Estimator"
End Sub
Sub AddNewButton()
  Application.CommandBars("Standard").Controls.Add _
    Type:=msoControlButton, ID:=2950, Before:=25
  Application.CommandBars("Standard").Controls(25).Caption =_
     "QueueEstimator"
  Application.CommandBars("Standard").Controls(25).OnAction =_
     "'" & ThisWorkbook.Name & "'!Call_Estimator"
End Sub
Sub SetupBoth()
 AddNewMenuItem
 AddNewButton
End Sub
```

Running the SetupBoth macro calls the AddNewMenuItem and AddNew- Button macros in turn. The AddNewMenuItem routine adds a new item called QueueEstimator to the Tools drop-down menu, and assigns the Call_Estimator macro (also included in this workbook, regardless of whether we've renamed the workbook) to that menu item. Similarly, the AddNewButton routine adds a button called QueueEstimator to the command bar. Figure 13.17 shows the final result when this code is run in Excel 2003.

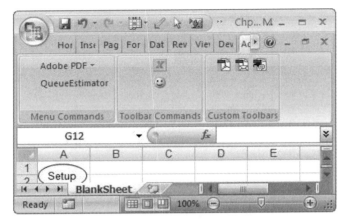

Figure 13.18. Appearance of forced menu and command button implants.

Along with the item's presence on the drop-down menu, we also get the smiley face button on our tool bar (not shown in the above clip, but present if the code is run in 2003), and we know we can easily modify it. Interestingly, this code also works if you run it in Excel 2007. The buttons and drop-down menus will appear under the Add-Ins tab, under MenuCommands (for the menu item loads) and under Toolbar Commands (for button loads), as shown in Figure 13.18. Unfortunately, changing the appearance of buttons forced this way into the toolbar in Excel 2007 is not straightforward (at least, at this point). You might be stuck with that smiley face if you need it to be under Toolbar Commands, but given that you could opt either for the menu item form (text) or the Quick Access form (where you have at least some graphical choices), there's little reason to feel penned in here.

13.3.4 Fully Automating Button and Menu Cleanup

Customized buttons and menu items can also easily be removed manually from use in Excel 2003 by dragging them "out" of toolbars and menus after right-clicking and getting into "Customize..." Similarly, buttons can be removed by right-clicking and selecting Delete Custom Command from the shortcut menu. Alternatively, if you are interested in providing an automatic cleanup of added customized items and buttons, something similar to the following code could be used in either version.

```
Sub RemoveMenuItem()
  Dim CmdBar As CommandBar
  Dim CmdBarMenu As CommandBarControl
  Set CmdBar = Application.CommandBars("Worksheet Menu Bar")
```

```
   Set CmdBarMenu = CmdBar.Controls("Tools")
   CmdBarMenu.Controls("QueueEstimator").Delete
End Sub
Sub RemoveButton()
   Application.CommandBars("Standard").Controls(25).Delete
End Sub
Sub RemoveBoth()
 RemoveMenuItem
 RemoveButton
End Sub
```

Here, both menu-item deletion and button deletion are described, along with a single macro that might be used to remove both customized elements if present in the workbook (also functional in Chp13_CustomSetup).

13.4 Ribbon Editing for Packaged Add-Ins

As a final note, all these methods can become part of the installation protocol of a larger add-in you might save and pass on to others for use. However, there are also some very elegant solutions to developing ribbon controls to accompany add-in saves. The most powerful and easiest to use that I've come across in the last few years is Andy Pope's RibbonDeveloper (available on the Excel Blackbelts add-ins directory). In fact, many of the ribbon launch buttons for the MapPointDeveloper, GoogleWriter, and Bivariate Normal Confidence Plotter were developed using this tool. I won't rehash Andy's instructions on use here because they are posted on the add-ins site. Suffice to say, this is an add-in that anyone interested in packaging their own custom add-ins should check out.

13.5 Don't Give Up on the Spreadsheet

If we can build interfaces that reduce user interactions to menu buttons and dialog boxes, why would we create elements such as user-defined functions that are callable through the spreadsheet? If we could get the same result with a dialog box, isn't that preferable?

There's a significant drawback to limiting user interfaces to dialog box menus. The spreadsheet landscape is still a great arena for laying out multiple calculations that can be updated in real time as other parameters and calculations change, and whose updates can be visualized (that is, changes depicted graphically) in real time. Replicating that kind of an environment strictly through the use of dialog box is both cumbersome and unnecessary for developers. Similarly, given the fantastic integration between live spreadsheet updates and live graphical updates in Excel, the ability to make

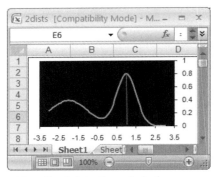
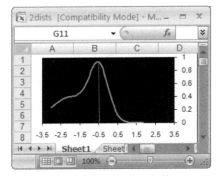

Here the "global" mode is 1   Here it's -0.6 (not quite -0.5)

Figure 13.19. Examples of two compound distributions and associated modes.

abundant use of functions (as opposed to dialog box and button-activated macro-based calculations) should not be underappreciated.

As developers, it's increasingly beneficial to be able to offer the best of both worlds in interface designs – allowing routine calculations to be menu driven and providing a function infrastructure that permits a wide range of user creativity and experimentation in the spreadsheet environment.

PRACTICE PROBLEM

Population distributions are often assumed to be normal, or bell curved in their shape, with the most members of the populations represented at the center of the curve. In statistical terms, this location of greatest frequency is referred to as the *mode*. In management scenarios, we are often faced with multiple populations that have some overlap (for example, clusters of demographically related customers that geographically overlap to some degree). Managers interested in dealing with multiple populations simultaneously may be interested in the associated points of greatest frequency (that is, where the greatest number of people in the combined population live). However, several forms can arise when combining two normally distributed populations. Figure 13.19 shows a couple of simple examples generated in the Ch13_2dists.xls workbook. The first shows a bimodal structure (with one peak representing the global mode); the second shows a single composite mode structure. Numerically, the two pictures differ only in the location of the mean of the second distribution: +1 versus −0.5, respectively.

Build your own function for determining the mode of a distribution resulting from the merger of two normal distributions. Your inputs should be the means and standard deviations for the two distributions, as well as a cell location to dump any resulting output. The output should be the global mode of the composite distribution, and whether a second local peak exists (just give a yes or no response).

Create a dialog box that prompts users to enter the input information into dialog text boxes, and a button that makes VB go through some kind of loop to determine the outputs required. Use a fresh workbook (not a version of 2dist.xls) for your work. Do not use any portion of the workbook's spreadsheet to store numbers or do the calculations. This exercise should all be done in VB.

To help you, the following is the code needed to calculate the frequency of a single distribution given a mean and standard deviation:

```
f1 = WorksheetFunction.NormDist (x, mean1, stddev1, 0)
```

Remember, you'll want to calculate a frequency for each and then add the frequencies together. You can conduct your search by constructing each composite frequency in turn (on 0.01 intervals of x; -3.0, -2.99, -2.98, and so on) and checking whether each new composite has a greater composite frequency than the maximum previously encountered.

Glossary of Key Terms

Add-In *[2.8, 3.3.4, 3.Supp.]*: An additional application compatible with Excel, designed to extend the capabilities of the spreadsheet environment. Examples include Solver, the Data Analysis tools, and a variety of free user-developed tools available through www.excel-blackbelt.com. The VBA developer content of any workbook (forms, subroutines, functions) can be saved as an add-in and made available to any workbook opened on a computer in which the add-in is installed.

Cluster Analysis *[5.4.4]*: A computational technique used to identify a set of fairly-distinct groups of observations (entities, records) in a data set. It operates by attempting to place individual observations in groups whose attribute values are most similar, while simultaneously attempting to ensure that the general characters of all formed groups are significantly different from one another.

Conditional Formating *[2.2.2]*: A mechanism enabled by Excel by which cells in a spreadsheet take on varous visual formats based solely on the nature of their content and ostensibly the content of the range of cells that they were co-formatted with.

Conditional Logic *[See Decision Trees]*

Constraints *[4]*: Those issues that restrain decision making and the pursuit of objectives; Technically, they prevent decision variables from taking on certain values either in isolation or in tandem with other decision variables (for example, relational constraints). Binding constraints in particular are those that work to prevent certain kinds of changes to the best of decision sets (that is, objective-optimizing decisions) that might otherwise lead to still greater levels of achievement in the objective.

Controls *[8.Supplement]*: A range of mechanisms in Excel through which to develop visually appealing and user-friendly object interfaces for modifying and/or displaying content within a workbook. Controls (and Forms) can reside entirely as embedded objects in a workbook or can appear as needed through the use of pop-up forms callable through Visual Basic code. In many cases also capable and ideally used in referenced calls to user-developed Macros.

Dashboard *[13]*: From a general decision-making perspective, a computer interface that allows individual users to simultaneously view various depictions of data and information, as well as various subsets of data relevant to a particular task and user-context.

Data Tables *[8.2]*: An automated mechanism for generating multiple evaluations of a computational model. The top row and/or left column of a Data Table can contain inputs to the model. One of the following can contain the output reference(s) from the manipulated model for populating the bulk of the Data Table: upper left-most cell, the top row or left column. Data Tables are typically used to describe joint effects of inputs on final or intermediate outputs. They are also very useful in simulation assessments and the calculation of distributions of effects in the presence of noise. *[See Design of Experiments]*

Decision Support System (DSS) *[1]*: An application designed to support, not replace, decision making. Often characterized as providing eased access, facilitated analysis, and rich communication – all of which is greatly augmented through intelligent and effective use of visualization.

Decision Trees *[2.Sup]*: Structures that outline sequential systems of compound logic. Useful in mapping the course of decision-making processes, the course of questions to be asked in order to determine identity or state, or the course of likely events in order to assess the value/cost of early decisions.

Decision Variables *[4]*: The elements of a decision-making process over which a decision maker has either direct or indirect control (for example, change as a consequence of other decisions made). These variables in turn impact the value taken on by the "objective function" and hence the relationship between these variables and that function mitigates the pursuit of the overall objective of the decision-making process, which is also subject to the presence of additional constraints on these variables.

Design of Experiments (DOE with Data Tables) *[8.2.4]*: An approach to leveraging Data Table capabilities, and working around their inherent limitations. In a DOE approach, a codex table is created in which a reference number is used to refer to the combination of levels of multiple inputs in a model. Those reference numbers (also occupying the left column or top row of a Data Table) serves as the primary input that the Data Table will send to the model. Translation of the reference number into its separate variable components (for example, using VLOOKUP on the original codex table) is done prior to model evaluation.

Discriminant Analysis *[5.5]*: A statistical method aimed at making use of a select set of predictive attributes to attempt to create some simple formulation that places specific observations/records/entities (characterized by those attributes) into groups (for example, clusters) that they are thought to belong to.

DoEvents *[See Loops]*

Drawn-Path Extraction *[10.Supplement]*: A technique through which developers can leverage standard object-drawing capabilities to derive graphical paths and path-coordinates that can subsequently be used to develop path-direct flow graphics as a feature of a system simulation visualization.

Error Handling *[11.5]*: VB code available for identifying and handling errors as they occur during run-time. Generally useful in safeguarding the effectiveness of complex applications developed in workbooks where macros and user-defined functions are active.

Filtering *[See Pivot Table and Section 4.2 in general]*

Forms *[See Controls]*

Formulae *[See Functions]*

Functions *[2.6]*: Built in formulae that can be executed within cells of spreadsheets. Under most scenarios, (similar to most graphs built in Excel), functions are automatically updated when changes take place in the content of workbooks or when forced updates: for example, through the use of F9 in the spreadsheet or 'Calculate' in VB code. These functions can also be automatically updated in conjunction with Web-query and iteration mode functionality (also see User-Defined Functions)

Genetic Algorithm *[See RISKOptimizer and Chp7 Supplement in general]*

Heuristic *[5]*: Codified approaches to developing ideas, decisions, and/or solutions to problems. Fast and frugal heuristics employ a minimum of time, knowledge, and computation to make adaptive choices in real environments. Heuristics, in general, typically do not guarantee optimal solutions but can be extremely capable in developing high-performing solutions (relative to random decision making).

Hill Climbing *[See Solver]*

Iteration Mode *[3.5]*: A calculation mode in Excel that allows for the step-wise calculation of functions within a spreadsheet that are based on previous calculations, even if the calculation referenced is stored in the same cell that the called function resides in (that is, circular loop calculations). In Excel, the sequence of cell calculations under iteration mode is very specific, and needs to be understood before accurately used.

Labels *[2.3]*: Text that can be associated with cells, cell-ranges, worksheets or objects embedded within an Excel workbook, for use in referencing these items in an intuitively meaningful fashion. Labels are also useful in both locating items in workbooks with considerable added content in addition to referencing these items from behind the scenes through Visual Basic code.

Link Data Wizard *[See MapPoint]*

Living Data Records *[3.5]*: Data records that typically consist of a range of cells containing data that are updated on an iterative basis. These records typically represent sequences of calculations or observations, and hence typically have some temporal meaning associated with them.

Locking *[See Protecting]*

Loops *[11.3.5]*: VB code structures designed to allow for iteration as a part of a subroutine's (Macro's) run. Two commonly used loop structures include fixed-finite repetion loops (For Loops) and condition-dependent repetition loops (While Loops). Given that loop structures are often associated with lengthy run times, the availability of flexibility and auto-exit mechanisms such as DoEvents script can become highly useful to DSS developers.

Macros *[8.3]*: Subroutines coded in Visual Basic (VB), often generated through the recording of changes within the spreadsheet environment, that enable specific changes to the workbook content, structure, and associated elements (for example, pop-ups) to take place. Only a limited set of activities can actually be directly recorded and translated into VB code; however a wide range of actions can be coded for directly through use of the VB Editor. External calls to applications and add-ins are also possible through the use of Macros. Activation of Macros typically takes place through the use of embedded buttons, customized menu items, or control-key shortcuts (or indirectly through calls by other Macros).

MapPoint *[3.2]*: A Microsoft application that provides both geographic visualization, mapping, and routing capabilities. While typically associated with a purchased database of geographic data, the use of tools such as the Link Data Wizard allows for regular imports of data from Excel spreadsheets. MapPoint graphs can also be imported to function as Embedded Maps in an Excel workbook.

Names *[See Labels]*

Objective *[4]*: The main pursuit of a decision-making process. Entirely context and orientation specific, and often unique in form, depending on the nature of the problem faced by the decision maker. Also entirely dependent upon the range of decisions available for consideration, as well as the constraints placed upon the decision-making process. Typically viewed as compound calculation (for example, expected total satisfaction, average total risk, and so on) to be either maximized, minimized, or set as close to a particular value as possible.

Objects *[2, 11.2]*: In general, noncell elements imported or created in the Excel spreadsheet environment. Objects can include anything from imported images and sound clips to MapPoint embedded map graphics. All objects have a unique set of attributes that may differ largely from those available to other kinds of objects; however, all can be characterized by position, reference label, and specific visualization. Such attributes and many more can be manipulated either through menu-driven interfaces or through VB code.

Optimization *[6]*: The process by which values of decision variables are altered computationally (or derived mathematically) in order to obtain the best possible results in an objective function, subject to constraints on both decision variables and the objective (as well as on any computational method used to drive the process)

Path-Directed Flow *[10.3]*: The flow of elements through a system based on a structured network of paths and interpath flow dynamics (logic and stochastic mechanisms). Graphically, the mechanism through which entities travel along meaningful attribute-space in their transitions between interpretable states (points on a graph).

Pivot Table *[4.2]*: A compound filtering mechanism available in Excel that enables the summarizations of multiple related records based on similarities across specific attributes. These attributes can be organized along rows and columns, and specific values of attributes associated with specific blocks of data can be filtered to allow focus and comparison on key subsets of data. As with other tools in Excel, Pivot Tables do not automatically update themselves when input data changes (manual or coded refreshing is needed).

Plot-Pulled Extraction *[10.Supplement]*: A technique through which developers can leverage graphical plotting capabilities (for example, those of Excel 2003) to derive graphical paths and path-coordinates that can subsequently be used to develop path-direct flow graphics as a feature of a system simulation visualization.

Pop-Ups *[13.2]*: Compound user forms that present numerous input and output options on an as-needed basis, appearing only when called for as by the user or as a portion of a Macro run sequence. These new form windows are not embedded in the spreadsheets in the same way that many fixed and standard controls may be, and can be designed to "float" out of the way of the spreadsheet or exist visually apart from the spreadsheet entirely, while simultaneously allowing for continuous interaction with the Excel workbook that generates them.

Principle Components Analysis (PCA) *[5.3.2]*: A statistical technique that attempts to create a reduced subset of attributes based on a larger set of potentially highly related (and perhaps redundant) attributes. The result is typically a condensed set of higher-level concepts that can ideally be used to more efficiently distinguish the nature of observations in a data set.

Protecting *[13.1]*: In general, a means by which to prevent certain kinds of changes from taking place in a developed spreadsheet or workbook as a whole. A critical part of the protection mechanism involves specifying the extent to which actions are limited under protection and whether or not certain cells are "locked" from modification. Password protection is an option in both spreadsheet and workbook protection cases.

RISKOptimizer *[7]*: An application developed to search out solutions to highly complex problems, often characterized by features such as nonlinearity and discontinuity in the objective function (as well as within relational constraints that involve decision variables that are under consideration). Moreover, the tool is designed to enable searches across simulated scenarios of complex problems where various attributes of these problems are subject to uncertainty. In order to tackle these problems, the application makes abundant use of Genetic Algorithms as a robust globalized search method (see Chapter 7 Supplement), thereby avoiding some of the difficulties that hill-climbing procedures might encounter. Callable both through menu interaction and/or through VB code.

Simulated Variants *[8.1.1]*: Generally, a set of structured problems or decision-making scenarios that are equivalent in structure but differ in the actual values of the parameters used to describe them. Extremely useful in "what-if" analysis, where the conditions of a problem-solving context (and hence the value of decisions constructed) are highly dependent on certain elements of uncertainty.

Simulation Optimization *[9.1]*: The task of seeking out optimal solutions to complex problems involving either critical elements that are known to be characterized by uncertainty and/or sequentially dependent across time (for example, as in System Simulations). Generally speaking, simulation optimization is an iterative process that involves multiple randomized assessments of a range of decision policies. RISKOptimizer provides an example of an application designed to conducted such searches.

Solver *[6]*: The standard mechanism provided through Excel to conduct a search for optimal solutions (values of decision variables) to an objective function, subject to constraints. Solver is technically another add-in tool and is therefore subject to the same strengths and limitations of many other tools in Excel. In its most typical use, it pursues optimization by means of a hill-climbing mechanism (local sensitivity search). It provides rich details regarding the nature of its final solution with respect to its view of the search through elements such as Answer Reports.

Stochastic Processes *[8.4]*: Processes in which key elements (for example, workers, jobs, patients, and so on) have the potential for passing through multiple states prior to completion or exit. Each state is associated with a particular probability of being visited in turn depending specifically on what the state the element has most recently been in (among other factors). System simulations often make abundant use of stochastic processes in an attempt to capture real-world dynamics. The visualization of changes within simulated systems can also leverage stochastic structures to provide rich depictions of these dynamics.

System Simulation *[8.1.2]*: Generally, the computational representation of a complex set of sequential interactions, designed in an attempt to more realistically capture the intertemporal (across time) dependencies of the processes and resources involved in real-world settings. The performance impact of decisions applied to these systems typically are assessed across multiple periods, and hence such multiperiod computations must be built into any search for ideal or at least improved decision making for the modeled settings.

Tools *[2.6]*: Additional mechanisms that are often built into Excel to facilitate the organization and analysis of information in workbooks. These include mechanisms by which to sort information and conduct complex statistical computations, among others. However, unlike other features of Excel (such as most functions and graphs), the functionality of these tools are typically not characterized by live updating – that is, changes in the content of workbooks, including the data that they are intended to operate on, do not typically alter their results automatically. Whereas other means by which to automate updates of their results exist, this is a necessary caveat to consider when relying on their use.

Types *[See VB Editor]*

User-Defined Functions *[11.4]*: VB code that allows inputs to be specified, complex calculations made or information derived, and individual results to be posted to cells or other Macros that make calls to the code. In spreadsheet usage, these can operate more or less like any other function built into Excel, including providing automatic updates to results as data relevant to its calculations are modified (also see Functions).

VB Editor *[11]*: The fundamental interface that allows developers to view, edit, and generate code (for example, macros and user-defined functions) for use in Excel-based DSS; A critical key to leveraging the various capabilities of Excel and linked applications in a seamless and integrated manner. The VB Editor includes multiple mechanisms through which to facilitate development include debugging tools, help mechanisms, and step-through execution (as needed). Key to the leveraging of complex code strucutres is an understanding of the role of user-defined variables and variable types that can make the best use of data resources and calculations toward a particular programming goal.

Appendix: Shortcut (Hot Key) Reference

Popular Function Keys (F#)

F1 Key	Pop-up Help	**F7 Key**	Spell Check
F2 Key	Edit cell content	**F9 Key**	Recalculate
F4 Key	Toggles hard references ($)	**F12 Key**	Save File As...
F5 Key	Pop-up Goto menu		

F6 Key   Hit twice – activates key-driven menu (provides guide to F6-# shortcut commands; for example, F6-f opens the Office Button menu)

Some Popular CTRL-# shortcuts (assuming they are not overwritten by user-defined macro shortcuts)

CTRL-A	Select entire worksheet		
CTRL-B	Toggles Bold Text (CTRL-2 does same)		
CTRL-C	Copies the item(s) selected to the Clipboard (can be pasted elsewhere using CTRL-V)		
CTRL-D	Copies Down the top cell in a range of selected cells to rest of range		
CTRL-F	Displays the Find dialog box		
CTRL-G	Pop-up Goto menu (as does F5)	**CTRL-1**	Displays Format Cells Dialogue Box
CTRL-H	Displays the Replace dialog box	**CTRL-2**	Toggles Bold Text (CTRL-B does same)
CTRL-I	Toggles Italic Text	**CTRL-3**	Toggles Italics (CTRL-I does same)
CTRL-K	Insert/Edit Hyperlink dialog	**CTRL-4**	Toggles Underline (CTRL-U does same)
CTRL-L	Displays Create List dialog box	**CTRL-5**	Toggles Strikethrough Text
CTRL-N	New File	**CTRL-6**	Toggles display of objects
CTRL-O	Open File	**CTRL-7**	Toggles to show Standard toolbar (2003)

CTRL-P	Print	**CTRL-8**	Toggles symbol outline display (2003)
CTRL-R	Copies Right the left-most cell in a range of cells to the rest of range	**CTRL-9**	Hides the selected rows
		CTRL-0	Hides the selected columns
CTRL-S	Save File		
CTRL-U	Toggles Underlined Text	**CTRL-LeftArrow**	Go to End of Column
CTRL-V	Paste the contents of the clipboard	**CTRL-Home**	Go to Top of Worksheet (A1)
CTRL-W	Closes selected workbook window	**CTRL-End**	Go to End of Worksheet
CTRL-X	Cut the selected item	**CTRL-PageDown**	Go to Next Worksheet
CTRL-Y	Redo the last undone action	**CTRL-Spacebar**	Select the entire Column
CTRL-Z	Undoes the last action		
CTRL-;	Insert Current Date	**CTRL-&**	Applies the outline border
CTRL-:	Insert Current Time	**CTRL-**	Removes the outline border
CTRL-~	Applies the General number format	**CTRL-^**	Exponential format (2 decimals)
CTRL-$	Currency format (two decimals)	**CTRL-#**	Date format
CTRL-%	Percentage format (no decimals)	**CTRL-@**	Time format
CTRL-!	Number format (two decimals)	**CTRL-'**	Copies formula from cell above into active cell
CTRL-`	Toggles display of cell values versus display of formulas in the worksheet	**CTRL-"**	Copies the value from cell above into active cell

Some Popular ALT-# shortcuts

ALT-=	Autosum	**ALT-F11**	Opens Visual Basic Editor
ALT-F8	Opens Macros		

Index